Managing Screen Time in an Online Society

Lídia Oliveira
University of Aveiro, Portugal

A volume in the Advances in Human
and Social Aspects of Technology
(AHSAT) Book Series

Published in the United States of America by
    IGI Global
    Information Science Reference (an imprint of IGI Global)
    701 E. Chocolate Avenue
    Hershey PA, USA 17033
    Tel: 717-533-8845
    Fax: 717-533-8661
    E-mail: cust@igi-global.com
    Web site: http://www.igi-global.com

Library of Congress Cataloging-in-Publication Data

Names: Oliveira, Lidia, 1968- editor.
Title: Managing screen time in an online society / Lidia Oliveira, editor.
Description: Hershey, PA : Information Science Reference, [2019]
Identifiers: LCCN 2018046996l ISBN 9781522581635 (hardcover) l ISBN
  9781522581642 (ebook)
Subjects: LCSH: Information technology--Social aspects. l Internet and
  children. l Information society. l Time management. l Quality of life.
Classification: LCC HM851 .M356 2019 l DDC 004.67/8083--dc23 LC record available at https://
lccn.loc.gov/2018046996

This book is published in the IGI Global book series Advances in Human and Social Aspects of Technology (AHSAT) (ISSN: 2328-1316; eISSN: 2328-1324)

British Cataloguing in Publication Data
A Cataloguing in Publication record for this book is available from the British Library.

All work contributed to this book is new, previously-unpublished material.
The views expressed in this book are those of the authors, but not necessarily of the publisher.

For electronic access to this publication, please contact: eresources@igi-global.com.

Advances in Human and Social Aspects of Technology (AHSAT) Book Series

ISSN:2328-1316
EISSN:2328-1324

Editor-in-Chief: Ashish Dwivedi, The University of Hull, UK

MISSION

In recent years, the societal impact of technology has been noted as we become increasingly more connected and are presented with more digital tools and devices. With the popularity of digital devices such as cell phones and tablets, it is crucial to consider the implications of our digital dependence and the presence of technology in our everyday lives.

The **Advances in Human and Social Aspects of Technology (AHSAT) Book Series** seeks to explore the ways in which society and human beings have been affected by technology and how the technological revolution has changed the way we conduct our lives as well as our behavior. The AHSAT book series aims to publish the most cutting-edge research on human behavior and interaction with technology and the ways in which the digital age is changing society.

COVERAGE

- ICTs and human empowerment
- Cyber Bullying
- Public Access to ICTs
- Activism and ICTs
- Technology Dependence
- Gender and Technology
- Human Rights and Digitization
- Technology and Freedom of Speech
- ICTs and social change
- Computer-Mediated Communication

IGI Global is currently accepting manuscripts for publication within this series. To submit a proposal for a volume in this series, please contact our Acquisition Editors at Acquisitions@igi-global.com or visit: http://www.igi-global.com/publish/.

Titles in this Series

For a list of additional titles in this series, please visit:
https://www.igi-global.com/book-series/advances-human-social-aspects-technology/37145

Gender Gaps and the Social Inclusion Movement in ICT
Idongesit Williams (Aalborg University, Denmark) Olga Millward (Aalborg University, Denmark) and Roslyn Layton (Aalborg University, Denmark)
Information Science Reference ● ©2019 ● 325pp ● H/C (ISBN: 9781522570684) ● US $195.00

Gender Inequality and the Potential for Change in Technology Fields
Sonja Bernhardt (ThoughtWare, Australia) Patrice Braun (Federation University, Australia) and Jane Thomason (Abt Associates, Australia)
Information Science Reference ● ©2019 ● 366pp ● H/C (ISBN: 9781522579755) ● US $195.00

Automatic Cyberbullying Detection Emerging Research and Opportunities
Michal E. Ptaszynski (Kitami Institute of Technology, Japan) and Fumito Masui (Kitami Institute of Technology, Japan)
Information Science Reference ● ©2019 ● 180pp ● H/C (ISBN: 9781522552499) ● US $165.00

Analytical Frameworks, Applications, and Impacts of ICT and Actor-Network Theory
Markus Spöhrer (University of Konstanz, Germany)
Information Science Reference ● ©2019 ● 327pp ● H/C (ISBN: 9781522570271) ● US $175.00

Analyzing Human Behavior in Cyberspace
Zheng Yan (University at Albany (SUNY), USA)
Information Science Reference ● ©2019 ● 333pp ● H/C (ISBN: 9781522571285) ● US $175.00

Handbook of Research on Technology Integration in the Global World
Efosa C. Idemudia (Arkansas Tech University, USA)
Information Science Reference ● ©2019 ● 535pp ● H/C (ISBN: 9781522563679) ● US $195.00

For an entire list of titles in this series, please visit:
https://www.igi-global.com/book-series/advances-human-social-aspects-technology/37145

701 East Chocolate Avenue, Hershey, PA 17033, USA
Tel: 717-533-8845 x100 ● Fax: 717-533-8661
E-Mail: cust@igi-global.com ● www.igi-global.com

Paula Alexandra Silva, *University of Aveiro, Portugal*
Olga Y. Strizhitskaya, *Saint Petersburg State University, Russia*
Mário Vairinhos, *University of Aveiro, Portugal*
Enrickson Varsori, *University of Aveiro, Portugal*
Cláudio Xavier, *University of the State of Bahia, Brazil*
Nelson Zagalo, *University of Aveiro, Portugal*

Table of Contents

Detailed Table of Contents

Chapter 1
Sedated by the Screen: Social Use of Time in the Age of Mediated
Acceleration 1
    Lídia Oliveira, University of Aveiro, Portugal

The social use of time has been progressively affected by the presence of screen devices in people's daily lives. These devices are of various types: television, tablet, computer, smartphones, etc. However, all of these have a power of seduction that makes people want to use them. In reality, a significant part of tasks are mediated by screens, whether they are playful tasks, socializing, work or training. In this chapter, the authors reflect on some quasi-paradoxical situations triggered by screen time, which shows that one is sedated by the screen. Then, they present the results of a systematic review of the literature focused on the concept of "screen time," which shows that the excessive use of the screen is causing various health problems, especially in children and young people. And, the results of two empirical studies are presented, one with young people between 12 and 18 years old, and the other with university students. The results of both studies demonstrate the need to develop competences in the management of the social use of time, that is, to develop time literacy.

Chapter 2
Running After Time: Temporality, Technology, and Power 31
    Ivone Neiva Santos, University of Porto, Portugal
    José Azevedo, University of Porto, Portugal

We live in a paradoxical age marked by the widespread perception that life is faster than it used to be, that quick access to people and information will free us to do other things, and simultaneously, most of us have experienced this creeping sense that time is slipping out of our control. That perception is a source of concern and even anguish considering the need we feel to follow the pace "imposed" by technology. The chapter starts by exploring the concept of time, from Heidegger's notion of time as temporality, the lived time, to the concept of real time, inherited from human-computer interaction studies, reflecting the immediacy and simultaneity that characterizes temporality in the digital age. The chapter discusses different perspectives of temporality, considering its relations to technology and power in four main intersections: temporality and technology, temporality and real time, temporality and power, and temporality and deceleration.

Chapter 3

In this chapter, the authors will attempt to answer two related questions: How is our cognitive experience with time enacted and extended? Has the cognitive dimension of the experience of time lost its reference in the body? The background reviews relevant literature and shows the motivation for the main discussion of the chapter, especially the contrast between the authors' approach and the traditional symbolic-representational view. The principal argument will be that the dimension of the organism's coupling with the environment that can be called engagement with material culture—or things—has been undertheorized in the literature. Bringing this dimension into the analysis can, the authors argue, help explain how we experience psychological time. What's more, it can help understand the kinds of extra-bodily extensions that might explain why the use of technologies does not threaten disembodiment.

Chapter 4

Digital consumer devices have penetrated our everyday lives, providing a platform to—with great efficiency and easiness—solve problems, communicate and exchange information, participate in remote activities, and even socialize. This increasing popularity provides the impetus for a rising dependency, which translates into a growing number of hours spent with the various types of media available. However, while the time we dedicate to media increases (at the cost of other activities), the number of hours that we have available (per day, per week, per month, etc.) cannot, giving rise to media multitasking behaviors. Some studies suggest that time orientation—either as a cultural construct or an individual preference—can influence one's media use habits, predicting (or not) multiple media use. There are, however, other perspectives suggesting that media use can actually affect one's time orientation. This chapter will attempt to assess both of these outlooks.

Chapter 5
Cynthia H. W. Corrêa, University of São Paulo, Brazil

This theoretical perspective situates the notion of neo-tribalism or tribalism characterized by fluidity, punctual gatherings, and dispersion, independent of the encounter's purpose and interest, as a generator of networks of sociality in the postmodern cyberspace, from the formation of virtual communities or tribes. In this context, the imaginary occupies a central space in everyday life, because, as a representation, it reveals a meaning that goes beyond appearance. The analysis comprises the communication phenomenon as responsible for the constitution of a social bond in the cyberspace, structured under a postmodern condition, a different and a more tolerant style of seeing the world, unlike modern standards. Rather than well-defined roles to perform as it dominated in modern times, in the postmodernity prevails a full integration of the citizen into several communities by affinities and proximity, led by the logic of identification.

Chapter 6
Mikael Wiberg, Umeå University, Sweden
Britt Wiberg, Umeå University, Sweden

Despite the increasing interest in understanding screen time and its effects, there are very few papers published on how the notion of "screen time" is conceptualized – both in terms of what "time" refers to in this context and in terms of what a "screen" denotes nowadays. In an attempt to contribute to this lack of theoretical grounding, the authors outline four theoretical grounds for understanding time. Further, they suggest that the notion of "screen" needs to be problematized in similar ways. In this chapter, the authors illustrate how the four different conceptualizations of "time" in relation to this broader understanding of screens open up for a new range of studies of "screen time," and they suggest that this conceptualization is necessary in order to move toward.

Jorge Abreu, University of Aveiro, Portugal
Pedro Almeida, University of Aveiro, Portugal
Ana Velhinho, University of Aveiro, Portugal
Enrickson Varsori, University of Aveiro, Portugal

Given the continuous transformation of the video consumption across multiple devices, this chapter has the main goal of characterizing the viewer behaviors at home, including the motivations for specific interactive television (iTV) features. An online survey was conducted with the aim of clarifying if the consumption patterns at home are contributing to the demand for unification services that combine videos from internet sources with TV content. The results highlight some insights regarding the preferred devices depending on age and the content source, as well as limitations and valued features to be considered in the development of future unification and personalization services. The results from this study are useful, not only to understand the dynamics of audiovisual consumption regarding the "future of television," but can also be applied to foster product-oriented projects based on the synergies between behavioral factors, technological innovations, and industry trends regarding audiences' needs and UX.

Enrickson Varsori, University of Minho, Portugal
Sara Pereira, University of Minho, Portugal

Several studies value the importance of technologies in everyday social processes, stressing loudly its positive effects for time control and management. However, the use of digital technology is increasingly said to co-produce the ways youngsters experience daily lives, as these are increasingly weaved in media hyperconnections, in several insidious and multiple forms, and in a continuous and enduring manner. This text focuses on the state of the art about the extension and nature of these co-productive processes, highlighting the effects of the technological means of communication on youngster's time representations and experiences, namely considering the social networks and other interactional devices that are now constituting increasingly more the individual identity, despite its intangibleness. The goal is to critically analyze the existing literature on time, technology, and youth, presenting its main contributions from a conceptual, methodological and practical point of view, including the use and the ways in media hyperconnections.

This chapter presents and discusses the results of a qualitative study developed in Portugal and Brazil regarding PhD time and the scientific supervision processes, focusing on the manner in which digital technologies are used during the preparation time of doctoral theses. Based on the analysis of data collected by 20 semi-structured interviews with students and supervisors, the main advantages and disadvantages of screen time during scientific supervision are examined. In an academic and social context of high acceleration and time fragmentation, research presents valid development perspectives for a re-evaluation of supervision processes, more specifically in the current context marked by high presence of online platforms.

Chapter 10

This chapter is looking into the emerging concept of "futurization," which is being used in the context of policy making; however, without clear definition, it creates ambiguous reactions. What does "futurization of politics," "futurization of thinking," or "futurization of behavior" actually mean? This chapter looked into the associations citizens or laypeople have with terms "future" and "futurization," and what were their expressed and unexpressed hopes, dreams, fears, and anxieties. The study, using surveys and focus-groups, revealed a rather lifeless image, future without photosynthesis, without female presence, and overall a wasteland scenario. However, when speaking about "futurization" in comparison to "future," there is much less inevitability, more personal agency, and both believe in and fear the technological advancement. The working definition of "futurization" is offered in the chapter as well as a comparative analysis of "future" vs. "futurization." The implications for sustainability policymaking and curriculum development in education are discussed.

In recent years, the concept of time perspective has acquired a prominent position within the psychology of time. After Zimbardo and Boyd´s seminal work, thousands of papers have cited its work and within the last decade; several books and papers of other authors have been dedicated to exploring and expanding its theory. Even when considering other relevant authors about this topic, such as Nuttin and Lens, among many others, Zimbardo´s theory has become a synonym of time perspective research. This chapter represents an effort to identify some of the existent shortcomings in subjective time research and more specifically in time perspective topics. This chapter intends to encourage a mostly needed discussion about what the actual state of the research being developed is and what precautions should be taken into consideration in future researches.

Chapter 12

World of Warcraft (WoW), a game of the genre MMORPG (massive multiplayer online role playing game), has proven to be a valuable field of study for researchers interested in understanding the functioning of online communities and social relationships in those communities. This chapter seeks, through literature review and interviews conducted within the game itself, from player/researcher immersion, to discuss the relationships of a group of players in a new context of relationship and (in)formation, considering the significant screen time, communication processes, identifications, and identity building.

The aim of this chapter is to examine the relations between time perspective and well-being considering two groups with different cultural backgrounds between Turkish and French. Instruments tapping into positive and negative affect, ontological well-being, flourishing, and five types of time perspective were administered to 615 late adolescents ages between 18 and 24 (Mean of age= 20.95, SD= 3.28). In this study, a recently created subjective well-being construct, known as ontological well-being (OWB), was utilized for measuring eudaimonic happiness based on time perspective in a cross-cultural study. Cluster analysis showed that Turkish people had higher levels of positive affect, negative affect, and psychological flourishing compared to French people, but the levels of regret and nothingness were similar in both groups. Differences between clusters in terms of negative affect were mainly driven by differences in ontological well-being (OWB).

This chapter intends to interact and integrate different perspectives that address temporality as a dimension that shapes the human being's life. On the other hand, temporality as a variable or universal dimension structures both the normal and abnormal life of people, having approached the subject from the perspective of psychiatrists of the Franco-German tradition to explain and phenomenologically understand the experience of time in psychosis. At present, understanding and interdisciplinary work should be taken into account and integrated for their application in the psychosocial rehabilitation of people with this pathology, recognizing also that the subject has not obtained concrete or satisfactory answers even today.

Preface

Life is time. We are time. Societies are time.

Time comprises a net in which phenomena suddenly appears in a wholly different light. The phenomena include feelings, memories, happiness, language, scholastic and professional achievements, one's sense of self, consciousness, stress, mental illness, and mindfulness of one's own self and body. (Wittmann, 2017, pp. xi–xii)

Time is essential and how you use time is crucial in the way we live. We all have 24 hours each day. However, the way these 24 hours are used varies greatly from person to person, it also varies according to culture and geography. This diversity and complexity creates a huge field of study, called Time Studies (CTUR, n.d.). But within Time Studies lies a great variety of focuses and approaches, since it is a subject of great complexity.

This book concerns all that investigates or studies about time and society. In general, it interests researchers and students of philosophy, sociology, psychology, anthropology, medicine, geography, new media, etc. The study of Time and Temporality is present in many scientific areas ranging from physics to philosophy. Where there are humans there is an interest in the investigation of the social uses of time.

THE CHALLENGES

Nowadays, the number of hours spent in front of screens is enormous. Screen time plays a very important role in work contexts, but even more significantly in contexts of leisure, social interaction and cultural consumption.

In the network society the screen time seduces the person to stay in the online interaction, leaving it in a state of alienation from its face-to-face context.

This almost compulsive relationship with screens is more evident in children and young people, although adults also spend a significant amount of their time using and consuming screens.

In this context, it is very important a book that brings together research contributions on the uses of time, and in particular the screen time, coming from various disciplinary areas, namely, sociology, psychology, new media, anthropology, medicine, etc. This is a clearly complex and interdisciplinary topic.

SEARCHING FOR A SOLUTION

This publication will contribute to the knowledge on time and society, in particular, on screen time and well-being, through a set of interdisciplinary contributions that demonstrates the complexity of the study of time.

Understanding how people manage their time in society is a challenge that involves many facets of everyday life and the personality and behavior of each person. This book is a clear contribution to understanding time in a contemporary society and how time management, and, in particular the time screen management, is critical.

ORGANIZATION OF THE BOOK

The book is divided into 14 chapters, with diverse contributions that contribute to understand the complexity of the phenomenon of time, in the life of individuals and in social organization. A brief description of each of the chapters follows:

Chapter 1, "Sedated by the Screen: Social Use of Time in the Age of Mediated Acceleration," discusses the impact of Screen Time on the lives of individuals, particularly children and young people. The author, through a systematic review of the literature focused on the concept of "Screen Time", shows that the published results show negative impacts on the physical health and mental health of children and young people who spend many hours in front of screens. The author uses the concept of paradox to show the existence of ambivalence in the society of screens, that is, what appears to be positive, in fact tends to present a negative face. In this reflective process, are treated some paradoxes that allow to reinforce the idea of alienation and sedation. This shows that young people are "Prisoners of the Screens". In addition, the author presents empirical results from two youth surveys, in which the tendency to be hyperconnected is evident, as well as the difficulty in managing the use of time in the face of tasks that have to be performed. These results point to the need for training to acquire time management skills, i.e., Time Literacy.

Chapter 2, "Running After Time: Temporality, Technology, and Power," analyzes the time in digital age underlining the idea of immediacy and simultaneity. The authors make this analysis from Heidegger's notion of time as temporality, the lived time, to the concept of real time, inherited from human-computer interaction studies. Considering the relations between technology and power, the authors discuss four main intersections: temporality and technology, temporality and real time, temporality and power, and temporality and deceleration. The authors emphasize the strong relationship between technology and society, although without advocating the existence of technological determinism. Different perspectives are confronted, namely those of P. Virilio, H. Rosa, J. Wajcman, among others. They conclude by stressing the need to continue to deepen the study of the dynamics between Temporality, Technology, and Power.

Chapter 3, "Screen Time, Temporality, and (Dis)embodiment," focuses on two main issues: first is the relationship between technology use and our experience and perception of time; second is the suspicion that the use of digital technologies can negatively interfere with the embodiment of the mind. Throughout the chapter the authors aim to answer some central questions, among them: How is our cognitive experience with time enacted and extended? Has the cognitive dimension of the experience of time lost its reference in the body? Is it possible that screen time can provoke a disembodied effect in our temporal and developmental architecture? Throughout the chapter the authors argue in the sense of answering the questions and evidencing how temporality is embodied and extended through our engagement with material culture. The authors launch future research challenges, defending the idea that the human body is no less involved in screen time use than in any other form of cognitive projection.

Chapter 4, "Time Orientation and Media Use: The Rise of the Device and the Changing Nature of Our Time Perception," considers the current communicational scenario which is characterized by the existence of multiple media and the increasingly intensive use of these media for hours and hours, typically in a multitasking approach. It is against this media saturated scenario that the authors make their analysis from different perspectives: Time orientation as a cultural construct; Time orientation as an individual preference; time orientation as a predictor for (multiple) media use and media use as a predictor for (a new time) orientation. In conclusion, the authors consider that there is bidirectional interference between time perception and technology.

Chapter 5, "Screen Time and the Logic of Identification in the Networked Society," analyzes the communicational scenario promoted by the Internet, which generated the possibility of new social aggregations (new tribes) and dynamics of sociability. The author starts off from classic authors of Cyberculture, as M. Maffesoli, P. Lévy, M. Castells, H. Rheingold, A. Lemos e D. Wolton to substantiate his reflection and analysis and makes the historical course of how cyberspace was constituted as a symbolic / virtual space that allows to create community and the symbolic construction of personas and, thus, the existence of a temporality of the online presence (screen time). The discussion of the theme is framed in the problematic of postmodernity. The author also discusses the issue of deterritorialization associated with the formation of virtual communities, and the typical communication scenario (cybersociality) thus mediated by the screens.

Chapter 6, "The Screens of Our Time: On 'Time' – Implications for Screen Time Research," contributes to the definition of screen time with the assistance of four different conceptualizations of "time": biological time, psychological time, social time and cultural time. The authors discuss each of these four perspectives on time. The authors emphasize that the "Screen time" can be understood in different perspectives: as objective measurable screen time; e.g. clock, calendar or mathematical time, respectively as experiential screen time, which can be defined as psychological screen time and also as subjective or social screen time and finally cultural screen time. The authors underline the importance of theoretical work around the concept of time and screen time, in order to be able to continue empirical studies with a solid theoretical framework.

Chapter 7, "Returning to the TV Screen: The Potential of Content Unification in iTV," contributes to understand the dynamics of audiovisual consumption regarding the 'future of television' through the characterization of the viewer's behavior at home, including the motivations for specific interactive television (iTV) features. The authors present the results of the survey conducted with the objective of characterizing the audiovisual practices and demands in the domestic environment along with a contextualization of the current trends in the TV ecosystem of a European country, Portugal. The results gathered from the survey aimed to answer some emerging questions: Do audiovisual consumption preferences impact the choice of which device to use at home?; Do unification and personalization features lead to a preference for audiovisual consumption on the TV screen?; Are the audiovisual consumption patterns at home contributing to the emergence of a unification scenario?; If having access to a unified TV system, would consumers prefer the TV screen for watching OTT audiovisual content instead of their current services? The analysis of the results obtained through the survey contribute to understand the behaviors and motivations associated to audiovisual consumption and the screen time spent by users from different age groups at home.

Chapter 8, "A Critical Review of Social Screen Time Management by Youngsters in Formal Educational Contexts," contributes to the realization of the state of the art about social screen time management by youngsters in formal educational contexts, namely considering the social networks and other interactional devices, which characterize the current society as a multi-screens society. The authors emphasize in their conclusion that the metasyntactic outcomes put in evidence the complex interactions between screen devices and personal time management. The authors highlight opportunities for future research, namely: investigate in order to identify the educational factors surrounding the screen time problematic among juvenile audiences; investigate the perceptions and causes of the technology use time impact on students and verify the potential of technologies use for the training and education. These are some of the topics for future research, which the realization of the state of the art has made evident and that have high potential to understand the management of screen time that young people do, namely, in formal educational contexts.

Chapter 9, "The Era of Hyperconnectivity: Investigating the Times for PhD Supervision," addresses the following dimensions: 1) the modes in which supervisors and students use screen time; 2) the advantages and the difficulties posed by the screen time both for supervisors and supervisees; and finally, 3) the type of strategies used to manage and master screen time usages during the PhD supervision. Based on the analysis of data collected by 20 structured interviews with students and supervisors, the main advantages and disadvantages of online technologies during scientific supervision are examined. This analysis contributes to know the opinion of PhD students and supervisors about the role that mediation technology and screen time as mediator can, or cannot, play in a scientific supervision processes. Although the contemporary society has consolidated the meeting in screen-mediated environments, one of the main conclusions of this study is that both doctoral students and supervisors consider it essential to conduct face-to-face meetings, especially in the theoretical research phase and in moments of decision-making on methodological options.

Chapter 10, "Futurization of Thinking and Behavior: Exploring People's Imaginings About the Future and Futurization," focuses on presenting in depth the emerging concept of 'futurization'. Also making the confrontation between the concept of Futurization and Future. The authors point out how important decision-making processes are for the individual and for society, and how these decision-making processes are influenced on what is thought / felt about the present and influenced on the imagery that each one has about the future. The authors state that the term 'futurization' has been used in processes associated with scenario planning and scenario analysis as a way to incorporate future thinking into present decisions, but that has been installing a lot of ambiguity around this term. This chapter describes the empirical work carried out, in which the participants had to define what they understood by Futurization. The result is that the interpretations given by the participants can be categorized into three distinct interpretations of the future: the future as a dystopic reality, the future as an extrapolation of the present and the future as a utopic result of an orchestrated intervention in the present. The main question that the authors aim to answer is: What images of the future people have and how those affect the daily life and behaviors?

Chapter 11, "If It Ticks Like a Clock, It Should Be Time Perspective: Shortcomings in the Study of Subjective Time," aims to identify some of the existent shortcomings in Subjective Time research and more specifically in Time Perspective topics, to contribute to a more enlightened discussion and to take precautions in future investigations. In order to create knowledge of what has been published within Time Perspective, the author advocates the importance and usefulness of meta-analysis as a research method and bibliometric analysis. These methodological approaches allowed us to know what has been investigated in this field and the impact that these publications and projects have had. The author presents a set of questions around which the debate over the study in Time Perspective should occur: 1) Which dimensions (or temporal frames) compose Time Perspective?; 2) Temporal extension, density, as many other concepts, should be considered as independent constructs or as composite properties of Time Perspective?; 3) Time Perspective should be considered as a trait or a process?; 4) What is the stability of these constructs, not only from a temporal point of view but from a situational perspective? It is thus launched the challenge of the discussion about the quality of studies to be undertaken to ensure the theoretical and methodological quality of future investigations.

In Chapter 12, "*World of Warcraft*: Screen Time and Identity Building," through a literature review and interviews with *World of Warcraft* (WoW) players, the authors analyze the game environment and screen time as factors of (in) formation of the subject and creation of identities. According to the authors, there are World of Warcraft players who feel more comfortable in the online game environment, which allows them to create their identity without constraint, than in the physical world. One of the main ideas to retain is the presence of the Psychological Feeling of Community among the players of the WoW. And that *World of Warcraft* was conceived as an effective space where players can establish relationships, built identities. In addition, it should be emphasized that a significant part of current relationships take place in online spaces / services, so screen time plays a significant role in consolidating the identity of individuals. The social relations built in *World of Warcraft* contribute to build the Self and to build communities. These entities play a role in the on-line world of the game, but eventually build up the construction of the identity of the subject, which exists in the material world, promoting a process of flow between these two worlds that have the meeting point on the screen.

Chapter 13, "Measuring the Relationship Between Time Perspective and Well-Being," examines the relationship between time perspective and well-being considering two groups with different cultural backgrounds between Turkish and French. The empirical study involved 615 late adolescents ages between 18 and 24 (Mean of age= 20.95, SD= 3.28), and it was used a recently created subjective well-being construct, known as ontological well-being (OWB), was utilized for measuring eudaimonic happiness based on time perspective in a cross-cultural study. The Turkish sample was composed of 307 undergraduate students, 208 female and 99 male ($\bar{x}$ = 20.96, SD = 3.15). The French sample was composed of 245 undergraduate students, 198 female and 63 male ($\bar{x}$ = 20.88, SD = 3.05). Each participant was invited to complete a scales set including perceived parenting behaviors, affect, and well-being. The authors present the differences of results obtained between the Turkish sample and the French sample, and point out as one of the main reasons, the structure and the cultural process, which play an important role in the temporal perspective.

Chapter 14, "The Destructuring of Time in Psychosis," shows, on the one hand, that Time is an universal variable, valid for all people regardless of their mental health. And, on the other hand, Time is an interdisciplinary topic with philosophical, biological, physiological, psychological, neuroscientific, astronomical, etc. approach. The authors present the historical evolution of Time in the psychiatry of the XX century and in the psychology of today. The authors underline the changes in the perception of Time in situations of psychic pathology and how this manifests clinically. The subjective experience of time in psychopathology shows how much time management becomes a major challenge. The chapter highlights the importance of empirical data and theoretical knowledge of the Time in pathological scenarios to rethink and adjust the effectiveness of Mental Health policies and programs, in contemporary society.

This book has the value of bringing together contributions from different points of view about Time and Temporality, converging approaches from various disciplinary domains and various methodological approaches. This fact gives a wealth of theoretical and empirical contributions, which make it a book with a great breadth and originality, useful to researchers and students of various fields, especially psychology, sociology and communication.

Lídia Oliveira
University of Aveiro, Portugal

REFERENCES

CTUR. (n.d.). *Centre for Time Use Research*. Retrieved December 5, 2018, from https://www.timeuse.org

Wittmann, M. (2017). *Felt Time: The Science of How We Experience Time*. The MIT Press.

Acknowledgment

The editor would like to acknowledge the help of all the people involved in this project and, more specifically, to the authors and reviewers that took part in the review process. Without their support, this book would not have become a reality.

First, the editor would like to thank each one of the authors for their contributions. Our sincere gratitude goes to the chapter's authors who contributed their time and expertise to this book.

Second, the editors wish to acknowledge the valuable contributions of the reviewers regarding the improvement of quality, coherence, and content presentation of chapters. Some of the authors also served as referees; I highly appreciate their double task.

Lídia Oliveira
University of Aveiro, Portugal

Chapter 1
Sedated by the Screen:
Social Use of Time in the Age of Mediated Acceleration

Lídia Oliveira
https://orcid.org/0000-0002-3278-0326
University of Aveiro, Portugal

ABSTRACT

The social use of time has been progressively affected by the presence of screen devices in people's daily lives. These devices are of various types: television, tablet, computer, smartphones, etc. However, all of these have a power of seduction that makes people want to use them. In reality, a significant part of tasks are mediated by screens, whether they are playful tasks, socializing, work or training. In this chapter, the authors reflect on some quasi-paradoxical situations triggered by screen time, which shows that one is sedated by the screen. Then, they present the results of a systematic review of the literature focused on the concept of "screen time," which shows that the excessive use of the screen is causing various health problems, especially in children and young people. And, the results of two empirical studies are presented, one with young people between 12 and 18 years old, and the other with university students. The results of both studies demonstrate the need to develop competences in the management of the social use of time, that is, to develop time literacy.

DOI: 10.4018/978-1-5225-8163-5.ch001

INTRODUCTION

The densification of events, information and images makes it impossible to delay. The rapid chaining of fragments leaves no room for contemplative delay. The images that pass fleetingly on the retina, fail to capture lasting attention. Propagates their force of attraction and fade away. (Han, 2016b, 55)

Time is a fundamental element of the organization of individual life and collective life. Societies are organized according to time rituals, whether religious or profane. There continues to be a circularity dimension of the present tense in the repetition of the daily, weekly, monthly and annual cycle. As if the mythical circular time had remained forgotten within the calendars. This circularity allows organizing the routines and establishing predictable cycles. However, in the last century social time underwent a strong acceleration process (H. Adams, 2005) (Rosa, 2013a) (Torres, 2016). This social acceleration was essentially produced / driven by the development of transport technologies. First of transporting people and goods and then transporting streams of various kinds (information flows, energy flows, financial flows, etc.), which becomes an acceleration of social life and the generation of dynamics of alienation (Rosa, 2013b).

The social use of time was modified according to individual objectives and social, cultural and economic dynamics. And these depending on available resources, namely, technological resources. The contemporary context is characterized by an exponential proliferation of digital information and communication technologies, storage, treatment and sharing of information in volume, variety and speed never before existing, which contaminates all psychosocial, political, cultural and economic routines.

The objective of this essay is the time in screen society (Cardoso, 2013), the era of hyperconnection (Oliveira & Baldi, 2014) and hyperconsumption (Lypovetsky, 2007), which leads to screen culture (Ana Melro & Oliveira, 2017). Screen time in a paradoxical society in which social acceleration is a central element, but where people are sedated by the screens, remaining for many hours consuming and / or sharing content, socializing and / or working online or performing tasks in which the screen plays a crucial role.

In a society where the tendency is to spend more and more hours online looking at a screen, which assumes the role of mediation access to information and relationships, it is crucial to understand what role this screen-time plays in people's lives. What consequences does the increase of occupation of time with the consumption and relationship mediated by the screen have? There will be screen time to cannibalize other types of time (Oliveira, 2017) - time to walk, time to cook, date, participate, study, etc. Considering the lack of time reported by a significant amount of people and what has been called the time pressure, which consists in the person feeling unable to do everything he has to do in the time he has available, we are led to conclude that there are new variables that consume time. In addition, the telepresence in which being connected makes the individual feel permanently pressured to respond to requests online (Barber & Santuzzi, 2016). Paradoxically, today's societies are the ones that have the most facilitators of everyday dynamics, cars, washing machines and dishwashers, piped water systems, ovens, stoves, etc. - which apparently saves time, which means people should have more time available, but the general complaint is lack of time.

The initial thesis is that the time spent on the screens (television, tablet, smartphone and computers) intensifies the use of time, making people never having "in-between times", that is, free time between tasks or displacements because the person has the smartphone and with it saturates your time, it fills. In such a way the screen-time is full, that leads individuals and societies to a state of sedation - society sedated by screens.

The present work is structured as follows: i) begins with a reflection based on a bibliographical survey centered on the concept of time, namely, with the identification of what are considered paradoxical situations of contemporary society; with the objective of establishing a theoretical framework that demonstrates the complexity of the time theme and, in particular, of social time and psychosocial perception of temporality; ii) the two main methodological procedures are presented, namely: the systematic review of literature based on the concept of screen time and having as corpus the basis of scientific documents indexed in Scopus (for being considered as one of the bases with better coverage of publications in the social sciences and humanities)[1], and the completion of two questionnaire surveys [2]. One of the surveys aimed at young people aged between 12 and 18 years in Portugal, in order to understand the extent to which the use of screen devices interferes with the social use of time (in which 406 valid answers were obtained) (Varsori, 2016) and another questionnaire, with the same objective aimed at university students from Portugal (in which 516 valid answers were obtained) (Campos, 2016); iii) we present some of the results obtained and their analysis in which we intend to understand screen time and its impact on the various dimensions of social relations and to what extent it generates alienation; iv) finally, the conclusions presented that aim to systematize the main ideas and contributions.

BACKGROUND: TIME IN THE SCREEN SOCIETY

The hypermodern era is contemporary with true screen inflation. Man has never had so many screens, not only to see the world, but also to live his own life. And it appears that the phenomenon, sustained by the prowess of high-tech technology, will expand and accelerate even further. (Lipovetsky & Serroy, 2010)

Time is a transversal and essential element in personal and organizational management. All of us, every day, decide what we do with our time according to our goals, our desires and our relationships. Decisions about the use of time impact on all other dimensions of our lives, namely our physical and mental health (Babic et al., 2015, 2017, 2016, Carson & Kuzik, 2017), our school success and / or professional, in our financial management, in our relational success, in our well-being and leisure, etc. (J. Adams & Nettle, 2009, Escobosa, 2012). What we do over time determines who we are.

It is in this sense that the use of the Time Organization Scale (Leite, Tamayo, & Günther, 2003a, page 63) becomes very pertinent, allowing the analysis of how subjects manage and perceive the management of their time. As can be seen in the items of the Time Organization Scale presented below (Table 1), it is possible to infer the style of relationship that the subject has with time management.

Table 1. Time organization scale

I leave what I have to do for the last hour
I postpone today's tasks for the next day
I take some time before initiating a task
I often interrupt what I am doing
It is difficult to keep my obligations up to date
I give up easily after starting an activity
Once I start an activity, I persist until I finish it
I have difficulty completing started activities
I plan my activities following an order during the day
I plan my activities everyday
I follow a daily routine
When I finish a task, I know what I should do next.
I am late for my appointments
I do enough with my time
I have trouble knowing what is most important for me to do in the day
I finish my tasks before the deadline

Source: (Leite et al., 2003a, p. 63)

These items of time organization are of particular interest if they are crossed with a range of values and media presence (Sora, 2016) in the decision-making ecosystem that leads to the use / distribution of time. If we add as a criterion of analysis the rhythm (Wajcman, 2008; Alhadeff-Jones, 2017) we can easily understand that acceleration is the dominant brand introduced by modernity (Rosa, 2013a).

This scale was used in both the empirical studies presented in the scope of this chapter and whose objective was, among others, to understand how students from 12 to 18 years and university students position themselves regarding the social use of time in relation to the consumption of screen devices in your everyday life.

Time is not a category that can be appropriated linearly. In reality time is a highly complex entity that has been studied under different perspectives according to several areas, namely, philosophy, physics, anthropology, sociology and psychology. Here we are interested in cultural time, time lived (Hall, 1984), time perceived by individuals. This perception is built within a social, family, group and personal worldview.

Nowadays time is assumed to be a tradable commodity, capable of being segmented, fragmented, more or less well managed - "Time is seen in this [Western contemporary] society as a commodity or a valuable resource to be filled with productive activities. Like other resources, time can be negotiable, sold, spent, saved or wasted, and can be well or poorly managed." (Leite, Tamayo, & Günther, 2003b, p.57). It is in this sense an indispensable resource that becomes a challenge of reflection in the context of the hyper connection society. The central question is: What are digital networked information and communication technologies making to the use of time?

Parallel to a society of connection, we developed a society of acceleration (Rosa, 2011, 2013b, 2013a), and as Harmut Rosa evidences, the processes of acceleration are not all of the same kind, and from that we can distinguish three orders of acceleration: technical acceleration, acceleration of social change and acceleration of the rhythm of life (Rosa, 2013a, 187); the process of social acceleration being a self-powered process in a spiral of acceleration – "l'accélération social de la modernité est devenue un processus autoalimenté, qui place les trois registres de l'accélération dans la spirale d'une relation synergique. L'accélération engendre alors en permanence plus d'accélération et elle se renforce elle-même dans un processus circulaire." (Rosa, 2013a, pp. 187–188).

The acceleration is felt in an almost paradoxical way given that if on the one hand there are immense physical flows of people in space, on the other hand there is an apparent stillness of people. Display devices absorb the attention of their users by placing them in a state of alienation from the context. We've all been confronted with pictures of friends at dinners where everyone is looking at their smartphone or pictures of people walking the streets while they look absorbed by the screen of their smartphone, or families that are apparently in the same place do not look, nor they communicate because they are alienated from the context of proximity, by an imperative of connection and interaction with what is absent, as if the screen was the place of an epiphany of the absent (Varsori & Oliveira, 2015) that keeps them sedated.

Display devices tend to suspend individuals from their circumstances and generate a perceived shortening of time, as if the time spent online was short, passing so fast that they do not even feel it, even though they have spent quite a bit of objective time. This effect is called the Subjective Paradox of Time which shows that the time of experience and the time of remembrance (of the memory of that time) are inverse qualities (Rosa, 2013b, pp. 127-129). When the lived experience is felt as pleasant and desired, time is perceived as rapid, but this time leaves in the subject many memories, for example, the holiday week passes quickly and of them are immense memories (short-long time); but a week of boring and monotonous work is perceived as an eternity, the days are hard to pass and this week little or nothing remains to be remembered (long-short time). The question is: how is the relation between perception and memory regarding screen time? When surfing the internet, playing online, watching TV, and other screen activities, the perception is that time goes by fast, even dedicating many hours to this activity (those who have young people at home know clearly how much they ask for to stay a little longer on television, on the computer or on the mobile phone, or in several at the same time, generating a small daily battle for these display devices to be turned off for sleeping or studying. The question is: what memory is left of that time? And the answer tends to be that it too is brief. Thus a new category of relation is called, that is, the brief-brief (brief as duration and brief as memory of that time).

This brief-brief time refers to the idea of civilization of the slightness (Lipovetsky, 2016), namely, the lightness-distraction that the media and the screen devices potentiate.

We live in the age of the triumph of lightness, both in the literal and metaphorical sense of the term. It is a daily culture of lightness mediated by the mass media that govern us, the universe of consumption that does not fail to exalt the hedonistic and playful references. Through objects, entertainment, television and advertising, an atmosphere of permanent amusement and incitement to the enjoyment of immediate and easy pleasures is spread. It is replaced by coercion by seduction, duty by hedonism, solemnity by humor ... lightness ... has become one of the great mirrors where our age is reflected. (Lipovetsky, 2016, p. 14)

The civilization of the slightness has in the sex appeal of the interaction with the smooth surface of the screens, its manifestation par excellence. Users are stuck to the screens between the seduction of the almost dermal caress, anticipating the soft / light encounter with the Other of Like - "The polished, clean, smooth and flawless is the sign of the identity of the present time. (...) The smartphone also complies with the aesthetics of the polished. (...) The polished is not limited to the outside appearance of the digital device. The communication carried out by means of the apparatus is also polished and softened, since its contents are mainly signs of complacency and, in short, positive things. Sharing and Ticking are modes of polite communication. Negative aspects are eliminated because they represent obstacles to accelerated communication "(Han, 2016a, pp. 11-12). This politeness and lightness make a great contribution so that the time spent on the screens is perceived as a short time, which passes quickly, which does not generate boredom, although it may be the manifestation of deep existential boredom, since this experience tends not to contribute for the constitution of memories to which to tie meaning for life.

The time-screen, online time, hyperbolize the present (Baldi, 2011b, 2011a), individuals are stuck to the present moment, sedated by the permanent interaction of having to update their profile in social networks, assign Likes, respond in chats, view the videos of the vlogers they follow, respond to the permanent avalanche of new publications, new e-mails or sms that always request urgent response, which when not answered generate a frustrated expectation in the interlocutor, who indignantly tries to understand why the other does not respond. This saturated screen time prevents the subject from feeling its context. It is suspended in the circumstances, from the polyphony of the images, sounds, smells and textures of the place, to be situated in between here and somewhere, where their interlocutors meet. This circumstance generates the Paradox of Stillness, that is, there is an apparent stillness, physical (with all health problems associated with sedentary life), and permanent mental excitement normally associated with performing several simultaneous tasks, in a mental state called the Popcorn Brain phenomenon, jumping from task to task in an intensive multitasking approach, in an approach of superficiality that led Nicholas Carr to ask the question: What is the Internet doing to our brains? (Carr, 2012). This is a time-consuming, life-threatening hyperactivity, with consequences also on mental health (sleep disorder, difficulty focusing attention in depth on a task, social anxiety, etc.) (Babic et al., 2017; Domingues-Montanari, 2017, Wu et al., 2017).

From this infocommunication scenario stands out another paradox - Paradox of Sociability - glued to the screens, ignoring the physical presence of other people or being effectively alone, individuals socialize online. Circumstance that Sherry Turkle characterized in his work *Alone Together* (Turkle, 2011) emphasizing how being always online creates new solitudes. But nevertheless, people never seem to have had so many social networks and so many friends. And they maintain conversation and sociability with these friends, what can be questioned is not the dimension of sociability, but the nature of sociability in the society of screens, in the perspective of the sociology of mediation (Cardoso, 2013). This hyper-sociability in the screen-time puts us in interaction with many people, but in conversation with few, in the sense that the conversation refers to the attentive and time-consuming dialogue that builds in empathy, in the management of silence and arguments. And the most crucial conversation is that the subject does with himself, but the inner encounter involves having time to listen to oneself.

Some of the most crucial conversation you will ever have will be with yourself. To have them, you have to learn to listen to your own voice. A first step is to slow down sufficiently to make this possible. Online life ramped up the volume of what everyone sees on any day and the velocity with which it whizzes by. We are often too busy communicating to think, create, or collaborate. We come to online life with the expectation that we ask a question and get an almost immediate answer. In order to meet our expectations, we begin to ask simpler questions. We end dumbing down our communication and makes it harder to approach complex problems. (Turkle, 2015, p. 319)

The dynamics of online sociability has incorporated an infernal spiral of resumption - Sisyphean Time - even if you consult documents online, no matter how you respond and / or delete all e-mails before bed, however much I have followed the posting on blogs and vlogs, in a few moments, hours, the next day when we wake up the mailbox is full again, new issues have been posted, new likes, photos and related posts posted, as well as new comments and videos - and Sisyphus has to climb the mountain again.

The pressure to perform many tasks of a diverse nature simultaneously generates a high pressure and dispersion of attention (the empirical data presented later in this chapter show the tendency to multitask and dispersion of attention from the age of 12 to university students). In addition, the permanent connection creates in the interlocutors the sensation and the expectation of the permanent availability of the others. However, this permanent availability tends to become its inverse, that is, in permanent occupation, without time for the duration, for tasks and meetings that require an extended temporality.

On the other hand, although technologies have made it easier to carry out many daily tasks and reduce the time spent on commuting, in other words, generating free time, paradoxically, the feeling is that less and less time is spent, since in reality the permanent online connection fill the entire temporality.

Mobile communication technologies because of their tendency to ubiquity in everyday life have brought flexibility, given that one can access and perform tasks wherever one is. However, this flexibility has meant that the symbolic and real boundaries between work, family and leisure places tend to disappear, or to be less marked, and people hybridize in these places, tending to be in permanent link with the tasks / concerns of some spaces in the other spaces, disorganizing the use of time in function of the context.

There is a sociocultural organization of time in large temporal blocks - time to be child, young, adult, old - these temporalities affect in a structural way what is expected of the social use of time. However, it turns out that everyone is being overwhelmed by the screens, it can vary the type of screen of dominance of the tablet to the smartphone passing by the television that is the great company of the elderly. In the society of speed, mediated by the screens, there is little time for lasting social and affective bonds. On the screen, relationships are built in silence, no one hears. Lack of listening, in the process of sedation that the screen causes, which sucks attention and suspends the future, sticking to the moment.

The programs to promote digital inclusion and the development of infocommunication competences that the various governments promote, do not include the development of skills of social use of time, in other words, Time Literacy, when this is a key element.

The use of online services that put us in front of the screens is extremely useful facilitating the daily dynamics of access to information, streamlining communication and putting at the disposal of each one an immensity of resources that would not otherwise be available. This is an opportunity no one denies. But where there is light there is shade and it is necessary to analyze the shadows of life online. Using the Greek concept of *pharmakon*, what is remedy is, simultaneously, poison, will depend on the quantity. If the globalized and generalized connection can be the opportunity for the promotion of Collective Intelligence, as Pierre Lévy argues, as well as the alert itself, it can be the means to generate new forms of isolation, cognitive overload, dependence, domination, exploitation and idiocy (Lévy, 2000: 31). The data collected through the systematic review of the literature and through the two empirical studies show that we are drawn to scenarios of excessive and compulsive use whose perverse effects begin to gain visibility. Glued to the present, glued to the screen, glued to the immediate rewards of likes.

The paradox is that everything is a simultaneous gift, everything has the possibility, or must have, of being now. The present is shortened, loses its duration. Your time frame is getting smaller and smaller. Everything is pressing simultaneously in the present. What has as consequence an agglomeration of images, events and information that make impossible any contemplative delay. This is how we do zapping in the world. (Han, 2016b, 56)

METHODOLOGY

The first strategy consisted of a systematic review of the literature that allowed us to understand the existence of studies that had used the concept of screen time. This systematic review was carried out on September 7, 2018 on the basis of scientific documents *Scopus*[3] throughout its temporal scope. The research was carried out in the sense of retrieving all the publications that used in the title the expression "*Screen Time*"[4], of this research, 515 publications were obtained.

From these 515 publications the abstracts were analyzed in order to understand the approach taken in the use of the concept of "*Screen Time*" and what variables it was associated with and the conclusions reached.

In addition to the systematic review of the literature, two empirical studies were carried out through an online questionnaire in the context of conducting master's dissertations under my guidance (Campos, 2016) and under the researcher Ana Melro's guidance (Varsori, 2016). In the empirical study of students between the ages of 12 and 18, although the answer to the questionnaire was carried out online, as a way of promoting their completion, a request was made for the collaboration of Public Schools of Portugal. It was considered as a population to investigate Portuguese students between the ages of 12 and 18, born after 1998 and enrolled in Portuguese public education that is, attending between 7 and 12 years of schooling. In order to obtain a territorial distribution of the respondents, two public school groups were selected for each of the eighteen districts of the Portuguese mainland and two from each of the autonomous regions (Azores and Madeira), in a total of forty schools groupings (Varsori, 2016).

In the following image we can understand the distribution of the districts in the territory of Continental Portugal and verify the number of islands of the Archipelagos of Madeira and the Azores.

As the Schools were partner entities in the study, it was necessary to submit the study to the approval of the Directorate General of Education (DGE), Ministry of Education (ME), with the presentation of data collection instruments, the data collection strategy and its objectives. The Directorate General of Education approved the study because it considered it methodologically appropriate and relevant to its objectives. The main objective is to understand how the use of screen devices intervenes in the way young people in Portugal structure their social use of time.

The questionnaire surveys were answered online during the month of May 2016 and 406 valid answers were obtained.

With regard to the survey of university students, it was held from the beginning of May to July 5, 2016 and was addressed to the students of the Portuguese Public Universities, to which correspondence was sent requesting the dissemination of the study and the request for collaboration of its students. The request for collaboration

Figure 1. Map of districts of Portugal
(Source: http://apogk.pt/dojos/ - consulted on 2018-06-09)

was also disseminated online in the pages of the Universities on Facebook and in student forums, in particular, with the help of Academic Associations of the Universities involved in the study, to which requests for collaboration were sent. There were 516 valid answers, with participation of students from 12 Universities (Campos, 2016).

Results from both questionnaires were treated using SPSS Software (Version 24)[5].

PRESENTATION AND ANALYSIS OF RESULTS

Systematic Review of Literature

The systematic review of the literature (Collaboration, 2001; Khan, Kunz, Kleijnen, & Antes, 2003) was carried out on the basis of the *Scopus* scientific document, in its entirety, on September 7, 2018, with selection criteria publications that use the expression "Screen Time" in the title. This procedure allowed to collect 515 publications.

The analysis of the documents collected in the systematic review process made it possible to understand that "Screen Time", - the time spent using screen devices such as television consumption, Internet browsing, playing with consoles, playing with computers (on or off line), use of mobile phone and tablet, - is surveyed in its dimension of excessive consumption and how this consumption impacts on several aspects of the daily life of the individual. The studies underline the extent of addiction in media consumption, because individuals, with a particular focus on children and young people, spend an excessive number of hours in screen-mediated activities. This consumption is carried out in a context of sedentary lifestyle that reveals its consequences in terms of physical health, correlated with increased rates of obesity, cardiovascular problems, Type 2 diabetes and sleep disturbances (decrease in the number of hours of sleep, increase in sleep of daytime sleepiness and poor sleep quality). In addition to physical health, mental health is also affected young people's sense of great pressure and social anxiety associated with how online peers will react to their publications and sharing, sometimes seeing themselves in situations of bullying, depression and low self-esteem. Besides addiction, it is already a dependency, it tends to become pathological, causing individuals, especially children and young people, to be aggressive when they are deprived of the possibility of using screen devices.

Figure 2 systematizes areas of impact of excessive consumption of screen time.

It is evidenced that Screen Time is a behavior that impacts structurally on people's lives and social dynamics and, as such, should be the object of sociological analysis.

Figure 2. Impact of excessive screen time on quality of life

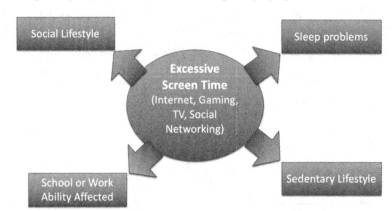

Doing a check of the occurrences of the words in the titles of articles retrieved from *Scopus* whose expression "Screen Time" is used in the title it turns out that the issues related to health are dominant. As can be seen in the Figure 3.

The infographic shown in Figure 4 expresses the intensity and transversality that the use of digital technologies in the way of life, especially the young, but increasingly also in the life of children and adults.

Sociology, and in particular the sociology of mediation, needs to be mindful of how Screen Time determines social, cultural, and political dynamics. This systematic review of the literature shows that there is a considerable impact on people's quality of life.

Empirical Study: Young People Between the 12 and the 18 Years

Regarding the characterization of the 406 respondents, aged between 12 and 18 years, the questionnaire survey shows that 217 (53.4%) are male and 189 (46.6%) are female . Regarding the possession of technological devices, the results indicate that: 99% have television and mobile, 60.6% have a laptop, 49% have a tablet, 43% have a fixed computer, 20.68% have a game console and only 8.13% have Smartwatch. Regarding the age at which they had the equipment, there are expressive values of those who always remember that in their home there is television (97.78%), portable computer (69.45%) and fixed computer (60.06%). Of note, 61.10% had their first mobile phone between 8 and 10 years old and 20.45% between 12 and 18 years old (Varsori, 2016).

Figure 3. Incidence of repetition of terms in titles of articles retrieved from Scopus whose expression "Screen Time" is used in the title[6]

Figure 4. Teen on Screens
(Source: Infografics by Alissa Scheller for The Huffington Post. Available in: http://www.huffingtonpost. com/2013/10/17/teens-on-screens_n_4101758.html)

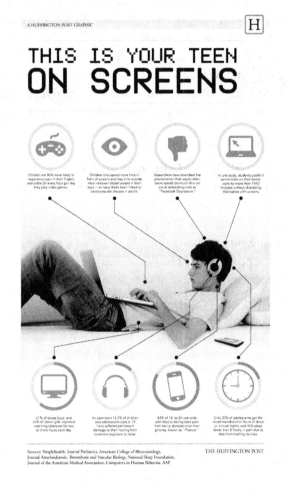

To complete the characterization of the access to the technologies by the young, it is verified that within their families there is a media ecosystem strongly populated with screen devices as can be seen in Figure 5.

This domestic context is of course an enhancer of a way of life in which the various elements of the family have habits of use of the screen devices, what makes these equipment already naturalized in the homes, that is, the natural way is that they exist and that are incorporated in the dynamics of social use of time.

As regards frequency of use, as can be seen in Figure 6, television and mobile phones are the dominant screens in the daily lives of young people.

Figure 5. Average number of screen devices per residence
Source: adapted from (Varsori, 2016, pp. 86–87)

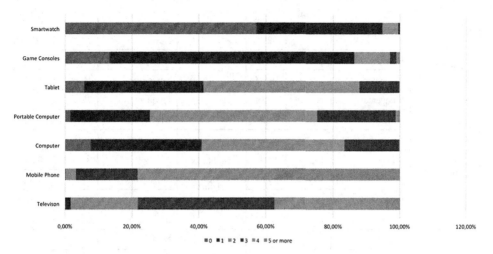

Figure 6. Frequency of use of the display devices
Source: adapted from (Varsori, 2016, p. 88)

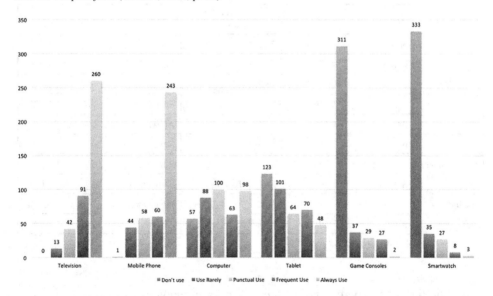

Also, in the sense of understanding the social use of time by young people and the use of technology, they were asked about the use of free time. Table 2 shows that screen devices have an expressive presence in leisure activities.

It was intended to understand the perception that young people have of the influence of past time in the use of screens in other activities of their daily lives

Table 2. Occupancy of free time associated with the use of display devices

		Total	% Total			Total	% Total
Watch TV / Interact with TV	Never	9	2.2%	Surf the Internet	Never	1	0.2%
	Rarely	30	7.4%		Rarely	3	0.7%
	Sometimes	78	19.2%		Sometimes	10	2.5%
	Frequently	79	19.5%		Frequently	78	19.2%
	Always	210	51.7%		Always	314	77.3%
Study / Do Homework	Never	5	1.2%	Read books, online magazines, etc.	Never	20	4.9%
	Rarely	10	2.5%		Rarely	82	20.2%
	Sometimes	106	26.1%		Sometimes	177	43.6%
	Frequently	193	47.5%		Frequently	63	15.5%
	Always	92	22.7%		Always	64	15.8%
Play games	Never	4	1.0%	Visit websites and use conversation apps (facebook, whatsapp, etc)	Never	3	0.7%
	Rarely	60	14.8%		Rarely	35	8.6%
	Sometimes	44	10.8%		Sometimes	102	25.1%
	Frequently	258	63.5%		Frequently	115	28.3%
	Always	40	9.9%		Always	151	37.2%
Listening to music	Never	3	0.7%	Talking on the phone	Never	4	1.0%
	Rarely	5	1.2%		Rarely	78	19.2%
	Sometimes	66	16.3%		Sometimes	87	21.4%
	Frequently	216	53.2%		Frequently	208	51.2%
	Always	116	28.6%		Always	29	7.1%
Use computer for activities not linked to the Internet	Never	87	21.4%	Texting	Never	4	1.0%
	Rarely	157	38.7%		Rarely	90	22.2%
	Sometimes	60	14.8%		Sometimes	59	14.5%
	Frequently	43	10.6%		Frequently	216	53.2%
	Always	59	14.5%		Always	37	9.1%

Source: (Varsori, 2016, pp. 90–91)

regarding the overall perception of the difficulty in managing time due to the use of screen devices, as shown in Figure 7, there is a considerable percentage of young people who recognize that the use of the screens presents them with difficulties of managing the time, 56.16% consider that this happens to them almost always and 9.36% always. If we add up these two values, we have that 65.52% of the young people realize that their Screen Time negatively impacts the way they manage time.

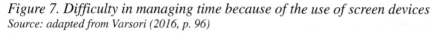

Figure 7. Difficulty in managing time because of the use of screen devices
Source: adapted from Varsori (2016, p. 96)

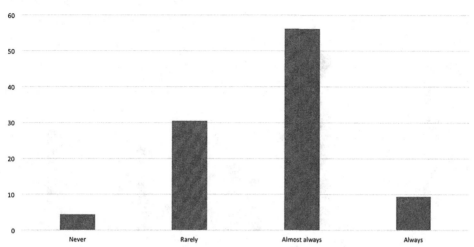

In order to deepen in what kind of activities the young people feel that the screen time influences the performance of other activities were surveyed and can be verified in Figure 8.

The analysis shows that in a clear way the use of the screens makes it more difficult to concentrate (83.5%), to be with the family (47%), to be with friends (39.7%) and curiously makes it more difficult to entertain / play 31.3%. Considering that studying in a concentrated way is essential for young people between the ages of 12 and 18 to undertake compulsory schooling, this result shows the need to develop in these young time management skills that allow the screen time to be in their favor, given that it is recognized as favorable when it comes to doing research with school purpose. The family that is another essential pillar in the development of young people of these ages sees communication threatened due to the screen time of their children. Here too, there is an alert to be done, so that young people are not alienated / sedated by the screens in the face of the two fundamental dynamics in their formation, school and family.

Considering the responses to the items of the Time Organization Scale (Figure 9), the predisposition to multitasking, which is an indication of scatter of attention, reinforces the already presented value of the screens making the focused / focused study process difficult.

It is also evident that, although young people follow a routine, which is natural since they have a weekly school schedule that they have to fulfill, it is noted that

Figure 8. How the use of the screens influences the performance of other activities
Source: adapted from Varsori (2016, p. 92)

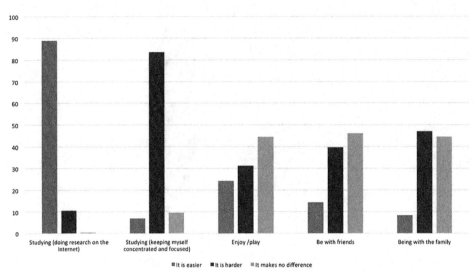

Figure 9. Answers to Time Organization Scale items
Source: adapted from (Varsori, 2016)

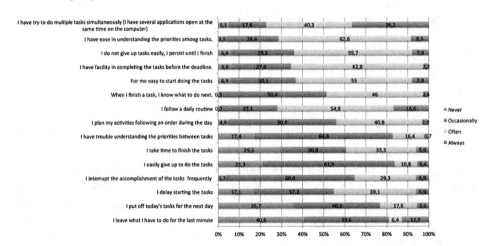

they take time to start the tasks, have some difficulty in understanding the priority between tasks and postpone what they have to do for the next day. The results of the responses to the items of the Time Organization Scale show the need for a training strategy / promotion of time management skills, so that these young people optimize their social use of time.

Empirical Study: Young University Students

The study of 516 valid answers from 12 Portuguese universities had 69.2% of female respondents and 30.8% of male respondents (Campos, 2016).

In higher education the ages can have a greater amplitude, as you can see in Table 3.

Regarding the distribution of the sample by the various University there are clearly asymmetries (Table 4), yet it is considered very interesting to have answers from several institutions, from students living in different contexts, most of whom study in medium-sized cities (Covilhã, Funchal, Aveiro, Évora and Braga).

Regarding the difficulty in managing the time, by the university students participating in this study, we can see the results in Table 5 and in Figure 10, which follow.

There is an important percentage that expresses that sometimes it is difficult to manage their time (48.4%), with 15.9% who usually have difficulty in managing the time plus 5.4% who always have difficulty. The sum of these values indicates that 69.7% have some degree of difficulty of time management. This result shows that although university students, in terms of age, have greater maturity, this is not sufficient for the acquisition of skills to social use of time that allows them to make good management of this fundamental resource that is the time. Therefore, also in the University there should be training for the development of skills in time management (Time Literacy). It is all the more important that these students will be the future professionals, senior managers who in addition to having to manage their own time, often perform management functions in organizations and as such have to manage the time of others and the organization.

Table 3. Distribution by age

Age	%	N
17-20	23,3%	120
21-24	37,0%	191
25-30	17,1%	88
31-35	5,6%	29
36-40	6,6%	34
> 40	10,4%	54
	100,0%	516

Source: adapted from (Campos, 2016, p. 48)

Table 4. Distribution of answers by University

University where you are a Student	N	%
University of Évora	208	40,2%
University of Aveiro	135	26,2%
University of Madeira	86	16,6%
University of Minho	53	10,3%
University of Beira Interior	21	4,1%
University of Lisbon	4	0,8%
University of Coimbra	3	0,6%
University of Algarve	2	0,4%
ISCTE - Lisbon	1	0,2%
University of Porto	1	0,2%
University of Azores	1	0,2%
New University of Lisbon	1	0,2%
	516	100,00%

Source: adapted from (Campos, 2016, p. 52)

Table 5. Frequency of difficulty in time management

How often do you find it difficult to manage your time?	%	N
Never	3,7	19
Sometimes	48,4	250
Usually	15,9	82
Occasionaly	26,6	137
Always	5,4	28
	100	516

Source: adapted from (Campos, 2016, p. 91)

As is shown in Table 6 with the crossing of data between the time spent on the internet and the difficulty of managing time, the tendency is to have a positive correlation and the greater the number of hours spent online the greater the degree of difficulty felt in time management.

Considering the answers to the items of the Time Organization Scale (Figure 11) it is clear that university students are also predisposed to multitasking.

It should be stressed how positive the persistence in the tasks and the demonstration of concern in arriving at the hours to the commitments. There is evidence that there is a high potential for dispersion both by multitasking and by the level of

Figure 10. Frequency of difficulty in time management
Source: adapted from (Campos, 2016, p. 91)

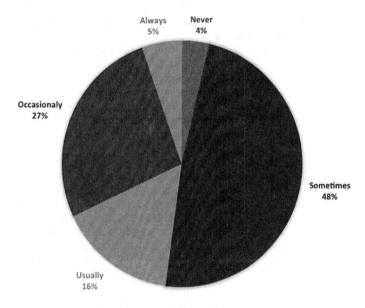

Table 6. Tabulation between the number of hours online and the frequency with which it feels difficult to manage the time

Tabulation between the number of hours online and the frequency with which it feels difficult to manage the time							
		How often do you find it difficult to manage your time?					
		Never	Sometimes	Usually	Occasionally	Always	Total
How many hours a day are you connected to the Internet?	Between 6 and 8 hours	5	63	19	33	9	129
	Between 3 and 6 hours	2	85	21	44	5	157
	Between 1 and 3 hours	4	31	9	26	1	71
	More than 8 hours	6	69	33	34	13	155
	Less than 1 hour	2	2	0	0	0	4
	Total	19	250	82	137	28	516

Source: (Campos, 2016, p. 330)

high frequency recognition of interrupting the tasks they are doing, which is an indicator of lack of concentration. Procrastination is also present in the way they manage time, with a high percentage indicating that they postpone tasks for the next day (49.4% occasionally, 16.5% often and always 2.7) and also a high tendency to leave for the last hour the accomplishment of the tasks (41.7% occasionally, 19.6 often and 3.7% always).

Whereas university students are users of high frequency display devices: 30% access more than 8 hours a day to the Internet, 25% between 6 and 8 hours and 30% between 3 and 6 hours a day. Being 100% holders of at least one personal display device that tends to be on 24 hours a day. Then, and also considering the

Figure 11. University students' response to the time organization scale
Source: adapted from (Campos, 2016)

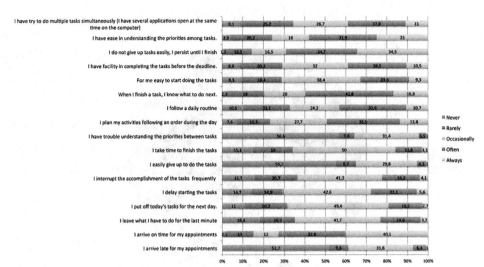

results obtained in the Scale of Organization of Time, it is necessary to promote metacognitive practices on the social use of time in order to mitigate the negative effects of excessive use that were presented in the topic of the systematic review of the literature.

FUTURE RESEARCH DIRECTIONS

The results presented in this chapter suggest the need for Time Literacy research to understand the level of awareness that people have of the consequences of screen time in their lives and in particular their quality of life (physical health, health mental and quality of face-to-face relationships). On the other hand, it is important to investigate which are the fundamental competences in the management of the social use of time; and how to develop these skills in children and young people. In particular, knowing how to manage Screen Time in daily life is crucial for personal and social balance, therefore, there is a great challenge for research on both the family and work context and the school context.

There is a need for future research that relates the individuals' temporal orientation profile (past, present or future) and the amount of hours spent online, namely to perform hedonistic activities. One of the issues that should be investigated is: people who spend a high number of hours online in leisure activities tend to be present oriented?

CONCLUSION

In contemporary society the mediation of access to information and communication is mostly performed through technological devices whose surface interaction is a screen, this allows to use the designation of society of the screens or talk about the emergence of the screen culture (A Melro & Silva, 2013). The proliferation of screens in daily life progressively occupies a significant time and absorbing other temporalities leading to dynamics of alienation from the context of proximity to lead the individual into a sedated state, which makes him oblivious to what surrounds him.

The screen society, paradoxically paralyzes individuals, who despite being hyperactive in online interactions, chatting online chats, updating profile in social networks, sharing photos, commenting, giving likes, watching videos, following playing, navigating among various simultaneous tasks, are physically quiet, with no physical activity reflected in rates of obesity, type 2 diabetes, and other psychophysical weaknesses.

Excessive use of screen and online activities promotes a sedated, contented society while online, under the hypnotic effect of the connection, losing the sense of self and context, forgetting the time to go to sleep and management of the time of social and school commitments, tending to multitasks, procrastinating what has to do, and forgetting the limit between personal and professional life, mixing contexts, establishing a fluidity of those who have little solidity, sedated someone who does not evaluate properly their actions, and have difficulty projecting the consequences in the future. The screen society, tendentially sedated and oriented to the present (Zimbardo & Boyd, 2008) (Chittaro & Vianello, 2013), where hedonic activities are privileged, where the enjoyment of being online suspends the subject of his daily reality, in its context and also of its responsibilities with itself and with the face-to-face context.

This reality of "Screen Prisoners" calls for the emergence of a screen-time literacy, that is, that time-management skills be developed, so that screen time cannot cannibalize the remaining temporalities (Oliveira, 2017). In this context we identify some initiatives as the application "Screen time - Manage the time your kids spend on their tablets and smart phone"[7]

The existence of applications such as *Screentime* that aims at parental control of the time that children spend on the screen shows that the paradoxical point has been reached, that digital integration has gone from access to information and knowledge construction to disruptive, fragmentation of attention and blurring of the concrete goals that children and individuals in general need to achieve.

Figure 12. Screentime Application
(source: https://screentimelabs.com/)

The screens promote a sedated society, which is alienated, which makes a consumption stuck to the present in fruition, a fast-food consumption from the portable screen, which is always present. It requires an ethics of deliberate disconnection as hygiene of the spirit and reconnection with context, contemplation, others and the aroma of time. This need is also reflected in the architecture that begins to design a building with a "white zone" without electromagnetic emissions, where there is no access to the Internet, where technological devices and artificial raw materials are excluded, with natural materials such as wood, clay, cork, wool, linen, cotton - these are spaces of recollection that enhance the subject's approach to himself, with the silence that reconnects with him, with the place, but also with the dialogue with the one next to him, promoting the exit of the state of sedation potentiated by the screen.

To accompany the promotion of the use of digital technologies should be triggered a program of development of management skills the social use of time, which integrates the challenge of the management of Screen Time, for the development of citizens with greater critical awareness and social and political participation.

ACKNOWLEDGMENT

Thanks to Enrickson Varsori and Sara Campos for their work in the scope of their Master's Dissertations. Thanks also to the Researcher Ana Melro for the co-supervision work of the Enrickson Varsori research. In this chapter I retake a small part of the empirical work done together with them to support my reflection about the paradoxical dimension of screen time.

REFERENCES

Adams, H. (2005). A Law of Acceleration. In The Education of Henry Adams (pp. 473–482). San Diego, CA: Icon.

Adams, J., & Nettle, D. (2009). Time perspective, personality and smoking, body mass, and physical activity: An empirical study. *British Journal of Health Psychology, 14*(1), 83–105. doi:10.1348/135910708X299664 PMID:18435866

Alhadeff-Jones, M. (2017). *Time and the Rhythms of Emancipatory Education - Rethinking the temporal complexity of self and society.* Routledge.

Babic, M. J., Morgan, P. J., Plotnikoff, R. C., Lonsdale, C., Eather, N., Skinner, G., ... Lubans, D. R. (2015). Rationale and study protocol for "Switch-off 4 Healthy Minds" (S4HM): A cluster randomized controlled trial to reduce recreational screen time in adolescents. *Contemporary Clinical Trials, 40*, 150–158. doi:10.1016/j.cct.2014.12.001 PMID:25500220

Babic, M. J., Smith, J. J., Morgan, P. J., Eather, N., Plotnikoff, R. C., & Lubans, D. R. (2017). Longitudinal associations between changes in screen-time and mental health outcomes in adolescents. *Mental Health and Physical Activity, 12*, 124–131. doi:10.1016/j.mhpa.2017.04.001

Babic, M. J., Smith, J. J., Morgan, P. J., Lonsdale, C., Plotnikoff, R. C., Eather, N., ... Lubans, D. R. (2016). Intervention to reduce recreational screen-time in adolescents: Outcomes and mediators from the 'Switch-Off 4 Healthy Minds' (S4HM) cluster randomized controlled trial. *Preventive Medicine, 91*, 50–57. doi:10.1016/j.ypmed.2016.07.014 PMID:27471018

Baldi, V. (2011a). Oltre il presentismo. *Critica Sociologica, 45*(178), 75–80.

Baldi, V. (2011b). Su tiempo! Más allá de la ubiquidad del presente. *Interartive. A Platform for Contemporaney Art and Thought, Abril/Maio*(31–32).

Barber, L., & Santuzzi, A. (2016). Telepressure and College Student Employment: The Costs of Staying Connected Across Social Contexts. *Stress and Health*. Retrieved from http://onlinelibrary.wiley.com/doi/10.1002/smi.2668/pdf

Campos, S. (2016). *StudentSurfer: Afinal o que fazem os estudantes universitários com a Internet?* Universidade de Aveiro.

Cardoso, G. (Ed.). (2013). *A Sociedade dos Ecrãs*. Lisboa: Tinta da China Edições.

Carr, N. (2012). *Os Superficiais - O que é que a Internet está a fazer aos nossos cérebros?* Lisboa: Gradiva Publicações.

Carson, V., & Kuzik, N. (2017). Demographic correlates of screen time and objectively measured sedentary time and physical activity among toddlers: A cross-sectional study. *BMC Public Health*, *17*(1), 1–11. doi:10.118612889-017-4125-y PMID:28193271

Chittaro, L., & Vianello, A. (2013). Time perspective as a predictor of problematic Internet use: A study of Facebook users. *Personality and Individual Differences*, *55*(8), 989–993. doi:10.1016/j.paid.2013.08.007

Collaboration, C. (2001). *Guidelines for preparation of review protocols*. Retrieved from https://scholar.google.com/scholar?hl=en&btnG=Search&q=intitle:Guidelines+for+Preparation+of+Review+Protocols#8

Domingues-Montanari, S. (2017). Clinical and psychological effects of excessive screen time on children. *Journal of Paediatrics and Child Health*, *53*(4), 333–338. doi:10.1111/jpc.13462 PMID:28168778

Escobosa, A. (2012). Los Usos Del Tiempo En La Relación: Familia, Trabajo Y Género. *Contribuciones a Las Ciencias Sociales*. Retrieved from http://www.eumed.net/rev/cccss/18/ape.pdf

Hall, E. T. (1984). *La Danse de la Vie - Temps culturel, temps vécu*. Paris: Seuil.

Han, B.-C. (2016a). *A Salvação do Belo*. Lisboa: Relógio D' Água.

Han, B.-C. (2016b). O Aroma do Tempo - Um Ensaio Filosófico sobre a Arte da Demora. Lisboa: Relógio D' Água.

Khan, K. S., Kunz, R., Kleijnen, J., & Antes, G. (2003). Five steps to conducting a systematic review. *JRSM*, *96*(3), 118–121. doi:10.1177/014107680309600304 PMID:12612111

Leite, U., Tamayo, Á., & Günther, H. (2003a). Organização do uso do tempo e valores de universitários. *Avaliação Psicológica*, *1*, 57–66. Retrieved from http://pepsic.bvsalud.org/scielo.php?pid=S1677-04712003000100007&script=sci_arttext&tlng=en

Leite, U., Tamayo, Á., & Günther, H. (2003b). Organização do uso do tempo e valores de universitários. *Avaliação Psicológica*. Retrieved from http://pepsic.bvsalud.org/scielo.php?script=sci_arttext&pid=S1677-04712003000100007

Lévy, P. (2000). *Cibercultura*. Lisboa: Instituto Piaget. Retrieved from http://www. google.com/books?hl=pt-PT&lr=&id=7L29Np0d2YcC&oi=fnd&pg=PA11&d q=cibercultura&ots=ghVxxEUwbm&sig=-39WptJB1He-abTbu0DdGCkBGOQ

Lipovetsky, G. (2016). *Da Leveza - para uma civilização do ligeiro*. Lisboa: Edições 70.

Lipovetsky, G., & Serroy, J. (2010). *O ecrã global*. Lisboa: Edições 70.

Lypovetsky, G. (2007). *A Felicidade Paradoxal - ensaio sobre a sociedade do hiperconsumo*. Lisboa: Edições 70.

Melro, A., & Oliveira, L. (2017). Screen Culture. In Encyclopedia of Information Science and Technology (4th ed.). Hershey, PA: IGI Global.

Melro, A., & Silva, L. (2013). A ecrãcultura emergente nas vivências dos jovens portugueses: poderá falar-se de uma geração de ecrãs? *Observatorio (OBS*)*. Retrieved from http://obs.obercom.pt/index.php/obs/article/view/694

Oliveira, L. (2017). Hiperconexão: o pensamento na era da canibalização do tempo. In H. Pires, M. Curado, F. Ribeiro, & P. Andrade (Eds.), Circum-navegações em Redes Transculturais de Conhecimento, Arquivos e Pensamento (pp. 73–84). Famalição: Edições Húmus.

Oliveira, L., & Baldi, V. (Eds.). (2014). *Insustentável leveza da Web: retóricas, dissonâncias e práticas na Sociedade em Rede*. Salvador da Bahia: Edufaba.

Rosa, H. (2011). Aceleración social: consecuencias éticas y políticas de una sociedad de alta velocidad desincronizada. *Revista Persona y Sociedad, 1*(25), 9–49. Retrieved from http://onlinelibrary.wiley.com/doi/10.1111/1467-8675.00309/abstract

Rosa, H. (2013a). *Accélération - Une critique social du temps*. Paris: La Découverte. doi:10.7312/rosa14834

Rosa, H. (2013b). *Aliénation et accélération: vers une théorie critique de la modernité tardive*. Paris: La Découverte.

Sora, C. (2016). *Temporalidades Digitales - Análisis del Tiempo en los New Media y las Narrativas Interactivas*. Barcelona: Editorial UOC.

Torres, F. (2016). A secular acceleration: Theological foundations of the sociological concept "social acceleration.". *Time & Society*, 25(3), 429–449. doi:10.1177/0961463X15622395

Turkle, S. (2011). *Alone Together: why we expect more from technology and less from each other*. New York: Basic Books.

Turkle, S. (2015). *Reclaiming Conversation - The Power of Talk in a Digital Age*. New York: Penguin Press.

Varsori, E. (2016). *Os Dispositivos-Ecrã no Quotidiano dos Jovens Portugueses - A mediação-ecrã no uso social do tempo*. Universidade de Aveiro. Retrieved from http://hdl.handle.net/10773/17738

Varsori, E., & Oliveira, L. (2015). Ecrã-quotidiano: Epifania do ausente. In *Atas do IX Congresso Sopcom*. Coimbra: SOPCOM.

Wajcman, J. (2008). Life in the fast lane? Towards a sociology of technology and time. *The British Journal of Sociology*, *1*(59), 59–77. doi:10.1111/j.1468-4446.2007.00182.x PMID:18321331

Wu, X., Tao, S., Rutayisire, E., Chen, Y., Huang, K., & Tao, F. (2017). The relationship between screen time, nighttime sleep duration, and behavioural problems in preschool children in China. *European Child & Adolescent Psychiatry*, *26*(5), 541–548. doi:10.100700787-016-0912-8 PMID:27822641

Zimbardo, P., & Boyd, J. (2008). *The Time Paradox - Using the new Psychology of Time to your advantage*. London: Rider.

ADDITIONAL READING

Añez, E., Fornieles-Deu, A., Fauquet-Ars, J., López-Guimerà, G., Puntí-Vidal, J., & Sánchez-Carracedo, D. (2018). Body image dissatisfaction, physical activity and screen-time in Spanish adolescents. *Journal of Health Psychology*, *23*(1), 36–47. doi:10.1177/1359105316664134 PMID:27557652

Cadoret, G., Bigras, N., Lemay, L., Lehrer, J., & Lemire, J. (2018). Relationship between screen-time and motor proficiency in children: A longitudinal study. *Early Child Development and Care*, *188*(2), 231–239. doi:10.1080/03004430.2016.1211123

Dong, F., Howard, A. G., Herring, A. H., Thompson, A. L., Adair, L. S., Popkin, B. M., ... Gordon-Larsen, P. (2017). Longitudinal associations of away-from-home eating, snacking, screen time, and physical activity behaviors with cardiometabolic risk factors among Chinese children and their parents. *The American Journal of Clinical Nutrition*, *106*(1), 168–178. doi:10.3945/ajcn.116.146217 PMID:28539376

Hewitt, L., Benjamin-Neelon, S. E., Carson, V., Stanley, R. M., Janssen, I., & Okely, A. D. (2018). Child care centre adherence to infant physical activity and screen time recommendations in Australia, Canada and the United States: An observational study. *Infant Behavior and Development*, *50*, 88–97. doi:10.1016/j.infbeh.2017.11.008 PMID:29223777

Levine, R. (2006). *A Geography of Time: The Temporal Misadventures of a Social Psychologist or How Every Culture Keeps Time Just a Little Bit Differently*. Oxford: Oneworld.

Mullaney, J. L., & Shope, J. H. (2015). Feeling the Hands of Time: Intersections of Time and Emotion. *Sociology Compass*, *9*(10), 853–863. doi:10.1111oc4.12301

Przepiorka, A., & Blachnio, A. (2016). Time perspective in Internet and Facebook addiction. *Computers in Human Behavior*, *60*, 13–18. doi:10.1016/j.chb.2016.02.045

Santos, A., Silva-Santos, S., Andaki, A., Mendes, E. L., Vale, S., & Mota, J. (2017). Screen time between Portuguese and Brazilian children: A cross-cultural study. Motriz. *Revista de Educacao Fisica*, *23*(2). doi:10.1590/S1980-6574201700020006

Swartz, M. K. (2017). Taking Another Look at Screen Time for Young Children. *Journal of Pediatric Health Care*, *31*(2), 141. doi:10.1016/j.pedhc.2017.01.006 PMID:28215218

Wajcman, J. (2016). *Pressed for Time: The Acceleration of Life in Digital Capitalism (1a)*. Chicago, London: The University of Chicago Press.

KEY TERMS AND DEFINITIONS

Alienation: Act and effect of detaching itself from the real and being suspended from the surrounding reality. The alienation promoted by the screen time causes the individual to shift their attention from the material context in which they find themselves, to a virtual context in which they interact in the pursuit of fruition.

Hyperconnection: The permanent and excessive use of internet services/social networks. The act of being permanently online and the feeling of absolute need to have an Internet connection, felt by the individuals; who have symptoms of stress due to the fact that they do not have an internet connection.

Paradox: An ambivalent situation, in which, after all, what appears to be evident finally contains its quasi-opposite.

Screen Time: The time individuals spend interacting with screens. Being that this interaction can have diverse purposes: to have fun, to socialize, to study and/or to work.

Sreenlife/Onlife: Lifestyle overly dependent on online interaction, which characterizes contemporary society in which a significant part of the activities are carried out through the connection to the Internet network.

Sedation: A psycho-physical state in which the individual is alienated from the context in which he or she is and presents a low level of self-awareness.

Social Use of Time: Time is a fundamental existential resource. All use of time realized by humans is a social use, since time acquires meaning in the social context, where each individual inserts itself. All uses of time are social, from bedtime, to hygiene, to work, to dating, to studying, to having fun, etc. The way time is used is clearly marked by each person's socio-economic and psycho-social context.

ENDNOTES

[1] Scopus - https://www.scopus.com/

[2] These surveys were carried out by students of the Masters in Multimedia Communication (Sara Campos and Enrickson Varsori Silva), University of Aveiro-Portugal, under my guidance and under researcher's Ana Luísa R. Melro guidance.

[3] https://www.scopus.com/home.uri - Web address of the database of scientific publications used in this research.

[4] Scopus research was conducted in English because it is mandatory that all indexed documents, even if written in another language, have the title, abstract and keywords available in English. In this way, the researcher is sure to retrieve all available information.

[5] Website where the software is located: https://www.ibm.com/analytics/us/en/technology/spss/ (accessed on 2018-09-15).

[6] This word cloud was developed using Wordle Software - http://www.wordle.net/create (last accessed on 2018-09-14).

[7] Screentime Application Site - https://screentimelabs.com/ (last accessed on 2018-09-23).

Chapter 2
Running After Time:
Temporality, Technology, and Power

Ivone Neiva Santos
University of Porto, Portugal

José Azevedo
University of Porto, Portugal

ABSTRACT

We live in a paradoxical age marked by the widespread perception that life is faster than it used to be, that quick access to people and information will free us to do other things, and simultaneously, most of us have experienced this creeping sense that time is slipping out of our control. That perception is a source of concern and even anguish considering the need we feel to follow the pace "imposed" by technology. The chapter starts by exploring the concept of time, from Heidegger's notion of time as temporality, the lived time, to the concept of real time, inherited from human-computer interaction studies, reflecting the immediacy and simultaneity that characterizes temporality in the digital age. The chapter discusses different perspectives of temporality, considering its relations to technology and power in four main intersections: temporality and technology, temporality and real time, temporality and power, and temporality and deceleration.

DOI: 10.4018/978-1-5225-8163-5.ch002

INTRODUCTION

We live in a paradoxical age marked by the widespread perception that life is faster than it used to be, and that quick access to people and information will free us to do other things. Simultaneously, most of us have experienced this creeping sense that time is slipping out of our control. This perception is a source of concern and even anguish, considering the need we feel to follow the pace "imposed" by technology.

For this reason, temporality in modern societies has been a subject of reflection and debate in social sciences. It is possible to find divergent perspectives, namely in what concerns to acceleration or its relationship with technological development, phenomenon, and relation that we usually associate to contemporaneity. This chapter starts by exploring the concept of time, from Heidegger's (2003) notion of time as temporality, the lived time, to the concept of real time, inherited from human-computer interaction studies (Sora, Jordà & Codina, 2017), reflecting the immediacy and simultaneity that characterizes temporality in the digital age. It then discusses different perspectives of temporality, considering three main intersections: Temporality and technology, temporality and real time, and temporality and power.

The sensation of being "pressed for time" or "against the clock" became common in modern life, that now goes hastily at the rhythm of real time. It is the rhythm of the immediacy, which digital media made possible, that transforms our temporal experiences, now increasingly characterized by speed and ubiquity. This results in the perception of a continuous time, homogeneous and globalized, over which we have no control. In literature, real time appears frequently associated to astronomic time. It is a unique, universal time that overlaps the chronology of events that happen in a local, historical moment. On the other hand, chronological time, allowing for the organization and synchronization of human activities, had and still has a fundamental role in our daily life and in societies, and is recognized as an essential factor in the development of capitalism. If, as Castells (2010) or Virilio (2000) state, real time is a key-element of the current phase of the development of capitalism, which Jameson (1991) baptized as "late capitalism", the relation between the two dimensions of time reveals itself complex. This complexity is reflected in the paradoxical character of contemporary temporality and in the diversity of perspectives that can emerge in its analysis. Indeed, it is possible to find approaches that identify temporality as univocal and characterized by acceleration (as in Virilio's view), but also others that recognize different temporalities with different and interdependent speeds (for instance, Sharma, 2017). This second field may include authors that find mainly social reasons to that differentiation and authors, such as Wajcman (2008), that value personal appropriation, signing the individual capacity to define personalized temporalities.

The difficulty to define time and temporality makes the construction of a theoretical body hard. According to Rosa (2013), social scientists' approaches to the subject may be organized in three main fields. The first systematizes the existing literature and reflections from different perspectives, generally presenting this systematization as an argument to claim the importance of temporal structures in society and the need to study them deeply. Rosa refers, for example, Lauer (1981) and Bergman (1992). The second field is dedicated to the study of specific dimensions of temporality, as Levine (1997) did. Indeed, this author concentrated his attention on the study of the acceleration of the pace of life, not questioning but assuming "time" as a "self-evident quantity" (Rosa, 2013, p. 2). Lastly, the third field is dedicated to clarify the concept of time in philosophical, scientific, and social terms. Here, Rosa (2013) mentions, for instance, Nassehi (1994), who, inspired by Luhmann's system theory, produced theoretical reflections about the subject, but points out the tendency for rather abstract approaches that hamper a common scientific definition of the concept. In fact, there is not even an agreement whether if time is a natural, rational, or social category. The dimension of time to which this text refers is close to the "lived time" that Heidegger (2003) relates to our existence in counterpoint to eternity. According to the philosopher, the "dasein", the "being there", is time itself. Time would therefore be temporality. For this purpose, Rammstedt (as cited in Rosa, 2013) identifies four forms of experienced time along history (although these forms may coincide in time), from the "occasional" consciousness of time in primitive societies, in which past and future merge, resuming the experiences of time to "now" and "not now", a cyclical time consciousness, where past and future are structurally identical, and then to a clear distinction of past, present and future in modern societies, with an irreversible and closed linear evolution and a clearly defined future. Functional differentiated societies are characterized by a linear consciousness of time with an uncertain future, resulting, for this reason, in a temporal experience of a continuous movement of acceleration, so typical of contemporaneity. In Simondon, the first phase corresponds to the "magical mode of being", that is followed by the phases of technicity and religion, where relations of human with the world are "mediated" and result in the thickening of time experience (as cited in Mills, 2016, p. 118). For Simondon, the new phase created by the development of industrial technology creates a new unity that resembles the primordial magic state.

TEMPORALITY AND TECHNOLOGY

The approach that establishes a close connection between acceleration of modern life and technological development is headed by authors such as Innis (1950). The author's earlier writings gave rise to a distinctively approach on the interconnection between the vitality and durability of countries and empires and the modes of communication that where dominant in them. In this perspective, time is a cultural effect of technology. Departing from his studies in political economy, Innis identified the determining role of the means of transport and communication in social evolution. In the author's view, technology is a mean through which civilizations expand themselves, make connections, and exercise power. In Innis's work The Bias of Communication (1950), he defends that each society has a dominant media, and therefore a bias related to time and space. In this approach, media can be divided into time-biased and space-biased types. In societies which are biased towards time, heavy media predominate. They are hard to carry, but also hard to destroy and, therefore, durable (as the oral traditions or cave paintings, for instance), preserving knowledge until the present. They are adapted to our limited capacity of memorization over time. On the other hand, space-biased societies prefer more light and flexible media, yet with great storage capacity. It would be the case of Western modern societies, which are oriented to long-distance communication and the privatization of media in general, and which the author associates to the decline of democracies.

This is also the opinion of Virilio (2000), Castells (2010), and Giddens (2002), who enhance the effects of the acceleration of transport and communication technologies in the changing of our perception of time and space. McLuhan (1996), who was Innis's pupil and quite influenced by him, also meets this perspective when he defends that each new media introduces a change of scale, rhythm, or pattern in human subjects.

Virilio's contribution to this reflection is particularly relevant. This author sustains historical revolutions are mainly speed revolutions. The author proposes concepts such as dromology[1] or dromocratic revolution to describe the role of the different vehicles of speed along history. According to Virilio, in each revolutionary moment, a new vehicle allowed more speed, as well as new ways to communicate and travel (Hauer, 2016). For Virilio, the Industrial Revolution, which was triggered by the invention of the steam engine, was mainly a Revolution of Transportation, which he classifies as a time-space revolution. The development of the navy in colonial societies and of aerial power in the fifties, with the appearance of supersonic planes that transposed the sound barrier, are other examples. From transports to photography and cinema, for the French philosopher, the development of technology and the correspondent speed causes the growing suppression of time and space until the era of real time, our own, that the author claims to be one of inertia, associated to the nonsense of any movement. Virilio (2000) considers the emergence of the aesthetics of disappearance (photography and cinema) that follows the aesthetics of appearance (painting and sculpture) as another transforming revolution in the XIX century. The speed of capture in instantaneous photography and the speed of projection in film (24 images per second), based on retinal persistence, revolutionized perception, the way of seeing, moving "from the persistence of a material -- marble or the painter's canvas to the cognitive persistence of vision" (Virilio, 2000, p. 24). Cinema reveals itself to be capable to offer the spectator, in a fraction of a second, the unknown sensation of ubiquity, transporting him/her to a fourth dimension that suppresses time and space (Virilio, 1989). Afterwards, cinema would be substituted by the automobile, by the trip, corresponding this to Virilio's (2000) idea that our lives are associated to "accelerated journey prosthesis of which we are not even conscient" (p. 68), as the train, the automobile, the plane, the telephone, the television or the computer. For the author, speed has taken roots in the lives of individuals and societies. It changed, and continues to change, our values and perceptions.

Other perspectives frame technology in a larger set of social dynamics that affect temporality. It is the case of Rosa (2013), for whom the principle of acceleration is part of the modernity culture itself, preceding its technological concretization. The author follows Virilio when he identifies two waves of acceleration in the history of Western civilization, connected to the technological innovations which were brought, first, by the Industrial Revolution and, secondly, by the digital revolution and globalization. On the other hand, Rosa criticizes the French author's thesis to accommodate a general view that social change is not determined by technology acceleration, being this rather a symptom of the acceleration of social change. Sharma (2014) also criticizes the ones she calls "speed theorists", accusing them of a simplistic analysis of temporality. She considers that, although the discourse about speed has become hegemonic, it does not reflect the complexity and the pace variability of different temporalities. She contests that temporality should be understood as a homogeneous experience associated to a certain epoch or dominant technology. In Sharma's perspective, temporality is a mechanism of social differentiation. Another author that contests technological determinism is Wajcman (2008), who states that media are cultural and social artefacts and not inevitable, for this reason.

Simondon (as cited in Mills, 2016) proposes an intermediate perspective. He defends that the harmony between technological development and culture was broken with industrialization. As technology tends to be progressively autonomous and able to auto-regulate itself, it becomes "natural", "to the extent to which it operates in conjunction with its environment" (Mills, 2016, p. 112)[2]. For Simondon, culture failed to react to this naturalization of technology. He claims technological development produces new values and desires that must be acknowledged, criticizing the perspective of technology just as purely instrumental or utilitarian, when it is in fact part and constitutive of culture.

TEMPORALITY AND REAL TIME

As Rosa (2013) states, the linear and chronological quality of time seems to be dissolving with the development of speed and record capacity of digital technology. Virilio (2000) defends that, since Einstein and his relativity theory, a new reality emerged, in which speed overrides time and space, in the same way that light transcends matter, turning, for this reason, as mentioned before, any travel extemporaneous. When we reach the limit of the speed of light, we replace historical time, domain of history, and physical space, domain of geography, by the unique present, without human dimension, which, according to Virilio, corresponds to Foucault's (as cited in Virilio, 2000) "great incarceration", according to which we would be not in a prison, but "in the speed and inanity of any movement" (Virilio, 2000, p. 61). Although all history happens in a local time, real time has no relation to historical time. The author is worried about the ubiquity, immediacy, and interactivity digital media have allowed[3]. He believes that they result in the tyranny of the continuous present and the substitution of reflection by reflex. Being this a fertile ground for manipulation, the author states, as Innis (1950), that it results in the crisis of democracies Virilio,1989).

The same perspective is shared by authors such as Harvey (1999), who, inspired by Marx's (as cited in Harvey, 1999) idea of annihilation of space by time, proposes the concept of space-time compression, meaning a process that alters the relation between space and time, namely through technological innovation (Rosa, 2013). In the same direction, Giddens (2002) presents the notion of time-space distanciation to mean the fact that social events appear now disconnected from the spatial-temporal matrix, which allows us to reorganize and recombine them by increasing spatial and temporal distances, and thus transforming the nature and content of our everyday experiences.

Castells (2010) proposes the concept of timeless time to describe what he considers to be the dominant time form of networked societies, which occurs whenever there is a systematic disturbance in the sequential order of social practices, diluting our temporal experience in a "timeless cyberspace" (Sora, Jordà & Codina, 2017, p. 197). Since the Internet has no limits of time and space, it can constantly reconfigure itself. This reconfiguration may take the form of compression or may introduce discontinuity in the sequence. By compressing time, at the limit, time itself disappears, which would be an equivalent to eternity. This perspective is also in line with Giddens' reading when he points out that the discrepancy between a limited individual life-time and the time of the world perceived as unlimited was "solved" by almost all developed societies with the introduction of a new category of time: the "sacred time", which transcends the linear time of life and history. In this perspective, we may risk saying that real time replaces the sacred time of religions. As Chabot (2013) declares, technology and sacred are intimately connected, since archaic societies, although in modern era we tend to forget it and privilege the connection between technology and science. Invoking Simondon's thought, Chabot states that "Technology creates a world. Its impact is cosmic, like that of the sacred" (2013, p. 129).

In turn, Hassan and Purser (as cited in Sora, Jordà & Codina, 2017) defend that asynchrony is the real current temporality, turning time into something simultaneously homogeneous and fragmented in multiple temporalities, synchronous and asynchronous, that coexist in the Web. In this perspective, the experience of modernity would not then be one of acceleration, but one of simultaneity of different times. In the same direction, Tomlinson emphasises the role of digital media in the transition to a culture of immediacy, rather than speed (as cited in Keightley, 2013), and Rosa (2013) identifies the fragmentation of different spheres of action that turn time dedicated to each task each day shorter.

TEMPORALITY AND POWER

As referred in the previous point, the relationship between temporality and technology varies according to different authors. However, the same authors agree when they associate temporality to power and capitalism. It is the case of Virilio, Castells or Sharma, through the concepts of chronopolitics (Virilio, 2000) informational capitalism (Castells, 2010), and power-chronography (Sharma, 2014).

According to Virilio (2000), speed is a privilege of the powerful, the strongest, a synonymous of wealth and, consequently, power. The author articulates speed and politics, and considers acceleration as the other side of capitalism. The dromological revolution is then mainly a production speed revolution (and also destruction, when Virilio addresses the evolution of war machines). This notion of production speed revolution meets the thought of Marx, when he talks about time as a scarce resource in the capitalist system, and Weber, when presenting the efficient use of time as an imperative of the capitalist ethic. For Virilio if the XIX and XX centuries were the centuries of geopolitics, in which the power was mainly linked to space, the XXI century is already the time of what he calls the chronopolitics. This new form of political organization would institute the rule of domination of the fastest, which is also the one that determines the rhythm, duration, sequence, and synchronization of human activities (Rosa, 2013). In chronopolitics, the new frontiers would therefore be more related to the use of time than of space, since acceleration would lead to a contraction of space and its devaluation. For Virilio (2000), contemporary Western societies are characterized by the conjugation between a phenomenon such as the speed of light and the automatic quotations in the stock exchanges. Worried about the future of humanity, the author defends deceleration and the return to the physical world of cities and human relations, as a way out of the paradox of immobility. This results from the fact that the speed of light renders the physical world tendentially irrelevant and puts us before the futility of any displacement. For this reason, Virilio (as cited in Hauer, 2016, p. 323) believes that the modern history of acceleration leads us to what he calls "polar inertia, inertia of absolute speed".

Castells (2010) also attributes the phenomenon of temporal compression to the development of capitalism in the network society, calling it informational capitalism (p.18). Giddens (2002) points out that in capitalism time is both linear and polarized, determined by the logic of this economic system, but also by the technical logic of industrial production. For this author, the invention and diffusion of the mechanical clock and the generalization of the use of instruments of time control already pointed to changes that were not only local, but universal. In Giddens's view, globalization is a new level of the process of separation of spatial and temporal dimensions, augmenting the capacity of social coordination of space and time.

Although departing from what she calls the "culture of speed", Sharma (2014) also proposes an understanding of temporality as the "awareness of power relations as they play out in time" (p. 4.), arguing that these multiple and interdependent relationships are framed in global contemporary capitalism (Sharma, 2017). In her work, temporality is understood as a mechanism of social differentiation, which is the reason why she prefers to speak about temporalities. According to this author, these temporalities are supported in relations of power in what she calls "power-chronography"[4]. In this regard, Sharma explores the figure of the corporate warrior, simultaneously vulnerable (as a victim of jet lag or stress, for instance) and privileged, considering, among other reasons, the cultural capital associated with the public display of overwork. Wajcman (2008), too, highlights this dimension when she points out the fact that our culture values being busy. Wajcman also defends that temporality is complex and prefers to talk about different temporalities. Nevertheless, she presents a more benign view of technology, defending that its appropriation brings new practices that personalize individual time experience. Tomlinson and Keightley (as cited in Pentzold, 2018) share this view of the "domestication of media" by individuals who have the capacity to accommodate to different experiences of temporality. On the other hand, in Sharma (2014), the figure of the corporate warrior is dependent on the availability of others with less valued temporalities (e.g., taxi drivers or hotel employees). The temporality would thus be simultaneously differentiating and shared, forcing a permanent adjustment of expectations or recalibration (Sharma, 2017). In short, for the author, it is not speed that produces inequality, but its explanatory and normalizing power, as if it was a uniform experience in the contemporary moment that values the time of some in the detriment of others and excludes those who experience time in a different way. According to Sharma (2014), it is an ideology that does not consider other temporalities. In this line of thought, she criticizes the strategies of ideological slowness, such as those adopted by the slow movements, drawing attention to the fact that the capacity to slow down is itself a form of privilege that presupposes an individualistic and depoliticized position. Sharma then proposes that time is a new field of collective struggle, advocating the construction of "public times" with a vocation like that of "public spaces". Noys, in his analysis of the relation between accelerationism and capitalism, also points out that "the few scattered anti-accelerationist critiques of our present moment [that] often seem to leave untouched the libidinal core of accelerationism" (2014, p. 93). Alternatives such as the slow movements are considered by the author "tepid" and even "reactionary". For Noys, to fight accelerationism it is crucial to reconfigure pleasure, as an alternative mode of choice "rather the compulsive exercise of 'choice' offered and demanded by contemporary capitalism" (p. 94) and "to struggle for decommodification of our lives" (p. 97). This because the author believes that the seduction of accelerationism is to turn "labour under capitalism as site of extreme and perverse enjoyment" (p. 10) although simultaneously "impossible" (p. 11), establishing a relation between capitalism and the development of modern psychopathologies.

Rosa (2013) also looks mainly for social causes to understand temporality. When he proposes the concept of social acceleration to approach modernity, he is also talking about power. Social acceleration is defined as a process at several levels, but involving a profound transformation of the temporal structures and horizons that have a social nature. Globalization, in this perspective, would be an unprecedented process of synchronization. The author quotes Norbert Elias, for whom time has a primarily functional character, serving to coordinate and synchronize social processes. The individual consciousness of time would be socially produced, but it would also be a social habitus, an inextricable component of the individual personality, being this, for Elias, the explanation for the accelerated time of modern societies. Moving away from technological determinism, Rosa identifies three kinds of acceleration: technical acceleration, acceleration related to social change, and faster pace of life. Nevertheless, the author denounces that the idea that acceleration produces a faster pace of life is a fallacy, considering that acceleration should have an opposite effect, providing us more free time. He defends that the reason why it does not is because of growth: the free time which is gained with acceleration is being used to do more things (e.g., produce more and consume more). On one side, the "potential time savings are turned into increased output or improved quality" (Rosa, 2013, p. 69). On the other side, the author advances with a second explanation related to the fact that new technologies create new possibilities of action that are also time consuming. For example, in Rosa's view, more relevant than the amount of information in circulation is the fact that both asynchronous and synchronous communications are now possible at any time, regardless of the location of the actors.

As Sharma, Rosa (2013) also identifies deceleration as an essential element of contemporary societies. He identifies five categories of deceleration or inertia:

The natural limits to speed; the existence of what he calls "islands of deceleration", which are constituted, for example, by socially excluded groups; deceleration as a side effect (e.g., traffic jams, unemployment, and waiting times); intentional deceleration (as an ideology or as an acceleration strategy); the structural and cultural rigidity that is complementary, according to the author, to the acceleration itself, including cultural values such as individualism or rationalism, and political and administrative institutions or the industrial organization of labor. According to the author, these rigidification processes occur simultaneously and in interdependence with acceleration, that would not be possible without them.

Wajcman (2008) offers us a micro-sociological approach to the issue, arguing for the need to develop empirical studies on the temporal practices individuals have adopted and their relationship with technology that allow the construction of a theoretical framework. At a first level, the author also considers that acceleration has become an essential concept to understand modernity, although safeguarding, as Sharma (2014) does, that it should not be analyzed as a collective experience, given the different observable temporalities. If everybody notices acceleration, the temporal experiences are, however, differentiated. The author notes how the experience of time scarcity is particularly felt by working mothers in their attempt to reconcile work, family, and leisure, alerting to gender differences at this level, which are often "masked" by "average times." Nevertheless, she stresses the difficulty in measuring daily temporalities, highlighting the need to verify the social tendency to perform more tasks in a given period, which she calls temporal density, concurring with Rosa (2013) on this point.

Following Southerton and Tomlinson's (2005) analysis, Wajcman (2008) names three mechanisms responsible for the sensation of "haste": the volume (of tasks and of time needed for its accomplishment), the coordination (that may result in the sense of disorganization related to the difficulty of coordinating with others), and the allocation of social practices (the density of assumed practices, including multitasking), thus transforming it into a multidimensional experience differentiated according to different social groups and practices. However, Wajcman departs from the critical perspective by arguing that people find ways to appropriate and shape the use of technology to gain greater control over time. In this context, the author presents the use of mobile phones as an example of how technology can evolve in conjunction with new social practices that change time experiences. If, on the one hand, the constant availability these devices have provided is potentially invasive, on the other hand, they allow that individuals organize their lives in "flexible compartments of time" (Wajcman, 2008, p. 60) and create new temporal practices. This is also the point of view of Keightley (2013), who proposes the notion of "zones of intermediacy" to describe the constant negotiation between the temporalities technology has made possible and the individual and social uses of time. In this view, technologies or socioeconomic configurations do not necessarily accelerate, rather they allow new practices and new meanings of temporality.

CONCLUSION

Temporality conceptualization varies along a continuum of technological determinism with different weights on how to encompass the effects of technology into a set of social dynamics that go beyond it. However, criticisms of technological determinism to the "speed theorists" may be somehow unfair, considering that, as Castells (2010) points out, technology and society are inseparable. As the author states: "the dilemma of technological determinism is probably a false problem, since technology is society, and society cannot be understood or represented without its technological tools" (p. 5). In this perspective, focusing on the role of technology is not the same as devaluing the role of social structures and dynamics, as the relationship between technology and capitalism that authors such as Virilio and Castells perceive reveals. Nevertheless, their position is still criticized because it considers the effects of technology, namely digital technology, as having irreversible impacts, leading to "disruptive" social revolutions. This critique is expressed, for instance, by Wajcman (2008), who advocates technology "neutrality". As pointed out, these authors defend the active role that people may have in the appropriation of technology and that may even help them to take control of their time. In this perspective, individuals would have the power, in articulation with available technology, to reconfigure the practices of time use, defining their own temporalities. However, is it not true that this power exists only within the limits imposed by the devices themselves? This turns out to be a capacity of quite conditioned self-determination, remembering Virilio's (2000) critique to the interactivity digital media provide. To what extent is it possible to speak about autonomy in this context? Simondon (cited in Chabot, 2013) outlines an answer, when advocates an integrative approach to culture and technology, recognizing its tendency to naturalization and the need for culture to frame its evolution.

On the other hand, if, for example, as Wajcman proposes, the mobile phone, although invasive, allows gaining greater control over time, it is perhaps important not to disregard aspects such as digital divide, access or media literacy, but also the somehow coercive features of technology and the possibility, and consequences, of deciding not to use the devices. Rosa (2013) also approaches this topic critically when he talks about the progressive fragmentation of the spheres of action, noting that the possibilities offered by technology and its associated social demands play an important role in this regard. These remarks may be perceived as indicators of how the development of digital technology seems to carry unforeseen and transformative consequences on temporality. Thus, rather than advocating or challenging the determinant role of technology, in our perspective, it is important to perceive the social transformations associated with it, either as an instrument or as an agent of change. Rosa (2013), while criticizing Virilio for understanding acceleration as technologically driven, does not fail to consider that "technical innovations represent a powerful instigator of social change" (p. 308).

Nonetheless, a particularly pertinent critical approach is that of Sharma (2014) when she notices the ideological character of the "culture of speed", arguing that temporality is a form of social differentiation and considering different temporalities. It is thus distinguished from Wajcman's approach by observing that temporal experience is simultaneously differential and collective, sustained in relations of power. However, if Virilio presents deceleration as a way out to avoid the shock of the time barrier to where the absolute speed of light leads us, Rosa and Sharma see it critically, as the "other side" of a culture which capitalizes time, distributing it unevenly in function of different positions in social structure. In this perspective, time is power, and the "appropriation" capacity Wajcman describes would be a privilege accessible only to a few. Thus, more than acceleration or deceleration, it is the ability to determine it, to impose rhythms that determine temporality.

In conclusion, it seems clear that the real time of technology has imposed itself as a new structuring element in modern society. It is then important to study and critically evaluate its implications, both positive and negative, but refusing its inevitability or "sacralization". As Hauer (2016) points out, the question of how much speed we need and what acceleration rate is tolerable for the economy, society, and environment remains unanswered. More empirical studies, as Wacjman (2008) and Pentzold (2018) propose, are needed, but also more critical and interdisciplinary analysis of technology, in a context in which its rampant evolution makes both more difficult. On the other hand, it is also important to analyze the relationship between temporality and technology in the broader context of social structures, and to see in what ways this relationship can constitute a factor of social inequality. Temporality, technology, and power are three corners of a triangle whose study is necessary to deepen, if we want to regain control over our lived time.

REFERENCES

Bergmann, W. (1992). The Problem of Time in Sociology. *Time & Society*, *1*(1), 81–134. doi:10.1177/0961463X92001001007

Castells, M. (2010). *The Rise of the Network Society*. Blackwell Publishing. doi:10.2307/1252090

Chabot, P. (2013). *The Philosophy of Simondon Between Technology and Individuation*. London: Bloomsbury.

Giddens, A. (2002). *Modernidade e Identidade*. Rio de Janeiro: Jorge Zahar Editor.

Harvey, D. (1999). Time-Space Compression and the postmodern condition. *Modernity: Critical Concepts*. doi:10.1037/0278-7393.11.1-4.629

Hauer, T. (2016). Globalization and Political Economy of Speed. In M. S. Eva Kovářová, Lukáš Melecký (Ed.), *3rd International Conference on European Integration 2016* (pp. 319–325). Ostrava: VŠB - Technical University of Ostrava.

Heidegger, M. (2003). O conceito de tempo. Lisboa: Fim de Século.

Innis, H. A. (1950). *Empire and Communications*. Toronto: Toronto University Press.

Jameson, F. (1991). *Postmodernism, or The Cultural Logic of Late Capitalism*. Durham, NC: Duke University Press. Retrieved from http://socium.ge/downloads/komunikaciisteoria/eng/Jameson.Postmodernism,orTheculturallogicoflatecapitalism(1991).pdf

Keightley, E. (2013). From immediacy to intermediacy: The mediation of lived time. *Time & Society*, *22*(1), 55–75. doi:10.1177/0961463X11402045

Lauer, R. (1981). *Temporal man: the meaning and uses of social time*. New York: Praeger.

Levine, R. (1997). *A geography of time: The temporal misadventures of a social psychologist, or how every culture keeps time just a little bit differently*. New York: Basic Books.

Massey, D. (1991). A Global Sense of Place. *Marxism Today*, *35*(June), 315–323. doi:10.1016/j.pecs.2007.10.001

Mcluhan, M. (1996). Os meios de comunicação como extensões do homem. *Buscalegis*, *407*. doi:10.1590/S0034-75901969000300009

Mills, S. (2016). *Gilbert Simondon: Information, Technology & Media*. London: Rowman & Littlefield International.

Nassehi, A. (1994). No Time for Utopia: The Absence of Utopian Contents in Modern Concepts of Time. *Time & Society*, *3*(1), 47–78. doi:10.1177/0961463X94003001003

Noys, B. (2014). *Malign Velocities - Acceleration and Capitalism*. Zero Books.

Pentzold, C. (2018). Between moments and millennia: Temporalising mediatisation. *Media Culture & Society*, *40*(6), 927–937. doi:10.1177/0163443717752814

Rosa, H. (2013). *Social Acceleration_ A New Theory of Modernity (New Directions in Critical Theory)*. New York: Columbia University Press. doi:10.7312/rosa14834

Sharma, S. (2014). In the Meantime. *Temporality and Cultural Politics*, *9*, 2014–2016. doi:10.1215/9780822378334

Sharma, S. (2017). Temporality. In Keywords for media studies. New York: NY UP.

Sora, C., Jordà, S., & Codina, L. (2017). Chasing real-time interaction in new media: Towards a new theoretical approach and definition. *Digital Creativity*, *28*(3), 196–205. doi:10.1080/14626268.2017.1355323

Southerton, D., & Tomlinson, M. (2005). "Pressed for time" - The differential impacts of a "time squeeze.". *The Sociological Review*, *53*(2), 215–239. doi:10.1111/j.1467-954X.2005.00511.x

Virilio, P. (1989). *Esthétique de la disparition. Collection l'Espace Critique*. Retrieved from http://www.sudoc.fr/00151766X%5Cnhttp://www.worldcat.org/search?q=no%3A300078551

Virilio, P. (2000). *Cibermundo: a política do pior*. Lisboa: Editorial Teorema.

Wajcman, J. (2008). Life in the fast lane? Towards a sociology of technology and time. *The British Journal of Sociology*, *59*(1), 59–77. doi:10.1111/j.1468-4446.2007.00182.x PMID:18321331

KEY TERMS AND DEFINITIONS

Real-Time Interaction: Direct and immediate communication, independent of time and space, simultaneously synchronous and asynchronous, global, and fragmented.

Social Acceleration: The transformation of the temporal structures of societies caused by social dynamics.

Technological Acceleration: The pace of technological progress—especially information technology—speeds up exponentially over time; possibilities offered by technology, in each historical phase, to do more and better in less time.

Technological Determinism: The idea that technology dictates the direction of its social structure and cultural values. Changes in technology are the primary source for changes in society.

Temporality: The condition of being bound in time. The perception of lived time.

Time Acceleration: Subjective perception that time tends to speed up in our contemporary daily lives. Rushing to do more in less time. Fragmentation of time dedicated to different activities.

Time-Space Compression: The term defined by David Harvey in *The Condition of Postmodernity* is often linked to the change of space-time conceptions associated with the rise of the Modern Era that has had a disorienting and disruptive impact upon political-economic practices, the balance of class power, and upon cultural and social life.

ENDNOTES

[1]   From the Greek *dromos*, meaning "racetrack."

[2]   The author states that a plant nurtured in a greenhouse would, in this sense, be "artificial."

[3]   Wajcman states that there is no empirical evidence that *"instantaneous time"* is *"socially destructive"* (2008, p. 67).

[4]   An appropriation of Massey's "power-geometry" (1991), according to which some groups would be more responsible than others for the compression of space-time, making use of this compression and turning it into an advantage.

Chapter 3
Screen Time, Temporality, and (Dis)embodiment

Eduardo J. Santos
University of Coimbra, Portugal

Ralph Ings Bannell
Pontifícia Universidade Católica do Rio de Janeiro, Brazil

Camila De Paoli Leporace
Pontifícia Universidade Católica do Rio de Janeiro, Brazil

ABSTRACT

In this chapter, the authors will attempt to answer two related questions: How is our cognitive experience with time enacted and extended? Has the cognitive dimension of the experience of time lost its reference in the body? The background reviews relevant literature and shows the motivation for the main discussion of the chapter, especially the contrast between the authors' approach and the traditional symbolic-representational view. The principal argument will be that the dimension of the organism's coupling with the environment that can be called engagement with material culture—or things—has been undertheorized in the literature. Bringing this dimension into the analysis can, the authors argue, help explain how we experience psychological time. What's more, it can help understand the kinds of extra-bodily extensions that might explain why the use of technologies does not threaten disembodiment.

DOI: 10.4018/978-1-5225-8163-5.ch003

INTRODUCTION

Human beings are living in the digital age. One perceives an avalanche of events during a few hours or a day; communicates with a number of people at the same time, sending and receiving dozens of messages and e-mails; faces and solves different issues simultaneously. Humans are connected to a world of rapid changes, and this connection occurs through different screens, in a multitasking way.

Screen time is a concept that reflects contemporary reality, especially the quantity and modalities of time in the use of digital technologies. It is something that is recent and therefore still involves much discussion. The importance of temporality in the construction of human experience and the organization of social systems is well known. Is screen time qualitatively different from the temporalities experienced so far? And, what is its impact on our psychological and social functioning? Are there thresholds for good use, abuse and misuse?

Since the 1950s, when television was born and became a revolutionary phenomenon in the Western world, the discussion of the effects of technologies on the human mind and society has grown, especially with regard to the mental health of children. The time they spend watching television programs, and nowadays in front of other screens, and the impact that this has, for example, on the quality of sleep and the balance of circadian rhythms (Lissak, 2018; Moffat, 2014; Parent, Sanders, & Forehand, 2016; Wiecha et al., 2006), has been a constant theme of debate. With the great development of the Internet since the 1990s, and digital technologies in general, this discussion is exacerbated and also extends to its use by adolescents and adults. An important question here is how our temporality and cognition are intimately linked, through a circular causality, to our corporality. There are a variety of ways to analyze this relation in cognitive and developmental psychology and within the broader interdisciplinary area of cognitive science. The authors will review some of this literature below.

What the authors want to focus on in this chapter are two basic issues. The first is the relationship between technology use and our experience and perception of time. The second is the suspicion that the use of digital technologies can negatively interfere with the embodiment of mind. Is it possible that screen time can provoke a disembodied effect in our temporal and developmental architecture?

The authors will look at these issues through the prism of the embodied mind. The concept of embodied mind (Varela, Thompson, & Rosch, 1991; Shapiro, 2011, 2014) has developed extensively over the past few decades. Many different approaches can be included within this broad label, including enactive (Gibson, 1979; Noë, 2004, 2012; Gallagher, 2005, 2017; Hutto & Myin, 2013; Gallagher & Zahavi, 2008), embedded (Piaget, 1968; Triphon & Vonèche, 1996; Vygotsky, 1978) and extended (Clark & Chalmers, 1998; Clark, 1997, 2003, 2008, 2014, 2016; Menary, 2010;

Wheeler, 2005) conceptions. In what follows the authors will refer mainly to the enactive and extended mind theses, because these approaches have specifically tied cognitive experiences to our active coupling with the environment and, in the case of the extended mind thesis, incorporated technologies into its analysis of cognition. These approaches are already interdisciplinary but the authors will include in our discussion work from philosophy and cognitive science, cognitive and developmental psychology and cognitive archeology and anthropology.

BACKGROUND

If one looks at the analysis of time from an historical perspective, one finds that psychological time has a biological texture, our body. From a neurophysiological point of view, the body undoubtedly constitutes the rhythmic "nature" of human behavior in interaction with environmental synchronizers (Santos, 1992), which include natural markers, such as the rhythms of night and day, and artifacts, such as watches and their ticking. In parallel with this chronopsychological dimension is the experience of the body as an "imaginary space" (Sami-Ali, 1974), which, through the experience of its anatomy and its motricity, establishes a preoperative temporality (Piaget, 1968). In other words, the origin of time is in the symbolic/ imaginary life of the body, because the body is understood as a space for representation, including time. The idea of the body as a space of representation has been extended recently in work, some of which the authors will discuss later, that shows how our body is involved in the constitution of perception, meaning, imagination and reason (Gibson, 1979; Noë, 2004, 2012; Johnson, 1987, 2007, 2017).

However, recent work has shown that this emphasis on the symbolic and representational character of the body has been challenged by the idea that the body creates meaning in ways that do not require internal representations, at least as these are normally understood as images or in symbolic terms. The enactive approach to mind explores the idea that cognitive experience is enacted directly in our coupling with the world, thereby eliminating, or at least reducing, the need to postulate mental representations.

Now, as well as the body, cognition and our experience of time also involve artifacts, as the reference to watches above suggests. These are part of the cultural environment with which the organism is coupled, together with the physical environment. Most theories of embodied mind take cultural factors into account but few analyze them in depth[1]. Theories of enactive and extended mind are an exception in that they emphasize how external factors actually *constitute cognitive processes*. Cultural artifacts enter here as central constitutive elements. In the main part of this paper the authors will focus on a theory of material engagement that analyses the constitutive intertwining of cognition and material culture.

However, it is worth looking briefly at other ways of relating culture and cognition. As a significant example, we have the semantic temporality of "cradle stories", which in rhythmic and cyclic transitivity dilute infantile consciousness into a dream state (Santos, 1992). Similar effects can be found with adults with respect to both symbolic content (semantic) and material engagement (enactive), in motherese language (Saint-Georges et al., 2013) and in lullaby singing (Baker & Mackinlay, 2006; Cevasco, 2008). In fact, the differences in the conception of time at different life stages is interesting (Santos, 1992) and is plausibly related to how we perceive events, the perception of time being an abstraction from event perception, something the authors will explore in more detail below. This raises the general question of the relationship between narrative and time (Ricoeur, 1984). Some psychotherapies have used this strategy for years (Santos, 1992), where the use of metaphors, through their kinesthetic logic, connects cultural representations and behavioral and corporeal experiences (Santos et al., 2012).

An important contemporary approach analyzes how psychological time is transmuted into cultural and cognitive representations. If we analyze time from the cultural point of view, it should be noted that there has been an evolution in its representations. Time has not always been conceived of in the same way (Eliade, 1949). As Santos (1992) states, the time of Antiquity is not the same as that of the Modern Age. However, there are themes that remain structurally constant in the evolution of cultures. They are universal themes. This is the question of the representation of origins, a question which is itself universal, cosmological. And there is also the question of the end, of death. This is also a universal, cosmic question, which erupts in the most diverse cultures and traverses literary productions. This is a question that is resolved either by conceptual solutions, such as the continuity of time, where beginning and end lose their importance as referents, or symbolic solutions, such as the architectural materialization of the great temporal cosmological questions in the stones of cathedrals and their iconographic clocks. In contemporary times these representations are somewhat ambiguous. Stoetzel (1983), for example, found pessimism about the future in European culture. But he found both confidence and optimism about the individual's future and the disposition to master "destiny".

Nevertheless, our approach in this text will not focus on symbolic representations as either anchors or producers of psychological time, presented here essentially as part of an historical context of the study of time, hoping to get clearer about the evolution of conceptualizations and research. On the contrary, without going into the vexed question and debate on representations in mental life, the authors will look at theories that give much less importance to this concept, arguing that mental life is enacted and extended beyond the brain and the body of the cognizer.

Within the broadly representational view of cognition, another dimension to consider is how social and economic organization can influence the individual conception of time. Nuttin, Lens, Van Claster, and De Volder all point out that some temporal representations constitute "modes of use of time" (as cited in Santos, 1992). Knapp and Garbutt (as cited in Santos, 1992) have shown that certain dynamic temporal representations are highly associated with the motive of realization, integrating this issue into the theme of the "achieving society" addressed by McClelland, Atkinson, Clark and Lowell (as cited in Santos, 1992) and corroborated by Fraisse (1957). It is in this interaction between the temporal framework and human behavior that systems of temporal representations are constituted, as Cottle (as cited in Santos, 1992) shows. For example, Gonzalez and Zimbardo (as cited in Santos, 1992) in research on what they called "temporal perspectives" have concluded that there are "seven time zones", each represented by specific behavioral contents: futurity-motivation for work; fatalism-present; hedonism-present; temporal planning; temporal anxiety; temporal-future instrumentality; planning.

Here religions are viewed as fundamental matrices from a psychosocial point of view. The time of modernity that we live in is an heir of the conception, simultaneously linear and circular, which since Zoroastrianism has been extended by Judaism, Christianity and Islam (Boyce, 2001). It is a prophesied, messianic time where there is a past-present-future trinity, a notion of beginning and end, a historicizing of experiences, represented by the spatial analogy of an arrow's flight. But it is also an earthly and material time, of the days and nights, of the seasons, of the dates celebrated each year, represented by the analogy of the boomerang, and of increasingly secularized social and technological evolution. In this text, the authors propose to go further, and will discuss the relationship between time and culture through theories that focus on our active engagement with material culture rather than cultural representations and their symbolic manifestation.

In addition to these issues, we continue to have experimental evidence that time has a sensory-motor dynamic of embodiment. As examples, the perception of time changes according to how we incorporate the other's body postures (Nather, Bueno, Bigand, & Droit-Volet, 2011), being together in time depends on the dynamics of intersubjective embodiment (Laroche, Berardi, & Brangier, 2014), spatial embodiment influences past-future temporal location of events (Kranjec & McDonough, 2011), the effects of stimulus movement impact on temporal perception (Brown, 1995), and the relationship between motor representation of actions and time influences perception of visual motion (Gavazzi, Bisio, & Pozzo, 2013). There is also evidence that agency (voluntary action) enhances spacial and temporal processing of proprioceptive information, also modulating time perception (Tsakiris et al, 2005; Haggard et al, 2002). The sensory motor dynamic of embodiment will be a central theme of our argument below.

Articulating this background with the precise relationship between screen time, experience and temporal cognition, body, and cognitive development, shows that the issue of screen time and the uses of digital technologies, since the early pediatric concerns, has evolved into much broader views (Becker, 2000), which include approaches to developmental psychology and its life-span disorders, with special focus on the cognitive aspect. Here the extended mind thesis has gained considerable importance in the studies and experiments carried out, in a wide range of reflections on the very essence of the extended mind (Greif, 2012), and of the coupling problem that dynamical systems models have chosen as a central research question (Froese, Gershenson, & Rosenblueth, 2013), or even from the historical point of view when reviewing its origin in the work of authors such as Mead and Dewey [2] (Madzia, 2013). The question of coupling is also central to enactive and extended approaches to mind and cognition.

It should be noted that the anthropological approach has the question of coupling on its research agenda, for example in the paradigmatic study of Gärdenfors and Lombard (2018) on the relation between causal cognition, force dynamics and early hunting technologies. This diversity of studies may be extended further with sociolinguistic approaches where words are considered as social tools in an extended embodied mind perspective (Borghi et al., 2013), or with approaches on extended affectivity as a cognition of primary intersubjectivity (Candiotto, 2016). However, these approaches emphasize symbolic or even linguistic representations as central cognitive mechanisms, even in early infant cognition. Our approach, although not denying the important role of symbolic representations in cognition in general and the psychological experience of time in particular, will try to show how meaning is enacted in our direct engagement with material culture.

Because human memory is one of the most used cognitive resources in our society, much research has been produced on its relations with digital technologies (Sutton, 2009). Here we encounter the themes of E-memory (Clowes, 2013), of the "Google effect" in memory (Sparrow, Liu, & Wagner, 2011), or of Web-Extended Mind (Smart, 2012). In this regard, it should be emphasized that dichotomous thinking about the virtues and harms of the use of digital technologies is now less frequent, since we know that uses are always social practices contextualized by cultural parameters, and thus any technology will always be a sociotechnology. Below, the authors will emphasize that use of technologies involves material engagement with them as artifacts or material culture. Here the agency involved is as much determined by the technology as by the human being using it. The parameters are 'material cultural' practices. More on this in the discussion below.

However, because diabolization of new technologies still exists, we need to include studies in which its use has very positive effects, for example, in the compensation of anterograde amnesia through the use of smartphones (Svoboda & Richards, 2009).

With respect to the interface between technologies and cognitive processes, the authors highlight Henkel's (2014) study on the "photo-taking-impairment effect", which shows that, in a museum environment, when photographing pieces in their totality causes an impoverishment of the memory of them, if the photo taken is only of details of these pieces, we gain in richness of memories. This allows us to argue that it will be the way we use new technologies and set up extended minds that will determine their potential for psychological development.

In order to synthesize this question and apply it to the relation between screen time and experience and temporal cognition, once again we find studies that highlight its negative effects, namely psychosomatic, but also its positive effects (Blatchley et al., 2007). A study that shows the influence of the use of new technologies in the development of depressive disorders, where body experiences are altered, and consequently the experience of time and temporal cognition (Owen et al., 2015), is that of Primack and collaborators (2009), which, although using a longitudinal methodology, sufficiently robust from the point of view of the establishment of cause-effect relationships, draws attention to the fact that, even controlling the baseline of predictors and criteria, we cannot fail to consider the hidden presence of other variables. In this same sense, we find other studies (Hardie & Tee, 2007; Selfhout et al., 2009) where, from the point of view of research methodology and conceptual framework, the possible existence of moderating and mediating variables, personal and situational, in explaining the effect of the behavioral consequences of screen time, even psychopathological ones, has to be central, because even in disorders of this nature the issue of comorbidity is fundamental (Þórarinsdóttir, 2015).

This wide range of studies on the use of screen time, from different perspectives and with differing conclusions, provokes a need for a cautious approach to these issues, especially since other studies highlight the positivity of the use of new technologies in the subjective well-being of people (Sum et al., 2008), or even question whether they will not be responses to psychological disorders (Campbell, Cumming, & Hughes, 2006). As for the relationship between screen time and experience and temporal cognition, the study by Agarwal and Karahanna (2000) emphasizes the positive role of the use of information technologies in the production of cognitive absorption, very close to the flow experiences that positive psychology has investigated (Csikszentmihaiyi, 1990).

Also, we need to take into account that the archaeological evidence of tool use and tool making since the very early hominid species shows that we are *homo sapiens* because we are *homo faber*. Tools and technologies are "enactive cognitive prostheses" (Malafouris, 2013, p. 154). Stiegler (1998, in Malafouris, 2013) goes further, suggesting that "the prosthesis is not a mere extension of the human body; it is the constitution of this body qua 'human'". Tools and technologies are "cognitive artifacts". If this assumption is correct, could we expect the use of digital technologies, as tools, to alter the basic nature of the human mind? We might expect the development and use of different tools to alter cognitive experience and capacities. After all, the development of more and more sophisticated tools by *homo sapiens* throughout evolution has been accompanied by ever greater cognitive capacities. Although other factors partially account for this, tool use must be a major part of any explanation of cognitive advance.

The authors will end this review with some comments on the philosophical background to the issues to be discussed. In 1998, philosophers Andy Clark and David Chalmers published an article in which they state that human bodies and brains extend themselves through technologies. As a consequence of this human coupling with technologies, Clark asserts that we become cyborgs, even though we don't have chips or internal implants in our bodies. According to Clark, the technologies we use are more than props and aids: they are a constitutive part of our cognitive systems – for example, a smartphone would be part of our memory, glasses would act as extensions to our own eyes, and when we use a pen or pencil to write, or a software such as a word processor, we would extend our reasoning skills (writing is thinking).

Clark and Chalmers, together with others, are part of a growing group of philosophers, cognitive scientists, psychologists and neuroscientists who work to overcome Cartesian dualism, causing a mind-body paradigm shift. As well as eliminating the 'ghost in the machine' (Ryle, 1949), they argue that the brain is not all there is to mind, but acts as one of the pieces in our cognitive puzzle, the body also acting not as a machine in the service of the brain but as a fundamental part of the cognitive system. Therefore, there is no disembodied cognition; the body as a whole is indispensable for the existence of mind.

Our coupling with the environment and, later, with technologies wouldn't be possible if we were not embodied creatures. Extending our minds like Clark postulates depends on having bodies as essential parts of our cognitive systems, hence extending our bodies through the environment. Our brains, according to Clark, were developed to couple with the world. There would be no cognition without brains, bodies and the world; and, nowadays, without digital technologies. We transform the environment and the environment transforms us, as well.

However, despite Clark's evident enthusiasm for digital technologies, his own thesis exposes a series of problems that could derive from humans coupling with them. These include among others, the fear of disembodiment, in which Clark claims to have "a special stake", for the following reason:

I have long championed the importance of the body in the sciences of the mind. One of my books even bears the subtitle 'Putting Brain, Body and World Together Again'. Imagine my horror, then, to find myself suspected, in writing enthusiastically of technologies of telepresence and digital communication, of having changed sides, of now believing that the body didn't matter and the mind was something ethereal and distinct. (Clark, 2003, p. 189)

Clark's "horror" could certainly be connected to the fear of human beings becoming new versions of the Cartesian paradigm, characterized by two separate parts, being *Res Extensa* and *Res Cogitans*, as Descartes postulated. As humans use digital technologies and, even more, couple with them, Clark glimpses the risk of a new kind of a 2.0 Dualism, so to speak. Do our bodies still have meaning in a world of virtual reality, or do they become obsolete? Would our brains be transferred to the virtual world, while our bodies remain in the offline world, characterizing this new form of Dualism?

One of the roots of Clark's worries about disembodiment is "the popular image of the lonely keyboard-tapping adolescent, who prefers video games to human company, takes no interest in sports or direct-contact sex, and who identifies more closely with his or her own electronic avatar or avatars than with his or her biological body" (Clark, 2003, p. 190). Showing great optimism, however, Clark believes that human-centered technologies may shift the scenario of the isolated person sitting in front of a computer, playing games for hours, as new technologies may offer a "mobile, varied, and physically demanding social whirl" (Clark, 2003, p. 192); "wearable computing and ubiquitous computing are each, in different but complimentary ways, geared to freeing the user from the desktop or laptop. They are geared to matching the technology to a mobile, socially interactive, physically engaged human life form" (Clark, 2003, p. 193). Human-centered technologies would be those developed to act in an invisible way together with their users, leading them to feel as if they were their real extensions, with no hiccups or abrupt interruptions.

Another part of the philosophical background to our argument is the phenomenological tradition, which is gaining more and more attention within cognitive science, especially within the enactive and systems dynamic approaches. The roots of this are, of course, in Husserl, Heidegger and Merleau-Ponty but our principal reference is the work of Gallagher (2017) and Gallagher and Zahavi (2012).[3] What the authors want to take from this tradition is the basic idea of lived experience and its associated idea that the coupling of brain, body and environment actually constitutes mental processes, with no necessary mediation through mental representations, however they are conceived. Of course, the authors do not deny the role of representations for some mental processes and states, even the necessity of propositional representations for some. Our argument is simply that some mental processes, such as perception and action, do not always require such representations: the relationship between organism and world is more direct than that. Moreover, meaning is created in this enactive relationship.[4]

In this chapter the authors will focus on trying to develop some hypotheses that could help in answering the two following questions:

How is our cognitive experience with time enacted and extended?

Has the cognitive dimension of the experience of time lost its reference in the body?

The discussion is necessarily speculative, although the authors will refer to relevant empirical studies where appropriate. Our principal argument will be that the dimension of the organism's coupling with the environment that can be called engagement with material culture – or things – has been undertheorized in the literature. Bringing this dimension into the analysis can, the authors argue, help explain how we experience psychological time. What's more, it can help understand the kinds of extra-bodily extensions that might explain why the use of technologies does not threaten disembodiment.

THE DANCE OF PERCEPTION: HOW BRAINS, BODIES AND THINGS CONSTITUTE PERCEPTUAL EXPERIENCE AND TEMPORAL COGNITION

The authors start by looking at Gibson's (1979) seminal text on the ecological approach to visual perception. Although Gibson's theory deals primarily with how we perceive the visual world, it can also provide insights into our perception of time. It is interesting to note that, besides being an inspiration for Clark's work, Gibson's theory was, likewise, a meaningful source for the world of design and user experience, including in virtual environments. The theory was applied by Donald Norman (2013) in the development of theories for the design of everyday objects. Norman is co-founder of the Nielsen Norman group, a leading group in the user experience field.

As is well known, one of the central concepts in Gibson's theory is that of *affordances*. Physical and social environments afford (provide or furnish) different things to different animals. As Gibson points out, affordances are always relative to the animal. For example, a leaf affords a surface for an ant to stand on but not a human being. And it is what Gibson calls the 'ambient optic array' that provides the information for perceiving the world. Now, the 'ecological events' we perceive are neither at the subatomic level or the astronomic level; they occur at the level of the substances, surfaces and media that structure the ambient optic array that provides the information we can take up in perceiving the world. An ecological event is, for Gibson, a change that occurs at this level. These changes indicate a change in the affordances the environment offers the organism. For example, when a door turns, it affords entering into a room.

The important point to notice is that ecological events cannot be measured in terms of the concept of time in physics. They aren't homogeneous but differentiated. If we want to explain the psychology of time we cannot be tied to physics. The authors want to explain our phenomenological experience of time, which, as we all know, can vary. Time as measured by physics does not alter in this way. What this means is that "we should begin to think of events as the primary realities and of time as an abstraction from them – a concept derived mainly from the regular repeating events, such as the ticking of clocks. Events are perceived but time is not" (Gibson, 1979, p. 93). The principal point is that events are not stimuli, in the usual sense of this term, and that they have affordances for animals, including human beings. The main idea is that events will disturb the ambient optic array and, therefore, the information that can be taken up from the environment. Disturbances in this structure "carry the information about events in the environment" (Gibson, 1979, p. 100). Ecological events, in this sense, are meaningful and objective in the sense that they exist in the environment and not only subjectively. We distinguish events by the disturbances in the optic array that they produce.

If time is an abstraction from events in Gibson's sense, then if the events change and, consequently, the invariant structure of the ambient optic array also offers different information to be taken up, then our conception of time will also suffer a modification. Gibson refers to natural events but also observes that artificial environments are produced by human beings. Now, although Gibson wasn't thinking of digital technologies, we can extend his analysis to include such technologies. In what way could cognitive technologies alter events? However, before trying to answer this question, we need to look at self-perception.

In order to perceive the world, we need to be able to perceive ourselves. Some of the information taken up from the environment is *propriospecific*, which means it specifies the perceiver and not the environment. When we observe the world, parts of our bodies are near to the point of observation. In humans these parts include the head, the body and limbs. This gives us our sense of a self in the head, with the body as a peripheral part. We literally see our self. Parts of our bodies enter and leave the field of view; they occlude parts of the environment and reveal others. But the 'objects' that reveal and conceal the world, in this case, are attached to the viewer and they move as the observer moves. Now, all perceptual systems are *propriosensitive*, in Gibson's sense, because they provide information about the activities of the perceiver.

An individual not only sees himself, he hears his footsteps and his voice, he touches the floor and his tools, and when he touches his own skin he feels both his hand and his skin at the same time. He feels his head turning, his muscles flexing, and his joints bending (…) in fact, he lives within his own skin. (Gibson, 1979, p. 108)

Now, Gibson's main point is that the information to specify the self and that needed to specify the environment coexist: "the one could not exist without the other (…) Self-perception and environment perception go together" (Gibson, 1979, pp. 108-109). Apart from eliminating the dualism between subjective and objective, this analysis shows how the world is revealed through the movement of the body, such as turning the head, for example[5]. As we move our body, we sample the environment. In Noë's terms (2004), the world is virtually accessible to us and we access it through movement. As we move about, the field of view samples the ambient array and we take up information about ourselves and the environment. We perceive the world and ourselves together.

Limb movements are central to this process. Our manipulation of the environment through the use of our hands, for example, is guided by the information that is taken up from the ambient optical array. "All manipulations, from the crudest act of grasping by the infant to the finest act of assembly by the watchmaker, must be guided by optical disturbances if they are to be successful" (Noë, 2004, p. 113). As infants and later, we develop what Noë calls sensorimotor patterns that are relatively stable and allow us to access the world. What's more, "when an object grasped by the hand is used as a tool, it becomes a sort of extension of the hand, almost a part of the body" (Gibson, 2015, p. 113). Cognitive technologies are extensions of this kind. They allow us to perceive the world in new ways. Moreover, if the perception of the world and the perception of self are two sides of the same coin, as Gibson argues, then the extension of the body through technologies will have effects on proprioception as well.

As already noted, according to Gibson we perceive events and our perception of time is an abstraction from such events. For example, we perceive the rising and setting of the sun and the changes in surfaces and colours that mark the seasons, etc. We abstract from this and develop our perception of the passing of days and years. We notice disturbances in the continuity of events or in the layout of things. Some disturbances are regular and establish the parameters of our perception of time. Others are unexpected and interfere with our perception of time. The natural constraints on perceiving events – and, by extension, time – are fixed by the natural limits of our organism and its coupling with the environment. But what can happen if those natural constraints are overcome? Do we perceive events and time in a different way?

For example, a common phenomenon is the perception of time passing more rapidly, although age is a factor in the experience of time as flowing faster (Friedman & Jenssen, 2010). One possible hypothesis to explain this phenomenon might be that disturbances in the ambient array are more frequent and rapid than in the past, largely as a result of our coupling with an environment altered by man. Abstracting from this, we perceive time as flowing faster.[6]

To explore our experience of time further, the authors propose looking at a wider cognitive ecology than that proposed by Gibson. This is because although his theory states an important role for bodily movement in visual perception, and thus the perception of events, the claim that our experience of time is an 'abstraction' from our experience of events does not clarify sufficiently how our coupling with the environment can enact or bring forth meanings by processes of cognitive extension. In other words, the environment constrains – in the positive and negative senses of enabling and restricting – the affordances it offers, which provide opportunities for symbolic and material engagement, both of which are important for shaping cognition.

Let us start with Lakoff and Johnson's embodied theory of cognition. In this theory, basic cognitive structures emerge from our sensorimotor experience. That is to say, it is only because we have bodies like we do, that move in characteristic ways, that we can have basic-level structures. These are our capacities for perception and mental imagery, movement, etc. However, from this basic level structure emerges an image-schematic structure, comprising recurring patterns in sensorimotor experience and perceptual interactions that form abstract image-schema in the brain. A particularly interesting aspect of the theory is that we "project activation patterns from sensorimotor areas to higher cortical areas (…) Projections of this kind allow us to conceptualize abstract concepts on the basis of inferential patterns used in sensorimotor processes that are directly tied to the body" (Lakoff & Johnson, 1999, p.77).

The claim is that these metaphorical mappings are the basis of our thought processes such as categorization, concept formation and even reasoning. Metaphor is, in other words, at the ontological core of our cognitive capacities and is not simply a figure of speech. It is a basic process of thought (Malafouris, 2013, p. 62). Malafouris cites Núñez's (1999) example of the "time events are things in space" metaphor, which is particularly instructive for our purposes in this chapter. As Núñez (1999, p. 52, as cited in Malafouris, 2013, p. 64) says:

We simply don't observe the conceptual structure of time flow based on domains of human experience such as tastes, flavours, or colours. Given this, the future can't taste purple. (…) Human beings, no matter the culture, organize chronological experience and its conceptual structure in terms of a very specific family of experiences: the experience of things in space.

If this is true, we can immediately see its relevance for our perception of time and its compatibility with Gibson's theory of affordances. If our experience of things in space is the source of our conceptual structure of time flow, then it follows that any change in this experience will bring about a change in our understanding of how time flows.

However, although this theory puts bodily experience at the heart of human cognition, it can be criticized for not going far enough. Malafouris suggests that it extends the boundaries of the *res cogitans* whilst still keeping cognition inside the body. What is lacking is the material engagement with the world as a constitutive part of the human mind. The principal claim here is that material engagement produces meaning in a way not possible by any purely representational mechanism, even the non-propositional one suggested by Lakoff and Johnson. What does this mean and how can we analyze experience of this type? Malafouris (2013, p. 66) suggests two theoretical commitments that are shared by Clark's extended mind hypothesis: (1) what is outside the brain is not necessarily outside the mind; (2) cognition is not simply a matter of internal representations[7]. The first commitment focusses our attention on "cognitive events that include interaction among people, artifacts, space and time", the latter being particularly important, as it helps us understand that space and time can also be used as a cognitive artifact (Malafouris, 2013, p. 67). The second commitment helps us realize that representations can be external, as in maps, charts, tools, etc., as well as internal (in whatever form these representational structures might take). This means, amongst other things, that what matters in delimiting the mind is the functional relationships between the cognitive elements and not their specific location (inside or outside the head or even the body).[8]

The authors will now explore cognitive mechanisms that extend beyond the body and are anchored in material things, where the material engagement enacts meaning in a way that metaphoric projection does not. The basic idea is that much of our cognition is *enacted through our engagement with things* in real space and time. An example using digital technologies might be the process of thinking by writing on a computer using a word processor. According to the traditional approach, the thinking takes place inside our head and is simply registered on the computer screen. However, anyone who writes on computers these days will observe that they physically manipulate the representational medium and that this manipulation is part of the cognitive process. The writing is arranged in space on the screen and the word processing device allows us to move the position of words, phrases and even whole passages as we think and write. What's more, we can store parts in other files or even send them to colleagues for them to make alterations before we continue the process. As Malafouris (2013, p. 72) suggests, in relation to a much older writing system (the Linear B system of the Mycenean clay tablets, the oldest registered script in history), "the file (…) is also transforming the physical boundaries of the problem's space, and thereby structuring the problem-solving process".

In short, the manipulation of the material culture – in this case the computer screen and the files contained within the computer – cannot be separated from the cognitive process. The process is enacted in real space and time. One of the problems with Mycenean clay tablets was that they dried rapidly, thus restricting the freedom of the person registering transactions on them, who had to register everything within the same few hours, which wasn't possible given that a single person didn't have all the information necessary and couldn't remember it all in their biological memory. The solution was to use small leaf-shaped tablets and then arrange them in a larger tablet. The smaller tablets thus afforded the registration of records given the technology of the time. Nowadays, cognitive technologies such as computers and word processing programs afford the recording of facts and ideas in a way that permits revision, alteration and elimination over time and the sharing of the writing process over space, with a number of people contributing towards the final product. Here space and time are being used as cognitive artifacts and not simply as some kind of passive backdrop to cognition. By manipulating the space on the computer screen and on files, we can hide or emphasize parts; we can also facilitate perception by the way in which the material is arranged on the screen, sometimes temporarily in order to focus on a specific part; we can also facilitate problem solving by moving text around and saving bits for future use, etc., as well as distributing the whole process amongst various people. Such features were available in the Mycenaean pre-historic context, in limited form, but the technologies of today obviously augment these features, offering different affordances not available so long ago.

Now, Mycenaean tablets were a technology. It's important not to fall into the trap of thinking that only digital computers or other recent inventions are technologies. As Clark correctly says, we are "natural born cyborgs" and always have been. Just as, in the example of Mycenaean tablets, it's important to postulate "the dynamic interaction between [the] person [reading or writing on the tablet] and the physical properties of the medium of representation as a material thing" (Malafouris, 2013, p. 73), it is just as important to postulate the dynamic interaction between us and digital computers and other similar technologies.

Now, how can this interaction affect our perception of time? One hypothesis would be to suggest that the motion of things in space that digital technologies permit alters how they are present to us and, through the "time events are things in space" metaphor, this can alter how we cognitively structure time. The argument to support this hypothesis might go something like this. If Núñez is correct, the cross-domain mapping of the source domain and the target domain of this metaphorical extension of bodily experience would start out with the mapping of 'things' and 'times'. A further mapping would lead from the order of things in a horizontal one-dimensional landscape to the chronological order of times. This would imply that things in front of the observer are future times and things behind the observer are past times, with things at the location of the observer as present times. Finally, the sequence of events in time would be an extension of one object in front or behind of another object in the sequence (Malafouris, 2013, p.63). Now, we could argue that the motion of things in space is altered by computers in that not only the sequence of events is often altered but that their motion in space can also be drastically altered. If time events are mapped onto space, we would expect an alteration in the location and sequencing of things in space to produce an alteration of the perception of time. Of course, for this to happen the source domain of space would have to be consistently altered for long periods of time, for the neural substrate to be altered. But, as mentioned at the beginning of this chapter, one of the worries related to the use of digital technologies is the prolonged periods of time spent in front of computer screens, for example, especially by children and adolescents.[9]

But, if Malafouris is right, this hypothesis doesn't go far enough. One reason is that cognition can still be understood as something that happens inside the organism, even though the organism is coupled with the environment. A change in the environment might produce a change in cognition but this change is of something internal to the organism. Here there is a causal connection between the computer and the mind but not necessarily any cognitive extension. This hypothesis still assumes that mind is a property of the individual, who has priority in the enaction of cognitive processes, which are still seen as inside the organism (see Malafouris (2013, p. 81), for an extended critique of these assumptions). If we embrace the extended mind hypothesis, we need to break with these assumptions and see mind as something beyond the individual and his or her organism and as emerging from the intertwining of cognition with material culture. What hypothesis about the perception of time could be built on this theory? What is more, in the discussion of material engagement above, time is conceived, along with space, as a cognitive artifact. But what about our experience of time itself? If much of our cognition is *enacted through our engagement with things* in real space and time, how is space and time itself enacted? First let us elaborate the theory in more details and supplement it with insights from phenomenology before proposing a hypothesis.

One important aspect of this theory is that material culture is not simply a symbol for something that could be expressed and communicated through verbal language, although sometimes things can operate as symbols in this sense. This implies that we cannot use linguistic models for thinking about material culture and how it produces meaning. The process of creating meaning involves the physical properties of the things themselves. Put slightly differently, things are material signs that have an enactive logic (Malafouris, 2013, chapter 5). A material sign instantiates and expresses meaning rather than simply substituting a concept; without the material engagement with the sign, there is no meaning. In short, it's not the case that first there is the concept and then, temporally and ontologically, the material sign "carries" this message. On the contrary, ontological priority has to be given to the material sign itself. As Malafouris says, "material signs are the actual physical forces that shape the social and cognitive universe" (Malafouris, 2013, p. 97). In sum, the material sign enacts and "brings forth" the world. This is, of course, a semantic and semiotic process, although it doesn't involve symbolic signs.[10]

How does this happen? The basic idea, which we do not have the space to spell out in detail here, is that a mechanism of cognitive projection establishes an ontological correspondence between domains of experience. This is a non-representational mechanism, although it is, of course, conceptual[11]. The central point is that it permits a structural coupling between mind and matter. What's more, the mappings are not only internal, as in the case of conceptual metaphors, but between internal elements and external things. Malafouris' main claim is that this mechanism is a human capacity that is the basis for sense making.

But perhaps the most important point of this theory is that projection requires "material anchoring" (Hutchins, in Malafouris, 2013, p. 102). Without the material object, this process of cognitive projection cannot occur. In cognitive projections what happens is that elements in two domains are integrated or blended in a third, creating a hybrid meaning not contained in the original domains. The conceptual space that emerges is not identical to either of the original spaces but a "new hybrid or blended phenomenal domain" (Malafouris, 2013, p. 103). What is more, without the material anchoring this process would not occur.

What importance does this have for our perception of time? One possible idea is that it is not only the abstraction from events in space that give us our perception of time, if by abstraction we mean a purely symbolic process that does not require any engagement with material culture. Rather, it is also our engagement with the objects and other forms of material culture that gives us our perception of time. Or, perhaps more accurately, the process of conceptualizing time is enacted through our engagement with material culture as well as with symbolic forms. In short, meaning is not in the material sign before any engagement with it; it emerges from such engagement. This is not a purely hermeneutic process caught up in a hermeneutic circle. As Malafouris says,

in the case of material signs, we do not read meaningful symbols; we meaningfully engage meaningless symbols. Material signs have no meaning in themselves. They merely afford the possibility of meaning, as a door affords the possibility of being opened. In real life, to interpret a material sign (...) is to become habituated with the interactive possibilities and consequences of its performance in context (...). Material signs do not represent; they enact. They do not stand for reality; they bring forth reality. (2013, pp. 117-118)

How might this affect our experience of time? As the authors said in the background to this article, in our culture experience of time has been deeply influenced by religion as a fundamental matrix, as well as by economic and social organization. Now, these matrices are material as well as representational. In our previous comments the authors suggested that the principal mechanisms for establishing time in the Modern Age have been representational. However, we would like to suggest that such mechanisms do not capture the material engagement involved in the construction of the meaning of time. The authors mentioned how the great temporal cosmological questions are materialized in the architecture of cathedrals and their iconographic clocks (for Christian culture). However, this materialization was still seen as largely a question of representing an abstract conceptual domain by some kind of process of symbolic projection. Also, in our comments on the "modes of use of time" determined by economic and social organization, the authors suggested that temporal representations are associated with the motive of realization and the "achieving society", creating temporal perspectives represented by forms of behavior. The central suggestion was that temporal representations are constituted by the interaction between the temporal framework (understood in symbolic, representational terms) and human behavior.

What the authors would like to suggest now is that this is only partially true in that it does not give enough weight to material engagement with cultural artifacts, and that a theory of material engagement can help fill this gap. In short, representational temporality is, perhaps, not our primary experience of time; we experience time primarily through our material engagement with things. If the principal mechanism for this is conceptual integration, then the physical anchoring of this experience in the material thing is central. The cognitive process is extended beyond the body to involve material culture as part of the cognitive circuitry. But more importantly, experience of time would not be durable without the material anchors that constantly reinforce it. We might even go further and suggest that the experience of time is a phenomenal domain constituted by the mapping achieved by integrative projection; it is an emergent conceptual space made possible by the mapping not of two internal domains (the concrete concept of events in space with the abstract concept of events in time through metaphorical extension) but between internal domains and external material culture. The material culture operates as an anchor without which the experience of time would not be created and would not endure. So, not only do space and time operate as cognitive artifacts for the construction of other cognitive experiences but are also, themselves, enactively constituted as psychological experiences.

Let us try and put some flesh on these speculative bones by looking at the two examples already mentioned above. If time, in our largely Judaic-Christian-Islamic culture is experienced as linear – with a past-present-future and a beginning and end – as well as 'circular', in that it is repeated in the celebration of the rhythms of each day, dates in the year and seasons, etc., then we could argue that this experience requires engagement with material culture. It is well known that the Christian calendar, at least, incorporated the dates and events of pagan societies, based on the rhythms of nature. The rhythms of the day were then marked by the chimes of church and cathedral clocks, which are external, material elements, as well as the rituals of mass or other religious services, which also involve engagement with material culture. These were later substituted largely for the clocks in public spaces and factories, as well as the watches nearly everyone wears today, our engagement with which is almost constant throughout the day. Many religious dates are incorporated into the economic calendar, together with their material culture. Religious services were, over time, either substituted or transferred to the rituals of going to work by public transport or car, eating at certain times of the day and manipulating the tools associated with the production of goods and services.

Now, the point is that all of these events that mark time require engagement with material culture. And it is this engagement that anchors this experience but not simply as a support; it is a constitutive part of the experience of time. The experience of time has a sensorimotor dynamic of embodiment and a dynamic of material engagement. In fact, these two dimensions can be seen as two sides of the same coin. We need to move in order to engage with material culture but this also enters the process as a material agent, without which our experience of time would be very different.

What is meant here by a 'material agent'? Surely, one might argue, agency is a property of persons and some other higher animals and that inanimate material signs cannot be agents. What sense, if any, can be made of material agency? Obviously, the idea isn't that material things can act intentionally in their own right. Rather, it's the idea that "if there is such a thing as human agency, then there is material agency; there is no way human agency and material agency can be disentangled" (Malafouris, 2013, p. 119). In other words, agency and intentionality are properties of an organism's engagement with the world and not something exclusively internal to the human or other animal, prior to this engagement.[12]

Perhaps the most important idea is that agency and intentionality "are not properties of the isolated person or the isolated thing; they are properties of a chain of associations" (Malafouris, 2013, p. 129) that are human and non-human. To accept this, we need to overcome a deep prejudice in modern Western thought: the idea that persons and things are separate and independently defined ontological entities. Without going into the detailed arguments necessary to reject this assumption, for our purposes we only need to notice that objects are not secondary agents, on a comparison with people, but are active as part of a dynamic system that enacts meaning.

This is, the authors confess, the most controversial and difficult part of material engagement theory, in that it requires us to think of intentional states as something beyond the body and extended into things. If intentionality is a characteristic of mind and necessary for agency, then the concept of material agency requires us to extend both beyond human agents. And the concept of agency is necessary if we wish to retain the link between action and the processing of information, not only bodily information within the constraints of real space and time but also the possible modulation of time perception itself. And this is necessary because there is some evidence of a strong link between voluntary action and conscious awareness (Tsakiris et al., 2006, 2007; Haggard et al., 2002). Here Gibson's insight that proprioception is an integral part of perception is relevant. Just as we cannot see the world if we don't see ourselves, we also can't be aware of the world if we don't act in it.

Agency, in short, emerges as a property of material engagement and not of an isolated human agent and her intentions. This is contra-intuitive and, indeed, flies in the face of much philosophical discussion of mind (Searle, 1983) but the authors suggest that a strong commitment to the extended mind hypothesis leads us in this direction. Just as intentionality and agency have already been extended to non-human animals, we need to take the further step of extending them to things. The basic idea here is that when humans engage the world, their intentions are subject to the mediation of affordances that the material environment presents. These material affordances are part of what philosophers call the background of intentional action (Searle, 1983), that is, aspects that are not part of the specific intention of the human agent but are necessary constituent elements of the intention-in-action that is coextensive with the action itself. In other words, artifacts are not just things to act upon but things to engage with and, through this engagement, produce meaning and action (Malafouris, 2013, chapter 6). This makes the material world part of the intentional system that produces the action and not something merely passive and separate from it (Searle, 1983). We can here legitimately talk of an "extended intentional state". The effectiveness of our intentional actions is partly explained by the affordances the environment offers and our engagement with them. Without this material culture, our intentions would have no or very little practical effect. Things shape human intentions in both positive and negative ways.

Is screen time and our engagement with computers, smartphones, tablets, etc. changing our experience of time? Irrespective of the complexity of the topic addressed, and of the innumerable questions that arise, we can say that, nevertheless, some general consensus exists on substantive topics. Thus, through the review of the literature cited above, it is known that there is research that evidences an association between screen time and mental disorders, but that fail to prove that this relation is of a direct causal nature. On the other hand, the use of digital technologies is also associated with positive effects on people's well-being. Faced with this controversy it is necessary to reflect, to contemplate new conceptual models, such as those the authors propose, and to deepen research. It is also consensual that new technologies change the perception of time (Blatchley et al., 2007), as has always happened from the point of view of the anthropological and historical evolution of technologies, an example being the infinite impact that wheel vehicles had on society and human behavior.

And what about bodily experience? Of course technologies also had an impact there. What we might call the "thinking hand" (Soylu, 2014) also felt technological evolution. The current processes of embodiment defined as "how culture gets under the skin" (Anderson-Fye, 2012, p.16), or "bodily being-in-the-world" (Csordas, 1999, p.143), reflect the new relationships between body and technology (Ihde, 2001; Murray, 2000; Wasiak, 2009), but nothing that suggests an *a priori* suspicion of disembodiment, reinforced, on the other hand, by the possibility of re-embodiment through technology (De Preester, 2010; Zaina & Kaivanara, 2015), specifically at the level of symbiotic tools (Osiurak, Navarro, & Reynaud, 2018).

If the tentative argument elaborated above is on the right track, psychological experience of time will depend on the ways in which our material engagement with cultural artifacts, including screens, could alter forms of agency and intentionality and, therefore, our experience of time. If cognitive projection is anchored in material space and our engagement with material culture, then we need to look at how this space and culture is altered by screen technologies and, therefore, how this anchoring process is also altered. Also, if awareness of the body is essential to human action, and to time perception, we need to see how this awareness might be altered by screen time. We would then need to examine to what extent, if any, this is simply a substitution of material agency that does not significantly alter our experience of time or if it is a new form of agency that is causing a shift in that experience.

As far as we know, these are questions that haven't been answered and are only beginning to be formulated. However, material engagement theory helps us in this task in that it goes beyond examining representations of time (internal and external) and their correlations with human behavior and focuses our attention on how this behavior, in the form of our material engagement with things through practices, is part of the cognitive circuitry and, therefore, constitutive of the cognitive experience of time.

CONCLUSION

In this text the authors have tried to show how temporality is embodied and extended through our engagement with material culture. In doing so, the authors have suggested an approach for the explication of our experience of time that could generate a number of hypotheses that could be tested in future work. Our discussion has been speculative and tentative. The authors do not offer this as a clearly worked out theoretical perspective nor as a framework for experimental method. Much more theoretical, methodological and experimental work has to be done to see if this approach is fruitful. However, the authors see no *a priori* reason why it should not be. On the contrary, the authors think it might be able to offer a way of thinking about the experience of time that is consistent with enactive and extended conceptions of mind.

The authors have also indirectly addressed the worry that the cognitive dimension of time may be losing its reference in the body with the development of digital technologies and the phenomenon of screen time. The authors suggest that there is no danger of this happening because technologies can be understood as extensions of our bodies and that even screen time use has a sensory-motor dynamic of embodiment that is also an engagement with the material culture of screen technologies. The human body is no less involved in screen time use than in any other form of cognitive projection.

REFERENCES

Þórarinsdóttir, J. A. (2015). *The Impact of Screen-Use on Cognitive Function: A Pilot Study*. Retrieved from http://hdl.handle.net/1946/22566

Adams, F., & Aizawa, K. (2008). *The Bounds of Cognition*. London: Blackwell.

Agarwal, R., & Karahanna, E. (2000). Time Flies When You're Having Fun: Cognitive Absorption and Beliefs about Information Technology Usage. *Management Information Systems Quarterly*, *24*(4), 665–694. doi:10.2307/3250951

Anderson-Fye, E. P. (2012). Anthropological Perspectives on Physical Appearance and Body Image. In *Encyclopedia of Body Image and Human Appearance* (Vol. 1, pp. 15–22). San Diego, CA: Academic Press. doi:10.1016/B978-0-12-384925-0.00003-1

Baker, F., & Mackinlay, E. (2006). Sing, soothe and sleep: A lullaby education programme for first-time mothers. *British Journal of Music Education*, *23*(2), 147–160. doi:10.1017/S0265051706006899

Baym, N. K. (2010). New relations, new selves. In N. K. Baym (Ed.), *Personal Connections in the Digital Age* (pp. 99–121). Cambridge, UK: Polity Press.

Becker, H. J. (2000). Who's Wired and Who's Not: Children's Access to and Use of Computer Technology. *The Future of Children*, *10*(2), 44–75. doi:10.2307/1602689 PMID:11255709

Bermúdez, J. L. (2007). Thinking without Words: An Overview for Animal Ethics. *The Journal of Ethics*, *11*(3), 319–335. doi:10.100710892-007-9013-8

Blatchley, B., Dixon, R., Purvis, A., Slack, J., Thomas, T., Weber, N., & Wiley, C. (2007). Computer use and the perception of time. *North American Journal of Psychology, 9*(1), 131–142.

Borghi, A. M., Scorolli, C., Calisiore, D., Baldassarre, G., & Tummolini, L. (2013). The embodied mind extended: Using words as social tools. *Frontiers in Psychology, 4*, 214. doi:10.3389/fpsyg.2013.00214 PMID:23641224

Boyce, M. (2001). *Zoroastrians: Their Religious Beliefs and Practices*. New York, NY: Routledge.

Brown, S. W. (1995). Time, change, and motion: The effects of stimulus movement on temporal perception. *Perception & Psychophysics, 57*(1), 105–116. doi:10.3758/BF03211853 PMID:7885802

Campbell, A. J., Cumming, C. R., & Hughes, I. (2006). Internet use by the socially fearful: Addiction or therapy? *Cyberpsychology & Behavior, 9*(1), 69–81. doi:10.1089/cpb.2006.9.69 PMID:16497120

Candiotto, L. (2016). Extended affectivity as cognition of primary intersubjectivity. *Phenomenology and Mind, 11*, 232–241. doi:10.13128/Phe_Mi-20122

Cevasco, A. M. (2008). The effects of mother's singing on full-term and preterm infants and maternal emotional responses. *Journal of Music Therapy, 45*(3), 273–306. doi:10.1093/jmt/45.3.273 PMID:18959452

Clark, A. (1997). *Being There. Putting Brain, Body and World together again*. Cambridge, MA: MIT Press.

Clark, A. (2003). *Natural-Born Cyborgs. Minds, Technologies, and the Future of Human Intelligence*. Oxford, UK: Oxford University Press.

Clark, A., & Chalmers, D. (1998). The extended mind. *Analysis, 58*(1), 7–19. doi:10.1093/analys/58.1.7

Clowes, R. W. (2013). The Cognitive Integration of E-Memory. *Review of Philosophy and Psychology, 4*(1), 107–133. doi:10.100713164-013-0130-y

Csikszentmihaiyi, M. (1990). *Flow: The Psychology of Optimal Experience*. New York, NY: Harper and Row.

Csordas, T. J. (1999). Embodiment and Cultural Phenomenology. In G. Wiess & H. F. Haber (Eds.), *Perspectives on Embodiment: The Intersections of Nature and Culture* (pp. 143–164). New York, NY: Routledge.

De Preester, H. (2011). Technology and the Body: The (Im)Possibilities of Re-embodiment. *Foundations of Science*, *16*(2-3), 119–137. doi:10.100710699-010-9188-5

Dewey, J. (1925). *Experience and Nature*. Chicago: Open Court.

Eliade, M. (1949). *Le Mythe de l'éternel retour*. Paris: Les Essais.

Farr, W., Price, S., & Jewitt, C. (2012). *An introduction to embodiment and digital technology research: Interdisciplinary themes and perspectives*. NCRM Working Paper. NCRM. Retrieved from http://eprints.ncrm.ac.uk/2257/

Fraisse, P. (1957). *Psychologie du temps*. Paris: Presses Universitaires de France.

Friedman, W. J., & Jenssen, S. M. J. (2010). Aging and the speed of time. *Acta Psychologica*, *134*(2), 130–141. doi:10.1016/j.actpsy.2010.01.004 PMID:20163781

Froese, T., Gershenson, C., & Rosenblueth, D. A. (2013). *The Dynamically Extended Mind. A Minimal Modeling Case Study*. Retrieved from https://www.researchgate.net/publication/236661591_The_Dynamically_Extended_Mind_--_A_Minimal_Modeling_Case_Study

Gallagher, S. (2005). *How the Body Shapes the Mind*. Oxford, UK: University Press. doi:10.1093/0199271941.001.0001

Gallagher, S. (2017). *Enactivist Interventions. Rethinking the Mind*. Oxford, UK: Oxford University Press. doi:10.1093/oso/9780198794325.001.0001

Gallagher, S., Martínez, S. F., & Gastelum, M. (2012). Action-Space and Time: Towards an Enactive Hermeneutics. In B. B. Janz (Ed.), *Place, Space and Hermeneutics, Contributions to Hermeneutics 5* (pp. 83–96). New York, NY: Springer.

Gallagher, S., & Zahavi, D. (2008). *The Phenomenological Mind*. London: Routledge.

Gärdenfors, P., & Lombard, M. (2018). Causal Cognition, Force Dynamics and Early Hunting Technologies. *Frontiers in Psychology*, *9*, 1–10. doi:10.3389/fpsyg.2018.00087 PMID:29483885

Gavazzi, G., Bisio, A., & Pozzo, T. (2013). Time perception of visual motion is tuned by the motor representation of human actions. *Scientific Reports*, *3*(1), 1–8. doi:10.1038rep01168 PMID:23378903

Gibson, J. J. (2015). *The Ecological Approach to Visual Perception*. New York, NY: Taylor and Francis.

Greif, H. (2017). What is the extension of the extended mind? *Synthese*, *194*(11), 4311–4336. doi:10.100711229-015-0799-9 PMID:29200511

Haggard, P., Clark, S., & Kalogeras, J. (2002). Voluntary action and conscious awareness. *Nature Neuroscience*, *5*(4), 382–385. doi:10.1038/nn827 PMID:11896397

Hardie, E., & Tee, M. Y. (2007). Excessive Internet Use: The Role of Personality, Loneliness, and Social Support Networks in Internet Addiction. *Australian Journal of Emerging Technologies and Society*, *5*(1), 34–47.

Hartley, R. (2010). *Living on the Screen: Disembodiment to Embededness*. Retrieved from http://riahartley.com/wp-content/uploads/2013/07/Living-on-the-Screen-Disembodiment-to-Embededness.pdf

Henkel, L. A. (2014). Point-and-Shot Memories. The Influence of Taking Photos on Memory for a Museum Tour. *Psychological Science*, *25*(2), 396–402. doi:10.1177/0956797613504438 PMID:24311477

Hergert, P. (2017). How tangible is cyberspace? *Digital Culturist*. Retrieved from https://digitalculturist.com/how-tangible-is-cyberspace-dce550c52248

Hutto, D., & Myin, E. (2013). *Radicalizing Enactivism: Basic Minds whitout Content*. Cambridge, MA: MIT Press.

Ihde, D. (2001). *Bodies in Technology*. Minneapolis, MN: University of Minnesota.

Johnson, M. (1987). *The Body in the Mind. The Bodily basis of Meaning, Imagination, and Reason*. Chicago, IL: University of Chicago Press.

Johnson, M. (2007). *The Meaning of the Body. Aesthetics of Human Understanding*. Chicago, IL: University of Chicago Press. doi:10.7208/chicago/9780226026992.001.0001

Johnson, M. (2017). *Embodied Mind, Meaning, and Reason. How our Bodies give rise to Understanding*. Chicago, IL: University of Chicago Press. doi:10.7208/chicago/9780226500393.001.0001

Kranjec, A., & McDonough, L. (2011). The implicit and explicit embodiment of time. *Journal of Pragmatics*, *43*(3), 735–748. doi:10.1016/j.pragma.2010.07.004

Lakoff, G., & Johnson, M. (1999). *Philosophy in the Flesh. The Embodied Mind and its Challenge to Western Thought*. New York, NY: Basic Books.

Laroche, J., Berardi, A. M., & Brangier, E. (2014). Embodiment of intersubjective time: Relational dynamics as attractors in the temporal coordination of interpersonal behaviors and experiences. *Frontiers in Psychology*, *5*, 1180. doi:10.3389/fpsyg.2014.01180 PMID:25400598

Lissak, G. (2018). Adverse physiological and psychological effects of screen time on children and adolescents: Literature review and case study. *Environmental Research*, *164*, 149–157. doi:10.1016/j.envres.2018.01.015 PMID:29499467

Loizou, A. (2000). *Time, embodiment and the self*. Aldershot, UK: Ashgate.

Madzia, R. (2013). Chicago Pragmatism and the Extended Mind Theory. Mead and Dewey on the Nature of Cognition. *European Journal of Pragmatism and American Philosophy*, *5*(1), 279–297.

Malafouris, L. (2013). *How Things Shape the Mind. A Theory of Material Engagement*. Cambridge, MA: MIT Press.

Menary, R. (Ed.). (2010). *The Extended Mind*. Cambridge, MA: MIT Press. doi:10.7551/mitpress/9780262014038.001.0001

Merleau-Ponty, M. (2012). *Phenomenology of Perception*. London: Routledge.

Moffat, P. (2014). Screen time. How much is healthy for children? *Community practitioner: The journal of the Community Practitioners' & Health Visitors'. Association*, *87*(11), 16–18.

Munn, L. (2015). *Digital Disembodiment*. Retrieved from http://www.lukemunn.com/2015/digital-disembodiment/

Murray, C. D. (2000). Towards a phenomenology of the body in virtual reality. *Research in Philosophy and Technology*, *19*, 149–173.

Nather, F. C., Bueno, J. L. O., Bigand, E., & Droit-Volet, S. (2011). Time Changes with the Embodiment of another's Body Posture. *PLoS One*, *6*(5), e19818. doi:10.1371/journal.pone.0019818 PMID:21637759

Noë, A. (2004). *Action in Perception*. Cambridge, MA: MIT Press.

Noë, A. (2012). *Varieties of Presence*. Cambridge, MA: Harvard University Press. doi:10.4159/harvard.9780674063013

Norman, D. A. (2008). Signifiers, not affordances. *Interactions (New York, N.Y.)*, *15*(6), 18–19. doi:10.1145/1409040.1409044

Norman, D. A. (2013). *The Design of Everyday Things*. New York, NY: Basic Books.

Osiurak, F., Navarro, J., & Reynaud, E. (2018). How Our Cognition Shapes and Is Shaped by Technology: A Common Framework for Understanding Human Tool-Use Interactions in the Past, Present, and Future. *Frontiers in Psychology*, *9*, 293. doi:10.3389/fpsyg.2018.00293 PMID:29563891

Owen, G. S., Freyenhagen, F., Hotopf, M., & Martin, W. (2015). Temporal inabilities and decision-making capacity in depression. *Phenomenology and the Cognitive Sciences*, *14*(1), 163–182. doi:10.100711097-013-9327-x

Parent, J., Sanders, W., & Forehand, R. (2016). Youth Screen Time and Behavioral Health Problems: The Role of Sleep Duration and Disturbances. *Journal of Developmental and Behavioral Pediatrics*, *37*(4), 277–284. doi:10.1097/DBP.0000000000000272 PMID:26890562

Piaget, J. (1968). *Genetic Epistemology*. New York, NY: Columbia University Press.

Primack, B. A., Swanier, B., Georgiopoulos, A. M., Land, S. R., & Fine, M. J. (2009). Association between media use in adolescent and depression in young adulthood: A longitudinal study. *Archives of General Psychiatry*, *66*(2), 181–188. doi:10.1001/archgenpsychiatry.2008.532 PMID:19188540

Ricoeur, P. (1984). *Time and Narrative* (Vol. 1). Chicago, IL: The University of Chicago Press.

Rowlands, M. (2010). *The New Science of the Mind*. Cambridge, MA: MIT Press. doi:10.7551/mitpress/9780262014557.001.0001

Ryle, G. (1949). *The Concept of Mind*. London: Hutchinson.

Saint-Georges, C., Chetouani, M., Cassel, R., Apicella, F., Mahdhaoui, A., Muratori, F., ... Cohen, D. (2013). Motherese in Interaction: At the Cross-Road of Emotion and Cognition? (A Systematic Review). *PLoS One*, *8*(10), e78103. doi:10.1371/journal.pone.0078103 PMID:24205112

Sami-Ali, M. (1974). *L'Espace imaginaire*. Paris: Gallimard.

Santos, E. (1992). *Time, Affect and Project* (Unpublished doctoral thesis). University of Coimbra.

Santos, E., Almeida, J. G., Santos, G., Frontini, R., & Ferreira, J. A. (2012). Tempos e Afectos: para um paradigma ecossistémico na construção de projectos. In E. Santos, J. A. Ferreira & Colaboradores (Eds.), *Mudanças e Transições: pessoas em contextos* (pp. 11-24). Viseu: Psicosoma.

Schmid, H. (2017). The Embodiment of Time. In S. Broadhurst & S. Price (Eds.), *Digital Bodies. Palgrave Studies in Performance and Technology* (pp. 97–109). London: Palgrave Macmillan; doi:10.1057/978-1-349-95241-0_7

Searle, J. R. (1983). *Intentionality. An Essay in the Philosophy of Mind.* Cambridge, UK: Cambridge University Press. doi:10.1017/CBO9781139173452

Selfhout, M. H. W., Branje, S. J. T., Delsing, M., ter Bogt, T. F. M., & Meeus, W. H. J. (2009). Different types of Internet use, depression, and social anxiety: The role of perceived friendship quality. *Journal of Adolescence*, *32*(4), 819–833. doi:10.1016/j.adolescence.2008.10.011 PMID:19027940

Shapiro, L. (2011). *Embodied Cognition.* London: Routledge.

Shapiro, L. (Ed.). (2014). *The Routledge Handbook of Embodied Cognition.* London: Routledge. doi:10.4324/9781315775845

Smart, P. R. (2012). The Web-Extended Mind. *Metaphilosophy*, *43*(4), 446–463. doi:10.1111/j.1467-9973.2012.01756.x

Soylu, F., Brady, C., Holbert, N., & Wilensky, U. (2014). *The thinking hand: Embodiment of tool use, social cognition and metaphorical thinking and implications for learning design.* Paper presented at the AERA Annual Meeting (SIG: Brain, Neurosciences, and Education), Philadelphia, PA. Retrieved from https://ccl.northwestern.edu/2014/Soylu-2014-ThinkingHand.pdf

Sparrow, B., Liu, J., & Wegner, D. M. (2011). Google Effects on Memory: Cognitive Consequences of Having Information at Our fingertips. *Science*, *333*(6043), 776–778. doi:10.1126cience.1207745 PMID:21764755

Stoetzel, J. (1983). *Les Valeurs du Temps Présent: une enquête européen.* Paris: Presses Universitaires de France.

Sum, S., Mathews, M. R., Hughes, I., & Campbell, A. (2008). Internet Use and Loneliness in Older Adults. *Cyberpsychology & Behavior*, *11*(2), 208–211. doi:10.1089/cpb.2007.0010 PMID:18422415

Sutton, J. (2009). Remembering. In P. Robbins & M. Aydede (Eds.), *Cambridge Handbook of Situated Cognition* (pp. 217–235). New York, NY: Cambridge University Press.

Svoboda, E., & Richards, B. (2009). Compensating for anterograde amnesia: A new training method that capitalizes on emerging smartphone technologies. *Journal of the International Neuropsychological Society*, *15*(04), 629–638. doi:10.1017/S1355617709090791 PMID:19588540

Triphon, A., & Vonèche, J. (Eds.). (1996). *Piaget-Vygotsky. The Social Genesis of Thought*. New York, NY: Psychology Press.

Tsakiris, M., Prabhu, G., & Haggard, P. (2006). Having a body versus moving your body. How agency structures body ownership. *Consciousness and Cognition, 15*(2), 423–432. doi:10.1016/j.concog.2005.09.004 PMID:16343947

Tsakiris, M., Shcütz-Bosbach, S., & Gallagher, S. (2007). On agency and body-ownership: Phenomenological and neurocognitive reflections. *Consciousness and Cognition, 19*(3), 645–660. doi:10.1016/j.concog.2007.05.012 PMID:17616469

Tsatou, P. (2009). Reconceptualising 'time' and 'space' in the Era of Electronic Media and Communications. *PLATFORM: Journal of Media and Communication, 1*, 11–52.

Turvey, M. T. (1992). Affordances and prospective control: An outline of the ontology. *Ecological Psychology, 4*(3), 173–187. doi:10.120715326969eco0403_3

Varela, F. J., Thompson, E., & Rosch, E. (1991). *The Embodied Mind. Cognitive Science and Human Experience*. Cambridge, MA: MIT Press.

Vygotsky, L. S. (1978). *Mind in society: The development of higher psychological processes*. Cambridge, MA: Harvard University Press.

Wasiak, J. (2009). Being-in-the-City: A Phenomenological Approach to Technological Experience. *Culture Unbound, 1*(2), 349–366. doi:10.3384/cu.2000.1525.09121349

Wheeler, M. (2005). *Reconstructing the Cognitive World: the Next Step*. Cambridge, MA: MIT Press.

Wiecha, J. L., Peterson, K. E., Ludwig, D. S., Kim, J., Sobol, A., & Gortmaker, S. L. (2006). When children eat what they watch: Impact of television viewing on dietary intake in youth. *Archives of Pediatrics & Adolescent Medicine, 160*(4), 436–442. doi:10.1001/archpedi.160.4.436 PMID:16585491

Zani, L., & Kaivanara, M. (2015). Teaching Embodiment through Technology. Teaching Tools. *Cultural Anthropology*. Retrieved from https://culanth.org/fieldsights/682-teaching-embodiment-through-technology

Zelazo, P. D. (2013). The Oxford Handbook of Developmental Psychology: Vol. 1. *Body and Mind*. Oxford, UK: Oxford University Press.

ADDITIONAL READING

Chemero, A. (2009). *Radical Embodied Cognitive Science*. Cambridge, MA: MIT Press. doi:10.7551/mitpress/8367.001.0001

Di Paolo, E. A., Cuffari, E. C., & De Jaegher, H. (2018). *Linguistic Bodies: The Continuity between Life and Language*. Cambridge, MA: MIT Press.

Dreyfus, H. L. (2014). *Skillful Coping. Essays on the Phenomenology of Everyday Perception and Action*. Oxford: Oxford University Press. doi:10.1093/acprof:oso/9780199654703.001.0001

Hovhannisyan, G. (2018). Humanistic cognitive science. *The Humanistic Psychologist*, *46*(1), 30–52. doi:10.1037/hum0000074

Kyselo, M. (2018). Review of Enactive Cognition at the Edge of Sense-making by Massimiliano Cappucio and Tom Froese (Eds.), Palgrave Macmillan, 2014. Phenomenology and the Cognitive Sciences, 1-6. doi:10.100711097-018-9574-y

Shapiro, L. (2011). *Embodied Cognition*. London: Routledge.

Sheets-Johnstone, M. (2011). *The Primacy of Movement. Expanded* (2nd ed.). Amsterdam: John Benjamins. doi:10.1075/aicr.82

Thompson, E. (2007). *Mind in Life. Biology, Phenomenology, and the Sciences of Mind*. Cambridge, MA: Harvard University Press.

KEY TERMS AND DEFINITIONS

Affordances: Things in the environment that enable cognitive functions such as perception.

Agency: The capacity of a cognitive system to act.

Embodied Mind: An approach to mind that sees the body as a constitutive element of its architecture and functioning.

Enactive Mind: An approach to mind that puts the body in movement at the center of the explanation of how it works.

Extended Mind: An approach to mind that understands external artifacts as component elements of its architecture and functioning.

Intentionality: A basic characteristic of mental states as always having objects.

Material Engagement: An approach to cognition that emphasizes the constitutive role of the physical engagement with things.

ENDNOTES

1 Vygotsky's embedded theory of cognitive development is an exception, as well, of course.

2 Dewey's notion of feeling and sensing felt qualities in the environment as legitimate pre-linguistic, semantic processes of meaning making is a forerunner of some of these ideas. It's also close to Merleau-Ponty's analysis and to phenomenology in general. We do not have space to examine these connections. See Dewey (1925) and Merleau-Ponty (2012).

3 There are a number of deep philosophical problems associated with this approach, also shared with the extended mind approach, around the concepts of representation and constitution/causation. We have already touched on the question of representation above but it's worth adding here that the assumption that mental life has to be about the construction of mental representations as mental states is a very traditional view that is being challenged by these approaches, although not all want to remove representations from the picture altogether. The question of constitution is central to both phenomenological approaches and to the extended mind thesis, because both claim that the coupling of the brain, body and mind actually constitutes mental processes and is not simply a causal structure that, however much it might be necessary for cognition, is not actually part of the mental process itself. We do not have space to go into these debates here (but see Rowlands, 2010, Adams & Aizawa, 2008 and Gallagher, 2017 for discussion). We will simply assume that not all cognition involves mental representations and that coupling with the body and the environment actually constitutes cognitive processes.

4 It is important to emphasize that we are not rejecting the semantics of mental states and processes. What is enacted in this coupling process is meaning, as Dewey pointed out a long time ago. It's just not a symbolically or propositionally constituted meaning. Now some, even if they accept that not all meaning is propositional, will not accept that meaning can exist without symbolic representations. We cannot go into this question here. We simply assume that it can be.

5 There is also a close parallel with Merleau-Ponty's (2012) analysis of perception in *Phenomenology of Perception* and the central role he gives the lived body in our perceiving the world.

6 We thank one of the anonymous referees for suggesting literature that extends the concept of 'affordances', which includes Norman (2008), and Turvey (1992). However, since our use of this theory is to introduce the idea of enactivism, and not to discuss it in depth, we have not included this or other literature.

7   It is important to stress that Johnson shares these commitments, at least if the term 'representation' is used with its normal meaning and the body is included as part of the mind (see Johnson, 1987, 2007, 2017).

8   This is also consistent with Clark's external functionalism.

9   Some evidence suggests that a musician's brain can be re-wired over the cause of a lifetime playing an instrument, so perhaps the exposure does not have to be that long after all.

10   The distinction between iconic, indexical and symbolic signs comes from Peirce's semiotic theory, which Malafouris builds on in his own theory. See Peirce (1955). It's important to note that we are not suggesting that symbolic signs do not exist or that they are not operative in the production of meaning. Rather, we are suggesting that not all meaning is produced through symbolic signs.

11   This raises, of course, the question of whether concepts can exist without symbolic representation. We cannot go into this here but for an argument in favour of this possibility, at least with respect to linguistic representations in relation to non-human animals, see Bermúdez (2007).

12   This idea is also found in enactivist analyses of intentionality. For example, Gallagher (2017) draws on Merleau-Ponty's analysis of the bodily seat of intentionality in an attempt to develop an enactivist conception of this characteristic of agency. Malafouris takes his lead, however, from Latour's (2005) Action Network Theory, although he does make reference to Hubert Dreyfus, a phenomenologist. For our purposes, however, we need only outline the basic ideas of material agency.

Chapter 4
Time Orientation and Media Use:
The Rise of the Device and the Changing Nature of Our Time Perception

Cláudia Barbosa
University of Aveiro, Portugal

Luís Pedro
iD https://orcid.org/0000-0003-1763-8433
University of Aveiro, Portugal

ABSTRACT

Digital consumer devices have penetrated our everyday lives, providing a platform to—with great efficiency and easiness—solve problems, communicate and exchange information, participate in remote activities, and even socialize. This increasing popularity provides the impetus for a rising dependency, which translates into a growing number of hours spent with the various types of media available. However, while the time we dedicate to media increases (at the cost of other activities), the number of hours that we have available (per day, per week, per month, etc.) cannot, giving rise to media multitasking behaviors. Some studies suggest that time orientation—either as a cultural construct or an individual preference—can influence one's media use habits, predicting (or not) multiple media use. There are, however, other perspectives suggesting that media use can actually affect one's time orientation. This chapter will attempt to assess both of these outlooks.

DOI: 10.4018/978-1-5225-8163-5.ch004

INTRODUCTION

Speaking at a TEDx event in Stanford in May 2013, late Professor Clifford Nass described the relationship with media in an increasingly digital world, indicating that

every time a new technology or service appears, the first thing that happens is pretty obvious: it steals time from other information services. Movies stole time from books, radio stole time from movies, television stole time from radio, internet stole time from television, et cetera.

This phenomenon has been dubbed "partial media displacement": as new technologies are developed, they may overlap or compete for the user's attention or time, in those cases where the emerging media are perceived to offer the same gratification as the previous medium (Okazaki, S. & Hirose, M., 2009). If their pull is such, according to the authors, that they are considered to be more gratifying or more able to provide the users with further opportunities for satisfaction, they may replace existing technologies.

Also, as technologies evolve, the periods we spend using them tend to increase, overriding time that we usually dedicate to non-media related activities or as Nass indicates: "(..) media are seductive, so after they steal time from other information activities, they also steal time from non-media activities." Cue in the all too ubiquitous image of families or groups of friends sitting around a restaurant table and typing away at their screens while waiting for their meal.

What occurs, however, in a highly technological society, where new technologies emerge faster and in a higher number than ever before? Nass states

we did whatever we do when we have too many things to do, and too little time to do it: we started to double-book media. But the rate of media, new media, gradually accelerated and then increasingly accelerated. So what did we do then? Did we give up? No. We triple- and quadruple-book media (Nass, 2013)

How does this translate into our media use habits and behavior in the saturated media society we currently live in, in which a screen (any screen) is usually only centimeters away?

Time is a recurring word in the above extract by Professor Nass, in association with media use: of the little time that we have, different media are said to dictate how we spend our time, even "stealing" it. Can media actually (re)define how we perceive time, and inspire new priorities?

This chapter has a particular focus on the relationship between time orientation and media use, in detail, the use of multiple media or media multitasking. Firstly, it describes current trends in the media landscape, which favor an increased use of media and a rise in multitasking behaviors. Secondly, it considers and presents references for the concept of time orientation, both as a cultural construct and as an individual preference. The link between different time orientations (polychronicity/monochronicity) and media multitasking is exploited next, by drawing on the work of several authors who investigated time orientation as a predictor for multiple media use but also by reflecting on the somewhat newer perspective of the influence of media on what would be the expected cultural time orientation.

MEDIA USE: CURRENT TRENDS

A widespread tendency commonly reported is the *increase* – in the last decade - *in the use of media,* or the increased time spent with media, including a rise in screen time.

Ofcom, for instance, reported an uptake on all measures of digital take-up between 2005 and 2015 in the United Kingdom, with the amount of weekly online hours doubling (from 9.9 to 20.5) in that period. For the American market, Comscore reported, for the same reference year, that "total digital media usage has nearly tripled since 2010". The European Broadcasting Union also highlights in its reports a steadily rise in daily viewing time per individual between 1996 and 2012 in Europe, while forecasting a gradual growth of all TV viewing time until 2020. A similar trend is presented for Portugal in Obercom's *Anuário da Comunicação* 2017, where TV viewing hours, for example, rise from a daily average of 202 minutes, in 2000, to 284 minutes in 2017.

Zenith's Media Consumption Forecast for 2018 predicts a total of 479 minutes a day of media consumption, representing a 12% increase in relation to 2011. For 2020, Zenith Media's predictions consider a further increase, leading to a grand total of 492 minutes a day of media consumption, which represents more than 8 hours a day - the equivalent of the average working time in several countries (according to OECD) as well as the recommended sleeping time for adults. Nielsen's *Total Audience Report* for the first quarter of 2018 already surpasses these projections stating that "on average, U.S. adults are spending over 11 hours a day connected to linear and digital media and almost six hours a day with video alone", an increase of 19 minutes from the previous quarter.

This increased media use is likely to be promoted by a *significant rise in ownership of digital equipment*: the declared ownership of tablets and smartphones (much more versatile than the "dumb phone" and now the main medium for online access) has risen, in the UK, from 5% to 37% of all adults between 2010 and 2014 for the former, and from 30% to 66% between 2010 and 2015 for the latter, according to the British communications regulator, Ofcom.

Albeit in a wider group – users older than 10 years who own mobile phones – the 2016 findings from Ofcom's Portuguese counterpart – Anacom - regarding smartphone ownership show similar trends: smartphone ownership had doubled from 33,2% in 2012, to 66,7% in 2015. Marktest figures for December 2017 indicate that 6,8 Million individuals in Portugal now own a smartphone, which is roughly 75% of total mobile phones users. This for a population of a total of 10,2 Million people.

Similar figures are presented for the US market by Pew Research where smartphone ownership by American adults increased from 35% in 2011 to 77% in 2018. An even more staggering rise can be seen in the tablet ownership figures: while roughly 3% of US adults had acquired a tablet in 2010, figures from January 2018 show that now more than half (53%) own such a device.

Zenith's Media Consumption Forecast 2018 identifies the rapid expansion of mobile internet as a reason for the increase in the amount of time the average individual spends consuming media, given its ubiquitous characteristics, allowing for access to content at anytime, anywhere. However, while the time we dedicate to media increases – at the cost of other media or non-media related activities - the amount of hours that we have available (per day, per week, per month…) cannot, leading to a rise in the use of multiple media, either simultaneously, in rapid succession or switching- also known as *media multitasking*.

The American Psychological Association (2006) identifies the occurrence of multitasking in three possible situations, namely when "someone tries to perform two tasks simultaneously, switch from one task to another, or perform two or more tasks in rapid succession".

These three options fall under the two different multitasking types defined by Salvucci, Taatgen & Borst (2009): concurrent multitasking (as in the first example listed by APA); and sequential multitasking (when the person spends more or less time with one task until moving to the second one, or when one alternates between tasks).

Although the APA definition presented above does not specify the type of tasks that are conducted nor the means used, it is common to consider the concept of multitasking in association with one or several media, thus originating the term *media multitasking*.

Media multitasking is defined by Baumgartner (2014) as an activity involving interaction: with two different types of media; or between one type of media and a non-media related activity.

Wallis (2010), on the other hand, characterized it as a possible threefold event, stating that media multitasking can occur: between medium and face-to-face interaction; between two or more media; and within a single medium.

It is clear, from the definitions presented above, that media multitasking can occur in situations that combine media with non-media, but it is also worth pointing out that the media involved does not have to be of highly technological nature – in fact, this tendency for the simultaneous completion of different tasks or attendance to different things at the same time is not a new topic.

However, the impact that technological developments have had in the amplification of multitasking behaviors is undeniable. Hassoun (2012) considers that the "true birth of the multitasker occurs in the first decade of the twenty-first century" associating it with the "popularization of the personal computer", and marking the first instance that the term "multitasking" itself is associated with human behavior rather than with the capacities of processing systems.

Hembrooke & Gay (2003) highlight that the ubiquitous, pervasive and mobile nature of new technologies "encourage a simultaneity of activities that goes beyond anything our culture has heretofore ever known. Indeed the ability to engage in multiple tasks concurrently seems to be the very essence or core motivation for the development of such technologies".

The aforementioned rise of the smartphone would have irrefutably contributed to the rising figures for multitasking behaviors, given its ubiquity, pervasiveness and mobility, as pointed out by Hembrooke & Gay. Consumer data supports this view: Verto Analytics confirms the rise of media multitasking behaviors in its 2017 report, where it analyses both multitasking across multiple devices, as well as using multiple apps, within a single device. While multitasking occurs on all digital devices, Verto Analytics data shows that multitasking is far more prevalent on smartphones, with more than a third of all mobile device sessions being multitasking sessions, a number that continues to rise.

TIME ORIENTATION

How we conduct ourselves, perform tasks - be it with media or without -, schedule different actions or prioritize different events is inextricably linked to how we perceive our time and act in respect to it.

In what concerns trends on the use of media and the tendency to multitask with multiple media, most studies relating it to the users' time orientation address the concepts of *Monochronicity* and *Polychronicity*, which can be perceived as both a cultural construct as well as an individual preference.

The link between *Polychronicity* and *Multitasking* is so close, that some authors even argue that these are alternatives terms for the same phenomenon: Lin, Cranton and Lee (2015), for example, state that depending on the discipline, different expressions have been used for the phenomenon of "doing several things at the same time or switching quickly between several tasks": "multitasking, media layering and media multitasking have been used in information sciences, human-computer interaction, communication, psychology, and media studies", while "polychronicity has been used in anthropology, organizational learning, and human performances". Other authors, should as König & Waller (2010) suggest a needed clarification of both terms, stating that "the term polychronicity should only be used to describe the preference for doing several things at the same time, whereas the behavioral aspect of polychronicity should be referred to as multitasking".

In fact, most authors agree that although the concepts of multitasking and polychronicity are separate theoretical constructs, they are conceptually related (König & Waller, 2010, cited in Voorveld et al., 2014), assuming the former the behavior of engaging in simultaneous tasks concurrently and the latter the preference for doing so.

Time Orientation as a Cultural Construct

It is in the field of anthropology that the concepts of *Monochronicity* and *Polychronicity* first originate. As a cultural dimension – i.e. as a shared behavior that characterizes a large group of people - *Monochronicity* was first defined by the American anthropologist Edward T. Hall who, in *The Silent Language* (1959), simply described it as "doing one thing at a time", further developing the construct in subsequent works.

Hall was interested in the tacit cultural dimensions of *context*, *space* and *time*. In relation to the dimension of *time*, Hall argued that complex cultures organized time in at least two different ways: either scheduling events and actions one at a time (predominantly "monochronic") or participating in several things at once (predominantly "polychronic") (Hall, 1983). Countries such as the United States or the United Kingdom as well as most northern European countries were characterized by Hall as primarily monochronic, while regions such as the Indian sub-continent, Latin America, Southern Europe and Africa were considered to be chiefly polychronic.

Time in monochronic countries (the concept of *M-time*) is, in Hall's perception, a rather tangible and linear reality, and can be visualized as "a ribbon or a road stretching from the past into the future, which is divided into segments called minutes, hours, days, months and years" (Helman, 2005). The fact is that time in monochronic cultures is, according to Hall (1983) so

thoroughly woven into the fabric of existence that we are hardly aware of the degree to which it determines and coordinates everything we do, including the molding of relations with others in many subtle ways. In fact, social and business life, even one's sex life, is commonly schedule dominated.

Human actions are scheduled, segmented and therefore, only possible to be performed one at a time, with attention dedicated to the action at hand, in a culture oriented to tasks and schedules. This explains, according to Hall, expressions that we use and that reflect M-time's importance as a classification system that orders life, such as "saving", "spending", "wasting", "losing", "killing", "making up" and "running out of" time.

P-time, on the other hand, is considered as a less tangible reality. "For polychronic people, time is seldom experienced as 'wasted,' and is apt to be considered a point rather than a ribbon or a road, but that point is often sacred" (Hall, 1983). People are at the core of this time orientation, rather than tasks or schedules.

While Hall's initial focus was on the behavior aspects of the term, in an interview conducted in 1998 by Allen Bluedorn and published in the Journal of Management Inquiry, Hall expands the meaning of polychronicity by indicating that "a polychronic culture is a culture in which people value, and hence practice, engaging in several activities and events at the same time", a definition that reflects not only the act of engaging in several activities ("practice") but also of "valuing" it, thus adding a reflective perspective on the behavior.

While Hall mostly named - rather than ranked - cultures as mono- or polychronic, Morden (1999), in line with Hall's time duality, proposed a Monochronic-Polychronic Demographic Scale (Table 1). Morden's scale presents an extensive graded list of countries, which - in line with the perspective that rather than being the other end of the spectrum, Polychronicity is considered as "a point in a continuum ranging from monochronic to polychronic" (Slocombe, 1999, cited in Voorveld et al., 2014) - considers the following groups, by order of progression from Monochronic to Polychronic:

Time-related monochronic characteristics listed by Morden (1999) include the following features: doing one thing at a time, being punctual, being dominated by timetables and schedules, and completing action sequences. These characteristics are mirrored in the polychronic side of the table by: doing several things at once, working any hours, being unpunctual, timetable unpredictability, completing human transactions. Van Everdingen & Waarts (2003) further adapted Morden' scale by giving a score to the various categories of countries (while combining some adjacent ones), ranging from very monochronic (=1) to very polychronic (=20) .

A further model of time orientation is devised by Richard D. Lewis (1996), who introduced a tripartite model of cultural classification with the categories of "linear-active", "multi-active" and "reactive". The Lewis Model, rather than being a continuum, is presented as a triangle, with countries placed between two of its vertices, each presenting one of these three concepts (Figure 1).

Table 1. Monochronic-Polychronic demographic scale

- Germans,
- Swiss and Austrians;
- Americans;
- Scandinavians, Finns;
- British, Canadians, New Zealanders;
- Australians, (white) South Africans;
- Japanese;
- Dutch, Flemish Belgian;
- Other American cultures;
- French, Walloon Belgian;
- Koreans, Taiwanese,
- Singaporeans;
- Czechs, Slovakians, Croats, Hungarians;
- Chinese;
- Northern Italians;
- Chile;
- Other Slavs;
- Portuguese;
- Spanish, Southern Italians, Mediterranean peoples;
- Indians, and other Indian sub-continent;
- Polynesians;
- Latin Americans, Arabs, Africans.

(Morden, 1999)

Figure 1. Cultural types
(Lewis, 1996)

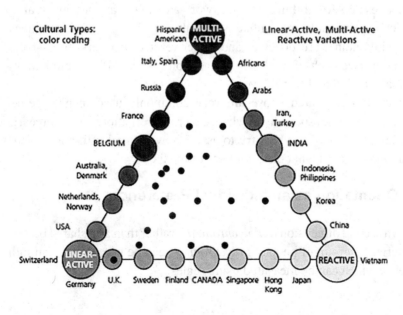

Cultures and countries - such as the Anglo-Saxon world in general, Switzerland, Germany, the Netherlands, Austria and Scandinavia - which share a linear vision of time and action are considered "linear-active". Such cultures, according to Lewis, are also monochronic, that is, "they prefer to do one thing at a time, to concentrate on it and do it within a fixed schedule", viewing this a way of getting more things done and in a more efficient way (Lewis, 1996).

The "Multi-active" perspective of time - fostered by Southern Europeans and Arabs - represents a focus on the present reality, and on current tasks, in such an extent that "the more things they can do at the same time, the happier and more fulfilled they feel". "Multi-active" people are not, according to Lewis, very interested in schedules or punctuality and time is "event- or personality-related, a subjective commodity which can be manipulated, molded, stretched, or dispensed with, irrespective of what the clock says".

The third type of culture – reactive – encompasses most cultures in Asia, with the exclusion of the Indian sub-continent. Reactive cultures prefer to – as the name indicates - react to actions by others and view time as neither linear nor event-related but cyclic, where "the same opportunities, risks and dangers will represent themselves when people are so many days, weeks and months wiser" (Lewis, 1996). In short, and in what concerns their attitude to task completion (and time management), linear-actives do one thing at a time, work fixed hours, are punctual and dominated by timetables and schedules (not unlike the characteristics of Morden's monochrons), multi-actives do several things at once, work any hours, are not punctual, have an unpredictable timetable (not unlike Morden's polychrons), while reactives react, have flexible hours, are punctual and rather react to partners' timetables. If we could summarize each of the types in one word, we would venture naming them sequential, parallel and responsive.

The models presented above are very commonly used in management and organization studies, especially in what concerns international workforces, but also on media-related studies which try to assess how cultural affiliation relate to the more or less predominant concurrent use of media.

Time Orientation as an Individual Preference

There is a second dimension to *Polychronicity*: rather than as a shared behavior that characterizes a group of people, *Polychronicity* can be perceived as an individual preference which can be measured using scales.

In this sense, Bluedorn et al. (1999, 2002) present a further definition of this phenomenon highlighting that it is "the extent to which people in a culture (1) prefer to be engaged in two or more tasks simultaneously; and (2) believe their preference is the best way to do things". According to Bluedorn et al. (1999), this definition touches on both values ("preferences") and beliefs ("believe"), rather than on behaviors, which lead the authors to develop a 10-item *Inventory of Polychronic Values (IPV)*, focusing on the user's preference to be engaged in two or more tasks or events simultaneously, together with the belief that this is the best way to do things.

Lindquist and Kaufman-Scarborough presented in 2007, a further model that attempts to "identify behaviors and attitudes that are predictive of an individual's polychronic or monochronic time use, relating these findings to individual's time management approaches" under the premise that people could choose to behave in either a monochronic or polychronic way within a culture, irrespectively of the cultural context. The PMTM (*Polychronic-Monochronic Tendency Model*), developed by the authors, accounts for "the level of engagement in one vs. multiple activities, liking to engage in one vs. multiple activities and feeling comfortable engaging in one vs. multiple activities at the same time" (Kononova & and Chiang, 2015).

Robinson & Kalafatis (2017) recently developed a multidimensional scale to measure the complex phenomenon of "multiple media use" or media multitasking. The authors state that this scale - *Polychronicity - Multiple Media Use* (P-MMU) - is the first to actually measure multiple media use, as all previous scales were mainly developed for an organizational, managerial or consumer-related context. The P-MMU addresses nine different dimensions: comfort, convenience, effectiveness and efficiency, compulsive addictive, emotional gratification, information and knowledge, multi-media channel preference, social benefits, and assimilation.

Media-related studies that consider these concepts as an individual preference try to assess how one's particular preferences relate to the engagement with one or more media-related activities. Although the P-MMU from Robinson & Kalafatis (2017) is the one mostly directed at multiple media use, the fact that it is quite recent hasn't allowed for its applicability in many - if any - studies so far.

TIME ORIENTATION AS A PREDICTOR FOR (MULTIPLE) MEDIA USE

Models that consider the concepts of polychronicity and monochronicity as cultural constructs are, as aforementioned, very common in management and organizational studies, especially in research concerning international workforces which have different cultural backgrounds and characteristics, but still need to find a common ground of understanding and a joint working routine.

In the field of media studies, such models are also considered, when authors try to assess how cultural affiliations relate to the more or less predominant use of different media, or the more or less predominant use of multiple media combinations. However, while the discussion on media use patterns and outcomes is multiple, "the literature about predictors of media multitasking calls for further development" (Kononova & Chiang, 2015). Geographical or cultural affiliation as a predictor for media multitasking, in particular, has received so far limited attention in the literature with the most relevant studies in this field being those of Kononova et al. (2013, 2014, 2015), Voorveld et al. (2014) and Bowman et al. (2014). From these studies, only Kononova et al. (2014), Kononova & Chiang (2015) and Voorveld et al. (2014) consider the impact of each of the countries' polychronicity/monochronicity profile or of the user's preferences as a predictor for media multitasking behaviors.

Voorveld et al. (2014) administered an online questionnaire to 5.973 participants in six different countries (Germany, United States, United Kingdom, the Netherlands, Spain and France). The authors reflected on the likelihood that the "cultural dimension of mono- versus polychronicity translates into different levels of media multitasking across countries", hypothesizing that the prevalence of media multitasking differs across countries and that media multitasking is more prevalent in polychronic countries than in monochronic countries, while also questioning to which extent differences exist between various media multitasking combinations in polychronic and monochronic countries. The results have demonstrated "significant overall differences among the six countries" with all forms of media multitasking being more prevalent in the United States, while the Netherlands exhibited the lowest level of media multitasking for different media combinations. Media multitasking with traditional media was found to be more prevalent in the United States and in the United Kingdom, while media multitasking with new media was more prevalent in the United States, Spain and France.

In order to test possible differences between monochronic and polychronic cultures, the six countries were organized into two groups, one representing polychronic countries (France and Spain) and one representing monochronic countries (the United States, the United Kingdom, Germany, and the Netherlands). While not reporting significant differences in the total amount of multitasking, results have demonstrated relevant differences in the type of media multitasking conducted: multitasking with traditional media was found to be more common in monochronic countries, whereas media multitasking with new media was more prevalent in polychronic countries. For this difference, the authors offer three possible explanations:

1. The characteristics of new media might correspond to the preferences of polychrons;

2. Differences in media use times can partially account for this difference, in that polychrons spend more time with – and have therefore the opportunity and the tendency to multitask more – newer media;
3. Since – according to Hall's and Morden's models – people in polychronic countries tend to value more human interactions and are more relationship-oriented, they lean more towards new media – such as social media, the Internet, and mobile media, which are more likely and suitable to establish and maintain social relations.

Kononova et al. (2014) addressed the subject of multitasking with traditional and new media with college students (N=532) in Kuwait, Russia and the United States. From the three countries assessed, the USA featured in Hall's description as a predominantly monochronic country, Kuwait appeared as a chiefly polychronic country, and Russia was somewhat placed between the two. Each country's positioning in the polychronicity continuum was not, however, the only cultural aspect considered, with the authors also taking into account other factors such as income per capita, development of ICT market and political freedom. The authors hypothesized that: Kuwait would indicate greater levels of media multitasking (given its status as a polychronic culture and its high indices of income per capita); the USA would show high levels of multitasking (in spite of its monochronic orientation) due to its highly developed ICT market, its income per capita and greater political freedom; while Russia would exhibit lower multitasking levels due to lower economic and political development indicators, and moderate positioning in the polychronicity scale. The authors' findings were consistent with their predictions that economic, political, and cultural differences may influence media use behaviors: Russian students multitasked significantly less than their Kuwaiti and American counterparts due to lower levels of both income and ICT development (leading to lower ownership of media devices), political constraints, and a moderate positioning in the polychronicity scale. Although similar to Russia in regards to overall democratization, the Kuwaiti students exhibited more media multitasking behaviors, which the authors explain in the context of their study by both economic and cultural – in the case of Kuwait, polychronic – characteristics. Of all the cultural aspects considered, the political landscape was considered to be the least relevant predictor for media multitasking behavior. In relation to the polychronic/monochronic range, the authors conclude that although the USA is considered to be a predominantly monochronic country, cultural, economic and political developments could possibly compensate for the preference of people in North America to do one thing at a time

Kononova and Chiang (2015) explored how media and audience factors, such as country of residence, media ownership, and polychronicity, predict media multitasking behaviors via a cross-cultural survey (N=1972) that included respondents from the

United States (a predominantly monochronic country) and Taiwan (a predominantly polychronic nation), implemented independently in each country. The authors analyzed here a two-fold perspective on polychronicity: both as cultural construct – centered around the country of residence – and as well as an individual preference. For the first dimension, the authors hypothesized that the respondents' country of residence will moderate the effects of polychronicity on the extent of media multitasking. For the latter, that preference for polychronicity would positively predict the extent of media multitasking, meaning that those who declare to prefer to perform several tasks at a time, will combine media activities more often than those who prefer to do one thing at a time. The authors used, in this study, Lindquist and Kaufman-Scarborough (2007) model of polychronic-monochronic tendency. While the country of residence did not appear to moderate the effects of polychronicity on the extent of media multitasking, the results validated the authors' hypothesis that a preference for polychronicity would positively predict the extent of multitasking, as "higher polychronics were more likely to multitasking with media than monochronics". Surprisingly, and in spite of their typical monochronic outlook, Americans were found to be the higher polychronics and the higher multitaskers of the two, while also reporting higher levels of media ownership. This last fact raises an interesting discussion by the authors, as they believe

it may suggest that media technology, indeed, has the power to change culture, in particular, perception of time, where engagement with multiple electronic media alters the ways people organize and act according to their schedules.

The authors further state that

Alternatively, and paradoxically, this finding may also suggest that media multitasking is a logically growing phenomenon in monochronic cultures. The increasing uses of electronic media may allow people in such cultures to deal with schedules and meet deadlines faster. Moving from one activity to another in a timely manner may create the illusion of multitasking with things happening one after another but so proximate in time that they seem to happen simultaneously.

In fact, and according to the definition of multitasking presented above, both examples are symptomatic of multitasking.

MEDIA USE AS A PREDICTOR FOR (A NEW TIME) ORIENTATION

While we had discussed so far whether time orientation (either as cultural-based orientation or an individual preference) can be a predictor for media use, Kononova & Chiang (2015) raised an interesting point, focusing on a possbile bidirectionality in the relationship between time and media. This proposition has been put forward by some authors, who postulate that technological devices may, themselves - and as a reverse action - affect the users' time orientation, causing a shift in perspective from monochronicity to polychronicity and encouraging a device-driven multitasking patterned behavior.

Chung & Lim (2005) proposed to assess how the time perceptions and lifestyles of Singaporeans may have been influenced by the growing ubiquity of the mobile phone. The authors conducted several focus group discussions and non-participant observations, with eight participants each, half being working adults and half adult students. The focus groups discussions were conducted to "elicit people's opinions on social codes informing mobile telecommunications use" while the observation focused on recording social exchanges or shifts in activity caused by the use of the mobile phone. The findings pointed towards the fact that while living in a culture which is characterized as being monochronic, Singaporeans exhibit traits commonly associated with polychronic societies, such as the ones pointed by Morden and Hall of unpredictable time-management, flexible time planning, unpunctuality, and attendance to multiple tasks focused on human interaction. The authors conclude that the "use of the mobile is encouraging polychronic practices", given its portability and connectivity, not very unlike the statement of Hembrooke & Gay (2003) above. But this is not a simple paradigm shift: Singaporeans still exhibit some monochronic patterned behaviours, and shift between the two temporalities. The monochronic/ polychronic dichotomy initially proposed by Hall seems inadequate to portray such a reality in which "Singaporean mobile users constantly negotiate between the two temporal modes, and informed by old and new social codes, decide when it is appropriate for polychronic uses of time mediated by the mobile". The authors propose the introduction of a new concept to reflect the effect that technological developments and new media had on the time outlook of different cultures - *Mobilechonicity* – a hybrid temporality dominated by and under the spell of the mobile phone. The word "mobile" stands here both for the fact that this particular temporal modus is "mobile(phone) induced" and that it is mobile, in the sense of shiftable in orientation (from mono- to poly-, and vice versa).

The impact of technology - especially mobile phones - in our society is such, that while Chung & Lim (2005) suggest that mobile phones propose a new sense of time, Meyrowitz (2005) reflects, in the same publication by Nyiri (2005) that they also offer a new sense of place, a "generalized elsewhere", a "glocality".

Hall himself had recognized the impact of technology in time perception stating that "all cultures with high technologies seem to incorporate both polychronic as well as monochronic functions" (Hall, 1983) and reflected on the use of what he called "extensions" to human behavior, which he defined as "a particular kind of tool that not only speed up work and make it easier but also separate people from their work". Examples of extensions included (we transcribe here solely the media-related ones): "(...) telephone extending the human voice, television extending both the eye and the ear, (...), computers extending the memory and some of the arithmetic parts of the central nervous system (...) cameras extending the visual memory (...)". Hall's perspective on these extensions is that when something is extended it "begins to take on a life of its own and quickly becomes confused with the reality it replaces" and "that any extension not only can but usually does eventually take the place of the process which has been extended". One can only wonder whether technology - let us consider the mobile phone with its manifold possibilities and capacity to assume so many functions as a prime example - can be taking the place of several human processes (and when the distinction between action and medium will be too blurred to be discernible).

CONCLUSION

The common description of our current society as "hypermediated" reflects both on the existence of a staggering amount of highly-developed media (due to unprecedented technological developments) as well as our growing dependence of said media. How we use media (or to a larger extent, how we choose to perform any given task in our daily lives) is considered to be related to the way we perceive time. But several authors point out that in such a developed society, and given our ever-present media use and our ever-growing media dependency, time orientation might not be filtering so much media use, as media use may be shaping time orientation. Several studies point out that cultures usually defined as monochronic exhibit polychronic features and behaviors and indicate as possible cause said cultures' advanced technological market and thereof following media use patterns. Although we acknowledge that these questions are not new (and can be traced in the media studies field discussion of the domestication theory that proposes a continuous negotiation and mutual adaptation of meanings and practices that emerge from the appropriation of technology devices in any social setting), we believe that this bidireccional interference between time perception and technological devices is especially relevant when the said device is an all-encompassing media device in which different types of media converge, different types of media behaviours - that include media consumption as well as media creation - are possible and multiple tasks can be performed, distributed and/or communicated with ease. The 'anytime, anywhere' motto associated with mobile devices appears then to be more than a catchy expression, reflecting the greater spatial and temporal fragmentation of our life and workstyles (Couclecis, 2004) and apparently is beginning to define the way we "perceptually attend to the world" (Richardson, 2005).

This line of thought, tecnhosomatic in nature (cf. Richardson, 2007), suggests that the relationship between body and devices is covalent and that devices are actually shaping the meanings of our environments (Richardson, 2005) and our behaviours as a species.

Fortunati (2005: 517-518) said it best: "Time, it has been said, has been stretched out. But in what sense? In the sense that, seeing that its temporal duration cannot be modified, its thickness has expanded. (...) The mobile in particular forces people to ask themselves about the compactness of what they are doing. It forces them to single out the pauses in their actions, the pores, the cracks in time, so as to get hold of and to make communicative use of them".

These spatial and temporal effects are changing the very fabric of our communicative acts and transforming our perception of time from a social-drive perspective to a device-driven one. The hiper-mediated reality that permeates our social acts surely gives hints in that direction.

ACKNOWLEDGMENT

This article reports research developed within the Program Technology Enhanced Learning and Societal Challenges, funded by Fundação para a Ciência e Tecnologia, FCTI. P. – Portugal, under contract # PD/00173/2014.

REFERENCES

American Psychological Association (APA). (2006). *Multitasking: Switching costs.* APA.

Autoridade Nacional das Comunicações (ANACOM). (2015). *Evolução da penetração dos serviços de comunicações eletrónicas.* ANACOM.

Baumgartner, S., Weeda, W., van der Heijden, L., & Huizinga, M. (2014). The Relationship Between Media Multitasking and Executive Function in Early Adolescents. *The Journal of Early Adolescence*, *34*(8), 1120–1144. doi:10.1177/0272431614523133

Bluedorn, A. (1998). An Interview with Anthropologist Edward T. Hall. *Journal of Management Inquiry*, *7*(2), 109–115. doi:10.1177/105649269872003

Bluedorn, A., Kalliath, T., Strube, M., & Martin, G. (1999). Polychronicity and the Inventory of Polychronic Values (IPV). *Journal of Managerial Psychology*, *14*(3/4), 205–231. doi:10.1108/02683949910263747

Capdeferro, N., Romero, M., & Barberà, E. (2014). Polychronicity: Review of the literature and a new configuration for the study of this hidden dimension of online learning. *Distance Education*, *35*(3), 294–310. doi:10.1080/01587919.2015.955249

Chung, L.-Y., & Lim, S. S. (2005). From Monochronic to Mobilechronic – Temporality in the Era of Mobile Communication. In K. Nyiri (Ed.), *A Sense of Place: The Global and the Local in Mobile Communication* (pp. 267–282). Vienna: Passagen Verlag.

Comscore. (2016). *Cross-Platform Future in Focus 2016*. Retrieved from https://www.comscore.com/Insights/Presentations-and-Whitepapers/2016/2016-US-Cross-Platform-Future-in-Focus

Couclelis, H. (2004). Pizza over the Internet – E-commerce, the fragmentation of activity and the tyranny of the region. *Entrepreneurship and Regional Development*, *16*(1), 41–54. doi:10.1080/0898562042000205027

European Broadcasting Union - Media Intelligence Service (MIS). (2014). *VISION 2020 - Media Consumption Trends*. Retrieved from https://www.ebu.ch/files/live/sites/ebu/files/Publications/EBU-Vision2020-Connect_EN.pdf

Fortunati, L. (2005). The mobile phone: Towards new categories and social relations. *Information Communication and Society*, *5*(4), 513–528. doi:10.1080/13691180208538803

Hall, E. (1959). *The Silent Language*. Garden City, NY: Doubleday.

Hall, E. (1983). *The Dance of Life: The Other Dimension of Time*. Anchor Press/Doubleday.

Hall, E. T., & Hall, M. R. (1990). *Understanding Cultural Differences: Germans, French, and Americans*. Yarmouth, ME: Intercultural Press.

Hassoun, D. (2012). Costly attentions: Governing the media multitasker. *Continuum, 26*(4), 653–664. doi:10.1080/10304312.2012.698041

Helman, C. H. (2005). Cultural aspects of time and ageing. Time is not the same in every culture and every circumstance; our views of aging also differ. *EMBO Reports, 6*, S54–S58. doi:10.1038j.embor.7400402 PMID:15995664

König, C., & Waller, M. (2010). Time for Reflection: A Critical Examination of Polychronicity. *Human Performance, 23*(2), 173–190. doi:10.1080/08959281003621703

Kononova, A., & Chiang, Y. (2015). Why do we multitask with media? Predictors of media multitasking among Internet users in the United States and Taiwan. *Computers in Human Behavior, 50*, 31–41. doi:10.1016/j.chb.2015.03.052

Kononova, A., Zasorina, T., Diveeva, N., Kokoeva, A., & Chelokyan, A. (2014). Multitasking goes global: Multitasking with traditional and new electronic media and attention to media messages among college students in Kuwait, Russia, and the USA. *The International Communication Gazette, 76*(8), 617–640. doi:10.1177/1748048514548533

Lemos, A. (2009). Cultura da mobilidade. *Mídia. Cultura e Tecnologia, 16*(40), 28–35.

Lewis, R. D. (1996). *When cultures collide: Managing successfully across cultures.* London: N. Brealey Pub.

Lin, L., Cranton, P., & Lee, J. (n.d.). Research Methodologies for Multitasking Studies. *Handbook of Research on Scholarly Publishing and Research Methods*, 329-348. doi:10.4018/978-1-4666-7409-7.ch017

Lindquist, J., & Kaufman-Scarborough, C. (2007). The Polychronic—Monochronic Tendency Model. *Time & Society, 16*(2-3), 253–285. doi:10.1177/0961463X07080270

Marktest. (2018). *3 em 4 utilizadores de telemóvel usa smartphone.* Retrieved from https://www.marktest.com/wap/a/n/id~2350.aspx

Meyrowitz, J. (2005). The Rise of Glocality: New Senses of Place and Identity in the Global Village. In K. Nyiri (Ed.), *A Sense of Place: The Global and the Local in Mobile Communication.* Vienna: Passagen Verlag.

Morden, T. (1999). Models of national culture – a management review. *Cross Cultural Management, 6*(1), 19–44. doi:10.1108/13527609910796915

Myíri, K. (2005). *A sense of place: the global and the local in mobile communication.* Vienna: Passagen Verlag.

Nielsen. (2018). *The Nielsen Total Audience Report*. Retrieved from: https://www.nielsen.com/us/en/insights/reports/2018/q1-2018-total-audience-report.html

Obercom. (2015). *Anuário da Comunicação*. Retrieved from https://www.ofcom.org.uk/__data/assets/pdf_file/0020/102755/adults-media-use-attitudes-2017.pdf

OECD. (2018). *Hours worked (indicator)*. Retrieved from https://data.oecd.org/emp/hours-worked.htm

Ofcom. (2015). *Adults' media use and attitudes Report 2015*. Retrieved from; https://www.ofcom.org.uk/__data/assets/pdf_file/0014/82112/2015_adults_media_use_and_attitudes_report.pdf

Okazaki, S., & Hirose, M. (2009). Effects of displacement–reinforcement between traditional media, PC internet and mobile internet. *International Journal of Advertising*, *28*(1), 77–104. doi:10.2501/S026504870909043X

Pew Research Center. (2017). *Mobile Fact Sheet*. Retrieved from: http://www.pewinternet.org/fact-sheet/mobile/

Richardson, I. (2005). *Mobile Technosoma: some phenomenological reflections on itinerant media devices. The Fibreculture Journal*. Sydney, Australia: TFJ Inc.

Richardson, I. (2007). Pocket Technospaces: The Bodily Incorporation of Mobile Media. *Continuum*, *21*(2), 205–215. doi:10.1080/10304310701269057

Robinson, H., & Kalafatis, S. (2017). The 'Polychronicity - Multiple Media Use' (P-MMU) scale: A multi-dimensional scale to measure polychronicity in the context of multiple media use. *Journal of Marketing Management*, *33*(17-18), 1421–1442. doi:10.1080/0267257X.2017.1383297

Salvucci, D., Taatgen, N., & Borst, P. (2009). Toward a unified theory of the multitasking continuum: from concurrent performance to task switching, interruption, and resumption. In *Proceedings of the SIGCHI Conference on Human Factors in Computing Systems* (CHI '09). ACM. 10.1145/1518701.1518981

Van Everdingen, M., & Waarts, E. (2003). The effect of national culture on the adoption of innovations. *Marketing Letters*, *14*(3), 217–232. doi:10.1023/A:1027452919403

Verto Analytics. (2017). *Multitasking and Mobile Apps: New Ways to Measure Consumer Behavior*. Retrieved from https://www.vertoanalytics.com/chart-week-multitasking-rise/

Voorveld, H., Segijn, C., Ketelaar, P., & Smith, E. (2014). Investigating the Prevalence and Predictors of Media Multitasking across Countries. *International Journal of Communication*, 8(23).

Zenith Media. (2018). *Mobile internet to reach 28% of media use in 2020*. Retrieved from: https://www.zenithmedia.com/mobile-internet-to-reach-28-of-media-use-in-2020/

ADDITIONAL READING

Foehr, U. (2006). *Media multitasking among American youth: Prevalence, predictors and pairings*. Menlo Park, CA: Henry J. Kaiser Family Foundation.

Kononova, A. (2013). Multitasking Across Borders: A Cross-National Study of Media Multitasking Behaviors, Its Antecedents, and Outcomes. *International Journal of Communication*, 7(23), 1–20.

Salvucci, D. D., & Taatgen, N. A. (2011). *Oxford series on cognitive models and architectures. The multitasking mind*. New York, NY, US: Oxford University Press.

Schuur, W. A., Baumgartner, S. E., Sumter, S. R., & Valkenburg, P. M. (2015). The consequences of media multitasking for youth: A review. *Computers in Human Behavior*, *53*, 204–215. doi:10.1016/j.chb.2015.06.035

The Guardian. (2018). Rise of the machines: has technology evolved beyond our control? Retrieved from: https://www.theguardian.com/books/2018/jun/15/rise-of-the-machines-has-technology-evolved-beyond-our-control-

KEY TERMS AND DEFINITIONS

Media Multitasking: Performing two or more tasks involving media, concurrently, in rapid switching or sequence.

Mobilechronicity: Time orientation perspective, that places the emphasis of the use of the media, especially mobile media. Used by some authors when cultures described as primarily monochronic, exhibit polychronic behaviors, due to the use of mobile media.

Monochronicity: Time management perspective, which focuses on performing one task at a time. It can be both a shared cultural behavior as well as an individual preference.

Multitasking: Performing two or more tasks concurrently, in rapid alternation or rapid sequence.

Polychronicity: Time management perspective, which favors performing multiple tasks at the same time. It can be both a shared cultural behavior as well as an individual preference.

Chapter 5

Screen Time and the Logic of Identification in the Networked Society

Cynthia H. W. Corrêa

https://orcid.org/0000-0002-9552-9235
University of São Paulo, Brazil

ABSTRACT

This theoretical perspective situates the notion of neo-tribalism or tribalism characterized by fluidity, punctual gatherings, and dispersion, independent of the encounter's purpose and interest, as a generator of networks of sociality in the postmodern cyberspace, from the formation of virtual communities or tribes. In this context, the imaginary occupies a central space in everyday life, because, as a representation, it reveals a meaning that goes beyond appearance. The analysis comprises the communication phenomenon as responsible for the constitution of a social bond in the cyberspace, structured under a postmodern condition, a different and a more tolerant style of seeing the world, unlike modern standards. Rather than well-defined roles to perform as it dominated in modern times, in the postmodernity prevails a full integration of the citizen into several communities by affinities and proximity, led by the logic of identification.

DOI: 10.4018/978-1-5225-8163-5.ch005

INTRODUCTION

Contemporary society highlights the adoption of information and communication technologies (ICT) in everyday activities. From this relationship between ICT and social life emerge new forms of aggregation in the virtual environment or cyberspace, spontaneously and attracted by the aesthetic pleasure, constituting the named Cyberculture. The social and cultural form that emerges from the symbiotic relationship amid society, culture, and digital technologies focused on communication (Lemos, 2003). In this respect, social relations in the virtual environment are understood through the combination of three main factors, capable of explaining the complexity of Cyberculture. The predominance of an aesthetic culture based on image enhancement, which distinguishes the postmodern age; the social sharing that refers to a tendency of people to form social groups through affinities, by the logic of identification; and the existence of the communication possibilities fueled by digital technologies.

Also, the need to belong to a group is essential to the individual can define its place in the world with the proposal to be recognized as different from many others. The search for identifying traits is a vital source of social significance in a context of extensive organizational disintegration, the progressive loss of legitimacy of institutions and weakening of critical social movements, which occurs during the period of modernity (Hall, 2014). The individual stripped of traditional references seeks for people to share common interests, a continuous action since it is part of the human nature to live in some association format; one needs to join others to form a society (Simmel, 1986). In recent times, this practice has been reinforced by the incidence of global computer networks, which make social contact more intense due to the resurgence of the notion of community as a tribe (Maffesoli, 1996, 1998, 2016) that operates in the arrangement of virtual communities (Rheingold, 1993).

This chapter presents an essay whose thesis statement situates the notion of neo-tribalism or tribalism, characterized according to Maffesoli (1996, 1998, 2016) by the fluidity, punctual gatherings, and dispersion, independent of the interest and purpose of the encounter, as an opportunity to generate networks of sociality in the postmodern cyberspace. Therefore, as a methodological approach, it is an approach based on a theoretical perspective, associating a description of the historical context and bibliographical research. Cyberspace is the symbolic environment where virtual aggregations, such as virtual communities or tribes, are structured and conceived as a sphere of information circulation that does not exist in opposition to the real (Lévy, 1996; Wilbur, 2000; Lastowka & Hunter, 2003). Indeed, the establishment of social relations in the virtual environment serves as a strategy of the individual inserted in a society connected via networks to be recognized and, thus, form sociality, according to the logic of identification and the opportunity of being together (Maffesoli, 1996,

1998, 2016). This natural form of aggregation becomes the assignment mode of identity traits, based on a personal and a subjective choice, of a symbolic dimension. That is the chief difference from the traditional model of the imposition of identity's characteristics, as the example of cultural identities.

At that point, the realm of appearance helps to comprehend the foundation of social bonds, the sociality, which characterizes the present period or the postmodernity itself (Maffesoli, 1996, 2016). In this setting, a symbolic dimension of the new social practices is also created, when the imaginary returns to occupy a central space in the day-to-day since as representation, it reveals or involves a meaning that goes beyond appearance (Durand, 1988). The investigation encompasses the communication phenomenon as responsible for the composition of a social bond in the postmodern cyberspace, which is organized under a postmodern condition (Lyotard, 1998), a unique style of seeing the world. When instead of pressures and constraints that restrict life in the modern age, one observes the voluntary participation of the citizen in several groups in postmodernity. After all, communication is what binds an individual to another, it is the social cement and the glue of the postmodern world, according to Maffesoli's conception (2004).

COMMUNICATION AND SOCIAL BOND IN POSTMODERNITY

The information society represents the social structure built around information networks, which connect the world without limit of time and location, with emphasis on the Internet and its graphical interface, the world wide web (WWW or Web). In this sense, Castells (2003, 2009a) declares that the Internet is much more than a simple technology, it is the means of communication that constitutes the organizational standard of nations, especially the western ones. A reconfiguration of local and global perspectives on the cultural level is also a striking element of the Internet, which has become famous worldwide because of the lack of borders. Something that is partly true, since information circulates at an incredible speed across the four corners of the planet via computer network systems. What is curious is that this mechanism of digital communication allows both the dissemination of data that may be of general interest and can attract many people, as it consents the diffusion of the characteristics of a specific culture, for instance, to arouse the interest of a group.

The potential of the global reach of the Internet, in this regard, can favor the manifestation of local aspirations, marking cultural diversity, the distinction of locals in the global panorama of cyberspace. It would be another paradox of the called Cyberculture based on a postmodern condition of life (Lyotard, 1998), and that would follow the trend of the relations between the global and the local or the glocalism (Castells, 2009a; García Canclini, 2015). Thus, the formation of aggregations that emphasize the place of origin and the culture of a people is significant, mainly, with the possibility of participating in communities on online social networking sites, whose phenomenon of popularity began with the Orkut network and today is spread via Facebook, Twitter, Instagram, among others. To Tsai and Bagozzi (2014), "The emergence of new information and communication technologies has initiated radical transformations in social interactions, which in turn have important implications for the formation of virtual communities" (p. 158). Cyberspace is at the same time the locus of territorialization (mapping, control, search engines, agents, surveillance) and likewise of reterritorialization (blogs, chats, peer to peer - P2P, mobile technologies). It is a question of affirming the deterritorializing, but as well as the ability to promote the reterritorialization, showing the power of Cyberculture technologies (Lemos, 2006).

That said, although society is connected worldwide via computer networks, the individual increasingly feels the necessity to get involved with people who share something in common, who has an identification. In short, there is a return to the search for characteristics that provide a kind of identity, to be recognized by others. It is a method for the individual to form a society or sociality (Maffesoli, 1996, 2016) since it is a product of different elements (Simmel, 1986). A sort of behavior that reflects some features of the postmodernity, which tends to promote in the contemporary megalopolis both the recollection of being in the group itself and a deepening of relationships within each group. For this, the individual wants to adopt an image or several images, different ways of being, meanwhile the author talks about a person (*persona*) that represents numerous social roles in their daily activities (Maffesoli, 1996, 1998).

The establishment of virtual social groups boosted by the existence of networks began before the consolidation of the Internet. For example, the cases of the Usenet network and the bulletin board system (BBS), which emerged in the United States in the 1970s. The social relationships originated via computer networks are developed in the cyberspace, an ambiance for the circulation of information, a space of communication, a virtual or digital background. Connecting in cyberspace also means, even if symbolic, the transition from modernity (where space is carved by time) to the postmodernity (where time compresses space); of a society discernable by the autonomous and isolated individual to the commitment in tribes in the collaborative digital panorama (Lemos, 2016). Cyberspace is the symbolic environment where virtual communities or tribes are constituted. It is relevant to mention that the conceptions of the virtual environment and cyberspace were associated with the field of science fiction in North American territory, with the author Gibson (2016) known as the inventor of the expression cyberspace registered in his novel of science fiction Neuromancer, published for the first time in 1984. In the book, he describes cyberspace as a consensual hallucination: "A graphic representation of data abstracted from the banks of every computer in the human system. Unthinkable complexity. Lines of light ranged in the non-space of the mind, clusters and constellations of data. Like city lights, receding" (Gibson, 2016, p. 65).

Continuing the debate, technological tools available also consent the person to create another identity to be able to relate to any other online, whose image can be determined by the name or nickname one adopts in a chat room, or the character (avatar) chooses to represent itself in virtual environments. Both the nickname and the chosen avatar serve to indicate some data about a person and its identity since each element contributes to embody a character that is wearing a type of mask.

The mask (of the persona) allows us to represent fear or anguish, anger or joy... In affections that are only valid because they are collectives. In general, theatricality, each one, in different degrees, and depending on the situations, plays a role (or roles) that integrates her/him into the societal whole (Maffesoli, 1996, p. 172).

Therefore, the adopted nickname or avatar functions as a real mask, which further reinforces the symbolic atmosphere of sociality in Cyberculture.

Among the various forms of sociality emerging in cyberspace, stands out the virtual communities, initially defined by Rheingold (1993). He stated, "Virtual communities are social aggregations that emerge from the Net when enough people carry on those public discussions long enough, with sufficient human feeling, to form webs of personal relationships in cyberspace" (p. 6). On the other hand, Maffesoli (1996, 1998, 2016) prefers to call these community groups of tribes or neo-tribes, the neo-tribalism underscored by fluidity and dispersion. Movement through which it is possible to describe the spectacle of a profusion of styles, of props, and adornments that invade the streets in the postmodern megalopolis and the cyberspace decentralized.

Nevertheless, of the designations that virtual relationships receive and the degree of permanence, ephemeral or not, the differential fact is that the person (*persona*), who plays the roles and changes costumes according to the moment, has the chance to participate in as many groups or tribes wishes. The pure subjective motivation is enough, what matter is the possibility of being together. This opportunity for integration with social groups by the affinity mechanism supported by the logic of identification is what sets it apart from the traditional model of cultural identity attribution. As the situation of national identity, in which a whole population is forced to adhere to certain symbols, to sing the anthem in schools during childhood, and to keep links to places and commemorative dates. In the virtual environment, the person selects which community she or he wants to be part of, being the primary motivation the interest in one or more subjects in which one perceives an identification and finds people to share ideas and discuss publicly. It is the common interest, the appearance and the will to be together that convey to the community a sense of belonging. From this point of view, Silva (2012) comments that although the social bond serves as cement for life in the society, it is only updated by the strength of shared values, revered images together and feelings and affections intensified by communion. Therefore, there is no social tie without imaginary.

Within a virtual community, feelings such as solidarity, emotion, conflict, imagination and collective memory, union, identification, communion, shared interests, and interaction can prevail. For the sense of communion to spread, it is necessary to happen the sharing of knowledge and opinions that may even be divergent, because, within the community, participants can and should have contradictory and conflicting thoughts, which is a form to verify the degree of tolerance amid its members. Also, the existence of conflicting ideas can result in the elaboration of new knowledge, constructed from debates.

Cyberspace enhances the emergence of social relationships outlined in around shared interests, of identifying traits, since she or he can approach, to connect individuals who may never have had the circumstance to meet in person. As clarified by the authors Garton, Haythornthwaite, and Wellman (1999).

When a computer network connects people or organizations, it is a social network. Just as a computer network is a set of machines connected by a set of cables, a social network is a set of people (or organizations or other social entities) connected by a set of social relations, such as friendship, co-working, or information exchange (p. 75).

Hence, the absence of a fixed geographical basis is another factor that discriminates virtual communities from traditional communities, making evident that what binds the individual to the other in the virtual sociality is the mechanism of identification, affinity, the mutual feeling, and the experience lived collectively. In any case, cyberspace presents itself as a public space for the occurrence of social contact.

Recognizing that identity is always under construction, Hall (2014) suggests thinking about identification, reasoning that meets the logic of identification in force in contemporary sociality (Maffesoli, 1996). According to Hall (2014), "Identity arises not so much from the fullness of identity that is already within us as individuals, but from a lack of wholeness that is 'filled' from our exterior, by the forms through which we imagine being seen by others." (p. 39). The person, consequently, when entering one or more virtual group, looks for traces of identification and not a unique identity. In this background of loss of reference, the contemporary sociality seems to be shaped by other values. Thus, are the appearance, the image, the senses, that the individual seeks, incessantly, to integrate it with others based on a real identification. Together they can live fully in the present moment (*Carpe diem*), to welcome each day, sharing a collective imaginary and motivating the resurgence of culture in social life, in the process of re-enchantment of the world (Maffesoli, 1996).

The incessant movement of identities' elaboration from the identification and recognition of the individual by the imaginary of others is additionally manifested in the constitution of virtual groups, when one pursues to approach people with similar interests, regardless of time, space and geographical location. In this way, the formation of virtual community aggregations understood as imagined communities, has helped to meet this requirement for identification. For Anderson (1989), all communities more massive than the first villages of face-to-face contact or even these have always been imagined. The author argues that the nation is imagined as a community, because, by ignoring the inequality and exploitation that prevail within them all, the nation is always conceived as a genuine and horizontal fellowship.

That said, the creation of community groups or virtual tribes is a strategy for the person to be recognized as different and unique in the face of so many other individuals. Notwithstanding of the name that this kind of social gathering may receive, one cannot overlook the force of the imaginary charge that gives inspiration to the relationships maintained through cyberspace. Moreover, considering Anderson's (1989) proposition of an imagined community, all communities would be formed by the belief in a notion of belonging to a group that would meet for living in a territorial area, that is, even if the community is related to a place, physical or symbolic, its motivation would always be from an imaginary order.

Thus, the search for identification mechanisms is a constant practice nowadays. There is a gradual slide of identity towards the idea of identification. The differentiating characteristic is in the form of identifying traits when a person has the chance to be part of as many communities as wishes. Indeed, this is possible due to a profound change in the understanding of the concept of identity, which is no longer seen as something fixed but elaborated continuously (Hall, 2014). With the advent of the postmodern period, there was a resizing of the role of people within societies, which had no single role to play, but rather a series of tasks (*persona*), consequently having to present a multiplicity of identities or even represent various characters in the theatrical plays of everyday life. "For a given individual, or for a collective actor, there may be a plurality of identities. Yet, such a plurality is a source of stress and contradiction in both self-representation and social action" (Castells, 2009b, p. 6). For this author, the conception of identities is stronger in meaning than roles to play in the social body, due to the mechanism of self-construction and individuation involved. In short, "identities organize meaning, while roles organize functions" (Castells, 2009b, p. 7). In this case, the meaning is defined as the symbolic identification by a social actor for her/his action. In the context of the network society, for most social actors, the meaning is organized around a primary identity that is self-sustaining in time and space.

Unlike the characteristics of national identities, today the individual has designated its identifying marks from what she or he is and what she or he wants to be, with the help of global networks such as the Internet that goes beyond the physical limits of ordinary life, whether at home or work, generating connections of consolidated affinities through virtual communities.

Lifestyle is not a useless thing, for that is what determines the relation to otherness: from pure sociability (politeness, ritual, civility, neighborhoods...) to a more complex sociality (collective memory, symbolic, social imaginary). Now, how can one apprehend the style of an epoch if it is not through what one lets oneself see? (Maffesoli, 1996, p. 160).

The aesthetic paradigm is the only one capable of justifying a whole constellation of actions, emotions, feelings, and environments precise to the spirit of the postmodern time (Maffesoli, 1996) or even a postmodern condition (Lyotard, 1998). A diverse style to see the world, when instead of the traditional duty of humanity, the full integration of the citizen into communities occurs, and it is to these plates of social sedimentation that the postmodern gaze is directed, seeking to comprehend both in their authenticity and precariousness. In this context, the old poles of attraction constituted by nation-states, political parties, professional labels, institutions of education and scientific research, and historical traditions lose their appeal, open space for what is varied, bordering, marginalized, corresponding to the daily life. That is, lost in grandeur, but gained concerning tolerance.

Consequently, it is imperative to understand the contemporary networked society in its multidimensionality, according to the Theory of Complexity, a sophisticated way of thinking that refutes mutilating and simplistic explanations considered rational. It does not aim at "The elemental - where everything is based on simple unity and clear thinking - but on the radical, where the uncertainties and antinomies appear" (Morin, 2002, p. 401). It seeks to contemplate the context and the complex on the assumption that it is compulsory to have a thought connecting what is separated and fragmented, able at the same time to respect the diverse and to recognize the unique, and that tries to discern the interdependencies. It is required to recognize that one lives in a world emphasized by differences and knowing how-to live-in front of so much diversity, without denying the existence of the other.

Postmodernity is antitotalitarian and democratically fragmented, rescues the poetic and rich detail of typical life. On the opposite side, conceptions of progress and emancipation of the rational subject, of the work proclaimed by science, were crumbling, describing the crisis of disbelief in the meta-narratives that had as their starting point the libertarian ideal of the French Revolution and as a foundation the principles of enlightenment reason. All these transformations profoundly affected the individual at the end of the twentieth century, when the so-called identity crisis manifests, inserted on a broader conjuncture of change, which displaced some vital constructions and processes of modern societies, and shaken the frames of reference that gave the individuals a stable anchorage in the social world (Hall, 2014). Thus, a different reality is born, in which the spatial, temporal and geographical barriers are no longer so meaningful, when global networks of exchanges connect and disconnect individuals, groups, regions and even countries under the global effects coming from the postmodernity or late modernity.

Because of the decomposition of the significant accounts, the social is taken in a more complex texture never seen before that is always, whether young or old, man or woman, rich or poor, placed on the knots of the circuits of communication. For Lyotard (1998), "The question of the social bond as a question is a play of language, that of questioning, which immediately positions the one who presents it, the one to whom it is addressed, and the referent which it questions: This question is already the social bond" (p. 29).

This form of social bonding through communication is equally accentuated by Maffesoli (2004), for whom communication is what reliance on, it is the social cement: "Communication is the glue of the postmodern." (p. 20). In this case, the idea of communication is implicit in the sociality in force, since one can only exist by the look of the other, each one is connected to the other by the mediation of communication. Besides, Maffesoli (2004) emphasizes that communication prevails in the notion of encounter, the fact that it vibrates with others around something, whatever it is, also serving to embody the return of an old concept: The imaginary, which as a representation of the real, is always a reference to an absent other (Durand, 1988).

For Lyotard (1998), the aspect of language takes on new importance and cannot be reduced to the alternative of the communication component that becomes more and more evident in society, both as a reality and as a problem, manipulating term or unilateral transmission of messages, or even free expression or dialogue. A line of reflection, shared by Morin (2004), when defending that a multidimensional view of human reality is essential to understand the communication phenomena and to abandon the idea that media is manipulative, represents evil, and influences the receiver, who is unable to discern between a program of good or poor quality: "There is always a receiver endowed with intelligence at the other end of the communication relationship. The media remain a medium. The complexity of communication continues to face the challenge of understanding." (Morin, 2004, pp. 18-19).

The existence itself has a funny part, since one does not live only for work and obligations. It is necessary to understand the complexity of the real that also encompasses passion, illusion, phantasm, that is, it is compulsory to rescue and value the creative act, the invention and the force of the imaginary as a chief aspect of the constitution of everyday life. For Morin (2004), it is undeniable that the media play a role in the public life, but that it is not central and much less determinant since its influence depends mainly on the individual experience, the context, and extra aspects.

FORMATION OF VIRTUAL TRIBES IN CYBERSPACE

The configuration of an original mode of relating to otherness appears as a remarkable trait of postmodern culture. According to the epoch, a kind of sensibility predominates, a type of style capable of specifying the relationships established with others. For Maffesoli (1998), the stylistic perspective authorizes to explain the passage from a political order, which privileged the individuals and their contractual associations, to the order of the fusion. When it is stressed the emotional and sensitive dimension; stressing a culture of feeling and sharing of affections structured by the logic of communication, responsible for promoting the bond or social interaction. Besides, the issue of building collective identities related to social movements and power struggles in the network society is very well explored by Castells (2009b) in the book named "The Power of Identity." Where the author also deals with the transformation of the state, politics, and democracy under the new conditions imposed by the combination of globalization and the new communication technologies.

In the scenario of a widespread and consolidated Cyberculture based on the growing use of ICT, this way of establishing sociality is highlighted by the possibility of meeting and socializing via cyberspace. Among the several social aggregations constituted in the network, the formation of the virtual tribes is distinguished, whose crucial components are the appearance, the image, and feelings of affection and emotion. The notion of neo-tribalism or tribalism is characterized by fluidity and dispersion, independent of the interest and purpose of the encounter. "Everything that connects with presenteeism, in the sense of opportunity, everything that refers to banality and aggregate power, in a word, to the emphasis of today's Renaissance Carpe diem, discoveries in the aesthetic matrix a place of choice." (Maffesoli, 1996, p. 55).

The meetings that lead to the formation of virtual tribes usually happen by chance, when the individual browses the Internet and encounters people with realizes to share affinities. Although it is an occasional meeting, it is valued because means being together, just as a commitment and a feeling of respect among members prevail while the interaction lasts. Some virtual communities often promote meetings and events outside the virtual environment to strengthen face-to-face contact, a way for people to meet in person, which would ultimately complement the social relationship maintained via social networking platforms.

Certain tribes adopt the so-called Netiquette, the norms and rules of conduct that in case of transgression, may result in the exclusion of the provoker. At this point, Maffesoli (1996) defines ethics a morality without obligation or sanction, that is, the person should have no other obligation than to be a member of a collective body, just as there should be no other sanction than to be excluded in situations of violation of behavioral norms. Besides, when the interest that connects the individual to the group ends, the person has complete autonomy to leave the group. On social interaction in virtual communities, Tsai and Bagozzi (2014) comment that: "If virtual community members experience constraints or perceive less freedom to act with volition, they can terminate their membership in the virtual community conveniently and effortlessly - often simply by ending the navigation session and never returning to the community domain" (p. 158).

Another feature is the absence of a custom hierarchy allowed by the Internet technology since it produces a distributed network environment, in which senior members remain on an equivalent footing as the average members. Usually, all members enjoy equality in speech as opposed to centralized systems or traditional and delimited communities that tend to bestow on certain members more privileges, coercive and legitimate power (Tsai & Bagozzi, 2014). These authors attempt to enhance current understanding of member contribution behavior in virtual communities, for example, delineating a framework that draws on the theory of collective intentionality to reformulate intentions inside a virtual community, not in individualistic terms, but rather to reflect shared volitions, which are more appropriate to social behavior associated with mutuality. Researchers have primarily ignored such group-based intentions, but they determine a variety of behaviors in virtual teams that seems particularly useful for characterizing voluntary participation behavior in virtual groups. They also advance on the comprehension of the cognitive, emotional, and social drivers of member contribution behavior in geographically distributed, electronically linked environments.

In the panorama of a planet joined by digital communication systems, there is still a tendency of people to close themselves in groups that worth a specific culture, exclusively reinforcing the bond between similar ones, a phenomenon designated by Alstyne and Brynjolfsson (1997) of cyberbalkanization. For the authors, the facilities of maintaining contact through emerging technologies could lead to a fragmentation of society in several associations of interests. The focus is on the potential of Balkanization or integration of interactions grounded on preferences, including social, intellectual, and economic affiliations, analogous to geographic regions: "Just as separation in physical space, or basic Balkanization, can divide geographic groups, we find that separation in virtual space or 'cyberbalkanization' can divide special interest groups" (Alstyne & Brynjolfsson, 1997, p. 4).

In some cases, fragmentation may be more intense in cyberspace because local heterogeneity can give rise to a virtual homogeneity regarding the subject of interest as it occurs in communities organized in the digital sphere, that agglutinate ignoring the geographical limits. On the other hand, with personalized access to online communication channels, individuals can focus their attention on career issues, leisure activities, making friends with people who have affinities, can read the specific news, all according to their predilection. In Putnam's view (2000), virtual communities may be more egalitarian than the real communities in which individuals live. Thus, by adopting a cyberspace-distributed access mechanism, virtual communities may be even more heterogeneous by considering factors such as race, gender, and age, although they may be more homogenous to interests and values.

In virtual communities, there is an express feeling of an elective affinity delimited by a symbolic territory, whose sharing of emotions and exchange of personal experiences are fundamental for group cohesion. Lemos (2006) explains that there is no standard for the procedure of elaboration of tribes since they do not have to originate from a geographically located place and migrate to the virtual, nor to be the exclusivity of the virtualization of social gatherings, predominantly, as some groups usually promote face-to-face meetings. Tribes can be born virtually, or from a physical location, a country, a city, a neighborhood, a school, a club, and can coexist and relate to the virtual environment and beyond. Besides, every space, regardless of physical or symbolic nature, can become a territory when it is appropriated by political, economic, cultural or subjective dynamisms. Hence, in the view of the author, a forum of discussion or a site structured in cyberspace, effectively deterritorializing, would be involved by a movement of symbolic reterritorialization.

In this sense, it would not be appropriate to speak of deterritorialization in isolation, since that it never occurs alone, it lacks a sort of compensatory process, the entitled reterritorialization (Haesbaert, 2004). By this bias, the cyberspace is an environment capable of promoting a series of reterritorializations, which would not be limited to the problematic of the geographic territory itself, extending to mechanisms of reterritorialization, reframing, and re-symbolization of culture and identity marks. In this perspective, one could think of cyberspace, above all, as a promoter of reterritorialization movements. Haesbaert (2004, p. 279) states that it would be possible to identify a "territory in the movement" or "by the movement," something that could be even the most significant innovation of the experience lived in the postmodern space-time. When controlling the space indispensable to social reproduction would not only mean controlling areas and defining borders, but also living in networks; where the own identifications and spatial-symbolic references would be made both in a relative stability, as in the mobility itself, since an expressive part of humanity is identified in and with space in motion. "Thus, territorializing means also today, to construct and/or control flows/networks and create symbolic references in a moving space, in and by the movement" (Haesbaert, 2004, p. 280). In addition, it is imperative to emphasize that similar units do not mold the territories because they are composed of different elements that provide configurations.

Another differentiating factor of this sociality is that the person (*persona*), who plays the roles and changes costumes according to tastes and moments, has the chance to participate in as many tribes as wants, so the motivation per se is enough. After all, the aesthetic paradigm consents one thinks of an alternative societal configuration, and at a time when the person lives amid a whirlwind of immediate uncertainties. Indeed, are these uncertainties of several kinds, including uncertainty about the existence of an identity that underlies the cultures sustained on emotions and feelings. In the author's conception, there is the slide from a logic of identity, individuality, to a logic of identification, which is much more collective.

There is a condition of possibility of all social experience, be it banal, scientific, literary or artistic, which is as an unavoidable foundation. It is what legitimizes the multiple conformities with an era, culminating in the known conformism (...). This is the shuttle that I have already analyzed: from mass to tribe, from conformity to conformism. The periods of cultural foundation live in this internal way, since they are times when the reaction against the values used elaborates new ways of being collective (Maffesoli, 1996, pp. 146-147).

This daily life, in its frivolity and superficiality, it is what makes any form of aggregation viable, whatever it may be. Moreover, although the logic of identity, which for centuries has served as the axis of the economic-political and social order, continues to function today, it is not capable of explaining the contemporary sociality. In this respect, Maffesoli (1998) appropriates the notion of aesthetics to approach social attitudes in postmodernity, since one cannot fail to point out the efflorescence and effervescence of neo-tribalism which, in the most varied forms, is based on any political project. Being the concern with a present lived collectively the unique reason to exist. On the other hand, the author underscores that the value of the everyday object only becomes interesting because it is a modulation of the form.

Thus, it is close to Simmel's thesis (1986) that man is a product of society, that is, the way of acting is directly linked to his place of origin, his environment and his interaction with other individuals. Man is formed according to his means and with the possibilities, including the techniques, available; only in this way society is possible. Therefore, Maffesoli (1998) assumes that the shared form founds a society, which has an erotic function, making a reading of this word in its most straightforward sense what leads to aggregation, generating an elective sociality, is the processes of attraction and repulsion by choice. This author, through the formalism of Simmel, as a category of knowledge or what was called presentation, reports very well the organic structure that is proper to nascent cultures, besides showing that the exterior or the surface has an undeniable function: The formalism permits people to grasp the random aspect and the deep coherence of social existence.

The person entering one or more virtual tribe seeks for traces of identification rather than a unique identity. Thus, the same individual can participate in various tribes and can adopt a pluralization of identities. To do so, he only needs to adapt himself to diverse situations of interaction, always trying to adjust the presentation of the self before each new situation. It is a person, while (*persona*), who "goes back and forth from one tribe to another, and wears, for the occasion, the costume appropriate to the space where it appears" (Maffesoli, 1996, p. 180). The requirement to be part of the group embodies an opportunity for the individual to strengthen social bonds or establish sociality since society is a product of different elements (Simmel, 1986). This need, according to Maffesoli (1998), reflects some components of the postmodernity, which tends to favor in contemporary megalopolis both the recollection of being in the group itself and a deepening of relationships within each group.

From the perspective of Lemos (2016), the postmodernity embraces the field of development of Cyberculture. Also, postmodern space and time can no longer be perceived as its modern correlates, since the other values are. In modernity, time is linear (progress and history), and space is naturalized and exploited as a place of things (direction, distance, volume). During this period, time is a way of sculpting space, for progress, understood as the incarnation of linear time, directly implies the conquest of physical space. In postmodernity, the predominant feeling is the compression of space and real time, where real-time (immediate) and telematic networks deterritorializes culture, having an impact on economic, social, political and cultural structures. The time is now a way to annihilate space. Such is the communications environment of Cyberculture.

For that matter, the opportunity of one can participate in virtual tribes is a strategy to form the sociality in cyberspace or the cybersociality. Having said this, it represents for the person a chance to take advantage of the present moment and, above all, to share a collective imaginary, promoting the resurgence of culture in social life, in the process of re-enchantment of the world, as proposed by Maffesoli (1996). From this point of view, the phenomenon of tribalism is captured as one of how cybersociality is possible - an adaptation of Simmel's idea (1986) about how society is possible, including the tribes of diversified interests, since they all integrate one or several tribes, even intellectuals, academics, and scientists. "What seems to us to be an individual opinion is, in fact, an opinion of all the groups belonging. Hence the creation of the doxas, which are a mark of conformism, and which form part of all groups of individuals, including the most distant of them, that of the intellectuals" (Maffesoli, 1998, pp. 106-107).

In other words, there is a process of taxing knowledge on the Internet, intellectual thinking, for example about authors, works, and a specific system, and an active participation of scholars, are self-taught, academics and/or scientists, with thoughts, are loaded with traits of subjectivity and imaginary. As Morin (2005) observes, attachment to ideas and the search for knowledge of the whole order always have a passionate/existential characteristic, as in any passion, so the author "Conceives *homo* no just like *sapiens*, and *economicus*, but also like *demens*, *ludens*, and *consumans*." (p. 18). When one recognizes a science of knowledge, which is much more scientific, more philosophical, and much more poetic, able to accept all these dimensions living side by side.

As a background, there is also the presence of communication technologies and computer networks that can collaborate to stimulate the ethereal network and the transfer of values and sensations shared concrete or virtually, which diffuses through technologies named by Silva (2012) as technologies of the imaginary. Such technologies function as devices for producing myths, world views, and lifestyles. They are elements that interfere with consciousness and sentimental territories below and beyond it, but they are not impositions, since the technologies of the imaginative work for the dissemination of the mental universe analyzed as a territory of fundamental sensations.

The technologies of the imaginary are devices of crystallization of an affection, imaginary, symbolic, individual or group patrimony, mobilizing of these individuals or groups. They are magmas that stimulate actions and producers of meaning. They give meaning and impulse, from the non-rational to practices that also present themselves rationally. Make a dream come true. They dream the real. (Silva, 2012, p. 47).

On the other hand, the virtual environment is a kind of mirror of society, which reflects the social practices and behavior occurred outside of cyberspace. Thus, everyday life is fueled by online and offline attitudes that always complement each other. They are by no means disconnected. In this case, new technology can only help to motivate a person's creative potential if she or he has the will and interest, as well as cultural and educational ability to enjoy the tool since no technology can transform a noncreative individual into a creative one. Not even the technology influences the way of communicating with a noncommunicative person. ICT may act as a driving force for human creativity and imagination, can motivate and promote socializing, contact, and a closer rapport between people, but only if they want to. It is not a determining factor, since the Internet, like any other media, does not have this power to manipulate the public.

In the panorama of the establishment of Cyberculture, the ICT revolution involves profound queries that surpass the technical advances of communication systems. According to Wolton (2012), it is common to reduce the phenomenon of communication to the purely technical question because the technique appears as the most visible element of communication since the machines and devices are concrete. For this author, the bottom line is to analyze the social side of the technique, which is incorporated in the way of communicating and interacting in Cyberculture, or the screen time invested and enjoyed. This new form of constituting cybersociality through which individuals unite with each other also by the ease of technological mediation, creating social bonds based on the principle of communication, contact with otherness and sharing of emotions and experiences in cyberspace. A concern that is also emphasized by Lemos (2016), for whom:

Considering the technical dimension of daily life means turning our gaze to the world of life. This is an attempt to recognize technique in the field of culture. If in modernity the imaginary of homogenization and instrumental rationality prevailed, the present age imposes a complex attitude of the technical phenomenon. (p. 19).

This proposition of the author is part of the sociology of uses, which aims to comprehend how society uses technical objects daily, remembering that all appropriation has a technical dimension (know how to handle the object) and other symbolic (a subjective, imaginary discharge). Thus, the appropriation is understood both as a form of use, learning, and technical mastery and as a form of deviance in relation to types of use, when a given object is applied differently for the purposes envisaged by the inventors or the institutions. In approaching this debate of digital communication technologies, Lemos (2016) points out that in the process of Internet research, one must overcome the perspective of the correct use or not of communication machines, always characterized by the stigma of the passive consumer and involved with strategies created by producers. It should, above all, consider the user an agent responsible for the social dynamics of the Internet.

According to Vaz (2004), the technological information network can stimulate the rapprochement of all, with all and breaks with the hierarchical distribution between transmitters and receivers, allowing each node/person to produce and transmit messages. It is the all-all models of production and transfer of content (Gillmor, 2005) when everything can turn into bits: sounds, images, and texts (Negroponte, 1995). Vaz (2004) states that the network represents the basis of a new understanding of contemporary society since in each period of human history a peculiar technical culture prevails that helps in the understanding of the actions and the behaviors in the course (Lemos, 2016). It is noteworthy that all media changes the space-time perception by offering a format and artifact with the purpose of sending information beyond space and time. The media transformations accompany humanity from writing, which takes off broadcaster and statement (space) and act as an instrument of memory (time), passing through the telegraph, telephone, radio, television until arriving on the Internet (Lemos, 2003), which introduces a culture marked by digital technologies: Cyberculture. Thus, one of the main characteristics of a cyberspace network is that it integrates all previous media, such as writing, the alphabet, the press, the telephone, cinema, radio, and television, all the communication mechanisms designed to create and reproduce signs, cyberspace being a kind of meta-media (Lévy, 2004). In this context, life is increasingly signaled by the appropriation of digital technologies used to carry out everyday activities such as contacting people, shopping, banking, according to the practices of a virtual culture or a digital life settled by people and bits (Negroponte, 1995).

In Lévy's ideal (2004), intellectual technologies would be able to refine some individual and collective cognitive systems when operated by companies, organizations, in various virtual communities and in humanity itself, the greatest of all the virtual communities, in the analysis of the author. Cyberspace would then encourage the call collective intelligence by presenting three modes of communication ("one-to-one", "one-to-many", and "many-to-many"), which could be articulated in real time: "The main meaning of cyberspace is the general interconnection of everything in real time, the virtual space where cultural and linguistic forms are alive" (Lévy, 2004, p. 166). Although it is accepted as a novelty the probability of the three models of communication in the virtual age, this innovation in the establishment of contact alone does not appear to be enough to promote the growth of intelligence, much less in the collective sphere, as proposed by the author. Since the substantive question of human behavior, the mind (imagination, creativity and willingness to acquire and improve knowledge) does not depend exclusively on technical support to manifest. There are many issues at stake.

The current technical relationship in Cyberculture could to some extent help in expanding the possibilities of communicating. To do this, the individuals need to show interest and have the cultural and educational capacity to interact from multiple locations and at the time chosen, synchronously or asynchronously, in a network of global dimension. As anticipated by Negroponte (1995), the digital life will require less and less that you are at a specific time and place. Soon, the notion of distance becomes less critical. Then, an Internet user does not even remember that it exists.

Silva (2012), in turn, contributes to the discussion by stating that the new technologies, together with their organic intellectuals, would give a new foundation to the man-nature pair. In this way, the control of reason would be converted into negotiation and interaction, since everyone is questioned, provoked, and produced by its own ideas.

Man lives in the techno sphere, where systems of locomotion and communication are articulated. All communication is a displacement: Of the message, of the interlocutor, of the broadcaster, of the collective imaginary. There is no idea, no belief, without the techniques of support and disclosure. (Silva, 2012, p. 46).

In other words, one must be aware that the symbolic dimension always affects the material, illustrating the mode of appropriation of the technique by an individual, who at one moment becomes the object of the technique and, in another, acts as if were the controller. Being conscious of this dialogical relationship between subject and technique that discriminates the social use of communication technologies in contemporary culture is fundamental to understanding the phenomenon of Cyberculture. The intertwining of technology with social life suggests that it is possible to apprehend the forms of the present-day technological imaginary through the existing spaces of production of sensations experienced collectively. As Lemos (2016) explains, the which count for the invention of the world of life is not merely the useful or the functionality, but an entire symbolic universe that is rooted in the lived spaces.

For Haythornthwaite and Wellman (2005), what is interesting to note after the moment of euphoria with the novelty is that the Internet, for instance, should no longer be comprehended as a unique system, but as something that is routinely incorporated into people's daily lives, being used to promote communication. The actions practiced in the virtual environment are usually not disjointed from the things people do when they are offline, so the authors argue that the focus of analysis must be on the appropriation of the Internet's graphical interface. They seek to develop research on a more integrated view of computer-mediated communication, noticing how performs practiced online fit in and complement each other's ordinary tasks.

CONCLUSION

Faced with a scenario in which a communicative sense prevails in postmodern Cyberculture, categorized by an aesthetic paradigm, valuation of the image, presenteeism, of the pleasure of sharing emotions collectively through technologies of the imaginary, this chapter concentrated on the comprehension of what society does with the media. In this specific case, about the social use of the Internet for the formation of virtual tribes. From a need to examine the relation of the media to social imaginaries, it was analyzed how the communication phenomenon and social interaction emblematic of a postmodern condition develops and manifests itself in the contact and formation of virtual tribes in cyberspace. When being together is the most crucial component, independent of the theme of interest that identifies and unites each group, which may be banal or intellectual. Moreover, life is distinguished by a complex social structure organized in multiple dimensions, composed of goodness and cruelty, of beauty and horror, emotion and reason, of order and disorder, of useful and useless, intellectuality and triviality, all the elements present in the day to day, sometimes competing, sometimes complementing each other. The articulations among these aspects reveal simultaneously the unity and multifaceted diversity of the human being, which was concealed throughout modernity by the discourse of a false, unidimensional and deterministic rationality, which excluded any contradiction (Morin, 2001).

In this context, the enhancement of the imaginary and its recognition as an essential element in daily practice and, consequently, present in all situations lived by any individual, are significant aspects to appreciate the world in its multidimensionality, exercising and assimilating a complex mode of thinking (Morin, 2002). According to Maffesoli (1996, 1998, 2016), since virtual tribes are structured by feelings of affinity and aesthetic pleasure, and that man joins another to form a society (Simmel, 1986), the phenomenon of tribalism in the networked society is a generator of cybersociality. That said, virtual tribes are one of the most representative groups of a postmodern Cyberculture, who devotes themselves to meetings and activities articulated around screen time. Besides, for Maffesoli (1998), social relations, those of everyday life, in the levels of institutions, work, and leisure, are no longer governed by transcendent instances. They are no longer guided by an objective to be achieved, which is delimited by an economic-political logic or determined by a moral vision. On the contrary, these social relations are structured on the actions that are living day by day, organically, and are increasingly focused on what is of the order of proximity.

Hence, contemporary Cyberculture replicates the characteristics of postmodernity that allowed the configuration of sociality from a stylistic perspective, that is, from the predominance of values such as appearance, image and the sensible. When one seeks, incessantly, to be part of tribes to enjoy the present moment and, above all, to share an imaginary collectively. Also, the prospect of being part of social groups from the system of the affinities of the logic of identification is what differentiates this current form of the social bond from the traditional model of attribution of cultural identities. Such as the case of national identity, in which a whole people are forced to adhere to specific national symbols, maintaining ties to places and celebrating commemorative dates, necessarily and artificially.

The virtual communities are a result of both the impact of new communication technologies on the structure of society (from the consolidation of Cyberculture) and the process of fragmentation of cultural identities (a direct reflection of the effect of globalization as an inherent characteristic of modernity). On the other hand, globalization by itself implies a movement away from the classical sociological idea of society as a well-delimited system in which all individuals share a sense of community. A credence that loses its strength due to its fragility, since the concept of a community, like that of a nation, are imagined constructions (Anderson, 1989). The composition of virtual communities is a way of conferring identities of the participants, based on one of the possible consequences of the aspects of globalization on cultural identities, which asserts that national identities are declining, but new identities - hybrid - take their place (Hall, 2014).

The acceptance of the world as it is by recognizing the question of sociality, which proposes a relativism of living by highlighting the greatness and tragedy of everyday life, differentiates contemporaneous from any other moment in history. Sociality appreciates the immediate, the present, and leaves aside the morality of must be, predominant in modernity, which would be succeeded by an ethic of situations, in which more attention is given to feelings as affections that are inseparable from the human being. The context in which the communication aspect plays a central role, acting as responsible for the constitution of the social bond in a society that devotes much attention to the screen time. Thus, communication is what connects one individual to another, representing the social cement and the glue of the called postmodern world (Maffesoli, 2004). Finally, it is decisive to clarify that the virtual environment is a sort of mirror and an extension of the behavioral phenomena of society, and therefore is neither better nor worse. The Internet does not change attitudes and social behaviors, and people take ownership of the available technologies to interact. With this perspective, a certain distance is still sought from an optimistic conception and even deification of communication technologies, seeing vital to investigate communication in its technical, cultural and social dimensions, and to confront them with an overall view of society, as proposed by Wolton (2012).

REFERENCES

Alstync, M. V., & Brynjolfsson, E. (1997). *Electronic Communities: Global village or cyberbalkans?* Retrieved May 12, 2017, from https://www.mediensprache.net/archiv/pubs/2809.pdf

Anderson, B. (1989). *Nação e Consciência Nacional*. São Paulo, SP: Ática.

Castells, M. (2003). A sociedade em rede. In D. Moraes (Ed.), *Por uma outra Comunicação. Mídia, mundialização cultural e poder* (pp. 255–287). Rio de Janeiro, RJ: Record.

Castells, M. (2009a). *The Rise of the Network Society: The Information Age - Economy, Society, and Culture: 1 (Information Age Series)*. Oxford, UK: Wiley-Blackwell.

Castells, M. (2009b). *The Power of Identity: The Information Age - Economy, Society, and Culture: 2 (Information Age Series)*. Oxford, UK: Wiley-Blackwell.

Durand, G. (1988). *A Imaginação Simbólica*. São Paulo, SP: Cultrix.

García Canclini, N. (2015). *Consumidores e Cidadãos: conflitos multiculturais da globalização* (8th ed.). Rio de Janeiro, RJ: UFRJ.

Garton, L., Haythornthwaite, C., & Wellman, B. (1999). Studying On-line Social Networks. In S. Jones (Ed.), *Doing Internet Research: Critical issues and methods for examining the Net* (pp. 75–105). Thousand Oaks, CA: Sage Publications. doi:10.4135/9781452231471.n4

Gibson, W. (2016). *Neuromancer* (5th ed.). São Paulo, SP: Aleph.

Gillmor, D. (2005). *Nós, os médias*. Lisboa: Editorial Presença.

Haesbaert, R. (2004). *O Mito da Desterritorialização*. Rio de Janeiro, RJ: Bertrand Brasil.

Hall, S. (2014). *A Identidade Cultural na Pós-modernidade*. Rio de Janeiro, RJ: Lamparina.

Haythornthwaite, C., & Wellman, B. (2005). Introduction: Internet in the everyday life. In B. Wellman & C. Haythornthwaite (Eds.), *The Internet in Everyday Life* (pp. 3–40). Hong Kong: Blackwell.

Lastowka, F. G., & Hunter, D. (2003). *The Laws of the Virtual Worlds*. Public Law and Legal Theory, Research Paper Series, Pennsylvania, PA. Retrieved May 12, 2017, from http://papers.ssrn.com/abstract=402860

Lemos, A. (2003). Cibercultura. Alguns pontos para compreender a nossa época. In A. Lemos, & P. Cunha, P. (Ed.), Olhares sobre a Cibercultura (pp. 11-23). Porto Alegre, RS: Sulina.

Lemos, A. (2006). Ciberespaço e Tecnologias Móveis: processos de territorialização e desterritorialização na cibercultura. In *Anais do Encontro Anual da Associação Nacional dos Programas de Pós-Graduação em Comunicação* (vol. 15., pp. 1-17). Bauru, SP: UNESP. Retrieved May 12, 2017, from http://www.facom.ufba.br/ciberpesquisa/andrelemos/territorio.pdf

Lemos, A. (2016). *Cibercultura, Tecnologia e Vida Social na Cultura Contemporânea* (8th ed.). Porto Alegre, RS: Sulina.

Lévy, P. (1996). *O que é o Virtual?* São Paulo, SP: Editora 34.

Lévy, P. (2004). O Ciberespaço como um Passo Metaevolutivo. In F. M. Martins & J. M. Silva (Eds.), *A Genealogia do Virtual: comunicação, cultura e tecnologias do imaginário* (pp. 157–170). Porto Alegre, RS: Sulina.

Lyotard, J.-F. (1998). *A Condição Pós-moderna*. Rio de Janeiro, RJ: José Olympio.

Maffesoli, M. (1996). *No Fundo das Aparências*. Petrópolis, RJ: Vozes.

Maffesoli, M. (1998). *O Tempo das Tribos: o declínio do individualismo nas sociedades de massa*. Rio de Janeiro, RJ: Forense Universitária.

Maffesoli, M. (2004). A Comunicação sem fim (teoria pós-moderna da comunicação). In F. M. Martins & J. M. Silva (Eds.), *A Genealogia do Virtual: comunicação, cultura e tecnologias do imaginário* (pp. 20–32). Porto Alegre, RS: Sulina.

Maffesoli, M. (2016). From society to tribal communities. *The Sociological Review*, *64*(4), 739–747. doi:10.1111/1467-954X.12434

Morin, E. (2002). *O Método 4. As ideias*. Porto Alegre, RS: Sulina.

Morin, E. (2004). A Comunicação pelo meio (teoria complexa da comunicação). In F. M. Martins & J. M. Silva (Eds.), *A Genealogia do Virtual: comunicação, cultura e tecnologias do imaginário* (pp. 11–19). Porto Alegre, RS: Sulina.

Morin, E. (2005). *O Método 5. A humanidade da humanidade*. Porto Alegre, RS: Sulina.

Negroponte, N. (1995). *A Vida Digital*. São Paulo, SP: Companhia das Letras.

Putnam, R. D. (2000). *Bowling Alone: The collapse and revival of American community*. New York, NY: Simon & Schuster.

Rheingold, H. (1993). *The virtual community: Homesteading on the electronic frontier*. Reading, MA: Addison-Wesley Publishing Co.

Silva, J. M. (2012). *As Tecnologias do Imaginário* (3rd ed.). Porto Alegre, RS: Sulina.

Simmel, G. (1986). Como la sociedad es possible. In *Sociología: estudios sobre las formas de socialización* (pp. 37–56). Madrid: Alianza.

Tsai, H.-T., & Babozzi, R. P. (2014). Contribution behavior in virtual communities: Cognitive, emotional, and social influences. *Management Information Systems Quarterly*, *38*(1), 143–163. doi:10.25300/MISQ/2014/38.1.07

Vaz, P. (2004). Mediação e tecnologia. In F. M. Martins & J. M. Silva (Eds.), *A Genealogia do Virtual: comunicação, cultura e tecnologias do imaginário* (pp. 216–238). Porto Alegre, RS: Sulina.

Wilbur, S. P. (2000). An Archaeology of Cyberspaces: virtuality, community, identity. In D. Bell & B. M. Kennedy (Eds.), *The Cybercultures Reader* (pp. 45–55). New York, NY: Routledge.

Wolton, D. (2012). *Internet, e depois? Uma teoria crítica das novas mídias* (2nd ed.). Porto Alegre, RS: Sulina.

KEY TERMS AND DEFINITIONS

Cyberculture: The social and cultural form emerged from the symbiotic relationship amid society, culture, and digital technologies focused on communication.

Cyberspace: A virtual or digital space built from the informational structure provided by global networks such as the internet.

Logic of Identification: The search for identification mechanisms is a constant practice nowadays. Hence, there is a gradual slide of identity towards the identification. The differentiating characteristic is in the form of identifying traits when the individual has the chance to belong, based on affinities, to as many communities as she or he wishes. Thus, there is a profound change in the understanding of the concept of identity, which is no longer seen as something fixed but elaborated continuously.

Sociality: A fluidity and natural manner of the establishment of relationships in a networked society, according to the logic of identification and the possibility of being together proposed by Michel Maffesoli.

Virtual Communities: Social aggregations that emerge from the Internet to people promote public discussions to form webs of personal relationships in cyberspace, according to Howard Rheingold.

Virtual Tribes: Social aggregations constituted in the cyberspace, whose essential components are the appearance, the image, and feelings of affection and emotion. The notion of neo-tribalism or tribalism is characterized by fluidity and dispersion, independent of the interest and purpose of the encounter.

Chapter 6
The Screens of Our Time:
On "Time" – Implications for Screen Time Research

Mikael Wiberg
Umeå University, Sweden

Britt Wiberg
Umeå University, Sweden

ABSTRACT

Despite the increasing interest in understanding screen time and its effects, there are very few papers published on how the notion of "screen time" is conceptualized – both in terms of what "time" refers to in this context and in terms of what a "screen" denotes nowadays. In an attempt to contribute to this lack of theoretical grounding, the authors outline four theoretical grounds for understanding time. Further, they suggest that the notion of "screen" needs to be problematized in similar ways. In this chapter, the authors illustrate how the four different conceptualizations of "time" in relation to this broader understanding of screens open up for a new range of studies of "screen time," and they suggest that this conceptualization is necessary in order to move toward.

DOI: 10.4018/978-1-5225-8163-5.ch006

INTRODUCTION

One of the most ubiquitous, and at the same time most visible aspect of computing is glowing computer screens. Screens increasingly occupy our attention and we spend more and more time in front of screens. Further, we surround ourselves with computer screens that comes in different formats – ranging from the small screens on our mobile phones - via the mid-size screens in the form of tablets, laptops and desktop computers - to larger screens for public use (e.g. TVs and other wall size displays). As we are increasingly spending time in front of these different screens, we also need a vocabulary for talking about this phenomenon. Here, the concept of 'screen time' has been set to address this particular fact.

BACKGROUND

One definition of "screen time" is that it is a demarcated period of time during which an individual is using technology with a screen in their everyday lives (ranging from the use of mobile phones, tablets, laptop computers, and computers, to the watching of television) and via the use of app's (health, well-being, transportations, games, and so on). In fact, some phone OS developers have even added functionality at the level of the operating system to track screen time (e.g. data about social network, productivity, reading and reference) in order to make its users more aware of the time spent on different apps. Along this increasing use of screens, questions have been raised whether time in front of these screens is beneficial or detrimental to children and studies around these questions have been done since televisions began to enter our homes in the mid twentieth centuries. Nowadays Internet and the social media platforms offers opportunities (and risks) for even more prolonged screen time sessions. Some researchers (e.g. LeMay, Costantino, O'Connor, & ContePitcher, 2014) have done studies on the amount of screen time for children and also looked into different kinds of screen time. The conclusion from their studies is that passive viewing of television and videos is fundamentally different from technology that requires navigation, tap and touch interaction, game play, whole body engagement and participation of others. As highlighted by Hiniker, Suh, Cao, & Kientz (2016) this does not reflect any particular emphasis on the amount of time spent with the screens. LeMay et al., (2014) also raise questions about different kinds of screen time, and the use of one screen or multiple screens and they also raise the question around personal tracking of screen time.

Against this background, current research on screen time is at the present moment 1) heavily focused on understanding questions related to how and why children and young people spend time in front of computer screens, and 2) this contemporary strand of literature is typically value-driven. Nowadays, the literature upholds a dichotomy that is concerned with screen time as either a good thing (children learn new things or are social online), or a bad thing (for instance it is advocated that if children play computer games there is an assumption that prolonged gaming might have a negative effect on their well-being and their ability to function in a social context). In this chapter the authors suggest that any such dichotomies are over-simplistic and that there is a need for more elaborated views on 'screen time'.

MAIN FOCUS OF THE CHAPTER

In relation to the need for a more elaborated view on ´screen time´, the authors review the current literature on 'screen time'. A point of departure for the literature review are concepts like the 'time', 'screens' and 'screen time' in order to find examples of studies of screen time. Based on these studies the authors suggest a model for further explorations of 'screen time' that takes into account not only time spent in front of a screen, but also 1) if the time spent is in an 'active' or 'passive' mode of watching; 2) if it is time spent in front of one screen or across multiple screens; 3) if it concerns prolonged watching (binge watching) or if it is a series of short watches over a longer period of time; and 4) if the activity that the watcher is focused on demands of her/his continuous attention. To address these different aspects of "screen time" the authors constructed a model with a basis in four different theoretical grounds for understanding time; including *biological time, psychological time, social time* and *cultural time*.

In this chapter the authors discuss each of these four perspectives on time. The authors relate the existing literature to each perspective of time and exemplify what to look for in each of these perspectives – ranging from aspects of the person spending time in front of screens and the personal experience of prolonged (or binge) watching, to clinical aspects of how such behavior stands in relation to the person that is occupied with the screen. With this as our conceptual ground the authors suggest that these four proposed perspectives on time will expand the current focus on 'screen time'. The authors also propose that these perspectives could work as a model for further studies of screen time. In short, the authors view these four perspectives on "time" as a theoretical ground for moving forward. The authors wrap up this paper by discussing the clinical and practical implications of this proposed conceptualization of time and its implications for screen time research and at last the authors outline some directions for future studies of screen time.

Related Work: Issues, Controversies and Problems

'Screen time' research has surfaces as an emerging research area devoted to understanding how time spent in front of computer screens; 1) can occupy our attention; 2) might lead to a withdrawal from the world outside of the computer; and 3) how prolonged 'screen time' might form the person involved in such sessions. Most of the studies on 'screen time' have been empirical studies on children (see e.g. Christakis, 2009; Lanningham-Foster, Jensen, Foster, Redmond, Walker, Heinz, & Levine, 2006; LeMay et al., 2014; Radich, 2013; Rooksby, Asadzadeh, Rost, Morrison, & Chalmers; 2016; Strasburger, Hogan, Mulligan et al., 2013) and how families manage screen media experiences for their children (see e.g. Hiniker et al., 2016; Livingstone, 2009), and teenagers' use of Internet (see e.g. Livingstone & Helsper, 2008), while less is known about how adults (see e.g. Shields & Tremblay, 2008) manage their screen time.

For instance, there is a strand of published research on the relation between 'screen time', physical activity and obesity (see for instance Laurson, Eisenmann, Welk, Wickel, Gentile, & Walsh, 2008; Shields, Gorber, & Tremblay, 2008). Here there are also examples of research on how to promote physical activity as to decrease sedentary screen time (see for instance the work by Maloney, Bethea, Kelsey, Marks, Paez, Rosenberg, & Sikich, 2008). From a related viewpoint others have explored sleep patterns and how 'screen time' affect sleep, depression and stress (Elder, Gullion, Funk, DeBar, Lindberg, & Stevens, 2012), mental health in general (Cao, Qian, Weng, Yuan, Sun, Wang, & Tao, 2011), and mortality (see e.g. Van er Ploeg, Chey, Korda, Banks, & Bauman, 2012).

In relation to these health related problems there are also studies that have examined the potential of interventions (Wahi, Parkin, Beyene, Uleryk, & Birken, 2011) or limit-setting and participation as to reduce youth screen time (Carlson, Fulton, Lee, Foley, Heitzler, & Huhman, 2010), while others have explored video-games as to promote physical activities while spending time in front of screens (Lanningham-Foster et al., 2006).

From this strand of literature it is clear that 'screen time' research has been heavily focused on understanding the relation between prolonged sitting and physical, biological, and mental health. However, less is still known about how the person engaged in prolonged 'screen time' sessions experience this (their sense of time), how others experience these persons who are occupied with screens, and the relation in between. While this can be seen as a lack of empirical studies that could fill this gap in the literature, the authors suggest that this is also a call for understanding the concept of "time" from other perspectives than how time passed affect our biological bodies.

"Time": Along Four Different Theoretical Perspectives

Time is central for functioning as humans and is crucial for human adaptive behavior. Much of human activity is time bound – both objective measurable and chronologically vs. subjective and experiential psychologically. Conceptualization of time in sciences is multilevel, so to say that different times apply to different levels of nature (Fraser, 1987). Human beings refer to different perspectives of time, e.g. *biological time, psychological time, social time* and *cultural time*. This four different theoretical accounts will be used in order to construct and get a deeper understanding and more theoretically informed ground for the concept of "screen time". Here below the authors will outline the concept of *time* from these different sciences and perspectives and then outlines its consequences for the concept of *screen time*.

Any scientific concept needs to be well-elaborated and clearly defined in order to be useful. Without a clear definition any concept becomes vague and it might be hard to understand what it refers to. As have been illustrated in the previous section there is still no elaborated definition of *screen time* and accordingly the authors will offer one such elaboration in this section, where the authors discuss the concept of "time" along four different theoretical accounts in order to construct a more theoretically informed ground for the concept of screen time. In this review the authors look closely at time from the viewpoints of 1) *biological time*, 2) *psychological time*, 3) *social time,* and 4) *cultural time*.

Perspective I - Biological Time: Human beings are biological organism, which are real and synchronized such as cycles, spirals, rhythms, linear to sustain life. Biological rhythms (such as circadian rhythm) are of central importance to human functioning. The circadian rhythm is defined as "the oscillations in the behavioral physiology and biochemical functions with a periodicity of approximately 24 hours" (Bhagwat, 2002, p.37). According to Bhagwat (2002) circadian rhythms have three basic features; 1) the circadian rhythms are endogenously generated; 2) the period of circadian rhythm is maintained at a constant value across a range of external temperatures; and 3) the circadian rhythms are entrained to the day-night cycle.

Biological time may be described by an orchestra metaphor, where the instant by instant synchronization of rhythms and cycles occurs in an organic present. This synchronization of biological reactions helps the cells and organism to remain alive. According to Duffy, Rimmer, & Czeisler (2001) morningness preference (or morning-type) respectively eveningness preference (or evening-type) explains the individual difference or circadian typology. The biological basis of preferences for morning activity patterns ("early birds") or evening activity patterns ("night owls") explains the variations in the rhythmic expression of biological or behavioral patterns. Biological times covers so to say biological clocks, oscillations and oscillatory processes at different levels of analysis.

Biological time permit future thinking, present thinking and past thinking. Carelli, Forman and Mäntylä (2008) reported that a number of patient studies suggest that impairments in frontal lobe functions are associated with disorders in temporal information processing. Clinical reports and observations of people with ADHD (and related frontal lobe disorders) have marked difficulties in temporal information processing. With evolution and brain development, human beings learned to represent real objects in a symbolic world, which according to Aylmer (2013) transform biological time to psychological time.

Perspective II - Psychological Time: Psychological time is a highly complex concept that constitutes a wealth of concepts. Four processes in temporal aspects in everyday life have been distinguished by McGrath and Tschan (2004); *time use*, *pace of life*, *time perception* and *time orientation*. *Time use* refers to an individual's distribution of time over daily activities such as eating, personal care, travel time, working time, leisure time, and sleeping time. *Pace of life* refers to the speed of doing everyday activities. *Time perception* is about how the individual judge the passage of time and has often been studied within individuals by their estimations of duration of specific temporal intervals judgements relating to time and feelings about the passage of time in general. *Prospective vs. retrospective time estimation* examines perceived duration and succession and describes the processing of time intervals in the range of seconds, minutes or larger time intervals. Succession refers to events that can be organized and perceived sequentially and it suggests a passage of our experience from present to past (Fraisse, 1984). Time estimation is an integrated part of people's everyday behaviors e.g. as the timing of motor behavior when walking or driving a car, and estimations of durations in concrete actions, or waiting for the elevator versus taking the stairs (Wittmann, 2009).

Time orientation refers an individual's view of the time and has a range of conceptualizations such as orientations to the past, to the present and to the future or the extension of the transcendental future and reflects the levels of involvement with theses temporal categories. According to Zimbardo and Boyd (1999) *time perspective* (TP) is considered to be an individual difference variable. They defined TP as "the often nonconscious process whereby the continual flows of personal and social experiences are assigned to temporal categories, or time frames, that help to give order, coherence, and meaning to those events" (Ibid, p. 1271). These authors identified five time perspectives; Past Positive, Past Negative, Present Fatalistic, Present Hedonistic and Future. Carelli, Wiberg and Wiberg (2011) completed their assumptions with dicotomizing the Future TP in two scales; Future Positive and Future Negative. Time perspective can be related to mental health through the concept "balanced time perspective" and to mental ill-heath through the concept of "biased time perspective" or stuck in time.

Also some other concepts have been used as psychological time such as *individual time styles* (time related individual differences) (Francis-Smythe, & Robertson, 1999) and the concept of *sense of time* (time related experiences). *Sense of time* means that subjective present experiences constitute time as mental constructs and in that way time is linked to past episodic memory and future thinking (plans). Most cognitive control functions - including planning, task initiation, and coordination - are time related in that they require compliance with temporal constraints (Carelli et al., 2008). Regardless of etiology, subjective experience of time is related to components of executive functioning.

Perspective III - Social Time: Social time may be regarded as an orientation tool, which refers to a relative framework, which help people to create points of orientation in a continual flow of changes. Social use of time is heterogeneous and have different meanings attributed to events in calendrical time. The sociologist Robert Lauer (1980) in his book *"Temporal Man: The meaning and uses of social time"*, made an attempt to introduce readers to the complex relations between man and time. These relations suggests the great richness of the topic and he conducted that the most fundamental difference in timekeeping throughout history has been between people operating by the clock versus people measuring time by social events. Lauer (1980) defined social or epochal time by events, which are dependent of time and he refers to patterns and orientations that relate people to social processes and the conceptualization of ordering of social life.

Social time is also constructed by norms, beliefs, the customs and practices of individuals and groups in the social world (Orlikowski & Yates, 2002). Some philosophers have also conceptualized time as having a social nature and emphasized its social construction, so to say the construction of the world as directly experienced by human beings. For example, Martin Heidegger in his book *"Being and Time"* (1927/1996) introduced the "temporal character of being and in doing" so he was also intellectually influenced by the philosopher Edmund Husserl and his phenomenology.

Perspective IV - Cultural Time: Cultural time deals with cross-cultural similarities and differences in time. Do persons from different cultures have similar or different views of time or the way persons deal with time? The anthropologist Edward Hall (1989) dichotomized time orientations into *monochromic* and *polychromic*. He argued that people with monochromic time orientation tend to prefer to do one thing at a time and rely on schedules and segmentation and people with polychromic time orientation tend to do several things at once and they stress the completion of transactions rather than adherence to preset schedules. Events may occur on regular basis or on-off-basis, e.g. tourist events and sports events. There are also some cross-cultural studies focusing entirely on time perspective and especially *time horizons* (e.g. Ashkanasy, Gupta, Mayfield, & Trevor-Roberts, 2004; Hofstede, 2011; Hofstede & Minkov, 2010). Time horizon refers to the length of the planning horizon and the length of time a person uses to think about the past or the future. Countries with short-term orientation (most western countries) foster values involving future-oriented rewards (in particular perseverance and thrift), whereas countries with a long-term orientation (such as China and Taiwan) foster respect for tradition, perseveration of "face", and fulfilling social obligations. Brislin and Kim (2003) suggested a dichotomy of *clock time cultures* and *event time cultures*. Robert Levine (2015) reports that in western countries we have clock time, the hour on the timepiece governs the beginning and ending of activities. His experiences in Brazil are that event time predominates, scheduling is determined by activities. Events begin and end when, by mutual consensus, participants "feel" the time is right. The distinction between clock and event time is profound.

The Concept of "Screen Time" Revisited From the Four Different Perspectives on "Time"

As illustrated in the previous section the concept of "time" can be elaborated on from a multitude of perspectives – ranging from biological time, to psychological time, to social time, and to cultural time. However, and despite this elaboration it is important here to bear in mind that; 1) so far such elaborations of this central concept of "time" is lacking in current "screen time" research; 2) that this has led to narrow focus on screen time research mainly based on a biological understanding of time; and 3) that an expansion of the concept of "time" can open up for a whole set of new studies on screen time. With this as a point of departure the authors will in this section go through each perspective of time as introduced in the previous section, and relate it to what it implies in relation to the concept of "screen time".

- **"Screen Time" From the Perspective of Biological Time:** As already introduced, biological time is concerned with synchronization of biological reactions so that an organism remains alive or at least comes to no harm. From a screen time perspective that implies screen time studies related to for example how our bodies react to prolonged sitting (as a typical effect of longer screen time sessions). A person's own biological time is often concretized with physical activities, weight and fatness, sleep, metabolic status (body mass index, lipoprotein, and cholesterol).

In one study, Lanningham-Foster and colleagues (2006) examined the effect of activity-enhancing screen devices on 25 children's (8-12 years) energy expenditure compared with performing the same activities while seated. Their hypothesis was that energy expenditure would be significantly greater when children played activity-promoting video games, compared with sedentary video games. They concluded that energy expenditure more than doubles when sedentary screen time is converted to active screen time. Such interventions might be considered for obesity prevention and treatment.

In another study, Mark and Janssen (2008) also found relationship between screen time and physical activity and metabolic syndrome during adolescence. They concluded that screen time was associated with an increased likelihood of metabolic syndrome in a dose-dependent manner independent of physical activity. These findings suggested that lifestyle-based public health interventions for youth should include a specific component aimed at reducing screen time. In a third study, Stamatakis, Hamer & Dunstan (2011) examined the independent relationships of television viewing or other screen-based entertainment ("screen time") with all-cause mortality and clinically confirmed cardiovascular disease (CVD) events. Also bigger studies (e.g. Stamatakis, Hamer, & Lawlor, 2009) have been conducted with a population sample of 4,512 (1,945 men) Scottish Health Survey 2003, respondents ($\geq$35 years) were followed up to 2007 for all-cause mortality and CVD events (fatal and nonfatal combined). Recreational sitting, as reflected by television/screen viewing time, is related to raised mortality and CVD risk regardless of physical activity participation.

- **"Screen Time" From the Perspective of Psychological Time:** As introduced in the previous section "Psychological time" is different from biological time in that it is subjective and less concerned with biological processes, but more focused on the experience of change or movement and also how time is perceived and understood. The foci here is on the *sense of time*, the experience of time, the individual's behavior relating to the sense of time, the experience of time, and the individual's behavior relating to time.

Ahrens and Sahani (2011) wanted to answer the question, "Where does our sense of time come from?" in two experiments. Their research indicated that people use their senses, e.g. the sense of sight, to help keep track of short intervals of time. According to them, people have learned to expect their sensory inputs to change at a particular average rate. They concluded that comparing the change they saw to this average value helped them to judge how much time has passed, and refined our internal timekeeping. Everyone's sense of time is different and, at least in part, dependent on what our senses are telling us about the external world. The sense of time is experienced by the self – both in normality and pathology – and the self is central for the understanding of time and the experience of time as duration. All individuals perceive time differently and the internal clocks do not match either. This means that one person's internal clock does not tick at the same rate as the other person's.

The development in infants – motor development, cognitive development, language development, development of executive functions, memory development and development of attentional capacity – is also the development of sense of time, speed and distance with reference to Ahrens and Sahani (2011). Neuroimaging studies support development of episodic memory and episodic thought (e.g. Okuda, Fujii, Ohtake, Tsukiura et al., 2003; Nyberg, Salami, Andersson, Eriksson et al., 2010; Szpunar, 2010; Tulving & Szpunar, 2012). These studies showed that the frontal and temporal lobes are linked with recollection of the past and envisioning the future. Aylmer (2013) wrote that damage to these areas means that a person lives in a "permanent present", where he/she is unable to access very recent or old memories.

In relation to screen time research this changes the focus from studies on bodily reactions and effected caused by prolonged sitting, towards studies focused on how persons engaged in screen time activities experience the flow of time, and how others perceive a person who is occupied in a screen time activity. Further, this perspective on time opens up for studies of how people engaged in screen time activities might lose the sense of time passing, and how they might experience a sense of flow, where they are so fully engaged in a screen time activity that they loses their sense of time, and loses the ability of estimate how long they have been engaged in a screen time activity (e.g. while playing a computer game).

- **"Screen Time" From the Perspective of Social Time:** The hallmark of social life (school, work, etc) is a shared temporal reference framework such as clocks, calendars and dating systems and these tools are used to distinguish different social groups. Calendars, clocks and "new media" (including cell phones, iPads, and social media) represent social artefacts that are imbued with meaning. In the social world – both in the real world and in the virtual world - associations with groups according to age, gender, race/ethnicity and sociodemographic status can be outlined.

Some studies of screen time have been done in families, where the parents' attitudes and beliefs toward time are illustrated. A couple of studies will be presented here. Hiniker and colleagues (2016) investigated children's transition to and from screen-based activities through parent interviews (n=27) and diaries through contextual details about the transitions to and from screen-based experiences from 28 families. The interview results showed that parents use strategies to reduce the frequency of painful transitions for fostering a smooth end to screen time. Eleven parents reported that they used "routine strategies" that occurred at predictable times around screen time. A majority of parents (21 out of 27) used "advanced warnings strategies" to attempt to improve transitions, and the majority of parents (20/27) also regularly used "support strategies from technology" itself. The majority of parents (20/27) brought up technology itself as an influential factor that predicts whether a transition will be smooth or painful. Parents value screen time for their young children but they want limits. This study showed that technology can be a partner to the parents or their adversary and the technology have to make design choices in order to facilitate the weekday for families with children. Parents permit their very young children to transition to screen experiences in order to keep them occupied because parents tend to do other essential tasks. In that way children have become routine users of newer technologies like smartphones and tablets.

Richards, McGee, Williams, Welch, & Hancox, (2010) reported that few studies have examined associations between attachment to parents and peers and different forms of screen time, and findings have been mixed. One study (Chowhan & Stewart, 2007) reported poorer family functioning among male adolescents who viewed programs with more violent content, but another study (Moore & Harre, 2007) reported no association between television viewing and family relationships. Brodersen, Steptoe, Williamson, and Wardle (2005) reported no association between screen time viewing (television, video, and gaming) and peer problems, although anecdotal concerns have been raised that limited television viewing may inhibit peer relationships through an inability to discuss popular shows and characters. Some studies (see e.g. Durkin & Barber, 2002; Cummings & Vandewater, 2007; Egli & Meyers, 1984) that specifically examined gaming (computer or video games) also reported conflicting findings.

- **"Screen Time" From the Perspective of Cultural Time:** Reinecke and colleagues (2013) found that event scheduling is a group decision-making process in which social dynamics influence people's choices and the overall outcome. As a result, scheduling is not simply a matter of finding a mutually agreeable time, but a process that is shaped by social norms and values, which can highly vary between countries. To investigate the influence of national culture on people's scheduling behavior they analyzed more than 1.5 million Doodle date/time polls from 211 countries. They found strong correlations between characteristics of national culture and several behavioral phenomena, such as that poll participants from collectivist countries respond earlier, agree to fewer options but find more consensus than predominantly individualist societies. Their study provides empirical evidence of behavioral differences in group decision-making and time perception with implications for cross-cultural collaborative work.

Methodological Implications for Doing "Screen Time" Research

In this chapter the authors have so forth outlined four different perspectives on time – including an understanding of time as *"biological time", "psychological time", "social time"* and *"cultural time"*. The authors have reviewed examples of the existing strand of literature that describe each perspective. In the presentation of each perspective the authors have made descriptions of what constitute the particular perspective and also presented some examples of studies in relation to each perspective. With this as a point of departure the authors now will discuss the methodological implications that follows from each of these perspectives for the study of screen time. Accordingly, for each perspective the authors first do a recap of each perspectives main focus, followed by a discussion of the methodological implications that follows.

- **Biological Screen Time Studies:** As we have presented in this chapter this perspective taken on time views it from the perspective of how it is concerned with synchronization of biological reactions so that an organism remains alive or at least comes to no harm (Aylmer, 2013). Further, this perspective highlight human beings as biological organism, which are real and synchronized along cycles, spirals, rhythms, linear to sustain life. According to Wittmann et al. "Humans show large differences in the preferred timing of their sleep and activity. This so-called "chronotype" is largely regulated by the circadian clock. Both genetic variations in clock genes and environmental influences contribute to the distribution of chronotypes in a given population, ranging from extreme early types to extreme late types with the majority falling between these extremes." (Wittmann, Dinich, Merrow, & Roenneberg, 2006, p. 497).

At the current moment, most existing studies of "screen time" take this perspective on time as its core point of departure. Accordingly, most "screen time" studies are focused on what happens in the human body – from a biological perspective - as an effect of prolonged sitting (binge watch or extensive screen time). As such, the focus is on how bodily "inactivity" effects the body and that is in return viewed as an effect of prolonged screen time. The methodological implications from this perspective is also clear. If one wants to understand "screen time" and its effect one should study the (measurable) bodily effects of prolonged sitting.

- **Psychological Screen Time Studies:** In line with our attempt to broaden the understanding of "screen time" – and along our proposed idea to first expand the concept of "time" to include additional perspectives - we now move to the methodological implications from adopting a perspective on time that focuses on "psychological time".

According to Carelli and colleagues (2008, p. 372) psychological time consists of cognitive constructs, images and symbolic representations, where most cognitive control functions, including planning, task initiation, and coordination are time related in that they require compliance with temporal constraints. In this perspective on time there is a focus on how people perceive the flow of time (rather than seeing time only as a factor that influences biological aspects of our bodies) and how they place situations in the present, in the past and in the future. As formulated by Ahrens and Sahani (2011) there is as important to understand "sense of time", that is how people formulate their understanding of time, as it is to measure what time passed does to our bodies. Further on, and as pointed out by Block and Zakay (2001) this perspective is focused on time related experiences, behaviors and judgements. And also people's retrospective and prospective timing according to memory, attention, and consciousness.

Here the methodological implications are also clear. In order to understand "screen time" we cannot just focus on biological processes in our bodies. Instead, we need to study how time is experienced by people, we need to study how people experience the duration of time, how they estimate time, and the perceived succession of time. Further, this perspective suggests that we also need "screen time" studies focused on understanding time related individual differences and to study individual time styles.

- **Social Screen Time Studies:** If now moving forward from the perspective on time as psychological time to also broaden it further to "social time" we can again see that it comes with a set of methodological implications for doing "screen time" studies. As presented in this chapter, the philosophers have also conceptualized time as having a social nature and they have emphasized its social construction, so to say the construction of the world as directly experienced by human beings. According to this perspective "social time" is constructed by norms, beliefs, the customs and practices of individuals and groups in the social world (Orlikowski & Yates, 2002).

Accordingly, and if doing "screen time" research one cannot only focus on either the biological or psychological aspects of time. Instead, studies are needed that contextualizes "screen time" in a social setting.

- **Cultural Screen Time Studies:** Finally, and if now expanding the time perspective to the forth perspective introduced in this chapter, that is to not only consider biological, psychological and social time, but also expand this to include an understanding of time as "cultural time" we can notice how this additional perspective again comes with a set of methodological implications for doing "screen time" research. As we have presented in this chapter, this perspective of time deals with cross-cultural similarities and differences in time and different time horizons. Do persons from different cultures have similar or different views of time or the way persons deal with time? Robert Levine (2015) reports that in western countries we have clock time, the hour on the timepiece governs the beginning and ending of activities. His experiences in Brazil are that event time predominates, scheduling is determined by activities. Events begin and end when, by mutual consensus, participants "feel" the time is right.

Accordingly, and if doing "screen time" research aimed at a richer understanding one needs to do screen time research with a clear focus on the cultural context as well. Here we propose that in order to do proper "screen time" research that captures "cultural screen time" one needs to engage in ethnographic and/or anthropological studies of not only how time is perceived, or how it is socially constructed. Here screen time must be studied around, but also how it is culturally embedded and formed, and how screen time as a cultural phenomenon in return affects and forms in the culture, in which the use of screens is socially, culturally and historically embedded.

FUTURE RESEARCH DIRECTIONS

"So, what is time"? In this paper we have proposed that this question has so forth been an overlooked, although so essential, question for the study of 'screen time'. Further, we have proposed that our understanding of "time", and even if that understanding is so forth only implicitly formulated, has implications for what "screen time" denotes and what it refers to as a conceptual construct - and as an analytical lens. In short, the way we define "time" has implications for what we study in "screen time research", and it has implications for what we look for, and for how we understand how people spend time with computers, and accordingly what effects we seek to observe and relate to this phenomenon.

In this chapter, and with this as a point of departure, the authors have elaborated on the concept of "time" as to theorize and explore how different perspectives on "time" opens up for different sets of studies of "screen time". In doing so we have as authors of this paper outlined four different theoretical perspectives on time – including understanding time as 1) biological, 2) psychological, 3) social, and 4) cultural. In this paper we have presented each perspective on 'time' and we have discussed how an understanding of time as "biological time" leads to studies of bodily effects of prolonged and inactive sitting (in front of screens), whereas an understanding of time as "psychological time" leads to studies of how people understand and perceive time, and the passing of time, as well as studies with a focus on how people lose their sense of time (in sessions of immersion). Further, and if adding two more perspectives on time we have in this chapter also explored this concept of time from the viewpoint of 'social time' which could for instance open up for studies on "screen time" as a matter of shared (or different) understandings of time passed (for instance differences in interpretations of what is a long 'screen time' session – between persons engaged in a screen time activity compared to a person observing someone who is occupied by a screen). Finally, we have explored time from the viewpoint of 'cultural time' where we have elaborated on how our conception of time might also be different in different cultural contexts.

"Screen time" is conceivable in several ways; as *objective measureable screen time*; e.g. clock, calendar or mathematical time, respectively as *experiential screen time*, which can be defined as psychological screen time and also as *subjective or social screen time* and finally *cultural screen time*. In addition to these perspectives the term "social jetlag" is getting increasingly established as a concept that points at a misalignment of biological and social time (Wittmann et al., 2006). Here a paper by Roenneberg, Allebrandt, Merrow and Vetter (2012) have reported results from a large-scale epidemiological study, which showed that, beyond sleep duration, social jetlag is associated with increased BMI. They concluded that their results demonstrated that "living against the clock" may be a factor contributing to the epidemic of obesity. This is of key importance in the pending discussions on the implementation of "daylight saving time" and on work or school times, which all contribute to the amount of social jetlag accrued by an individual. Their data suggest that improving the correspondence between biological and social clocks will contribute to the management of obesity.

In the psychological screen time the present includes the positions in time, which is the narrowest for the subjective observer. The events which happens before the present is called the past and the event that happens after the present is called the future. The user of screens can be a passive consumer of screen times or an active producer of screen time. In social screen time or we may call it "event time" because there are many people involved and it includes people from many cultures and cultures differences. "Clock-time cultures, like USA, adhere to schedules and punctuality, whereas event-time cultures, like Latin America, go more with the natural flow of social events. Although perhaps still prevalent, these distinctions may blur with globalization and the advance of technology and multitasking in all developed countries" (Sircova et al., 2015, p. 171).

Clearly, and as our review of the existing body of research on 'screen time' has illustrated it seems to be the case that 'biological time' is the dominant conceptualization of time as it frames time in relation to clock time, and in relation to how our bodies react over prolonged clock time. Of course, this perspective is useful for doing medical studies of how our bodies react to prolonged sitting, but it is at the same time a limiting perspective as it focuses solely on the individual who is engaged in a prolonged screen time activity.

In this paper the authors have broaden the meaning of 'time' and have added three additional perspectives and theoretical grounds. For instance, the perspective on 'psychological time' opens up for screen time research not only focused on bodily processes, but also on questions concerning perception, immersion, withdrawal (from the world outside of the screen), presence and engagement (with the things on the screen, and in relation to persons in the surrounding of the screen). As such the authors are confident that this chapter contributes both to a more theoretically grounded approach to screen time research. Further, the authors have demonstrated four ways of conceptualizing the concept of time, as well as to broadening the set of studies that can be conducted in the area of 'screen time' research – by showing how each theoretical framing of 'time' comes with a set of implications for what can be studied as a topic for screen time research. In doing so the authors suggest that the conceptual exploration we offer in this chapter contributes both *theoretically* and *methodologically* to expansion of screen time as a contemporary strand of research.

CONCLUSION

In this chapter the authors have addressed the importance of conceptualizing the notions of "time" and its implications for how we conceptualize "screen time" in order to further explore this phenomenon. Further, we have as authors of this paper stated that there is an increasing interest in studying screen time and its effects. At the same time, the authors have noticed that is evident from the increasing number of published empirical studies on this topic, is that we still lack theoretical discussions on the concepts of "time" although that time is a central aspect of "screen time" as a framing concept for these studies. Motivated by this need we have in this paper explored the notions of "time" along four theoretical perspectives. The authors have also revisited the concept of "screen time" in relation to each theoretical account. Further on, the authors have illustrated how each theoretical framing of "time" has implications for how to understand and study "screen time" and have provided examples for each perspective. In doing so our chapter contribute to this current strand of "screen time" research by offering a set of theoretical groundings for moving forward – not just empirically, but also theoretically in the development of a more precise vocabulary for addressing, describing and analyzing this concept. The authors suggest that this is a key for a deeper understanding of "screen time" and its effects, and suggest that this is a necessary step forward in order to move from empirical observations and studies to the development of theories on "screen time".

The authors envision that the four perspectives on time as presented in this paper will open up for further research, where each perspective on time might open up new research agendas in terms of new types of empirical studies on "screen time", and in terms of how each perspective will imply a set of future studies that will enrich each theoretical perspective on "screen time". The authors also envision that this will generate a range of studies that will contribute with examples and cases that illustrate how "screen time" can be understood as part of the continues emergence and development of our online society.

REFERENCES

Ahrens, M. B., & Sahani, M. (2011). Observers exploit stochastic models of sensory change to help judge the passage of time. *Current Biology*, *21*(3), 200–206. doi:10.1016/j.cub.2010.12.043 PMID:21256018

Ashkanasy, N. M., Gupta, V., Mayfield, M. S., & Trevor-Roberts, E. (2004). Future orientation. In R. J. House, P. J. Hanges, M. Javidan, P. W. Dorfman, & V. Gupta (Eds.), Culture, Leadership, and Organizations: The GLOBE study of 62 societies (pp. 282-342). Thousand Oaks, CA: Sage Publications.

Aylmer, B. (2013). *Continuity and Change in Time Perspective: A Longitudinal Field Study of Youth Workers* (Doctoral dissertation). Dublin City University, Business School.

Bhagwat, V. R. (2002). Cryptochromes and biological clocks. *Resonance, 7*(9), 36–48. doi:10.1007/BF02836184

Block, R. A., & Zakay, D. (2001). Retrospective and prospective timing: Memory, attention, and consciousness. *Time and Memory: Issues in Philosophy and Psychology*, 59-76.

Brislin, R. W., & Kim, E. S. (2003). Cultural diversity in people's understanding and uses of time. *Applied Psychology, 52*(3), 363–382. doi:10.1111/1464-0597.00140

Brodersen, N. H., Steptoe, A., Williamson, S., & Wardle, J. (2005). Sociodemographic, developmental, environmental and psychological correlates of physical activity and sedentary behavior at age 11 to 12. *Annals of Behavioral Medicine, 29*(1), 2–11. doi:10.120715324796abm2901_2 PMID:15677295

Cao, H., Qian, Q., Weng, T., Yuan, C., Sun, Y., Wang, H., & Tao, F. (2011). Screen time, physical activity and mental health among urban adolescents in China. *Preventive Medicine, 53*(4-5), 316–320. doi:10.1016/j.ypmed.2011.09.002 PMID:21933680

Carelli, M. G., Forman, H., & Mäntylä, T. (2008). Sense of time and executive functioning in children and adults. *Child Neuropsychology, 14*(4), 372–386. doi:10.1080/09297040701441411 PMID:17852120

Carelli, M. G., Wiberg, B., & Wiberg, M. (2011). Development and Construct Validation of the Swedish Zimbardo Time Perspective Inventory (S-ZTPI). *European Journal of Psychological Assessment, 27*(4), 220–227. doi:10.1027/1015-5759/a000076

Carlson, S. A., Fulton, J. E., Lee, S. M., Foley, J. T., Heitzler, C., & Huhman, M. (2010). Influence of limit-setting and participation in physical activity on youth screen time. *Pediatrics, 126*(1), e89–e96. doi:10.1542/peds.2009-3374 PMID:20547642

Chowhan, J., & Stewart, J. M. (2007). Television and the behaviour of adolescents: Does socio-economic status moderate the link? *Social Science & Medicine, 65*(7), 1324–1336. doi:10.1016/j.socscimed.2007.05.019 PMID:17587476

Christakis, D. A. (2009). The effects of infant media usage: What do we know and what should we learn? *Acta Paediatrica (Oslo, Norway), 98*(1), 8–16. doi:10.1111/j.1651-2227.2008.01027.x PMID:18793294

Cummings, H. M., & Vandewater, E. A. (2007). Relation of adolescent video game play to time spent in other activities. *Archives of Pediatrics & Adolescent Medicine, 161*(7), 684–689. doi:10.1001/archpedi.161.7.684 PMID:17606832

Duffy, J. F., Rimmer, D. W., & Czeisler, C. A. (2001). Association of intrinsic circadian period with morningness–eveningness, usual wake time, and circadian phase. *Behavioral Neuroscience*, *115*(4), 895–899. doi:10.1037/0735-7044.115.4.895 PMID:11508728

Durkin, K., & Barber, B. (2002). Not so doomed: Computer game play and positive adolescent development. *Journal of Applied Developmental Psychology*, *23*(4), 373–392. doi:10.1016/S0193-3973(02)00124-7

Egli, E. A., & Meyers, L. S. (1984). The role of video game playing in adolescent life: Is there reason to be concerned? *Bulletin of the Psychonomic Society*, *22*(4), 309–312. doi:10.3758/BF03333828

Elder, C. R., Gullion, C. M., Funk, K. L., DeBar, L. L., Lindberg, N. M., & Stevens, V. J. (2012). Impact of sleep, screen time, depression and stress on weight change in the intensive weight loss phase of the LIFE study. *International Journal of Obesity*, *36*(1), 86–92. doi:10.1038/ijo.2011.60 PMID:21448129

Fraisse, P. (1984). Perception and estimation of time. *Annual Review of Psychology*, *35*(1), 1–37. doi:10.1146/annurev.ps.35.020184.000245 PMID:6367623

Francis-Smythe, J., & Robertson, I. (1999). Time-related individual differences. *Time & Society*, *8*(2-3), 273–292. doi:10.1177/0961463X99008002004

Fraser, J. T. (1987). *Time - The Familiar Stranger*. University of Massachusetts Press.

Hall, E. T. (1989). *Beyond Culture*. New York: Anchor Books Edition.

Heidegger, M. (1996). *Sein und Zeit, 1927. Being and Time: A Translation of Sein und Zeit*. SUNY Press. (Original work published 1927)

Hiniker, A., Suh, H., Cao, S., & Kientz, J. A. (2016). Screen time tantrums: how families manage screen media experiences for toddlers and preschoolers. In *Proceedings of the 2016 CHI Conference on Human Factors in Computing Systems* (pp. 648-660). ACM 10.1145/2858036.2858278

Hofstede, G. (2011). Dimensionalizing Cultures: The Hofstede Model in Context. *Online Readings in Psychology and Culture*, *2*(1), 8. doi:10.9707/2307-0919.1014

Hofstede, G., & Minkov, M. (2010). Long-versus short-term orientation: New perspectives. *Asia Pacific Business Review*, *16*(4), 493–504. doi:10.1080/13602381003637609

Lanningham-Foster, L., Jensen, T. B., Foster, R. C., Redmond, A. B., Walker, B. A., Heinz, D., & Levine, J. A. (2006). Energy expenditure of sedentary screen time compared with active screen time for children. *The Journal of Pediatrics, 118*(6), e1831–e1835. doi:10.1542/peds.2006-1087 PMID:17142504

Lauer, R. H. (1980). *Temporal Man: The Meaning and Uses of Social Time.* New York: Praeger.

Laurson, K. R., Eisenmann, J. C., Welk, G. J., Wickel, E. E., Gentile, D. A., & Walsh, D. A. (2008). Combined influence of physical activity and screen time recommendations on childhood overweight. *The Journal of Pediatrics, 153*(2), 209–214. doi:10.1016/j.jpeds.2008.02.042 PMID:18534231

LeMay, S., Costantino, T., & O'Connor, S., & ContePitcher, E. (2014, June). Screen time for children. In *Proceedings of the 2014 Conference on Interaction Design and Children* (pp. 217-220). ACM.

Levine, R. (2015). Keeping Time. In M. Stolarski & N. Fieulaine (Eds.), *Time Perspective Theory; Review, Research, and Application* (pp. 189–196). Cham: Springer International.

Livingstone, S. (2009). Children and the Internet. *Polity.*

Livingstone, S., & Helsper, E. J. (2008). Parental mediation of children's internet use. *Journal of Broadcasting & Electronic Media, 52*(4), 581–599. doi:10.1080/08838150802437396

Maloney, A. E., Bethea, T. C., Kelsey, K. S., Marks, J. T., Paez, S., Rosenberg, A. M., & Sikich, L. (2008). A pilot of a video game (DDR) to promote physical activity and decrease sedentary screen time. *Obesity (Silver Spring, Md.), 16*(9), 2074–2080. doi:10.1038/oby.2008.295 PMID:19186332

Mark, A. E., & Janssen, I. (2008). Relationship between screen time and metabolic syndrome in adolescents. *Journal of Public Health, 30*(2), 153–160. doi:10.1093/pubmed/fdn022 PMID:18375469

McGrath, J. E., & Tschan, F. (2004). *Temporal matters in social psychology: Examining the role of time in the lives of groups and individuals.* American Psychological Association.

Moore, J., & Harre, N. (2007). Eating and activity: The importance of family and environment. *Health Promotion Journal of Australia, 18*(2), 143–148. doi:10.1071/HE07143 PMID:17663650

Nyberg, L., Salami, A., Andersson, M., Eriksson, J., Kalpouzos, G., Kauppi, K., ... Nilsson, L. G. (2010). Longitudinal evidence for diminished frontal cortex function in aging. *Proceedings of the National Academy of Sciences of the United States of America*, *107*(52), 22682–22686. doi:10.1073/pnas.1012651108 PMID:21156826

Okuda, J., Fujii, T., Ohtake, H., Tsukiura, T., Tanji, K., Suzuki, K., ... Yamadori, A. (2003). Thinking of the future and past: The roles of the frontal pole and the medial temporal lobes. *NeuroImage*, *19*(4), 1369–1380. doi:10.1016/S1053-8119(03)00179-4 PMID:12948695

Orlikowski, W. J., & Yates, J. (2002). It's about time: Temporal structuring in organizations. *Organization Science*, *13*(6), 684–700. doi:10.1287/orsc.13.6.684.501

Radich, J. (2013). Technology and interactive media as tools in early childhood programs serving children from birth through age 8. *Every Child*, *19*(4), 18–19.

Reinecke, K., Nguyen, M. K., Bernstein, A., Näf, M., & Gajos, K. Z. (2013, February). Doodle around the world: Online scheduling behavior reflects cultural differences in time perception and group decision-making. In *Proceedings of the 2013 conference on Computer supported cooperative work* (pp. 45-54). ACM. 10.1145/2441776.2441784

Richards, R., McGee, R., Williams, S. M., Welch, D., & Hancox, R. J. (2010). Adolescent screen time and attachment to parents and peers. *Archives of Pediatrics & Adolescent Medicine*, *164*(3), 258–262. doi:10.1001/archpediatrics.2009.280 PMID:20194259

Roenneberg, T., Allebrandt, K. V., Merrow, M., & Vetter, C. (2012). Social jetlag and obesity. *Current Biology*, *22*(10), 939–943. doi:10.1016/j.cub.2012.03.038 PMID:22578422

Rooksby, J., Asadzadeh, P., Rost, M., Morrison, A., & Chalmers, M. (2016). Personal tracking of screen time on digital devices. In *Proceedings of the 2016 CHI Conference on Human Factors in Computing Systems* (pp. 284-296). ACM. 10.1145/2858036.2858055

Shields, M., Gorber, S. C., & Tremblay, M. S. (2008). Estimates of obesity based on self-report versus direct measures. *Health Reports*, *19*(2), 61–76. PMID:18642520

Shields, M., & Tremblay, M. S. (2008). Screen time among Canadian adults: A profile. *Health Reports*, *19*(2), 31–43. PMID:18642517

Sircova, A., van de Vijver, F. J., Osin, E., Milfont, T. L., Fieulaine, N., Kislali-Erginbilgic, A., & Zimbardo, P. G. (2015). In M. Stolarski & N. Fieulaine (Eds.), *Time Perspective Theory; Review, Research, and Application* (pp. 169–187). Cham: Springer International.

Stamatakis, E., Hamer, M., & Dunstan, D. W. (2011). Screen-based entertainment time, all-cause mortality, and cardiovascular events: Population-based study with ongoing mortality and hospital events follow-up. *Journal of the American College of Cardiology*, *57*(3), 292–299. doi:10.1016/j.jacc.2010.05.065 PMID:21232666

Stamatakis, E., Hamer, M., & Lawlor, D. A. (2009). Physical activity, mortality, and cardiovascular disease: Is domestic physical activity beneficial? The Scottish Health Survey—1995, 1998, and 2003. *American Journal of Epidemiology*, *169*(10), 1191–1200. doi:10.1093/aje/kwp042 PMID:19329529

Strasburger, V. C., Hogan, M. J., Mulligan, D. A., Ameenuddin, N., Christakis, D. A., Cross, C., ... Moreno, M. A. (2013). Children, adolescents, and the media. *Pediatrics*, *132*(5), 958–961. doi:10.1542/peds.2013-2656 PMID:28448255

Szpunar, K. K. (2010). Evidence for an implicit influence of memory on future thinking. *Memory & Cognition*, *38*(5), 531–540. doi:10.3758/MC.38.5.531 PMID:20551334

Tulving, E., & Szpunar, K. K. (2012). Does the future exist? In B. Levine & F. I. Craik (Eds.), *Mind and the frontal lobes: Cognition, behavior, and brain imaging* (pp. 248–263). OUP USA.

Van der Ploeg, H. P., Chey, T., Korda, R. J., Banks, E., & Bauman, A. (2012). Sitting time and all-cause mortality risk in 222 497 Australian adults. *Archives of Internal Medicine*, *172*(6), 494–500. doi:10.1001/archinternmed.2011.2174 PMID:22450936

Wahi, G., Parkin, P. C., Beyene, J., Uleryk, E. M., & Birken, C. S. (2011). Effectiveness of interventions aimed at reducing screen time in children: A systematic review and meta-analysis of randomized controlled trials. *Archives of Pediatrics & Adolescent Medicine*, *165*(11), 979–986. doi:10.1001/archpediatrics.2011.122 PMID:21727260

Wittmann, M. (2009). The inner experience of time. *Philosophical Transactions of the Royal Society of London. Series B, Biological Sciences*, *364*(1525), 1955–1967. doi:10.1098/rstb.2009.0003 PMID:19487197

Wittmann, M., Dinich, J., Merrow, M., & Roenneberg, T. (2006). Social jetlag: Misalignment of biological and social time. *Chronobiology International*, *23*(1-2), 497–509. doi:10.1080/07420520500545979 PMID:16687322

Zimbardo, P. G., & Boyd, J. N. (1999). Putting Time in Perspective: A Valid, Reliable Individual-Differences Metric. *Journal of Personality and Social Psychology*, *77*(6), 1271–1288. doi:10.1037/0022-3514.77.6.1271

KEY TERMS AND DEFINITIONS

Biological Time: Refers to human beings as biological clocks, including real and synchronized processes such as cycles, spirals, circadian rhythms, oscillations and oscillatory processes, which are of central importance for human functioning and linear to sustain life. The biological basis of preferences for morning activity patterns ("early birds") or evening activity patterns ("night owls") explains the variations in the rhythmic expression of biological or behavioral human patterns.

Clock Time: Refers to the hour on the timepiece and what it governs (e.g., the beginning and the ending of activities which is most common in Western countries). On the opposite is event time, which predominates a scheduling determined by ongoing activities. Events begin and end when, by mutual consensus, participants "feel" the time is right. The distinction between clock time and event time is profound.

Cultural Time: Deals with cross-cultural similarities and differences in using digital technology with a display in everyday life (ranging from the use of mobile phones, tablets, laptop computers, and computers, to the watching of television) and via the use of app's (health, well-being, transportations, games, and so on). People from different cultures have different views of time or the way persons deal with time. Events may occur on regular basis or on-off-basis (e.g., tourist events and sports events). Different cultures have different time horizons, which refer to the length of the planning horizon and the length of time a person uses to think about the past or the future.

Psychological Time: Is a highly complex notion that constitutes a wealth of concepts. Several processes in temporal aspects can be noticed in everyday life for people learned to represent real objects in a symbolic world; e.g. time use, pace of life, time perception and time orientation. Also some other concepts have been used such as individual time styles (time related individual differences) and sense of time (time related experiences).

Screen Time: Refers to a demarcated period of time during which an individual is using digital technology with a display in our everyday lives.

Screens: Refers to computer displays (i.e., any piece of digital technology with a screen) that can display information (ranging from mobile phones, tablets, laptop computers, and computers, to television).

Social Time: Is a social construction and have different meanings attributed to events in calendrical time in the social world. Social time may be regarded as an orientation tool, which refers to a relative framework and is constructed by norms, beliefs, the customs, and practices of individuals and groups.

Time: Human beings refer to different perspectives of time and these different perspectives apply to different levels of human nature. In this chapter we present four different theoretical accounts of time including; biological time, psychological time, social time, and cultural time.

Chapter 7
Returning to the TV Screen:
The Potential of Content Unification in iTV

Jorge Abreu
University of Aveiro, Portugal

Pedro Almeida
iD https://orcid.org/0000-0001-5878-3317
University of Aveiro, Portugal

Ana Velhinho
University of Aveiro, Portugal

Enrickson Varsori
University of Aveiro, Portugal

ABSTRACT

Given the continuous transformation of the video consumption across multiple devices, this chapter has the main goal of characterizing the viewer behaviors at home, including the motivations for specific interactive television (iTV) features. An online survey was conducted with the aim of clarifying if the consumption patterns at home are contributing to the demand for unification services that combine videos from internet sources with TV content. The results highlight some insights regarding the preferred devices depending on age and the content source, as well as limitations and valued features to be considered in the development of future unification and personalization services. The results from this study are useful, not only to understand the dynamics of audiovisual consumption regarding the "future of television," but can also be applied to foster product-oriented projects based on the synergies between behavioral factors, technological innovations, and industry trends regarding audiences' needs and UX.

DOI: 10.4018/978-1-5225-8163-5.ch007

INTRODUCTION

Currently, the world is facing deep changes in audiovisual consumption habits that also have impact on the understanding of the role of TV, as a medium that nowadays is no longer confined to live broadcasting. Sustained by Streaming and Video-on-Demand (VoD) services, people are changing the way they watch audiovisual content, by migrating from the traditional approach of watching linear TV to non-linear TV and sources streamed over the internet, known as Over the Top (OTT) content (Abreu, Nogueira, Becker, & Cardoso, 2017). Simultaneously, the establishment of the new "Anywhere and Anytime" culture, mostly provided by constant advances on mobile devices, ensures ubiquitous access to Internet video, leading frequently to a transmutation of the primary screens (Vanattenhoven & Geerts, 2015a, 2015b). Pay-TV operators are, thus, working hard to make online video content available on their platforms. As they try to cope with the emergence of the cord cutters, they are committed to grant access to different mobile and web apps. Furthermore, personalized content can be provided by predicting which is the most appropriate content for each consumer, according to their viewing habits and reliable algorithms.

Pay-TV operators are also making the traditional line-up of TV content more flexible, offering services such as "catch-up TV" and "time-shift" in more engaging systems, supported by current User Interface (UI) paradigms (Abreu et al., 2017). In overall, Portugal is playing an important role regarding the offer of TV services by these operators, and is one of the most prominent countries in Europe where Pay-TV operators provide nonlinear alternative services (catch-up TV) to the linear-TV content offer (Abreu et al., 2017). The Pay-TV penetration in Portugal reached 89% of the households in 2017 and is expected to grow slowly but steadily to 94% by 2021, with Internet Protocol Television (IPTV) services having a prominent role since 2013 (Patel, 2017). Consumer demands and users' preferences for VoD content are heavily influencing how Pay-TV operators provide content beyond traditional linear TV. In the third trimester of 2017, about 5.5% of individuals aged 10 or over had access to subscribed to streaming services, such as Netflix, Fox Play, NPlay or Amazon Prime Video (ANACOM, 2017; Patel, 2017). Pay-TV Portuguese high competitive market is currently being occupied by operators, such as Altice and NOS, which offer many HD channels and OTT mobile services (e.g., MEO Go, NOS TV).

This backdrop leads to new unification approaches that aim to offer video from different sources (OTT and TV) at the same level, on unique and simple UI, while maintaining the user within the operators' TV ecosystem (Almeida, Abreu, Silva, Guedes, et al., 2018; Almeida, Abreu, Silva, Varsori, et al., 2018). This unifying opportunity is especially significant at home, where the big TV screen is still the preferred device for watching TV but isn't the favorite device for watching internet content by the youngest generations (Ericsson, 2017), which are becoming more demanding as more available options to watch audiovisual content arise. However, current solutions offering unified video content do not provide an optimal User eXperience (UX), considering that consumers still need to jump from TV-app to TV-app (e.g., jumping between the Netflix TV-apps to YouTube or Facebook videos) to access content from different sources/providers.

Taking in consideration this context, an online survey was developed and disseminated with the purpose of clarifying the motivations for using specific devices to watch audiovisual content in different contexts, as we move towards a possible scenario of unification and personalization in the TV. This data collection instrument is focused on the choice of device depending on the genre and source of the content; the use of connected devices to the TV; group or individual TV viewing; constraints found in their current Pay-TV service; and the most valued features on an Interactive Television (iTV) service, among other issues.

Using the results of this survey, the paper's main goal is to characterize the audiovisual practices and demands in the domestic environment along with a contextualization of the current trends in the TV ecosystem of a European country, Portugal. It is supported by the results of an online survey that aimed to collect information about the consumption of online video (e.g., from Netflix, YouTube or Facebook videos) and regular TV content through the TV set and other devices. This online survey was designed and disseminated taking into consideration that the information available in the literature was lacking a focus on the domestic environment habits, namely on the motivations behind the use of a specific device to watch a particular type of audiovisual content. An exploratory assessment of the interest in unification and personalization features in iTV was also contemplated in this survey. The results gathered from the survey aimed to answer some emerging questions:

- Do audiovisual consumption preferences impact the choice of which device to use at home?";
- "Do unification and personalization features lead to a preference for audiovisual consumption on the TV screen?";
- "Are the audiovisual consumption patterns at home contributing to the emergence of a unification scenario?";
- "If having access to a unified TV system, would consumers prefer the TV screen for watching OTT audiovisual content instead of their current services?".

This document is separated into 5 sections. After this introductory part, the next section presents the state of the art concerning known viewers' behaviors gathered in previous studies (Ericsson-Consumerlab, 2016, 2017; Nielsen-Company, 2015) that although not specific targeted to the domestic audiovisual consumption nor addressing the motivations behind the use of specific devices crossed with sources of content (as the online survey addressed in this paper does) provide very relevant data. The same section also presents the iTV industry trends relevant to the understanding of the unification concept. Next, the objectives and the sample of the online survey will be presented, followed by the results and discussion culminating in the most important conclusions and future work.

CHALLENGES AND OPPORTUNITIES FOR THE TV ECOSYSTEM

Viewers' Behaviors

With the emergence of new platforms and players, many studies have focused on understanding the new behaviors and consumption habits of video consumers. Results revealed that the TV and media landscape recognized as an ecosystem has suffered significant changes (Ericsson, 2017), often regarding the rise of new TV-viewer's clusters and the ways they watch TV over the available iTV services.

According to the 2017 Ericsson Consumer Lab study, six TV user groups can be considered. The classic "TV Couch Traditionalist" (heavy viewers of broadcasted TV via the traditional TV screen) is currently the less representative group with 13%, a reduction of 40% since 2010. This happened in favor of expanding user groups such as the "Screen Shifters" (consumers that use any screen, anywhere for all kinds of TV and video content) counting for 21% of the total number of users, and the "Mobility Centric" (firstly and mostly mobile screen users) with 22% (a mere 5% in 2010). These TV groups are related to generational clusters categorized as "Silent Generation" (ages 65+), "Baby Boomers" (ages 50-64)", "Generation X" (ages 35-49), "Millennials" (ages 21-34) and "Generation Z" (ages 15-20). The first three groups state to prefer watching video on the TV screen, especially sports, news and movies (Erickson, 2017 & Nielsen, 2015). However, computer, tablet and mobile phone-based viewing are more popular among younger consumers, not because they entirely dismiss the big TV screen but because they adopt multiple screen-viewing, along with multitasking practices. This has an impact on the number of hours dedicated to video consumption, with a total of 33 hours per week attributed to groups of users between 16-19 years old, with 54% of this time devoted to On-demand content. Users between 20-24 years old have similar behaviors. In contrast, the group of users aged 45-49 dedicates only 31% of their time watching On-demand content (from a total of 29 hours per week) whereas the 60-69 years old group have a similar total amount of viewing time, with only 21% of this period dedicated to VoD (Erickson, 2017).

The growing relevance of non-linear video over linear TV is highlighted as the central transformation within audiovisual consumption in recent studies, primarily due to the increase of OTT offers and the convenience of mobile viewing, as an alternative to the big TV screen (Erickson, 2017). To cope with this new context where OTT players are gaining ground in a market traditionally owned by telecommunications companies (TELCOS), Pay-TV suppliers counter with commodity bundle TV and Internet services, at competitive prices, that include Video-on-Demand, time-shifted, and catch-up TV features available on the move, anytime and anywhere (Abreu et al., 2017).

Despite non-linear TV content (from VoD and catch-up services) being already offered by most of the Pay-TV operators, users are increasingly subscribing on-demand services (SVoD) like Netflix (Erickson, 2017; Nielsen, 2015). Simultaneously, the consumption of free content (FVoD) is made available online by the leading video sharing platforms like YouTube and social networks like Facebook. Nevertheless, even when using advanced set-top boxes (STBs), SmartTVs or Media Players (e.g., Apple TV) this type of OTT content is offered in proprietary applications (app) fragmented in silos, with their own UI and UX, forcing the user to continuously jump from one app to another (Almeida, Abreu, Silva, Varsori, et al., 2018). This draws attention to other still unsolved issues within the existing iTV solutions, the effectiveness of content access and discovery in an overcrowded media context. Adding to this idea, Chorianopoulos (2008) recognizes that the profile of iTV users ranges from passive and ritualistic TV consumers to younger generations with a digital literacy mostly driven by the Internet, video games and mobile devices. In both cases, users must feel they own the control over their choices, without having to perform too many clicks to reach the intended content or to find a suitable recommendation for them.

Within this framework, the personalization of a content-first experiences, by aggregating and unifying content and sources may meet current users' media behaviors. In the 2017 rank of the six most valued factors concerning media attitudes users highlighted: (1) the preference for on-demand content over schedule viewing; (2) the use of the internet as a natural part of their TV habits; (3) having a fast internet connection to access unlimited TV and video streaming; (4) the release of full TV-series seasons; (5) the availability to access their TV/video content abroad; (6) the commodity of the bundled services provided by the traditional TV operator (Ericsson-Consumerlab, 2017). All these topics, along with the appreciation for content availability, video quality, content discovery, and cohesive UX at appealing pricing plans suggest a high standard and demanding audience that keeps pushing for new and innovative solutions.

Regarding Portuguese media landscape, according to the last available ERC (the Portuguese regulatory body for the media) report (Entidade Reguladora para a Comunicação Social, 2016), although consumer practices have changed significantly in recent years, television content continues to be the one that generates significantly more interest in the Portuguese population. In this sense, television is the preferred device for watching audiovisual content, with 99% of the respondents watching regularly (at least once a week). The report shows that, in addition to the TV, the Smartphone also has a significant presence in Portuguese domestic environment (75.2%), followed by the Laptop (52.9%), the DVD player/recorder (48.5%), Desktop Computer (32.5%), the Tablet (30.2%) and the Gaming Consoles (26.2%). Still according to ERC, respondents who watch television at least once a week, in terms of non-linear audiovisual consumption, the age group 25-34 years old watches the most deferred content (52.8%), followed by viewers between 15-24 years (46.6%), 35-44 years (45.4%), and, +65-year-old (7%). Only 6,9% of the respondents have access to more than the five Portuguese open channels, and, watch VoD content. From this group (6.9%), younger audiences (15-24) are also more likely to watch on-demand content (15.1%), with a progressive decrease to 55-64-year-olds (1.9%) – 25-34 years (9.7%), 35-44 years (7.9%) and 45-54 years (3.4%). The group of +65-year-old viewers presents a slightly higher value (2.8%) than the previous age group (Entidade Reguladora para a Comunicação Social, 2016). Although the consumption of Video-on-Demand seems to be reduced, the massive use of the TV suggests this could be the favored device to access content from different sources, namely OTT. Furthermore, the ERC report does not address the motivations behind the use of specific devices, as the presented survey aims to elucidate.

ITV INDUSTRY TRENDS

Achieving a unification framework that puts every player side by side with a content-first approach is not an easy task, because most content providers and producers have worked to preserve their commercial space encapsulated into mobile and web apps, resulting in an initiative called TV Everywhere (TVE). Initially, this was a technical and commercial approach designed to retain customers that were "cord cutting", and leaving the standard cable Pay-TV subscriptions, in favor of online On Demand services, such as Hulu, Netflix, YouTube, and others. The idea was to offer online services, both live and On Demand, but only to users already subscribing a traditional Pay-TV package. This can be considered as a kind of collusion between the channel owners and the traditional Pay-TV operators and, is, in fact, restricting the creation of pure OTT TV distributors, since most of these channels deny the rights for third parties to distribute their content online (Waterman, Sherman, & Wook Ji, 2013).

Although this initiative was presented to consumers as a "free" improvement to their subscription service, allowing them to watch TV "anywhere, everywhere", it brought a challenging UX problem as a byproduct. Not only the user must identify and install every TVE application (e.g., HBO Go, FOX Play, CNN Go, etc.), he needs to provide each app his username and password and must look up new content while copying with different settings and interaction models. The pure OTT providers like Hulu and Netflix are also following similar approaches, which can lead to frustrated users who are asked to use multiple apps and interfaces to get all the content they want. Other limitations of this approach include the lack of integrated search and no cross-operator recommendation and personalization solution.

There have been some industry tentative approaches to mitigate some of these issues. Apple added a "TV App" to the new AppleTV, that tries to consolidate some of the content from the apps already available on that platform. After an initial setup, the app provides an integrated search, recommendation system, and video consumption. However, the number of integrated partners is a small subset of the content available on the AppleTV, and although Apple keeps adding more providers, it still lacks big names like Disney, and naturally, Netflix.

Google has a similar approach in Android TV, allowing partners to provide metadata for the integrated search and highlights feature, and "channel feeds" for his "Live Channels" built-in app. Despite this, the metadata integration has attained greater collaboration from content producers than the actual channel playing. This makes search work (Google's area of expertise), and some features like "continue watching" its highlights, but the video playing is still done inside the partner app, resulting in distinctive UXs when facing different video players and user interfaces.

The Brazilian operator Oi has the Oi Play app with a similar metadata integration concept. This application aggregates metadata from most of the TVE providers in Brazil, and presents it in an integrated, cohesive interface, allowing for cross-catalog search and personalization. However, like in the Android TV approach, the content plays in the partner application or website, through a technique called "deep linking". Besides breaking the UX, this playing in another app also means that Oi will not be able to collect other consumptions done outside its app, reducing significantly the ability to make accurate recommendations.

Most recently, there appears greater openness for the creation of pure online integrated operators, utterly unrelated to traditional Pay-TV operations. YouTube TV, PlayStation Vue, Sling TV or Hulu are just some examples of that. In these initial stages, however, they are more a reimplementation of Pay-TV with an OTT streaming technology than a radical departure from the current business models, meaning there is still space for content aggregation and unification.

In this framework, it is worth to mention the research project [removed for blind review] that combines, at the same level over a unique user interface, TV content – both linear and non-linear – and OTT content – from Youtube, Facebook videos, and Netflix (Almeida, Abreu, Silva, Guedes, et al., 2018; Almeida, Abreu, Silva, Varsori, et al., 2018).

AUDIOVISUAL CONSUMPTION IN TELEVISION AND OTHER SCREENS: THE ONLINE SURVEY

Considering the information available in existing studies addressed in the previous section, a lack of focus on habits towards the aggregation of contents in the domestic environment was identified, specifically in audiovisual consumption, screen preferences and related value. Therefore, an online survey was designed and disseminated to address these shortcomings. In addition to characterize daily uses and motivations for the selection of devices to watch specific audiovisual content, an exploratory assessment of the interest in unification and personalization features in iTV were also contemplated in this study.

OBJECTIVES AND STRUCTURE

The survey was released online in January 2018. The data collection was intentionally divided into three streams: a version for individuals living in Portugal (PT version), another for Brazil (BR version) and an additional one for foreign countries (EN version). Only the data collected in the Portuguese version of the online survey was considered for this paper. The results provided an overview of the Portuguese context focused on motivational factors disregarded by other European studies. This approach outlines the viewers' profiles, based on their viewing behaviors. It aims to clarify the motivations for using specific devices to watch AV content in different contexts, as we move towards a possible scenario of unification and personalization in TV. For that reason, it focuses on the choice of device for each genre of content; its source (e.g., from TV channels, YouTube or Netflix); the use of connected devices to the TV; group or individual TV viewing; constraints found in their current Pay-TV service; and the most valued features on an iTV service, among other issues.

The survey consists of 20 closed questions, which are organized into five sections: (1) sociodemographic characterization, (2) device usage, (3) online consumption of audiovisual content, (4) TV content consumption, (5) Television of the future: unification of contents. The PT survey received 371 valid responses.

SCOPE AND DELIMITATION

The main research question prompting this survey was learning if audiovisual consumption preferences, and needs are influencing the choice of device and leading to an appreciation of unification and personalization features in iTV context.

Although the scope of the survey is broader as it includes the dynamics of audiovisual consumption between different screens, the analysis for this paper focuses specifically on the domestic environment. Additionally, age groups are considered relevant variables for correlations – namely the generation clusters used in the Nielsen study (2015) – and consumer types – resorting to Ericsson Consumer Lab's (2017) TV user groups, labeled on usage time amount and device.

Within this context, some hypotheses were identified, since it is important to identify if consumption patterns at home are contributing to the demand for unification services and potentially encouraging the development of commercial solutions. Thus, TV providers' weaknesses can be identified turning them into opportunities to meet this new type of users' needs. The reasons for choosing the TV screen over other devices are also examined. It was also considered relevant to identify if image quality and size affect the user's choice when facing the same services and content. Additionally, the verification of the dependence between the age and the type of consumer towards personalization features, like profiles, recommendations and UX continuity, was considered significant for analysis.

SAMPLE CHARACTERIZATION

The sample is composed of 371 persons, with men representing more than half of the respondents (58.8%). Regarding academic degrees, most of the individuals have Bachelor degree (29.1%) and K-12 diploma (28.6%), following other education levels: Master degree (17.8%), Trade/technical/vocational training (8.9%), Associate degree (6.2%), Professional or doctorate degree (5.7%) and Nursery school to 8th grade (3.8%). Concerning the household of the sample (mostly made up of adults), the distribution is as follows: Family without children (49.9%), Family with adults and children (24%), Housemates (15.1%), Single (8.1%), Other (1.9%) and Adult with children (1.1%). The age distribution ranged from 12 to 81 years old (Figure 1), with an average age of 28 years old. For comparison with other studies (Nielsen, 2015), the sample was also analyzed regarding age clusters, which includes: 94 individuals from Generation Z; 199 individuals from Generation Y/Millennials; 55 individuals from Generation X; 19 individuals from generation Baby Boomers and 4 individuals from the Silent Generation. The sample highlights three main clusters relevant for

Figure 1. Age / generation distribution

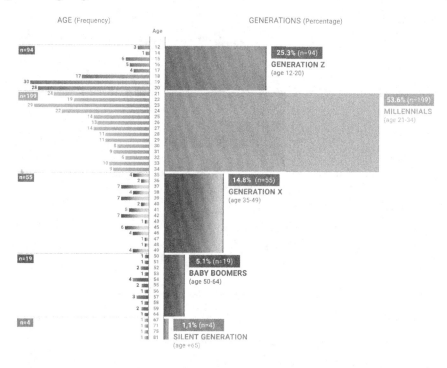

the current study: Millennials, between 21 and 34 years old (53.6%); Generation Z, until 20 years old (25.3%) and Generation X, between 35 and 49 years old (14.8%).

RESULTS AND DISCUSSION

Devices Used for Audiovisual Consumption at Home

Regarding television viewing at home, the sample reveals that most respondents watch television together (60.2%), with the following distribution: Family with other adults (38.8%), Alone (32%), Family with adults and children (13.7%), Housemates (6.5%) and Single adult with children (1.1%). Some respondents stated that they don't watch TV at home (7.8%).

With respect to the preferred device to watch AV content in the domestic environment (Figure 2), the three most common devices chosen by the respondents were: the Laptop (30.7%), the SmartTV connected to a set-top box or an antenna (26.1%) and the SmartTV connected to a Computer or Media Center, like Apple TV, Chromecast, Android TV, among others (18.6%). The ranking is the same for

Figure 2. Preferred device for watching audiovisual content at home (Question 1.3)

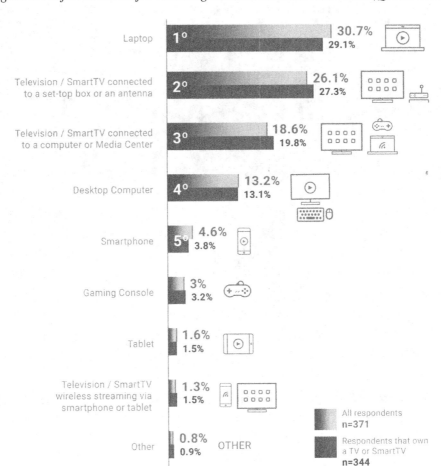

the group of 344 respondents (92.7%) that own a TV or SmartTV. Despite having a TV they chose the Laptop as the preferential device at home (29.1%). Only 7.3% of the sample do not own a TV or SmartTV.

In addition to traditional TV viewing, the survey also examined which devices are connected to the TV screen. A small share of the respondents (1.3%) prefer screen casting from their Smartphone or Tablet to watch audiovisual content on the television screen but 18.6% choose a Laptop or Media Center connected to the TV. Furthermore, when asked if they usually connect devices to the television 71.4% stated that they typically do and are likely to connect more than one device. The most popular devices connected to the TV are the Laptop (42%), Smartphone (21%) and Media Center (20.8%). The high percentage (71.4%) of this practice, despite not being the preferred way to watch AV content at home, may indicate that the respondents' TV services do not reflect their needs. In that sense, participants were also asked about the reasons that motivated the device choice at home and the limitations found on their Pay-TV services.

The distribution of reasons for choosing a device for watching videos at home, when analyzed individually by each device (Figure 3), shows that "practical and convenient access" is the most valued reason across all devices. Exceptions occur when the device is the Desktop Computer (it becomes the second most important reason in favor of the access to other applications and features) and when screencast is used on a SmartTV (where the screen size is the first reason). When it comes to mobile devices, such as the Smartphone and Tablet, and even the Laptop, mobility, portability and privacy are the main reasons for the choosing such devices at home.

Regarding content, the preference of device according to a specific source was also inquired. For watching traditional TV content, most of the respondents prefer watching it on a TV set connected to a set-top box or antenna (61.5%). Although 37.5% of the sample never or rarely watches Netflix, the most used device for this

Figure 3. Preferential device and related motivations for watching audiovisual content at home (Question 1.3 and 1.4)

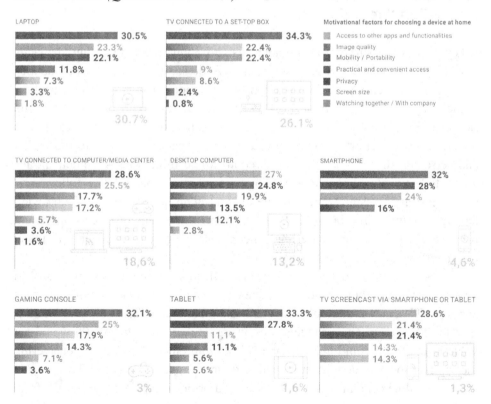

source was also the Desktop Computer or Laptop (32.3%), likewise for YouTube videos (62.5%) and other Internet contents (69.3%). As for Facebook videos, the respondents most often use the Smartphone (37.5%).

The estimated number of daily hours of video consumption at home was also gathered, distinguishing Internet sources from television channels. Most of the respondents spend about one hour (24.5%) or half an hour a day (24%) watching TV content at home. On the other hand, a considerable part of the individuals claimed not to watch TV at all (17.5%). As for content from various Internet sources (like Facebook, Instagram, Netflix, Popcorn Time, Snapchat, Vimeo and YouTube), the most frequent number of hours spent ranges between one and three hours a day – two hours (19.9%), one hour (14%) and three hours (12.1%), respectively. Nevertheless, considering the overall consumption of videos at home from Internet sources, the average a day was 5.8 hours, whereas for regular television content the consumption was considerably lower, with an average of 3.5 hours. Because this question refers only to audiovisual consumption at home, the number of hours indicated by the respondents suggests multitasking behaviors as using several sources and applications at the same time in the same device, or possibly simultaneous usage of several devices.

Motivational Factors Towards a Content Unification Scenario in the TV Screen

A key goal of this survey was to gather insights about expectations and demands towards an iTV content unification scenario. To do so, it was important to identify existing gaps, which could be inferred from the limitations identified by the consumers in their Pay-TV services (Table 1). These inefficiencies, identified by 65% of the sample (35% did not found any limitations in their services), can be explored as opportunities to support new systems and services, especially oriented to unification and personalization. Hence, the top three identified limitations – the demand for access to personalized content according to the users' habits (23.7%), followed by the interest in accessing sources of the Internet in an integrated way (22.6%) and having an intuitive interface (21.80%) – can represent the interest for a unified and more personalized solution offering at the same level and over a unique and simple user interface OTT content and TV content.

To clarify the respondents' interest in this unification concept, they were also asked about what features they would most value when faced with a potential simultaneous access to TV content and online content (e.g., YouTube, Facebook, and Netflix) over the TV screen. The average scores, using a Likert scale from 1 ("I would not value it") to 5 ("I would highly value it"), are presented in Table 2. Considering the top five most valued features – all with an average score above 3.5 – having access to online content on the TV screen is a priority, especially to benefit from

Table 1. Limitations identified in the operator's service (Question 3.4)

%	Do you encounter problems or limitations in your operator's service? If so, what limitations would you highlight?
35%	I do not find any limitations
23.7%	Not having access to personalized content, according to my habits and tastes
22.6%	Impossibility / difficulty in accessing content in an integrated way from Internet sources (YouTube, Facebook, Netflix)
21.8%	Type of interaction with the elements in the screen (menus, buttons, lists, etc.) is little intuitive
20.5%	Limited access to content and channels
14.6%	Difficulty finding and accessing the intended content
7.8%	Confusing and unintuitive remote control

the bigger screen size and image quality (4) and to take advantage of the size for collective viewing (3.8). Personalized controls over the content that emphasize the flexibility and continuity of the UX – such as bookmarking and "keep watching" – are equally valued (3.8). Mobile watching (3.7) and direct access without having to switch between apps (3.7) were the next more relevant features.

These results provide an overview of the dynamics of audiovisual consumption within the Portuguese sample. They show that viewing practices at home are scattered across devices (mostly the Laptop and devices connected to the TV) and express the interest in services that can provide an enhanced UX by using a personalized UI that gathers content from different sources. Conversely, the hypotheses of results discrepancy according to target groups, and the possible interdependence between variables led to the delineation of correlation factors to support a variance analysis.

Correlation Factors and Analysis of Variance

Based on current consumption practices and a near future context of unification of contents on the TV, the survey aimed to collect which behaviors and motivations are relevant depending on different target groups. The factors identified as potentially meaningful to differentiate those target groups were age (generation clusters), and their audiovisual consumption at home depending on the source (amount of time spent watching content from television versus from internet sources).

When looking at the average of time spent watching video content at home, there is a discrepancy between two clusters: younger generations (until 49 years old) with audiovisual consumption exclusively at home higher than 35 hours a week, and older generations with audiovisual consumption lower than 14 hours a week. In this sense, considering that Generation Z, Millennials and Generation X

Table 2. Ranking of the valued advantages of getting unified content on the TV screen (Question 4)

Average Score	Considering the possibility of simultaneous access to TV content and online content (e.g., Youtube, Facebook and Netflix) on the TV screen, please indicate how much you would value the following features
4	Enjoying a bigger screen and better image quality to watch content from Internet sources (e.g., YouTube, Facebook, and Netflix)
3.8	Taking advantage of the bigger size of the television screen to watch content from internet sources (e.g., YouTube, Facebook, and Netflix) with company
3.8	Having access to a personal area with content marked as favorite, "keep watching" or bookmarked for later viewing
3.7	Having access to this platform on mobile devices to allow mobile watching
3.6	Direct access to online content on the TV without having to switch between apps
3.2	Having the same kind of menus and features to interact with content from TV channels, YouTube, Facebook, and Netflix
3.1	Simultaneously searching for different sources (obtaining results from TV channels, YouTube, Facebook, and Netflix)
3.0	Previewing videos organized by themes and Internet sources on the TV screen
3.0	Having access to suggestions of other related videos depending on the content I'm watching (e.g., having access to related YouTube content following the viewing of a cable TV show)
3.0	Having access to recommended videos, depending on my profile, both TV channels and Internet sources (e.g., YouTube, Facebook, and Netflix)
2.9	Having access to advanced features of specific applications (e.g., subscribing, uploading videos, tasting content)
2.3	Interacting with others by sharing and recommending content from the television

are relevant target groups for the study and represent 93.7% of the current sample, these three generations were highlighted in Figure 4. Millennials have the highest average of video consumption regarding both sources, namely 48.4 hours a week of TV content and 58.8 hours of OTT content. Generation X present a more balanced content consumption between the two sources. Generation Z and Millennials have higher consumption of videos from Internet sources comparing to TV content, although Generation Z presents a decrease of about 2 hours per day. This decrease could be related to the consumption of shorter videos, namely, user-generated content from Internet sources. Still, Generation Z and Millennials present a similar proportion of watched content from Internet sources over television content. The higher consumption of both may be related to the increase of the SmartTVs and the use of devices connected to the TV, as depicted in Figure 5.

Figure 4. Average of daily hours of audiovisual consumption at home (TV channels content from television versus from internet sources) distributed by generations (Questions 2.2 and 3.2)

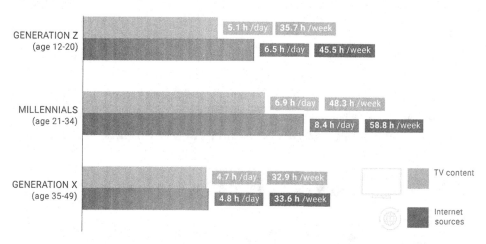

Regarding Generation X, Millennials and Generation Z, the device choice for audiovisual consumption at home was further analyzed according to these age groups (Figure 5).

In what concerns the preferred at home (Figure 5), there is a relevant divergence between individuals with less than 34 years old (Generation Z and Millennials) that choose the Laptop as their preferential device (41.5% and 34.1%, respectively) and Generation X where only 8.8% selected this device as preferential, and have the Television or SmartTV connected to a set-top box or an antenna (49.3%) as their top preference. As for their second choice in preferred devices, while Generation Z respondents favor the Desktop Computer, the Millennials choose a Television or SmartTV connected to a Computer or Media Center, suggesting an increasing appreciation for the TV screen over smaller screens, possibly favoring size and image quality. The choice for the Computer, either Desktop or Laptop, may be related to multitasking practices, as younger respondents are likely students regularly using this device in their daily activities. On the contrary, the television or SmartTV connected to a set-top box or antenna reveals an abrupt cut from 49.3% of Generation X to 13.8% regarding Generation Z´s preference for this device. This may indicate the teenagers' lack of interest for the Pay-TV offer and suggest possible shortcomings of the services' features towards their profile as consumers. Moreover, despite the intensive use and ubiquitous presence of mobile devices in our daily lives, as shown by relevant national and international reports in this domain (ERC, 2016; Ericson, 2017; Nielsen, 2015), the Smartphone and Tablet was a very residual choice to watch audiovisual content at home among the sample.

Figure 5. Distribution of the preferential device for watching AV content at home by generations (Question 1.3)

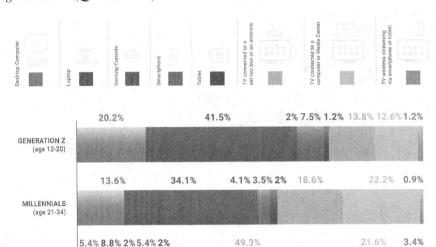

As for device choice at home according to a content source, the same generation distribution was considered: Generation X, Millennials and Generation Z (Figure 6). Generation Z is the age group that spends the least time watching TV and 34% of the sample claim they never or rarely watch content from TV channels. A considerable portion of the same age group never or rarely watches content from Netflix (35%) and Facebook Videos (29.6%). The set-top box connected to the TV is the most popular device to watch television content among these three generations, mainly by Generation X (72.5%). Regarding Netflix, Generation Z and Millennials watch mainly on the Computer (46.9% and 35.5%, respectively), while Generation X presents a more diffused device choice. They prefer to screencast from their mobile Netflix app to their TV (27.2%) or their TV (16.3%) before choosing the Computer (10.9%). Content from Internet sources like YouTube and other websites (e.g., downloads and streaming platforms) is preferentially watched at home on the Computer by the three generations, except for Facebook content with a slightly higher preference for the Smartphone followed by the Computer.

Concerning results of specific questions of the survey focused on a possible scenario of unification, namely on the limitations of the current Pay-TV service and valued features in TV systems, no substantial discrepancies between reasons and across age groups were found. Nevertheless, the ranking of the limitations and reasons varies between the three delimited generations, as presented in Table 3 and Table 4.

Figure 6. Distribution by generations of the preferential device for watching AV content at home by source (Question 1.8)

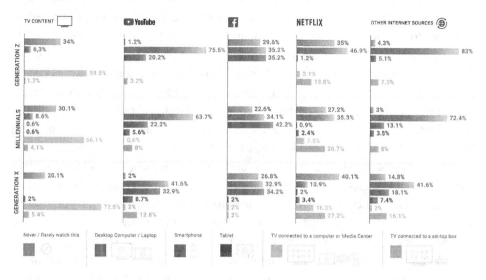

Table 3. Distribution of the top three of the limitations highlighted in the current Pay-TV service (Question 3.4)

		Generation Z		Millennials		Generation X
1°	17.2%	"Impossibility / difficulty in accessing content in an integrated way from Internet sources (YouTube, Facebook, Netflix)"	15.6%	"Confusing and unintuitive remote control"	19.5%	"Not having access to personalized content, according to my habits and tastes"
2°	15.7%	"Type of interaction with the elements in the screen (menus, buttons, lists, etc.) is little intuitive"	15.3%	"Difficulty finding and accessing the intended content"	15%	"Limited access to content and channels"
3°	14.8%	"I do not find any limitations"	14.9%	"Limited access to content and channels"	14.6%	"I do not find any limitations"

The identification of limitations in the Pay-TV service was a multiple-choice question. Like on previous questions, only Generation Z, Millennials and Generation X were considered for further analysis, due to their representativeness in the sample and relevance to the study. Considering the distribution of responses by age group (Table 3), the answer "I do not find any limitations" ranked third in the issues identified by Generation X and Z. However, for Millennials it is the least frequent answer, coming at the bottom of the ranking (12%). This indicates that Millennials are more critical of the offer provided by their current operator. Generation Z refer the impossibility or difficulty in accessing content from Internet sources in a unified way as the main limitation (17.2%), also expressing issues concerning the little intuitiveness of the UI (14.8). This suggests that the visual and interaction affordances from internet sources on this age group are not fully covered by the UX provided by the operator's television services, possibly disrupting the transition between devices and interfaces. Millennials, on the other hand, are more focused on problems concerning the remote interaction (15.6%) and the discovery and access to content (15.3%), while critical about the offer of content and channels (14.9%). Generation X highlights the limitations of access to personalized and recommended content according to their consumption habits (19.5%) and the diversity of content and channels (15%). Therefore, this ranking indicates that unification and personalization are concepts that can overcome the top limitations identified by our respondents. Furthermore, both concepts are not fully integrated into the current industry offer. This impacts the global UX that includes both hedonic and instrumental aspects (Bernhaupt, 2013) related to content, interface, and interaction in the specific context of iTV systems.

Regarding Table 4, that depicts the results of the average scores of valued features in a possible scenario of unification on the TV screen, there is an even distribution of scores among the several features and a concordance of the most valued features across the delimitation of the three generations. The distribution of the three generations confirms the global distribution of the sample (Table 2). The results indicate that the top features may be applied to product-oriented research without the need for a more granular segmentation of target. Thus, future unification systems must consider easy and direct access to both TV and Internet sources, based on profile recommendation and provide ways to manage personal content and settings. Additionally, they must be designed both with high-quality TV screens and mobile devices in mind.

Table 4. Distribution of the valued advantages of getting unified content on the TV screen by generations (Question 4)

	Generation Z	Millennials	Generation X
Enjoying a bigger screen and better image quality to watch content from Internet sources (e.g., YouTube, Facebook, and Netflix)	4.1	4.0	3.7
Direct access to online content on the TV without having to switch between apps	3.7	3.7	3.5
Having access to recommended videos, depending on my profile, both TV channels and Internet sources (e.g., YouTube, Facebook, and Netflix)	3.2	2.9	2.9
Previewing videos organized by themes and Internet sources on the TV screen	3.1	3.0	3.0
Having access to suggestions of other related videos depending on the content I'm watching (e.g., have access to related YouTube content following the viewing of a cable TV show)	3.3	2.9	2.9
Taking advantage of the bigger size of the television screen to watch content from internet sources (e.g., YouTube, Facebook, and Netflix) with company	4.0	3.8	3.7
Interacting with others by sharing and recommending content from the television	2.6	2.2	2.1
Simultaneously searching in different sources (e.g., obtaining results from TV channels, YouTube, Facebook, and Netflix)	3.2	3.2	2.8
Having the same kind of menus and features to interact with content from TV channels, YouTube, Facebook, and Netflix	3.3	3.3	3.0
Having access to advanced features of specific applications (e.g., subscribing, uploading videos, tasting content)	3.2	2.8	2.5
Having access to a personal area with content marked as favorite, "keep watching" or bookmarked for later viewing	3.8	3.8	3.5
Having access to this platform on mobile devices to allow mobile watching	4.1	3.7	3.3

To assure the reliability of the inferences, parametric tests were applied. The one-way ANOVA (analysis of variance) verifies the effect of an independent variable of qualitative nature (factor), with a dependent (or response) variable of quantitative nature (Field, 2018). The technique, with a significance level of 0.05, was used to determine if there were significant differences in the means of the groups of the independent variable. Three correlation factors were used: (1) age (generation clusters); (2) time consumption of contents from various Internet sources at home; (3) time consumption of television channels at home.

Regarding the verification of statistical confidence of correlations between devices preference and content sources, as well as motivational factors towards a unification, some specific questions of the online survey were considered for analysis of variance:

- 1.3. Select which device do you prefer to watch audiovisual content at home;
- 1.8. Select the device you use to watch the following content according to its source;
- 3.4. Do you encounter problems or limitations in your operator's service? If so, what limitations would you highlight;
- 4. Considering the possibility of simultaneous access to TV content and online content (e.g., YouTube, Facebook, and Netflix) on the TV screen, please indicate how much would you value the following features.

To sustain the results obtained by ANOVA, Levene's test was used to verify the homogeneity of the variances, and in cases where the assumption of variance homogeneity is violated Welch's robust test was applied considering sig. values that are different from 0 and 0.05.

The analysis of variance was applied for each of the four questions combined with the factors 'generations', 'consumption of television content at home' and 'consumption of videos from internet sources at home'. Only question 1.3 and 1.8 presented valid results for the correlation factor 'generations', as well as the feature "Having access to this platform on mobile devices to allow mobile watching" of question 4, regarding a unification scenario on the TV. Because the present paper reports only on the dynamics of audiovisual consumption concerning the domestic environment, this last result was not considered for further analysis.

Considering the valid results for variance analysis, there is a statistical variance among generational groups on the question 1.3 (focused on the preference of device to watch audiovisual content at home) and question 1.8 (focused on the preference of device depending on the source of the content). This confirms the significant correlation between choice of devices and content sources according to age, supporting the different patterns of behavior depicted in Figure 5 and Figure 6. In case of question 1.3, both Levene and ANOVA have a sig. 0, thus, there is homogeneity in the groups analyzed. In question 1.8, Facebook is the only case that confirms that there is no homogeneity among the variables (Levene with a sig. 0.06 and Robust Welch with 0.489). In other words, there are differences between generations and their use of Facebook.

Current limitations (Question 3.4) and motivations (Question 4) towards unification and personalization features in iTV are less age-dependent, suggesting that a comprehensive solution can be designed without target audience constraints.

CONCLUSION AND FUTURE WORK

Given that the Pay-TV penetration in Portuguese households is estimated to increase to 94% by 2021 (Portugal TV update, 2017), IPTV services qualify as a relevant context for research and development of more assertive services, that can better cope with the current consumers' behaviors. The behaviors and motivations of expanding target audiences regarding the use of devices, such as the "Screen Shifters" and "Mobility Centric" – that represent almost half of the AV consumers (Ericsson, 2017) – are essential to understand the next generation of viewers. Also, age clusters show that "Generation X" (ages 35-49), "Millennials" (ages 21-34) and "Generation Z" (ages 15-20) gather the highest amount of On-Demand content consumption, across multiple screens and multitasking practices (Nielson, 2015).

With the aim of clarifying if the consumption patterns at home are contributing to the demand for unification services that combine OTT content with linear TV, an international online survey was conducted. Preliminary results from the Portuguese version of the survey highlight some insights regarding devices preference depending on the content source and age, as well as limitations and valued features to be considered in the development of future unification and personalization services for iTV. The presented results aim to contribute with three streams of insights regarding screen time spent by users from different age groups at home, namely the motivations to use that time watching audiovisual content in a given device; the quantity of time (average of hours per day/week) regarding different sources of content; and the quality of time, in what regards content sources and preferred devices that have specific features and advantages associated.

Considering the three main target groups of the study – Generation X, Millennials and Generation Z – the video consumption only at home, regarding TV content and Internet sources, suggests parallel viewing on multiple devices given the high amount of hours spent per day (superior to 4 hours by source). These results reinforce the relevance of gathering data that can improve the development of services that may contribute to the quality of that screen time, taking a big part of people's lives in their households. According to the sample, the audiovisual consumption at home was higher in the Millennials age group (5.1 hours a day of TV content and 6.5 hours of OTT content), although presenting a similar proportion as the Generation

Z, being the internet content preferred over television content with a difference of 2 hours per day. The age group between 35 and 49 years old (Generation X) presents a lower but more balanced content consumption between the two sources (4.7 hours a day of TV content and 4.8 of OTT content).

Except for TV content, most likely watched in a TV connected to a set-top box or antenna, the most frequently chosen device to watch all the other sources of content at home was the Computer (Desktop and Laptop), across the three generation groups. The comeback of the TV screen among younger generations can be supported by their interest in benefiting from the dimension and image quality of this screen, especially for collective viewing, and enjoying Internet videos in a smooth way. According to the sample, 74% of the respondents watch television together and 71,4% stated they usually connect more than one device to the TV screen. The most used devices connected to the TV are the Laptop (42%), Smartphone (21%) and Media Center (20.8%).

Furthermore, the perceived willingness for a unified and more personalized offer of IPTV services is supported by the top three limitations identified in the respondents' current Pay-TV services: the demand for access to personalized content according to their habits (23.7%); the willing to get Internet sources in an integrated way (22.6%); and having an intuitive interface (21.80%). As highlighted by Chorianopoulos (2008), users must feel they have the control over their choices, quickly and efficiently as it may provide an optimal viewing experience that meets both the passive/ritualistic consumers and the younger/active generations.

Alongside this survey and aware of its results, an empirical study with an iTV prototype of a UI for content unification (Almeida, Abreu, Silva, Guedes, et al., 2018) is also being led in Portugal. Quantitative and qualitative data are being collected with a sample of 43 participants in the real context of use of the prototype, by applying online surveys, UX scales and following audiovisual consumption data retrieved from the Google Analytics. Preliminary results from this empirical study provided additional insights about a possible use case of unification and personalization at home. There are some valuable observations from the ongoing field trial with this prototype: the increase of audiovisual consumption from OTT and VoD sources and the rise of collective viewing practices over individual viewing.

In overall, the results from the survey allow us to get an overview of the Portuguese context focused on motivational factors at home, particularly regarding motivations and demands towards the TV screen. Within the foreseeable future, the results from the English and Brazilian version of the online survey may provide further insights and a comparison and verification of possible correlations with geographic and cultural patterns, dependent on each country's consumption dynamics and media landscape. The validation of the hypothesis and correlations, inferred from the online survey and the preliminary results from the empirical study, are crucial to understand the dynamics of audiovisual consumption regarding the 'future of television'. Furthermore, they may be employed to foster product-oriented practices based on the synergies between behavioral factors, technological innovations and industry trends regarding audiences' needs and UX.

ACKNOWLEDGMENT

This research was developed under the UltraTV - UltraHD TV Application Ecosystem project funded by COMPETE 2020, Portugal 2020 and the European Union through the European Regional Development Fund (FEDER) [grant agreement no.17738]. Authors are grateful to the project partners.

REFERENCES

Abreu, J., Nogueira, J., Becker, V., & Cardoso, B. (2017). Survey of Catch-up TV and other time-shift services: A comprehensive analysis and taxonomy of linear and nonlinear television. *Telecommunication Systems*, *64*(1), 57–74. doi:10.100711235-016-0157-3

Almeida, P., Abreu, J., Silva, T., Guedes, R., Oliveira, D., Cardoso, B., & Dias, H. (2018). UltraTV: an iTV content unification prototype. In *Proceedings of the ACM International Conference on Interactive Experiences for TV and Online Video - TVX '18*. Seoul: ACM. 10.1145/3210825.3213558

Almeida, P., Abreu, J., Silva, T., Varsori, E., Oliveira, E., Velhinho, A., … Oliveira, D. (2018). Iterative User Experience Evaluation of a User Interface for the Unification of TV Contents. In *Applications and Usability of Interactive Television* (pp. 44–57). Aveiro: Springer. Retrieved from https://www.springer.com/us/book/9783319901695

ANACOM. (2017). *Serviço de Distribuição de Sinais de Televisão por subscrição – 3º trimestre 2017*. Retrieved from https://www.anacom.pt/streaming/TVS3T2017public11dez2017.pdf?contentId=1423909&field=ATTACHED_FILE

Chorianopoulos, K. (2008). User interface design principles for interactive television applications. *International Journal of Human-Computer Interaction*, *24*(6), 556–573. doi:10.1080/10447310802205750

Entidade Reguladora para a Comunicação Social. (2016). *As novas dinâmicas do consumo audiovisual em Portugal 2016*. Retrieved from http://www.erc.pt/documentos/Estudos/ConsumoAVemPT/ERC2016_AsNovasDinamicasConsumoAudioVisuais_web/assets/downloads/ERC2016_AsNovasDinamicasConsumoAudioVisuais.pdf

Ericsson-Consumerlab. (2016). *TV and Media 2016: The evolving role of TV and media in consumers' everyday lives*. Retrieved from https://www.ericsson.com/assets/local/networked-society/consumerlab/reports/tv-and-media-2016.pdf

Ericsson-Consumerlab. (2017). *TV and Media 2017: A consumer-driven future of media*. Retrieved from https://www.ericsson.com/assets/local/careers/media/ericsson_consumerlab_tv_media_report.pdf

Field, A. (2018). *Discovering Statistics Using IBM SPSS Statistics (5th ed.)*. London: Sage Publications.

Nielsen-Company. (2015). *Screen wars: The battle for eye space in a TV-everywhere world. Nielsen Insights*. Retrieved from http://www.nielsen.com/apac/en/insights/reports/2015/screen-wars-the-battle-for-eye-space-in-a-tv-everywhere-world.html%5Cnhttp://www.nielsen.com/content/dam/corporate/us/en/reports-downloads/2015-reports/nielsen-global-digital-landscape-report-march-2015

Patel, I. (2017). *Portugal TV Update*. Retrieved from https://ovum.informa.com/resources/product-content/me0003-000831

Vanattenhoven, J., & Geerts, D. (2015a). Broadcast, Video-on-Demand, and Other Ways to Watch Television Content. In *Proceedings of the ACM International Conference on Interactive Experiences for TV and Online Video - TVX '15* (pp. 73–82). Brussels: ACM. 10.1145/2745197.2745208

Vanattenhoven, J., & Geerts, D. (2015b). Designing TV Recommender Interfaces for Specific Viewing Experiences. In *Proceedings of the ACM International Conference on Interactive Experiences for TV and Online Video - TVX '15* (pp. 185–190). Brussels: ACM. 10.1145/2745197.2755522

Waterman, D., Sherman, R., & Wook Ji, S. (2013). The economics of online television: Industry development, aggregation, and "TV Everywhere." *Telecommunications Policy*, *37*(9), 725–736. doi:10.1016/j.telpol.2013.07.005

KEY TERMS AND DEFINITIONS

Catch-Up TV: Service that offers recorded content from previous days based on an automated or editorial process of converting linear TV to on-demand videos.

Cord Cutters: Viewers that cancel their subscription and pay-TV services, usually opting for content available over the internet.

Non-Linear TV: A method based on using on-demand services to watch a show at any time allowing video replay actions (e.g. pause, fast forward, rewind, etc.). It is opposed to linear content broadcasted accordingly to a predefined schedule.

Over-the-Top (OTT) Content: Audiovisual content streamed over the internet, mostly using on-demand services.

Time-Shift: The ability to watch or replay a show after being broadcast.

TV Ecosystem: Social and technologic media landscape related to the audiovisual and TV field. Currently, this ecosystem includes industry players, managed operated networks, over-the-top services, multiple screens, and users with different viewing behaviors.

Unification of Content: Aggregation of content from different sources (TV and OTT) over the same user interface offering the same user experience.

User eXperience (UX): Is focused on several dimensions related with perceptions and emotions raised by the interaction with a product. Good user experience must encompass and enhance both the goals of the product and the users' needs.

User Interface (UI): A layer that allows the communication between a user and a system. It usually includes graphic elements like texts, images, buttons and icons within a surface like a screen or a page.

Video-on-Demand (VoD): Service that allows retrieving free or paid audiovisual content whenever required by the user.

Chapter 8

A Critical Review of Social Screen Time Management by Youngsters in Formal Educational Contexts

Enrickson Varsori
University of Minho, Portugal

Sara Pereira
University of Minho, Portugal

ABSTRACT

Several studies value the importance of technologies in everyday social processes, stressing loudly its positive effects for time control and management. However, the use of digital technology is increasingly said to co-produce the ways youngsters experience daily lives, as these are increasingly weaved in media hyperconnections, in several insidious and multiple forms, and in a continuous and enduring manner. This text focuses on the state of the art about the extension and nature of these co-productive processes, highlighting the effects of the technological means of communication on youngster's time representations and experiences, namely considering the social networks and other interactional devices that are now constituting increasingly more the individual identity, despite its intangibleness. The goal is to critically analyze the existing literature on time, technology, and youth, presenting its main contributions from a conceptual, methodological and practical point of view, including the use and the ways in media hyperconnections.

DOI: 10.4018/978-1-5225-8163-5.ch008

INTRODUCTION

The perspectives and understandings on the simultaneities of time in modern society (Araújo, 2007) include the analysis of transformations occurring in representations and often attributed to technologies. Several authors have devoted themselves to this phenomenon (Adam, 1990; Castoriadis, 1991; Zimbardo & Boyd, 2009), considering that the changes that have occurred in the last decades brought significant changes in daily life, including learning and education. In fact, time analysis constitutes a pertinent method of understanding modern society in many domains, including the processes of globalization, the penetration of technoscience and social imaginaries (Boltanski & Thévenot, 2006; Giddens, 1984). It is particularly important for analyzing youth cultures and how young people build their daily lives and attribute meaning. Agger (2011), for example, argues that the young people's rhythms of life are shaped by the their "ITime", a time that is attributed by the needs and desires of living the instantaneous present. Moreover, a wide range of authors (Manovich, 2002; Turkle, 2011) has proposed other approaches on the impacts of the progressive use of technologies as integral components of the self-identity.

Rivotella (2010) affirms that the current society is multi-screens, a consequence of the new literacies that reach youngsters in learning and socialization contexts. From the literature, it can be observed that the media, in general, including technologies, are a fundamental part of the discourses about contemporary social transformations of youth (Buckingham, 2008; Livingstone, 2002) and constitute important topics to study departing from the perceived experiences of the times and spaces in daily life.

Several studies address young people and their life experiences (Boyd, 2014; Pais, 2007; Selwyn, 2013). However, the literature on the representations of time in the use of these technologies and on how they shape the activities of these subjects in everyday life is scarce (Blanco, Miguel, & Arraz, 2016; Johnson & Keane, 2017). What we do know is that the reconfiguration of everyday life is often happening in the most diverse contexts of life and that the uses and perceptions of time are being shaped by the power of the technological culture construction (Fuchs, 2014; Lipovetsky, 2016), which is an agent of new cultures of time and temporality, against universes whose norms remain associated with linear and monochrome disciplinary models, as it happens in formal education contexts. To discuss these issues, in particular the technical acceleration diagnosed by Rosa (2015), it is crucial to problematize the time spent using the media, which is also part of young people's "daily budget" and become an extension of the continuous time non-use of media, along with other traditional time dividers, like work time, study time, among others.

In addition to the international contributions, studies on access to the media stand out. However, there is still a lack of indicators on the representations and literacies of young people in relation to technologies, which allow us to look at the current social moment.

Using a systematic review of the literature, this paper presents a critical review of the relevant contributions between 2007 e 2018 on prevailing modes of social use of time by youngsters in formal educational contexts, considering studies on the use of screen devices. Thus, it is central to reflect on the connection between the use of screen devices and the social use of the time nowadays, paired to the impacts caused by the continuous and excessive use of hyperconnection technologies in reference to the new social practices in everyday life.

The article is structured in six sections: (i) the Introduction, that provides a background to the topic of study; (ii) the Methodology, documenting the procedures of the systematic literature review; (iii) the Sample Characterization, describing the articles and proceedings under review; (iv) the presentation of main Results provided by the sample analysis, that culminate on (v) the Discussion, that addresses the main insights and limitations of these publications; and (vi) the Conclusion, that synthetizes the main contribution and opportunities to the current line of research.

METHODOLOGY

The systematic review was designed with the premise of using Scopus as the most extensive database of abstracts and citations of peer-reviewed literature, with in-depth studies published in scientific journals, books and congress proceedings. The initial research was driven by the search for keywords that emphasized the content to be analyzed, considering previous works on the subject "screen time" (Varsori, 2016; Varsori, Oliveira, & Melro, 2017). The following combinations of words were applied: "screen time", "social use of time", "education", "students", "youth" and "adolescents". The initial content analysis focused on the title, abstract, and keywords, considering only publications in the English language, namely articles and conference proceedings in the scientific areas of the Social Sciences and Humanities, and multidisciplinary fields combining Health and Socio-cultural indicators. Presentations, editorials, conference reports, program evaluation, unpublished manuscripts, dissertations and commentaries were excluded. The timeframe was between 2007 and 2018. Initiating in the year 2007 is because it can be considered a milestone regarding the insurgence of new digital technologies. With the launch of the iPhone by Apple Inc., a new understanding of touch technologies and User Experience (UX) created a significant impact on the world market. Also noteworthy is the launch, some years later, of devices such as the tablet, such as the iPad, also developed by Apple Inc.

The selection/exclusion of sources for the sample of the critical review was done through the filtering of the titles, abstracts and keywords of papers and proceedings, considering the most pertinent for the study. Articles that did not directly address topics associated with the focus of the research ("screen time") were dismissed. We also excluded studies that were not available online or were inaccessible for reading, such as corrupted links and documents not released in their full version.

After applying the exclusion criteria, the publications were examined by reading all the articles in full, followed by data coding and results analysis, using the software NVivo 12. The parameters for analysis aimed to verify and understand the type of studies that were more recurring in the timeframe defined for the systematic review. Therefore, the parameters (Table 1) for the classification and codification of the sources included the year of publication, country of origin, target audience, methods and techniques, along with the extraction of the main results provided by the sources. Using reference frequency, the data were codified with tags and categorized into nodes (categories) to identify cases that highlight relevant topics within the line of the research.

Table 1. Analysis parameters of the sample

Year	Country	Target Audience	Method/Technique
2009	Australia	Children	• Fitness test
2012	Brazil	Adolescents	• Interview
2013	Canada	Adults	• Physical measurements
2014	China		• Self-administered questionnaire
2015	Czech Republic		• School performance (grades)
2016	Estonia		• Diary
2017	France		• Literature review
2018	Germany		• Discourse analysis
	Iran		• Self-assessment
	Japan		• Diary
	Kingdom of Saudi Arabia		• Focus Groups
	Netherlands		• Survey
	New Zealand		
	Portugal		
	Slovakia		
	Spain		
	Taiwan		
	Turkey		
	United Kingdom		
	United States of America		

SAMPLE CHARACTERIZATION

A total of 94 articles were selected and imported into NVivo software. After a complete review of the titles, abstracts and keywords of these sources, the sample comprised a total of 47 articles, namely papers and proceedings. The sources excluded after review were related to specific health studies, and although including relevant keywords they did not match the purpose of the critical review. Regarding the origin of publication, the sample includes 13 countries, namely Australia, Brazil, Canada, China, Czech Republic, Estonia, France, Germany, Iran, Japan, the Kingdom of Saudi Arabia, the United Kingdom and the United States of America.

The indicators driven by the articles revised for the study of "screen time" as the key line of research were identified according to the recurrence of the themes (Figure 1). Four categories were delimited as the leading indicators for analysis: 1) Technology and media (n=45); 2) Physical activity (n=26); 3) Mental health (n=16); and 4) Socioeconomic status (n=13). Some articles are classified in more than one category and may address mixed audiences. Nevertheless, to facilitate the presentation of the results, the counts consider the categories and target groups separately. Within the sample, 14 publications (29.79%) work simultaneously with more than one target audience. Most of these studies are focused on adolescents (10-19 years old) – with an incidence of 36 articles (76.60%) – and children (0-9 years old) – covered by 21 articles (44.68%). Only one article (2.13%) targets an adult audience (over 20 years old).

Figure 1. Insidence of publications by thematic categories

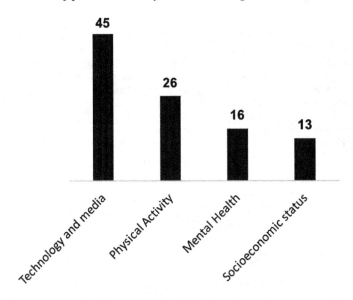

RESULTS

During the timeframe (2007-2018) applied to filter the sources of the sample, there is an increasing interest on the topics of study after 2013, with a peak of 16 publications in the years 2016 and 2017 respectively (*Figure 2*). When analyzing the origin of the publications, the United States of America (n = 17), Australia (n = 8) and Brazil (n = 5) were the most represented counties (Figure 3).

Figure 2. Incidence of publications by year

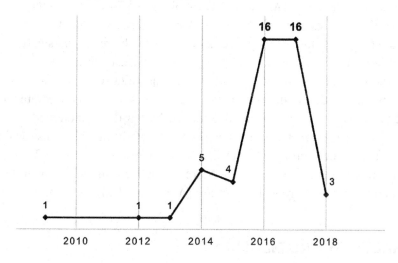

Figure 3. Incidence of publications by country

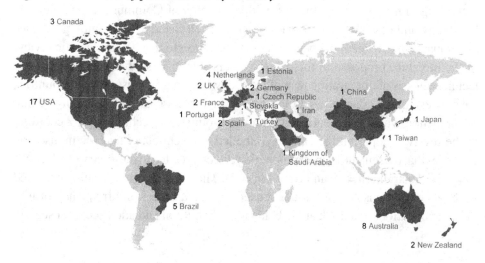

The main perspectives of researchers and study centers are translated in the four delimited categories for analysis (Table 2), which emphasize several relationships within the social processes regarding communication and information technologies towards establishing direct and indirect connections with digital technologies. Especially the screen, the key feature of televisions, smartphones, tablets and a myriad of other devices that afford indicators of the positive and negative effects of their presence in social contexts.

In this sense, the contributions of the reviewed texts were translated into the incidence of publications on each category, with a proviso that some sources may be classified simultaneously in more than one of the categories. As shown in Table 2, the most prominent theme was Media and Technology (95.74%), followed by Physical Activity (55.32%), Mental Health (34.04%) and Socioeconomic Status (27.66%).

Within the methodological approaches applied by the researchers in the studies under review, different sociological perspectives and data collection and analysis methods were identified, namely qualitative and quantitative. Some articles used a single technique of data collection, while other authors opted for the combination of techniques to corroborate and generalize results. Among the methods and techniques used, most articles conducted questionnaires ($n = 41$). Other authors chose qualitative methods such as focus groups ($n = 1$), discourse analysis ($n = 1$), ($n = 2$), interview ($n = 1$) and literature review ($n = 2$). More specialized investigations used field-driven parameters like physical fitness test ($n = 1$) and BMI measurement ($n = 1$).

TECHNOLOGY AND MEDIA USE

In recent years, the incidence of publications in the areas of Technology has been increasing in number. Nevertheless, within the area of Communication Sciences, Sociology and other Human Sciences, many articles study the technologies' uses and impacts in detriment of social issues. In response to that, the systematic review of the literature proposed in this paper gathers scientific studies that examine the technologies as an integrating part of everyday life. In this sense, several countries have invested and concentrated their research on the social understanding of that phenomenon which is accentuated with the evolution of technologies. According to the review sample, in the category labelled as Technology and Media use, the countries that present the highest production directly related to the topic were the USA ($n = 15$), Australia ($n = 9$) and Brazil ($n = 4$). The most recurrent results discussed in the investigations address issues related to media access and frequency of use. Some publications also look at the behaviors of children and adolescents at school.

Table 2. Classification of the categories and study parameters delimited by the nodes and the subnodes coded using NVivo.

Category / Study Parameter	Source	Reference
Technology and Media Use	**45**	**55**
Screen time	38	38
School performance	4	4
• Class size	1	1
Perceptions	2	2
Time management	1	1
Physical Activity	**26**	**40**
Body mass index	9	9
Diet	5	5
Obesity	5	5
Sedentary behaviour	4	4
Mental Health	**16**	**22**
Psychiatric symptoms	8	13
• Alcohol consumption	2	2
• Bullying	2	2
• Deficit and hyperactivity	1	1
• Drugs	1	1
• Immoral behaviour	1	1
• Problem behaviours	1	1
• Self-esteem	1	1
• Sexual intercourse	1	1
Sleep patterns	2	2
Social interaction	2	2
Socioeconomic Status	**13**	**13**
Family activities	5	5
• Parental control	3	3
• Leisure-time	1	1
Life satisfaction	3	3

Looking at the results on the use of ICT, several studies quested on how technology screens can offer benefits and harms, especially for the younger generations who were born in an age dominated by a range of technological devices of hyperconnection. The use time, commonly attributed as an indicator of social welfare, delimits whether it can be considered healthy or not. The World Health Organization, as well as the parameters adopted by the Commonwealth Australia and Center for Longitudinal Research of New Zealand, delineate that the healthy media use for children and adolescents is up to two hours. For the American Academy of Pediatrics, it is also necessary to limit the use of pre-bedtime technologies such as television and other devices.

Despite the recommendations on the limitation of media use time, several studies point to intensive technological consumption in everyday life. In terms of the results obtained, it is revealed that approximately 1 of 4 American children watch, daily, four hours of television or play video games (Gentile, Nathanson, Rasmussen, Reimer, & Walsh, 2012; Yilmaz, Caylan, & Karacan, 2015). Other studies indicate a direct relationship between technologies and the increase in suicide rates and depressive symptoms. Canadian studies reveal that children and adolescents in Canada can spend from six to eight hours in front of the screen, it being a practice associated with sedentary behaviors, weight gain and social well-being dysfunction (Cameron et al., 2016; Leatherdale & Ahmed, 2011; Leatherdale & Harvey, 2015). The time indicator in other countries is even higher. In New Zealand, the average interaction time with technologies reaches up to 11 hours per day (Kurek, Jose, & Stuart, 2017). The growth in television viewing hours by young people is also observed in India (Bapat, van Geel, & Vedder, 2017).

PHYSICAL ACTIVITY

The investigations that address indicators evaluating the relations of physical activity and the use of the media had a significant incidence in the results, totalizing 26 articles. The countries with the highest number of publications were the USA (n = 10), Brazil (n = 4) and New Zealand (n = 4). The publications based on indicators such as the behavior of children and adolescents is influenced by activities developed in school and leisure contexts, using Body Mass Index (BMI), diets and sedentary behaviors.

Sparse studies attempt to identify and understand how communication technologies influence school and leisure activities using the perceptions of education and health professionals. Physical activities have been neglected by students given the role that technology plays in their routines compared to structured activities such as sports and school games (Hyndman, 2017). The relationship that children establish with screen devices can also influence the way they perceive and create meaning in their daily lives. In this context, visual health indicators related to the brightness of the screen also play a crucial role in the sense that long-term use may lead to eye impairment and consequently affect school performance as a side effect (Chang et al., 2018).

Articles surveying the association between media use and physical activity show that children and adolescents are likely to have sedentary behaviors. As is well known, moderate and vigorous physical activity in daily life brings numerous benefits to young generations. Studies have shown that adolescents who engage in regular physical activity end up having less time to engage in screen-based sedentary activities and end up influencing their friends to have the same healthy behavior (Garcia, Sirard, Deutsch, & Weltman, 2016; Matin et al., 2017; Twenge, Joiner, Rogers, & Martin, 2018). Despite these results, other studies have shown that there is still a great cultural barrier to decrease the use of screen devices, for example, in Brazil, where a statewide survey shows that 1/3 of regular students spend an excessive period of time in front of the television, computer and video games screens (Munaro, Silva, & Lopes, 2016).

Correlations between a sedentary lifestyle and lack of activities are commonly established in several studies that use the BMI as an indicator related to activities on the screens. Research contributions point to the need for school-level prevention policies and social engagement with the community to achieve positive health outcomes (Carroll-Scott et al., 2013; Leatherdale & Papadakis, 2011; Magalhães, dos Santos, da Costa, Bones, & Martins Kruel, 2017; Suchert, Hanewinkel, & Isensee, 2016). The adverse consequences of poor diet and obesity are also directly related to the studies included in the category Physical Activity. The constant lack of energy and intake of food that have a high index of carbohydrates are addressed by studies that reinforce the need to think about juvenile overweight (Cameron et al., 2016; Morita et al., 2016). Sedentary behavior is often associated with problems of lack of attention and hyperactivity (Suchert, Pedersen, Hanewinkel, & Isensee, 2017) as well as other mental problems such as withdrawal (Schreck et al., 2016).

MENTAL HEALTH

Studies that cover mental health have been investigated in different fields of study, not being limited to Medicine or Health. Holistic perspectives combining different scientific domains flexibly shape the way topics and concerns are addressed regarding different lines of research. The direct relationships between technologies and mental health have been particularly studied in recent years. However, given the information overload in-built in the modern society, often the results depart from a bias that posits the use of media as harmful or unhealthy, thus being hardly considered from a neutral point of view. Within the sample, a total of 16 articles relate media consumption with mental health, being Australia (n = 3), the UK (n = 3) and the USA (n = 2) the countries that published more studies on the topic. Although mental health is a vast field, investigations have focused primarily on cases in which children's and adolescents' pathologies (depression, stress, addiction and anxiety) are associated with the use of technologies.

In several contexts, researchers have affirmed different perspectives on mental health and the use of technologies in everyday life. From the perspective of mental health outcomes, media education and the debate about contemporary standards have contributed to the understanding of how technologies affect daily life (Mavoa, Gibbs, & Carter, 2017). The regular use of technology can be positive for their recreational and informational potentialities (Przybylski & Weinstein, 2017). The usage typology of such technologies may determine, for example, that youngsters who have family consent in terms of access time to technologies have less aggressive behaviors (Yilmaz et al., 2015).

Regarding identity and behaviors associated with mental illness, studies indicate the need to verify how preferences of ICT usage influence the development of younger people (Kurek et al., 2017; Sanders, Parent, Forehand, Sullivan, & Jones, 2016). The correlation between sleep quality and the use of screens during night time have also been the object of study in several investigations. The use of screens, such as television and mobile phone, during the bed-time period is directly associated with sleep and development problems of children and adolescents (Cheung, Bedford, Saez De Urabain, Karmiloff-Smith, & Smith, 2017; Kubiszewski, Fontaine, Rusch, & Hazouard, 2014).

SOCIOECONOMIC STATUS

Socioeconomic status (SES) has been pointed as an essential factor in several investigations. The impact of SES is widely recognized by the attributions related to social stratification, economic status, health, and quality of life. The influence of SES on technology usage was presented in 13 of the 47 articles reviewed. The origin of publication was evenly distributed with a slightly higher incidence in the USA (n = 3) and Brazil (n = 2). The themes covered in the articles that used the SES as an indicator were mainly related to the types of activities developed at the family household, cultural issues about parental control over media usage, and also the effects of media usage on the school performance of children and adolescents from different social strata.

The influence of the household environment plays a key role in personal development for the healthy growth of children and adolescents. Based on the results, organized leisure-time activities (OLTA) are more frequent within families that support the direct involvement of young people, who in turn have higher SES (Badura et al., 2017). The relationship between parental control and media use has revealed important insights on children use practices according to media devices. In a study conducted in Estonia, mediation strategies performed by parents with children aged 0 to 3 years show that parental control effects on education, entertainment and behavior regulation (Nevski & Siibak, 2016). The perceptions about media usage also point out that young people who have time stipulated by their parents to use technology have better behavior during all development stages (Sanders et al., 2016). The effects of media on youngsters daily lives are measured by SES index parameters, such as the quality of leisure time (Carroll-Scott et al., 2013; Schreck et al., 2016).

DISCUSSION

The sample of articles analyzed (n = 47) contributes with a diverse range of parameters to be deepened and socially scrutinized. The importance of the debate on the status of technologies in everyday life makes it possible to highlight the related impacts of the devices that are daily used by the population. The themes addressed in this article depart from the conceptualization that the screen time exists in diverse contexts and practices. The recurrence of publications associated with this topic brings insights about what has been studied in the timeframe (2007-2018) that was delimited in the current systematic review of the literature.

In recent years, and according to the sample, there was an increase in the number of publications that focus on studying the use of the screens at home and in school environments by juvenile audiences. In this sense, from 2014 (n = 5) there was a growth of studies about digital technologies and social relations, with a peak of publications in 2016 (n = 16) and 2017 (n = 16). When looking at the recurrence of publications on this topic considering the origin of the sources, the USA (n = 17) and Australia (n = 8) dominate. Another important information to be considered in the discussion of the results is related to the methods and techniques for data collection and analysis. Most investigations use techniques that favor quantitative results (*Figure 4*), being the qualitative approaches negligible.

The quantification of results and the generalizations made based on inferential statistics are important, yet the number of studies that look at the perceptions and meanings that technologies socially and culturally provide to society is still lacking, especially regarding the new generations that live permanently connected to screen devices.

The themes addressed by the publications were classified in categories and subcategories that were tagged and sorted using NVivo software to facilitate the identification of relevant parameters for discussion based on the frequency of references. Hence, the four categories – Technology and Media use, Physical Activity, Mental Health and Socioeconomic status – have driven the discussion of results.

In detailing the results obtained, it is important to emphasize that the majority of the articles addresses the standards of what is considered healthy in terms of screen usage. Concerning the relation between Technology and Media, organizations such as WHO and AAP point out that the healthy use of screen technologies is a maximum of two hours a day. Despite this recommendation, the articles reviewed show that in practice average use time of young people is much higher in several countries. The WHO indicates that regarding the access to the computer, as the age increases there is also a significant growth in use time, exceeding the recommended two daily hours. Initiatives such as "The Campaign for Commercial-Free Childhood" cited by Sharkins, Newton, Albaiz and Ernest (2016) point to the lack of critical thinking about media education policies. The conscious use of technology is still far from ideal, although research is moving towards understanding the role of media in the lives of children and adolescents. Other investigations point out that it is necessary to reconsider school performance according to the role of technologies in everyday life (Busch et al., 2014; Chang et al., 2018; Cohen, 2018; Gentile et al., 2012). In general, the results of these studies consider that there is a lack of

Figure 4. Methods and techniques used in the publications

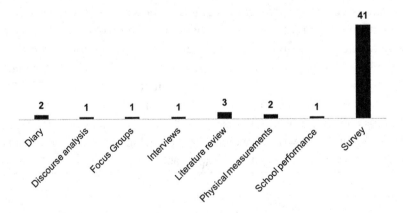

identification of contextual factors about how technology is used in everyday life. Only one publication of the sample assumes that the screen time indicator is not robust enough to allow for generalizations, even though they punctuate data that defy common sense assumptions and confirm others (Rideout, 2016). Despite this, the investigations disregarded the role of time management associated with the uses of the screen technologies, and the triggered by that use time as modern society is bound by processes of permanent management of the daily tasks that can cause symptoms of anxiety and other pathologies associated to the impact of pressure (or the lack of it) in the personal organization. The positive processes of technologies are evidenced in everyday life but ignore other forms that should be highlighted, which are labeled and mad in a generic way, such as the effects that extension of the use of technologies influences the decision making to do other tasks.

Regarding the articles related to Physical Activity and Mental Health, specific health indicators associated to the use of screen devices prevail (sedentary lifestyle, body mass index, obesity and other pathologic symptoms), ignoring the causes that activate and motivate those behaviors. In this sense, considering that the use time of devices such as the television, computer, smartphone, among others, may potentiate sedentary behaviors and other pathologies within younger audiences, it is important to study the discourses and perceptions related to such indicators.

Finally, regarding the Socioeconomic Status, parameters such as leisure time, family activities and parental control allowed us to contextualize how SES factors influence the different contexts and target groups of the investigations reviewed. From the results, we found a higher use time of media within families with lower SES, although the reasons for those rates are not clarified in the studies.

CONCLUSION

The systematic review of publications about screen time, between 2007 and 2018, allowed to unveil the scientific interest and projection of the subject in several fields of study. Despite the preliminary nature of the results, the metasyntactic outcomes put in evidence the complex interactions between screen devices and personal time management. The complexity of the subject in itself may constitute structural and conceptual limitations as research about the topic continues to grow. Another important insight is the fact that many investigations focus on quantitative studies rather than qualitative ones. This finding creates an opportunity for researchers to think about the scientific and educational policy possibilities for studies that contemplate a deeper and richer understanding of the emerging and complex phenomenon of how youths' time management impacts on the use of screens, especially in formal contexts.

Although there is a range of relevant indicators that can be extracted from the articles reviewed, further research is still needed to identify the educational factors surrounding the screen time problematic among juvenile audiences. Technological advances and the use of ICT at school can establish new ways of learning, new forms of student-teacher interaction, and additionally provide powerful tools for young people inside and outside the classroom. Hence, this brings opportunities for future publications to investigate the perceptions and causes of the technology use time impact on students, namely why they influence young people to seek the media as their main source of entertainment and social escape. In this sense, verify the potential of technologies use for the training and education of youngsters could be a new way to knowledge of screen management in contemporary society.

REFERENCES

Adam, B. (1990). *Time and Social Theory*. Philadelphia: Temple University Press.

Agger, B. (2011). iTime: Labor and life in a smartphone era. *Time & Society*, *20*(1), 119–136. doi:10.1177/0961463X10380730

Araújo, E. (2007). O desaparecimento do tempo nas sociedades modernas. In *Quando o tempo desaparece: Tempo e simultaneidade*. Porto: Edições Ecopy.

Badura, P., Madarasova Geckova, A., Sigmundova, D., Sigmund, E., van Dijk, J. P., & Reijneveld, S. A. (2017). Do family environment factors play a role in adolescents' involvement in organized activities? *Journal of Adolescence*, *59*, 59–66. doi:10.1016/j.adolescence.2017.05.017 PMID:28582651

Bapat, R., van Geel, M., & Vedder, P. (2017). Socio-Economic Status, Time Spending, and Sleep Duration in Indian Children and Adolescents. *Journal of Child and Family Studies*, *26*(1), 80–87. doi:10.100710826-016-0557-8 PMID:28111517

Blanco, S. R., Miguel, F. J. R. S., & Arraz, F. G. (2016). Los millenials universitarios y su interacción con el social mobile. *Journal of Communication*, 97–116.

Boltanski, L., & Thévenot, L. (2006). *On justification: economies of worth*. Princeton, NJ: Princeton University Press.

Boyd, D. (2014). *It's Complicated: The Social Lives of Networked Teens*. New Haven, CT: Yale University Press. doi:10.100710615-014-0512-3

Buckingham, D. (2008). *Youth, identity and digital media*. Cambridge, MA: MIT Press.

Busch, V., Loyen, A., Lodder, M., Schrijvers, A. J. P., van Yperen, T. A., & de Leeuw, J. R. J. (2014). The Effects of Adolescent Health-Related Behavior on Academic Performance: A Systematic Review of the Longitudinal Evidence. *Review of Educational Research*, *84*. doi:10.3102/0034654313518441

Cameron, J. D., Maras, D., Sigal, R. J., Kenny, G. P., Borghese, M. M., Chaput, J. P., ... Goldfield, G. S. (2016). The mediating role of energy intake on the relationship between screen time behaviour and body mass index in adolescents with obesity: The HEARTY study. *Appetite*, *107*, 437–444. doi:10.1016/j.appet.2016.08.101 PMID:27545672

Carroll-Scott, A., Gilstad-Hayden, K., Rosenthal, L., Peters, S. M., McCaslin, C., Joyce, R., & Ickovics, J. R. (2013). Disentangling neighborhood contextual associations with child body mass index, diet, and physical activity: The role of built, socioeconomic, and social environments. *Social Science & Medicine*, *95*, 106–114. doi:10.1016/j.socscimed.2013.04.003 PMID:23642646

Castoriadis, C. (1991). Time and creation. *Chronotypes: The Construction of Time*, 38–64.

Chang, F.-C., Chiu, C.-H., Chen, P.-H., Miao, N.-F., Chiang, J.-T., & Chuang, H.-Y. (2018). Computer/Mobile Device Screen Time of Children and Their Eye Care Behavior: The Roles of Risk Perception and Parenting. *Cyberpsychology, Behavior, and Social Networking*. doi:10.1089/cyber.2017.0324

Cheung, C. H. M., Bedford, R., Saez De Urabain, I. R., Karmiloff-Smith, A., & Smith, T. J. (2017). Daily touchscreen use in infants and toddlers is associated with reduced sleep and delayed sleep onset. *Scientific Reports*, *7*(May). doi:10.1038rep46104 PMID:28406474

Cohen, A. K. (2018). An instrumental variables approach to assess the effect of class size reduction on student screen time. *Social Science and Medicine*, *201*, 63–70. doi:10.1016/j.socscimed.2018.02.005

Fuchs, C. (2014). Digital prosumption labour on social media in the context of the capitalist regime of time. *Time & Society*, *23*(1), 97–123. doi:10.1177/0961463X13502117

Garcia, J. M., Sirard, J. R., Deutsch, N. L., & Weltman, A. (2016). The influence of friends and psychosocial factors on physical activity and screen time behavior in adolescents: A mixed-methods analysis. *Journal of Behavioral Medicine*, *39*(4), 610–623. doi:10.100710865-016-9738-6 PMID:27055818

Gentile, D. A., Nathanson, A. I., Rasmussen, E. E., Reimer, R. A., & Walsh, D. A. (2012). Do You See What I See? Parent and Child Reports of Parental Monitoring of Media. *Family Relations, 61*(3), 470–487. doi:10.1111/j.1741-3729.2012.00709.x

Giddens, A. (1984). *The Constitution of the Society: Outiline of the Theory of Structuration. Bulletin of the British Society for the History of Science* (Vol. 1). Cambridge, UK: Polity Press; doi:10.1017/S0950563600000038

Hyndman, B. P. (2017). Perceived social-ecological barriers of generalist pre-service teachers towards teaching physical education: Findings from the GET-PE study. *Australian Journal of Teacher Education, 42*(7), 26–46. doi:10.14221/ajte.2017v42n7.3

Johnson, N. F., & Keane, H. (2017). Internet addiction? Temporality and life online in the networked society. *Time & Society, 26*(3), 267–285. doi:10.1177/0961463X15577279

Kubiszewski, V., Fontaine, R., Rusch, E., & Hazouard, E. (2014). Association between electronic media use and sleep habits: An eight-day follow-up study. *International Journal of Adolescence and Youth, 19*(3), 395–407. doi:10.1080/02673843.2012.751039

Kurek, A., Jose, P. E., & Stuart, J. (2017). Discovering unique profiles of adolescent information and communication technology (ICT) use: Are ICT use preferences associated with identity and behaviour development? *Cyberpsychology (Brno), 11*(4). doi:10.5817/CP2017-4-3

Leatherdale, S. T., & Ahmed, R. (2011). Screen-based sedentary behaviours among a nationally representative sample of youth : Are Canadian kids couch potatoes? Screen-based sedentary behaviours among a nationally repre- sentative sample of youth : are Canadian kids couch potatoes? *Chronic Diseases and Injuries in Canada, 31*(September), 141–147. PMID:21978636

Leatherdale, S. T., & Harvey, A. (2015). Examining communication- and media-based recreational sedentary behaviors among Canadian youth: Results from the COMPASS study. *Preventive Medicine, 74*, 74–80. doi:10.1016/j.ypmed.2015.02.005 PMID:25732538

Leatherdale, S. T., & Papadakis, S. (2011). A Multi-Level Examination of the Association Between Older Social Models in the School Environment and Overweight and Obesity Among Younger Students. *Journal of Youth and Adolescence, 40*(3), 361–372. doi:10.100710964-009-9491-z PMID:20013351

Lipovetsky, G. (2016). *Da leveza: Para uma civilização do ligeiro.* Lisboa: Edições 70.

Livingstone, S. (2002). *Young people and new media: childhood and the changing media environment*. London: SAGE Publications Ltd.

Magalhães, R. L., dos Santos, N. S., da Costa, R. F., Bones, V., & Martins Kruel, L. F. (2017). Effects of two types of low impact physical training on screen time among overweight adolescents. *Journal of Human Growth and Development, 27*(3), 294–299. doi:10.7322/jhgd.118505

Manovich, L. (2002). Generation Flash. *Black Box White Cube, 2007*(2/10), 1–18. doi:10.1007/3-7643-7677-5_6

Matin, N., Kelishadi, R., Heshmat, R., Motamed-Gorji, N., Djalalinia, S., Motlagh, M. E., ... Qorbani, M. (2017). Joint association of screen time and physical activity on self-rated health and life satisfaction in children and adolescents: The CASPIAN-IV study. *International Health, 9*(1), 58–68. doi:10.1093/inthealth/ihw044 PMID:27836949

Mavoa, J., Gibbs, M., & Carter, M. (2017). Constructing the young child media user in Australia: A discourse analysis of Facebook comments. *Journal of Children and Media, 11*(3), 330–346. doi:10.1080/17482798.2017.1308400

Morita, N., Nakajima, T., Okita, K., Ishihara, T., Sagawa, M., & Yamatsu, K. (2016). Relationships among fitness, obesity, screen time and academic achievement in Japanese adolescents. *Physiology & Behavior, 163*, 161–166. doi:10.1016/j.physbeh.2016.04.055 PMID:27150913

Munaro, H. L. R., Silva, D. A. S., & Lopes, A. D. S. (2016). Prevalence of excessive screen time and associated factors in a school from a city in the northeast of Brazil. *Journal of Human Growth and Development, 26*(3), 360–367. doi:10.7322/jhgd.122821

Nevski, E., & Siibak, A. (2016). The role of parents and parental mediation on 0–3-year olds' digital play with smart devices: Estonian parents' attitudes and practices. *Early Years, 36*(3), 227–241. doi:10.1080/09575146.2016.1161601

Pais, J. M. (2007). Cotidiano e reflexividade. *Educação & Sociedade, 28*(98), 23–46. doi:10.1590/S0101-73302007000100003

Przybylski, A. K., & Weinstein, N. (2017). A Large-Scale Test of the Goldilocks Hypothesis: Quantifying the Relations Between Digital-Screen Use and the Mental Well-Being of Adolescents. *Psychological Science, 28*(2), 204–215. doi:10.1177/0956797616678438 PMID:28085574

Rideout, V. (2016). Measuring time spent with media: The Common Sense census of media use by US 8- to 18-year-olds. *Journal of Children and Media, 10*(1), 138–144. doi:10.1080/17482798.2016.1129808

Rivoltella, P. C. (2010). *A sociedade Multi-ecrãs: Das recomendações educativas à nova mídia-educação.* Retrieved from http://www.maxwell.vrac.puc-rio.br/acessoConteudo.php?nrseqoco=52514

Rosa, H. (2015). *Social Acceleration: A New Theory of Modernity.* New York: Columbia University Press.

Sanders, W., Parent, J., Forehand, R., Sullivan, A. D. W., & Jones, D. J. (2016). Parental perceptions of technology and technology-focused parenting: Associations with youth screen time. *Journal of Applied Developmental Psychology, 44,* 28–38. doi:10.1016/j.appdev.2016.02.005 PMID:27795603

Schreck, M., Althoff, R., Sibold, J., Giummo, C., Hudziak, J., Bartels, M., ... Rubin, D. (2016). Withdrawn behavior, leisure-time exercise behavior, and screen-time sedentary behavior in a clinical sample of youth. *Journal of Clinical Sport Psychology, 10*(3), 206–221. doi:10.1123/jcsp.2015-0031

Selwyn, N. (2013). *Education in a Digital World: Global Perspectives on Technology and Education.* New York: Routledge. doi:10.4324/9780203108178

Sharkins, K. A., Newton, A. B., Albaiz, N. E. A., & Ernest, J. M. (2016). Preschool Children's Exposure to Media, Technology, and Screen Time: Perspectives of Caregivers from Three Early Childcare Settings. *Early Childhood Education Journal, 44*(5), 437–444. doi:10.100710643-015-0732-3

Suchert, V., Hanewinkel, R., & Isensee, B. (2016). Screen time, weight status and the self-concept of physical attractiveness in adolescents. *Journal of Adolescence, 48,* 11–17. doi:10.1016/j.adolescence.2016.01.005 PMID:26854729

Suchert, V., Pedersen, A., Hanewinkel, R., & Isensee, B. (2017). Relationship between attention-deficit/hyperactivity disorder and sedentary behavior in adolescence: A cross-sectional study. *ADHD Attention Deficit and Hyperactivity Disorders, 9*(4), 213–218. doi:10.100712402-017-0229-6 PMID:28378132

Turkle, S. (2011). *Alone Together: Why We Expect More from Technology and Less from Each Other.* New York: Basic Books.

Twenge, J. M., Joiner, T. E., Rogers, M. L., & Martin, G. N. (2018). Increases in Depressive Symptoms, Suicide-Related Outcomes, and Suicide Rates Among U.S. Adolescents After 2010 and Links to Increased New Media Screen Time. *Clinical Psychological Science*, *6*(1), 3–17. doi:10.1177/2167702617723376

Varsori, E. (2016). *Os dispositivos-ecrã no quotidiano dos jovens portugueses: a mediação-ecrã no uso social do tempo*. Universidade de Aveiro. Retrieved from https://ria.ua.pt/bitstream/10773/17738/1/Dissertacao__Enrickson_Varsori.pdf

Varsori, E., Oliveira, L., & Melro, A. (2017). Jovens nos ecrãs : A fronteira invisível no quotidiano metodologia. In *CIBERCULTURA Circum-navegações em redes transculturais de conhecimento, arquivos e pensamento* (pp. 217–228). Braga: Edições Húmus. Retrieved from http://www.lasics.uminho.pt/ojs/index.php/cecs_ebooks/article/view/2803/2710

Yilmaz, G., Caylan, N. D., & Karacan, C. D. (2015). An intervention to preschool children for reducing screen time: A randomized controlled trial. *Child: Care, Health and Development*, *41*(3), 443–449. doi:10.1111/cch.12133 PMID:24571538

Zimbardo, P., & Boyd, J. (2009). *The time paradox: The new psychology of time that can change yout life*. New York: Free Press.

KEY TERMS AND DEFINITIONS

Daily Budget: A log or diary of the sequence and duration of activities engaged in by an individual over a specified period of time.

ITime: A time that is attributed by the needs and desires of living the instantaneous present.

Screen Time: Time allocated for the use of screen devices, usually attributed to the period of use of technology such as television, smartphone, or any screen device that allows man-machine interaction.

Socioeconomic Status: Social standing or class of an individual or group. In the chapter, it's used to describe the combination relating to education of family activities and life satisfaction.

Technical Acceleration: A term used to describe the speeding up of society in a self-propelling process, through of dimensions of social acceleration, regarding mechanical and manufacturing processes in the modern times.

Chapter 9
The Era of Hyperconnectivity:
Investigating the Times for PhD Supervision

Emilia Rodrigues Araujo

iD https://orcid.org/0000-0003-3600-3310
Universidade do Minho, Portugal

Kadydja Nascimento Chagas
Instituto Federal do Rio Grande do Norte, Brazil

ABSTRACT

This chapter presents and discusses the results of a qualitative study developed in Portugal and Brazil regarding PhD time and the scientific supervision processes, focusing on the manner in which digital technologies are used during the preparation time of doctoral theses. Based on the analysis of data collected by 20 semi-structured interviews with students and supervisors, the main advantages and disadvantages of screen time during scientific supervision are examined. In an academic and social context of high acceleration and time fragmentation, research presents valid development perspectives for a re-evaluation of supervision processes, more specifically in the current context marked by high presence of online platforms.

DOI: 10.4018/978-1-5225-8163-5.ch009

INTRODUCTION

How is PhD time being spent? How are digital information and communication technologies influencing the time available to carry out a PhD? How do supervisors and PhD students evaluate the use of these technologies? What advantages and what disadvantages do they attribute to screen time? These are the main questions to be debated in this text, which reiterates some discussions on the level of scientific supervision during the doctorate, whereas discussing some of the major changes introduced by digital media in the way time is experienced. Rosa and Scheurman (Rosa & Scheuerman, 2009, Rosa, 2010) discuss the acceleration trends in contemporary societies and in the increasing rise in the value of short and immediate time. On the other hand, Hassan (2003; 2009; 2010) examines more complex approaches to acceleration. He proposes that the centrality of immediacy is a by-product of an intricate transformation carried out by the development of digital media. For Hassan (2009), the internet provides a singular experience of time and nourishes other non-physical forms of coexistence and coexisting, although they can also bring about anomia and exclusion. It is factual that the theorists of enlarged modernity, globalization and postmodern societies identify themselves seriously with the need to consider the powerful effects and ramifications of technologies and science in the transformation of modes, lifestyles and work. Appadurai (1996), for instance, underscores the role of mediascapes in the construction of globalization, considering the interconnected platforms of human and non-human elements that persistently reconfigure social reality. Partially sharing this theoretical framework, other authors delve deeper into the field of academic time studies (Menzies & Newson, 2007; 2008; Ylijoki, 2010; 2013; Noonan, 2015; Smith, 2015; Spurling, 2015; Vostal, 2015) highlighting the effects of exceedingly time-transformative technological means on academic times. It is assumed that, along with the interest in studying working spaces and the manners in which technological platforms are taking over academic processes, there is a need to study time norms and time constraints, as well as type of experiences and their meanings (Muller, 2014).

A study such as this allows for the definition of strategies that can help institutions anticipate and cope with different ways of understanding and value educational work, especially at post/graduate levels. The need to grasp the manners in which time in academia is being instituted and made use of, especially given the increasing use of online means of communication, is essential. The transformation brought about by technologies and digitization are global. They spread into all directions and have influence on everything that happens. In the context of higher education institutions, they are modifying the manners in which students and teachers relate to time in many ways. They also deeply affect the way teachers and students build and experience time for learning processes. The aim of this chapter is to discern more accurately the way time is being utilized within the supervision processes, specifically how and to what extent are online technologies reshaping it and leading to different conceptions about the PhD itself. The profiles of the students attending PhD degrees have changed and multiplied. In some countries, such as Portugal and Brazil, the numbers of PhD students have increased exponentially, particularly after the Bologna reform (Pordata, 2018). Several authors have shown that there are many important implications of temporal nature which affect the time it takes to finish a PhD (Araújo & Bento, 2007). In the present situation, marked by the gradual incentive to reduce attendance times in supervision, and adopt increasing and diversified means of online communication, there is a need to think more in depth about what is happening to supervision practices concerning the uses of time and space. To learn more about how they are being moulded by online technologies and how they are perceiving these, it is also important to discern which strategies can be implemented to face the potential barriers and force higher education institutions to respond to this new order of technological times, without sacrificing the quality of the degree and the wellbeing of students and supervisors. Analysing Brazilian and European contexts, Bianchetti, Turnes and Cunha (2016) provided a seminal research on the topic of postgraduate education, arguing that the use of technologies may create the illusion of shortening the amount of time for personal contact between supervisor and student. However, it may augment the amount of time for supervision, as the range of requests made by students (part of them also demanded by institutions services) may get an increase. It cannot be argued that the increased use of virtual ommunication means during the time for the preparation of the thesis might also be a direct consequence of the development of the "industry", especially dedicated to innovations in academic work, including supervision and mentoring. Maor, Ensor and Fraser (2015) provide and in-depth analyses of the amount of literature produced concerning the use of remote technology devices in PhD supervision.

The authors assert that:

Doctoral supervision is an 'old profession' but new technologies may play a vital role in transforming traditional modes of supervision. Traditionally, the 'passing of the torch' of supervision wisdom has been conducted in an intuitive manner by professors who mentor students in an apprenticeship model to immerse them in their approach to research (Maor et al., 2015, p.2).

Maor et al. (2015) also proport, based on the work of Dron (2012), that pedagogy is inseparable from technology, when analysing the trends concerning PhDs. In his perspective, the use of technology is inevitably affecting the supervision process itself, therefore a new framework must be created and implemented that responds to the demands and quality of a PhD and allows for a better inclusion of remote technologies within the process. The authors say that:

Increasingly students are enrolled externally or from a distance and are not in the same location as their supervisors. Remote supervision creates new challenges and at the same time new opportunities to overcome the tyranny of distance through the creation of virtual spaces using web-based tools. Thus, face-to-face research training is giving way to a demand for flexible, available-at-all-times, distance-learning that is mediated by software that takes advantage of common computer literacies and is accessible regardless of the choice of device (Maor et al., 2015, p.3).

In fact, one of the most important changes taking place in a continued and irreversible manner is with regard to time conceptions and time management. New technological and digital devices have provided many different alternatives for performing the activity of supervision during online time. It is known from practice that PhD supervision, in almost every phase of the process, is being conducted through increasing screen times. It is assumed that screen time use allows students and supervisors to maintain optimal contact, despite the existing physical distance between them. Moreover, screen time also allows supervisors and students to attend to other demands during the same chronological time.

There are several research studies on the process of PhD supervision (Boud & Lee, 2008; Carpenter, 2012; Gray & Jordan, 2012; Borsen & Antia, 2013; Yarwood-Ross & Haigh, 2014). They analyse aspects such as the nature of the relationship between supervisor and student, the importance of institutional time regulations, the modes of planning and evaluating PhD progress and the supervision of work (Walker & Thomson, 2010). Other literature focuses more on prescriptions and guides for people to manage PhD demands and handle strict time constraints (Wellington, 2005; Taylor, Kiley & Humphrey, 2017; Wellington, 2010; Peelo, 2011; Wisker, 2012). However, few studies have been conducted which deepen the understanding concerning the process of completing the PhD and how new modes of ordering institutional time (which can include the amounts and the nature of the times ascribed by each supervisor to each thesis) are being considered within the process, as well as the institutional changes concerning the modes of organizing PhDs (plans, schedules, evaluation modes, calendars). Despite the absence of extact figures, the fact is that institutional and observational data concerning PhDs continue to reveal that many students have trouble with completion, with many dropping out prior to completion. Time planning and management appears to be a main variable which can be attributed to this issue. The use of screen time devices has been gaining momentum, with the promise of allowing people to master time more efficiently, allowing to avoid travel and other relocation costs, as well as other time barriers.

The goal of this text is to develop a better understanding of the times of supervision during the PhD, how they are being experienced, and what discourse is being generated to benefict PhD stundents in the future.

Concretely, this chapter addresses the following dimensions: i) the modes in which supervisors and students use screen time; iii) the advantages and the difficulties posed by the screen time both for supervisors and supervisees; and finally, vi) the type of strategies used to manage and master screen time usages during the PhD supervision. Along with the discussion based on the theoretical frameworks of academic times, the questions will be discussed in the light of the findings achieved in a study involving supervisors and supervisees in PhD programmes in Portugal and Brazil. This chapter is organized in four main sections: i) Theoretical framework; ii) Findings, ii) Discussion, and ii) Interrogations and other queries for the future.

BACKGROUND

The effects of information and communication technologies on modes and life have been a pivotal subject in several recent studies. Such studies align mainly with the theoretical paradigms that ensure the domination of science and technology in society. They share an optimistic point of view by analysing and anticipating the use of technologies of the most diverse types within the field of education. Typically, technophile visions advocate arguments that emphasize the benefits of technologies. They refer mainly to the potential they offer to deal with the increase in the volumes of information, to reduce the time spent on mobility, to foster innovation, to create new jobs and positively affect lifestyles. On the contrary, technophobic visions point to the perverse and unplanned effects of digital development. They have been shown to lead to the reduction of interpersonal communication, the increase in the impersonality of social relations, the increase in the intensification of work, isolation and unemployment, and the emergence of new forms of exploitation of individual time.

There is a growing debate regarding the interdependency of technologies and education which encompasses sociology, science and technological studies, as well as the disciplinary areas of technology, information systems and engineering. Some authors have glimpsed an almost radically new landscape in higher education, where technologies offer multiple possibilities for individual time management. This is favourable for autonomy and free will, leading to a healthier and sustainable environment in Academia. Taking advantage of time as a resource, and simultaneously ensuring the response to other needs, digitization in higher education is valued mainly because it reduces distances, broadening the scope of alternatives for individuals who may have to travel great distances, or simply are unable to physically attend the educational facility. Additionally, this is seen as a means for institutions to promote internationalization and increase the number of students. Most of these postures are rooted in the exaltation of the benefits that these devices offer or enhance, to dominate time and reduce waiting periods.

Studies indicate that social networks such as Facebook, Twitter and much of the online communication technology devices today are an integral part of the passage of time both in and out of the classrooms. Thus, these networks shape the practices as well as the expectations of students and teachers. The question is not, therefore, whether there is change, but how this is occurring, and what consequences these changes have on higher education. In fact, virtual learning environments, while allowing for the flexibility of time, also tend to reduce or be considered a face-to-face contact reducer (Schutte, 1997). Some authors have been pointing out the increasing scarcity of time in academy (Menzies & Newson, 2008; Yoliki, 2010; 2013; Noonan, 2015; Smith, 2015; Spurling, 2015, Vostal, 2015 Araújo, Oliveira & Bianhetti, 2014). Vostal argues that academy today is combining various processes of intensification and acceleration. Some of the main implications of this process end up reducing the time devoted to writing and reflection, an idea that coincides with that of other authors (Smith, 2015; Menzies & Newson, 2007; 2008), who speak of the effects on the reduction of time to read, to think, and to reflect. Yolijoki also agrees with the idea of the acceleration of academic time and declares that, today, research and academia are fundamentally based on projects with fragmented temporalities.

According to Nonaan (2015), the academy is being evaluated by its impacts, which makes deadlines and deliverables the most performative wars in academic daily life. Following this reasoning, the over presence of what one can name as "deliverables time", Muller (2014) examines the haste and acceleration researchers are facing throughout the course of postgraduate studies, which seem to be bringing in instability and exploitation of the time of junior researchers. Felt (2015) discusses academic time, criticizing the effects that acceleration has on the quality of participation in science and innovation. Spurling (2015) refers to the growing fragmentation of time at the academy, stating that education and research are valued in a differential way. Lima (2010) views knowledge as a public good in times of crisis as it increasingly responds to the temporalities of the market, which, in turn, demands for changes involving shortening the durations of training and supervision, at the expense of academic quality (Delamont, Atkinson, & Parry, 2004). Screen time devices such as those used in supervision work can be considered as ways to increase pressure on the supervisors and students to complete tasks (Bianchetti & Machado, 2005(At the same time, ICT can be considered as instruments of democratization, due to the fact that processes are more transparent and can be evaluated online by other participants, including colleagues and course directors. The PhD process is still documented as a solitary process, which lacks space and time for communication and debate, as has been found in several studies (Delamont et al., 2004; Lee, 2008; Zeegers & Barrona, 2012). In a very structured paper, Aghaee, Jobe, Karunaratne, Smedberg, Hansson, and Tedre (2016) suggest the use of online technologies to reduce the experience of anomy and build more collaborative and friendly PhD experiences. In their opinion, there is "insufficient online and structured information and lack of appropriate timelines" (Aghaee et al., 2016, p.364), in current PhD programmes, meaning "that the use of ICTSS in the PhD education may facilitate flexible and open learning and communication, which learners believe would be useful both on- and off-campus" (Aghaee et al., 2016, p.371). Despite signalling the highly controversial nature of the subject among students and supervisors, the authors presented a plethora of advantages and potentialities that the use of ICT can bring to supervision work, and part of them relate to time gains and time flexibility.

The authors say that ICT represents mostly the augmentation of control, organization and transparency as far as work planning, project development, timelines and milestones accomplishment are concerned. Therefore, they present some measures to reframe PhD time-space supervision with virtual supervision environments that maintain communication between the supervisor and the supervisee, reducing anomic sensations. Overall, these suggestions encompass the recommendations made in discussing the singular nature of the PhD supervision in academic contexts (McCallin & Nayar, 2012). The literature allows to define the dimensions of analysis concerning the use of screen time during the supervision of PhD theses, as follows: i) ways of usage of screen time; ii) advantages attributed to screen time by mentors and students; iii) disadvantages attributed to and evaluated by students and superiors; and iv) strategies of continuous availability, provided by access to screen time during supervision of the doctorate.

METHODOLOGICAL NOTE

This chapter is based on results from previous research carried out in Portugal regarding the experience of doctoral time (Araújo & Bento, 2007). It considers a more in-depth examination of recent research involving interviews of a group of Portuguese and Brazilian PhD students and their supervisors spanning different scientific areas. This research was designed to examine the modes in which PhD students and supervisors use time during the process of completing the PhD. Initially, the study encompassed the use of a survey conducted with supervisors and PhD students, and then a more detailed analysis through in-depth interviews involving the same respondents was used. Due to the low rate of answers collected until the present moment in the survey, this text only considers two types of information, as follows: i) interviews with PhD students; ii) interviews with supervisors of PhD students. The interviews were recorded and administered in person.

Sampling

Considering the goals of the study, variables such as scientific area, gender, race and age were not considered at this stage as being significant to delimiting the sample. In fact, as stated in the introduction, studies concerning this subject are scarce. We assume that an exploratory phase – opening new avenues for building a deeper understanding of the nature of time experiences during the preparation of the degree, and the importance that screen times and technological devices have – is essential for future study. In any case, a convenience sample was used following a snow ball process of identification. The qualitative principles of saturation and diversity (within the delimitation of those variables) were considered, as ways of exploring the importance of different variables in the shapping of the uses of screen time during the PhD. As stated, this chapter focusses only on the results obtained in personal interviews. In total, until now 20 interviews were conducted with 10 PhD students and 10 supervisors of different scientific areas in Portuguese and Brazilien institutions between October of 2017 and May of 2018.

Interview Guides

Among the several questions addressed in the interview guides, this text focused specifically on the collection of information regarding the use of screen time: modes of using it and the positive and negative aspects of access to screen time as understood by students and supervisors (Appendix). Personal interviews were carried out mainly within the university setting. After having agreed to participate in the study, both supervisors and PhD students were contacted again via email or phone to schedule the interview.

Data Analysis

After inserting information into a database (one for students and one for supervisors), data was analysed according to a set of dimensions, providing the tables shown in the text as well as the excerpts used to ilustrate each conclusion (Appendix). The process of analysing data was mainly dictated by the content analysis procedure, more specifically the thematic content analysis, as the dimensions (modes of using screen time, advantages and disadvantages) were taken as the major themes aggregating the answers to the questions addressed in the text.

Limitations

The sample is limited, considering the population of PhD students of the two universities, as well as the population of PhD supervisors. It was also noticed that written interviews provided contexts for achieving a higher level of information systematization. As Delamont et al. (2004) points out in the study of doctoral supervision, one important aspect to consider when basing the research on primary data, obtained through interviews and surveys, relates to the difficulties in apprehending actual social practices, as supervisors tend to answer according to what they believe will be valued by researchers, as opposed to their actual experiences. In any case, one should note that the results reveal high internal consistency, being in close correspondence with other studies. The aim of this text is to further investigate the phenomenon of screen time use during the PhD process.

FINDINGS

The results indicate that screen time is a part of the daily life of scientific supervision. However, both supervisors and students do not consider screen time as a replacement for face-to-face and personal contact. There are no standard practices or recommendations in doctoral programs regarding the use of digital media, both online and offline, during supervision. In addition, there is seemingly little space for discussing or sharing between professors concerning the experiences and challenges involved throughout the supervisory process.

Modes of Screen Time Use

Means and Tools

The first dimension analysed refers to the way in which supervisors and students use screen time. Most respondents claimed that they used screen time within disparate and variable ways during the day, week, or year. Email, Skype, Facebook, and WhatsApp are the most commonly used tools. The chance to update work and reply on time to students' queries is highlighted as a main advantage brought about by online means to the supervision process. Dropbox and Google Docs are also mentioned by some of the respondents. These items are easily usable for correcting written documents during more critical phases of the PhD process, such as project elaboration, the construction of data collection tools and data analysis. The phone is only used for interactions via WhatsApp and in cases of urgency. These technologies are said to tie relationships, allow direct connection and facilitate immediate communication.

Information concerning preferences in terms of media and online tools can be summarized as follows:

- Email/Online Documents (Dropbox, Google Docs)
- Chat/Instant Messaging (WhatsApp, Skype, Facebook)
- Video conferencing (Skype, WhatsApp)
- Collaborative platforms (University platforms)

The area of PhD study seems to have no influence on the type and the way that the students and supervisors use the supervision technologies during the doctorate. The same also applies to gender, number of students supervised, or age. Both supervisors and students speak with enthusiasm about the use of screen time which they use often. All of the interviews (20) reveal that screen time methodologies help in the process of supervision, but most of the participants say that supervision cannot be made only this way, that it needs face-to-face meetings, and this is an opinion expressed by respondents from social sciences and engineerings alike. On the one hand, it is apparent that each supervisor has her/his preferences as to to the means she/he uses, some of which technophilic. They use many kinds of digital means to supervise and keep in touch with their students and use these resources to send information, make comments and clarify any doubts or misconceptions within their students' work. Some refer that they "just keep in touch" with their students by having friendship links on Facebook and other networks or platforms, where they exchange information concerning everyday affairs, including politics and other issues. Others, despite saying they use online technologies, are apologetic about the use of technologies and the very exposure they allow or enable. Some supervisors speak about reducing purposively the use of online digital technologies (6 out of 10). Others admit they are having some resistance in changing and using remote, synchronous or asynchronous work platforms (2 out of 10).

Variability and Diversity in Use

The supervisors vary in opinion as to the degree of autonomy they expect from the students during the PhD process. This aspect is important in the use of screen time. Some supervisors expect a lot of autonomy from their students. Therefore, they help them to set up the goals and the objectives of the project. Then, they supervise according to this well-defined plan. Others foster little autonomy in their students and have a great need to determine and decide in detail what the students are doing at all stages of the PhD. In some of these cases, supervisors admit they feel the need to be in permanent contact with their students. Screen time, however, is said to be used in both situations, though differently. Most of the supervisors interviewed claim that they do not establish a precise schedule of meetings with the students.

They say they respond to the requests for clarifications made by students, according to their needs. This can happen even during the holidays. Supervisors say they do not have or follow a rigid planning as regards PhD supervision. The use of screen time is, therefore, strategic. It is usually motivated by the urgency of the situation, the interest in reducing the time spent on travel. The convenience in solving certain problems, which imply writing is also used as a motive for screen time. In any case, from the interviews with both students and supervisors, it is apparent that the use of screen time modalities does not provide a substitute for face-to-face meetings. One PHD student states that online plataforms helps making the writing process easier and more productive, since they allow the immediate evaluation of what is being written, permitting correction at the same time.

One thing is reading the text and say: "This idea is not okay". Another thing is to check the idea, to scratch it and see in concrete what in fact it does mean. (Interview, student, 1 PT).

Advantages

Time and Space Compression

Screen time brings together several features of modern simultaneous and networking time. It allows one to be in contact and work from a distance with many people at once. The PhD is becoming a more globalized degree where many people move from their homeland to complete a PhD programme. In this sample, a high number of students are now completing their thesis, in spite of having completed their initial PhD year in a different place or country where the PhD programme itself was offered. As a result, students claim that the use of screen time seems to be the best way to keep in touch while working on their PhD as it allows them to have feedback and guidance from supervisors, without having to relocate. Screen time allows PhD students to reduce the time spent on travel and expenses, allowing them to take part in the programme without having to move from their homeland. According to students, screen time has allowed them to ease communication, because:

The advantage is that, in case of email I can send an email at any time to her without restriction, there is not time zone, she will see the other day, she will respond (Interview, student, 8 BR).

Temporal Disciplinary Frame

The PhD can still be a very lonely process in all scientific areas, and screen time can be experienced as a time that creates the feeling of being permanently in touch. Even when not in use, one can experience the feeling of being in constant contact with the supervisors, as well as with colleagues. For students, the availability of screen time during supervision is a way to reduce the feeling of solitude during the trajectory, particularly when they are doing research in very specific and innovative topics. In addition, this "feeling of being in touch" can also help to keep focussed on their work, because they feel that supervisors can ask them to deliver outputs at any time. From this perspective, screen time helps to shape a rhythm for working, and for organizing time. Students claim that they struggle to use and manage time well during the day, saying that they often waste time doing unimportant things, often linked to internet searches. Therefore, screen time works as a sort of temporal disciplinary frame, supervisors use the screen time to send calls to students and ask them to submit the deliverables.

Gaining Time

Interviewees speak repeatedly about communication and how screen time strengthens the ties between supervisors and supervisees by facilitating contact. One of the biggest advantages of screen time, particularly focused on by supervisors, has to do with the rationalization of time. A PhD thesis involves many tasks, besides doing pure research. The PhD student is frequently stimulated to publish a certain number of papers prior to presenting the thesis before a jury. They are also advised to participate in seminars and congresses, as well as to respond to media inquiries. In an increasingly number of cases, PhD students are also expected to perform administrative tasks, and to assist with teaching. Disputable or not, most of these tasks are performed with the supervisor, further justifying the need for fostering contact between the two. In this line, screen time modalities of working are acknowledged as modes of time organization and rationalization. Additionally, screen time provides conditions for on line collaborative work between PhD students and supervisors. That is, more than facilitating oral interactions and the resolution of doubts, screen time also enables supervisors and students, individually or collectively, to give account of certain tasks in real time. The next excerpt expands on these effects and on how they are understood by supervisors:

Thus, to sum up, the main advantages identified by supervisors and students for the use of screen time are as follows:

- Time-space compression (6 out of 20)

- Contact speed (4 out of 20)
- Time rationalization and productivity in real time (5 out of 20)

Disadvantages

Time Non(Tuning)

Both groups agree that digital technologies are "great" and "excellent" in facilitating contacts, maintaining real-time correction, as well as in clarifying doubts, but they are also considered "insufficient" for effective communication when needed for the development of the thesis. Students and supervisors (7 out of 20) tend to argue that face-to-face meetings and environments which are freed from technological mediation are privileged time environments for interaction and learning during the PhD. They say they miss the interpersonal contact that screen time has reduced the need for. In fact, the lack or the reduction of face-to-face and personal communication is the most important negative point highlighted. Both supervisors and students claim that screen time methods can only be helpful once they are used in mindful ways. They say that before the use of these forms of mediation, supervisors and students need to be sufficiently socialized with each other. They need to be able to know and understand each other and to have incorporated tactical knowledge which is important to make communication flow when using screen time devices. Periods of face-to-face interaction are considered fundamental. Otherwise, screen time may not be satisfactorily utilized and may be a source of misunderstandings, potentially creating a negative effect on the entire PhD process.

A lot of people establish conversations over e-mail. Sometimes, there are people that talk through Skype. I do not like that very much. (...) I prefer the face-to-face contact, Skype allows to meet the other person, but it is not the best. (Interview, supervisor, 1 PT).

Time Disparity and Fragmentation

Two supervisors say that dealing with the excess and the diversity of requests/inquiries is the main negative point brought about using screen time during the supervision process. They also highlight the difficulty that online screen time creates, given the activities necessary during the supervision process, such as teaching, researching, and many others. Screen time brings about mental and physical fatigue, as supervisors feel they need to respond all at once to disparate demands. There are time conflicts which supervisors consider to be difficult to manage. In any case, supervisors consider that there is always a certain probability of losing time during screen time for PhD supervision, as online conversations are permeable to discussing other issues which are less important for developing the work. Supervisors say that this can happen mostly because during face-to-face communication, supervisors can experience difficulties being critical and may make more negative comments. Screen time is therefore an open space-time plane of ambiguities which characterize the power relations of the supervision relation itself (Manathunga, 2007).

Anyway, the advantage again is that we do not have to be close, it is faster, sometimes the supervisor is at home, or in another city and it is much easier to contact us. However, I like it more, at least in some phases, if I have the option to decide, I prefer face-to-face contacts, even because I think it is easier to feel, because sometimes through a message we do not understand well even the tone of the voice of the person with which we are talking, for me this is important, see if the person is agreeing, sometimes a look makes all the difference, so in this sense I prefer the face-to-face. But obviously it has many advantages as regards using digital media. (Interview, student, 5 PT).

The Problem of Constant Availability

Screen time presents itself persistently and continuously. It is built on a continuous emergent temporality. Anybody can access it and use it at any time. It thus creates an infinite time environment for interaction with no limits, schedules or boundaries for use. Supervisors and students (two) agree that they need to define their own screen time regulations, saying that technologies need to be controlled.

I only see there is a disadvantage if it is exclusive ...because it can not replace the face-to-face supervision. You have to impose rules, because sometimes the student takes a month to forward a particular document and wants an answer rigth a way. It is necessary to make a contract and agreement as regards the times to respond (Interview, supervisor, 9 BR).

Supervisors say that they sometimes feel that students are delaying their work and use the online contacts with the supervisors to avoid going deeper into the more challenging work; or they feel they are getting bombarded which constant communication and require time to concentrate on other tasks that are part of their responsibilities as researchers and teachers. It must be noted that supervisors claim that some students (not only PhD ones), when not receiving an immediate answer to their queries, try to contact them continually by repeatedly sending the same request, or trying to reach them via other means of contact. Supervisors mention several times the difficulties in managing "ever availability" (Zerubavel, 1981), giving account that some tasks, such as scientific writing, team meetings and laboratory tests are not entirely compatible with screen time. In this line, supervisors also consider that screen time can divert students' attention to less pertinent aspects.

The students participating in this study say that they are taking longer to complete the projects established and presented because they have difficulties in organizing time in a productive way. This issue of ever availability is more often a problem posed by the supervisors, than by the students. However, students also comment on the necessity to have some guidelines for using screen time during supervision and consider the compatibility of time with that of the supervisors.

Yes, for example. The fact that when we are writing, and if we are writing together, it is very common that the use of that writing is being monitored and we are being seen at the collaborative moment. It's one thing for me to read the text and say, "This idea is not right," it's another thing to tell the idea and stress it and scratch it and see in the concrete what it means. It's not just the very general idea that gets in the air and then we lose some time to know if it was a kilo or if it was something else. These platforms help identify exactly where I failed. It's almost as if I misspelled and I couldn't identify the error, and there the error underlined, it's concrete. This helps a lot when we are writing, ideas start to get more maturity, because we begin to see that all that logic of support and vision was better than the at this time. Especially since we've been seeing in the concrete, this whole process. From the point of view of writing, it is a very advantageous thing, we write in collaboration. (Interview, student, 1 PT).

The main strategies supervisors and students use to evade themselves from the potential ever availability are:

- Avoiding having skype or email-chat on
- Defining deliverables and deadlines
- Establishing priority online meetings
- Disconnecting online means during some periods
- Defining days for online meetings and collaborative work

DISCUSSION

The results assembled in the analysis support the understanding of PhD time as a singular learning period. The qualitative information collected in this study echoes the practicality and the usefulness of the online information and communication technologies during the supervision process. That is, concerning the extent to which screen time can affect individual time sovereignty, imposing their forms of implicit control and discipline with less pleasant effects on academic work and teaching settings. In fact, supervisors and students confirm that information and communication technologies produce an "emerging" time which can be highly beneficial during the PhD supervision due to its openness and flexibility. Nevertheless, they pointed out very firmly that screen time must not be understood as a condition to accomplish the PhD. In their view the elementary conditions for conducting a successful thesis are prior to the use of screen time devices. Skills, knowledge and a previous mutual understanding of expectations between supervisor and student are integral to the PhD process. They also consider that screen time should be used in conjunction with face-to-face communication between supervisor and student. Overall, there is a deep understanding that this relation comprehends fluxes and transactions of knowledge and wisdom, as well as of power that are maintained when using screen time. Therefore, there is a strong perception that this is a product of the use of technological means that provides the appearance of new forms of interaction between supervisors and students, which are extremely useful when they are geographically distant from each other. The study underlines the sociotechnical nature of screen time, insofar as individuals share the view that screen time devices are not something that all must adapt to. They are sought mainly as a tool that supervisors and students choose to use during the different phases of the PhD. The effects that it can produce depend on having and sharing a range of different skills that contribute to obtain the desired advantageous implications. Time mastering, time rationalization, collaborative work and communication flows are some of the main advantages pointed out. Overall, the data shows a conflict between the homogeneous time of the clock and the diverse timeless time produced during the thesis itself. In this sense, part of the interviwees mention that ICT during supervision process can bring about the risk of wasting time (4 of 20). Supervisors share the view that screen time may be a source of distraction and time loss. Besides, they also consider that it may lead to feelings of ever availability. The data reveals important conclusions about collaboration in science and the importance that time, and temporalization have in the generation of coherence and consistency of this collaboration. Each scientific area is involved in a time culture. Its members share patterns about the expected durations of activities or processes, as well as about the importance and the mode of relationship with the deadlines, deliverables and milestones. The data collected demonstrates that the effects of screen time in supervision (synchronous or asynchronous) depend, amongst other variables, on personal proximity as well as on the interpersonal contacts that occur prior to its usages, which are also constitutive of time cultures. This conclusion is in line with other studies which highlight the value of physical proximity and of interpersonal knowledge in academic collaborative work (Boschma, Marrocu & Paci, 2015). It shows that the doctorate is a process deeply ingrained in the development of tacit knowledge, requiring proximity as a source of trust, which will provide the context for information and interaction to flow.

In sum, interviews underscore the following advantages of using screen time, as it:

- Eases communication
- Lessens waiting times in the resolution of doubts
- Increases the possibility of verifying records
- Enables interaction between online participants, for writing articles or assembling projects
- Allows people to keep in touch
- Increases flexibility
- Increases the difficulty of imposing limits on what is or should be the focus of attention

The disadvantages identified are as follows:

- Makes communication difficult
- Can increase the waiting times depending on the type and diversity of information
- Can trivialize the importance of contacts in the supervisory context
- Does not allow the same type of interaction/personal verification found in face-to-face contexts
- Increases distance and impersonality
- Increases the range of simultaneous requests
- Requires a lot of discipline
- Increases variation and dispersion

SOLUTIONS AND RECOMMENDATIONS

Supervision is a time of intersection of several temporalities of objective and subjective nature. Recent years have witnessed an increasing relevance of studies that explain or promise to help teachers to accomplish the supervision work and lead students to successfully finish their theses. Important institutional discourses in higher education have been underlining the role that mobile communication devices have on the transformation of learning processes. Supervision work has a prominent role in thesis development and conclusion. Therefore, improvements on the use of online communication devices between supervisors and students may represent a way of ameliorating the supervision relationships by making them more effective in academic contexts. The use of screen time for doctoral purposes is part of the future of this level of education. Students and teachers can no longer resist to it, as post graduation is changing from within, demanding new educational practices that count with e/learning as a means of overcoming distance, responding to student needs and rationalizing equipment usages. Therefore, this singular type of time-space represents new challenges for doctoral education within an evolving technological context increasingly interweaved with hypermedia connections (Hassan, 2010) and increasing academic acceleration (Slaugther & Leslie, 1999, García, 2010). This matter has generated some indifference on the part of the regulatory institutions and the universities themselves to deal with the dilemmas of postgraduate education in the context of network societies (Albion & Erwee, 2011; Andrew, 2012). Information and communication technologies and, with them, a vast array of other devices, are transforming the professions, especially in relation to education and research, as well as the learning processes themselves, as they are also bringing about new forms of division of academic work, and new postures concerning the value and the goals of a PhD degree. This revolution requires adaptive models of intervention, but also brings awareness to the losses and gains that it implies, in relation to the objectives or ideologies of trainingIt is time to behave in psychological and subjective dimensions, in addition to the chronometric and quantitative dimensions. This means that the use of screen time cannot be understood in a deterministic or neutral way. In the relationship with the scientific and organizational cultures, screen time can be effective and mean resolution of the problems that still exist in supervision of PhDs.

These problems are dynamic and depend from the life circumstances, aspirations and pressures that students and supervisors feel. In fact, supervision is an activity that is easily taken for granted and can often bring about a lack of recognition. The data collected shows that students experience difficulties in organizing time and in the preparation of the projects that are reflected throughout doctoral processes, especially during the thesis. These issues are not resolvable using screen time alone, although this can make a difference in some cases. Scientific supervision remains a very individualized model of work, in which each single studenthas his/ her supervisor. Collaborative supervision is still looked upon with suspicion. At a time when there are more advisors and in which screen time becomes a tool with great potential, it is important to review the format of supervision times, making them more collaborative and open to external mediation. Students can benefit greatly from reviewing their projects collectively, having the chance to obtain feedback from more than one supervisor during the process. Academic mediation can foster the creation of an institutional frame adapted to deal with these new challenges, including the ways of improving the use of screen time.

As data indicate, the PhD process is an important phase in the lives of doctoral students. However, it is also highly valuable for present day academy, as a significant part of the innovatory research is due to PhD theses. As with the overall system of science, technology and higher education have coupled PhD graduation with other institutional research-interests. At the same time, it has increased the working pressure in the form of impact evaluation. Therefore, it is also important to investigate how and to what extent screen time acts as a source of transparency. It can also be a source of increasing pressure on students, from the side of the supervisors interested in the completion of a thesis. Regarding screen time, it is necessary to rethink the modalities of record keeping of meetings and of other useful information for the resolution of any difficulties. In this sense, it is important that the expansion of the modalities of online supervision be not mere means of evaluation, rationalization of time and resources and of standardization. It needs to contribute to the effective generation of diversity and improvement of the quality of the work and of the settings of work and of learning. Therefore, we found that institutions need to:

- Evaluate the forms and methodologies imposed and followed in different institutions
- Improve case studies
- Evaluate the form and the operationalisation of the doctoral schools and their relationship with supervision patterns, traditional and "modern"
- Evaluate and make available to supervisors tools and technological devices that privilege interaction and feedback
- Prepare students to make use of screen time in a manner where supervisor time is not dispersed and fragmented

FUTURE RESEARCH DIRECTIONS

The data presented in the text, not dissimilar from data encountered in other studies (e.g. Maor et al., 2015), indicates that further research is required to foster the use of technologies during the doctoral process for both students and supervisors. Future studies should provide an opportunity to examine in further depth the types of technologies in use, as well as strategies for mastering optimal time use and communication. It would also be relevant to go into more depth regarding the psychological and emotional characteristics of PhD students and that of their supervisors, assuming these are variables which affect the perception of time and, therefore, the uses of screen time technologies. On a more practical vein, this widening of the study would allow for planning and organizing PhD courses in a manner that technologies serve the interests of all involved, avoiding the risk of being sources of manipulation, distraction or loss of time. This is a complex endeavour, as it demands for an in-depth study of the demands and requisites of each PhD and the ways supervisors can effectively use technological devices, in a manner they can help overpass the solitude and time discrepancies that exist in the supervision processes. Eventually, it seems important to refer, as stated by Frigotto (1993, 1996) and Frigotto & Ciavatta (2001), that education is a crossing field that demands accurate analysis concerning time experiences and time mastering, as they can cause deep interferences and impacts on the learning process, depending on the way it is managed and conceptualized. A PhD is mainly a time experience, based on continuous and constant formulations, advances and drawbacks, strongly heterogeneous and variable along the years. The use of technology devices in learning processes is still in its infancy. It is important to research more in-depth how cultures affect that use, and to what extent supervisors and PhD students are engaged in that process. This suggestion would imply to interrogate also what universities want from a PhD thesis in the context of hyper connectivity.

CONCLUSION

The objectives of this chapter were threefold: i) analyse why, how and to what extent PhD students and their supervisors use screen time during scientific supervision; ii) study to what extent and how screen time creates a singular supervision time-space; and iii) examine to what extent and how this specific type of time-space represents new challenges for doctoral education within an increasing technological context. Supervision during the PhD time are complex matters that have attracted increasing attention for some years, as new changes have occurred within education and learning at postgraduate level, without changing too much in the experience of the PhD marked by solitude and significative unsuccess. The PhD process differs across scientific areas, and organisational strategies have an important role in promoting changes in the process of doing and supervising the PhDs. However, studies still document the singularity of this time, considering the individual struggles it brings about, both on the side of the student and on the side of the professor and supervisor. As indicated, when giving account of the interviews' trajectories, supervision is often naturalized and, at the same time hidden, or underestimated when compared with other times ascribed to teaching activities. What this paper conveys is the high importance of tackling supervision time, addressing more accurately its characteristics, and the ways it is conditioned and shaped using technological means. Moreover, it shows some of the important representations and resistances that both students and teachers have about using these devices during the process of PhD preparation.

It was ascertained that students and supervisors use screen times in several moments of the thesis preparation, without any order or sequence. Despite assuming to be familiarized with the use of these technological devices and having incorporated them in their daily practices (they are active in social networks, they are connected through skype and have videoconference equipment at their disposal), they show significative resistance to the use of distance learning devices. This needs to happen in conjunction with physical/personal (touchable) proximity, which is becoming increasingly difficult to have, considering the changes in course towards new forms of distance learning and working. This conclusion is valid for all the interviews irrespectively of nationality, organization or scientific area. What is said about the power of screen time to create singular nature of supervision relationships is of crucial importance here, as interviewees - both students and supervisors - say that screen time requires change and adaptation to their routines and ways of behaving. This is indicative of the fact that part of the disadvantages, as expressed by supervisors and students concerning the use of screen time technologies are more due to conformism and forms of resistance to change, than due to intrinsic negative aspects brouhght about by those devices. Interestingly, the results also indicate that users of these tools end up pointing to the need they feel of increasing the organization and the discipline of time, in order to resist and avoid the temptation to be always available, or to feel the need to respond all the time to requests that fall in the mail or are flagged by Skype, email, or Whatsapp to students and advisors.

REFERENCES

Abbott, C. (2003). *ICT: Changing education*. New York: Routledge.

Aghaee, N. (2013). Finding potential problems in the thesis process in higher education: Analysis of e-mails to develop a support system. *Education and Information Technologies*, *20*(1), 1–16.

Aghaee, N., Hansson, H., Tedre, M., & Drougge, U. (2014). Learners' perceptions on the structure and usefulness of e-resources for the thesis courses. *European Journal of Open, Distance and E-Learning, 17*(1), 154–171. Retrieved from: https://www.degruyter.com/downloadpdf/j/eurodl.2014.17.issue-1/eurodl-2014-0011/eurodl-2014-0011.pdf

Aghaee, N., Jobe, W. B., Karunaratne, T., Smedberg, A., Hansson, H., & Tedre, M. (2016). Interaction gaps in PhD education and ICT as a way forward: Results from a study in Sweden. *International Review of Research in Open and Distributed Learning*, *17*(3), 360–383. doi:10.19173/irrodl.v17i3.2220

Aghaee, N., Karunaratne, T., Smedberg, A., & Jobe, W. (2015). Communication and collaboration gaps among phd students and ict as a way forward: results from a study in sweden. In *Proceedings of E-Learn: World Conference on E-Learning in Corporate, Government, Healthcare, and Higher Education 2015* (pp. 237-244). Association for the Advancement of Computing in Education (AACE). Retrieved from: https://www.learntechlib.org/primary/p/152016/

Albion, P., & Erwee, R. (2011). Preparing for doctoral supervision at a distance: Lessons from experience. In Proceedings of Society for information technology & teacher education international conference 2011 (pp. 82-89). Academic Press.

Andrew, M. (2012). Supervising doctorates at a distance: Three trans-Tasman stories. *Quality Assurance in Education, 20*(1), 42–53. doi:10.1108/09684881211198239

Appadurai, A. (1996). *Modernity at large: cultural dimensions of globalization.* University of Minnesota Press.

Araújo, E., & Bento, S. (2007). *Como fazer um doutoramento? Práticas institucionais e gestão do tempo.* Porto: Ecopy.

Araújo, E., Oliveira, A., & Bianchetti, L. (2014). *Formação do investigador: reflexões em torno da escrita/pesquisa/ autoria e orientação.* Braga: CECS - Centro de Estudos de Comunicação e Sociedade Universidade do Minho / Braga. Portugal e CED - Centro de Ciências da Educação Universidade Federal de Santa Catarina / Florianópolis-SC, Brasil. Retrieved from: https://docs.wixstatic.com/ugd/18e49d_ddbc2b1dbe624a359281ea921dec573e.pdf

Bianchetti, L., & Machado, A. (2005). *Orientação/escrita de dissertações e teses em questão: produção científica e estratégias de orientadores e Coordenadores de PPGEs. Relatório final de projeto do CNPq, Edital Universal (Processo 479166/01-3).* Florianópolis: PPGE/UFSC.

Bianchetti, L., Turnes, L., & Cunha, R. (2016). O tempo de doutorado e o papel das TICS, questões para a pesquisa e análise. *Conjetura. Filosofia e Educação, 3,* 628–644.

Borsen, T., Antia, A. N., & Glessmer, M. S. (2013). A case study of teaching social responsibility to doctoral students in the climate sciences. *Science and Engineering Ethics, 19*(4), 1491–1504. doi:10.100711948-013-9485-9 PMID:24272332

Boschma, R., Marrocu, E., & Paci, R. (2015). Symmetric and asymmetric effects of proximities. The case of M&A deals in Italy. *Journal of Economic Geography, 16*(2), 505–535. doi:10.1093/jeg/lbv005

Boud, D., & Lee, A. (Eds.). (2008). *Changing practices of doctoral education*. London: Routledge.

Carpenter, J. (2012). Researchers of tomorrow: The research behaviour of generation y doctoral students. *Information Services & Use, 32*(1), 3–17. doi:10.3233/ISU-2012-0637

Delamont, S., Atkinson, P., & Parry, O. (2004). *Supervising the doctorate: A guide to success*. United Kingdom: McGraw-Hill Education.

Dron, J. (2012). The pedagogical-technological divide and the elephant in the room. *International Journal on E-Learning, 11*(1), 23–38.

Felt, U. (2015). *The temporal choreographies of participation: Thinking innovation and society from a time-sensitive perspective*. Vienna: Department of Studies of Science and technology, University of Vienna. Retrieved from: https://www.researchgate.net/publication/270451756_The_temporal_choreographies_of_participation_Thinking_innovation_and_society_from_a_time-sensitive_perspective

Frigotto, G. (1993). *A produtividade da escola improdutiva: um (re) exame das relações entre educação e estrutura econômico-social capitalista* (4th ed.). São Paulo: Cortez.

Frigotto, G. (1996). *Educação e a crise do capitalismo real* (2nd ed.). São Paulo: Cortez.

Frigotto, G., & Ciavatta, M. (Eds.). (2001). Teoria e educação no labirinto do capital. Petrópolis, RJ: Vozes.

García, T. (2010). La mercantilización de la educación. *Revista Electrónica Interuniversitaria de Formación del Profesorado, 13*(2), 16–21.

Gray, P. W., & Jordan, S. R. (2012). Supervisors and academic integrity: Supervisors as exemplars and mentors. *Journal of Academic Ethics, 10*(4), 299–311. doi:10.100710805-012-9155-6

Hassan, R. (2003). Network time and the new knowledge epoch. *Time & Society, 12*(2/3), 225–241.

Hassan, R. (2009). *Empires of speed: Time and the acceleration of politics and society*. Leiden, Boston: Brill. doi:10.1163/ej.9789004175907.i-254

Hassan, R. (2010). Social acceleration and the network effect: A defence of social "science fiction" and network determinism. *The British Journal of Sociology, 61*(2), 356–374. doi:10.1111/j.1468-4446.2010.01316.x PMID:20579058

Lima, L. (2010). Investigação e investigadores em educação – Anotações críticas. *Sísifo: Revista de Ciências da Educação, 12*, 63–72.

Manathunga, C. (2007). Supervision as mentoring: The role of power and boundary crossing. *Studies in Continuing Education, 29*(2), 207–221. doi:10.1080/01580370701424650

Maor, D., Ensor, J., & Fraser, B. (2015). *Doctoral supervision in virtual spaces: a review pf wev-basedtools to develop collaborative supervision*. Retrived from: https://espace.curtin.edu.au/bitstream/handle/20.500.11937/41864/236299. pdf?sequence=2

McCallin, A., & Nayar, S. (2012). Postgraduate research supervision: A critical review of current practice. *Teaching in Higher Education, 17*(1), 63–74. doi:10.10 80/13562517.2011.590979

Menzies, H., & Newson, J. (2007). No time to think: Academics' life in the globally wired university. *Time & Society, 16*(1), 83–98. doi:10.1177/0961463X07074103

Menzies, H., & Newson, J. (2008). Time, stress and intellectual engagement in academic work: Exploring gender difference. *Gender, Work and Organization, 15*(5), 504–522. doi:10.1111/j.1468-0432.2008.00415.x

Muller, R. (2014). Racing for what? Anticipation and acceleration in the work and career practices of academic life science postdocs. *Qualitative Social Research, 15*(3). Retrieved from: http://www.qualitative-research.net/index.php/fqs/article/view/2245/3726

Noonan, J. (2015). Thought-time, money-time and the conditions of free academic labour. *Time & Society, 24*(1), 109–128. doi:10.1177/0961463X14539579

Peelo, M. (2011). *Understanding Supervision and the PhD*. A&C Black. Retreived from: http://www.siecon.org/online/wp-content/uploads/2014/10/Boschman-Marrocu-Paci-106.pdf

Rosa, H. (2010). *Alienation and acceleration: towards a critical theory of late-modern temporality*. Malmo: NSU Press.

Rosa, H., & Scheuerman, W. E. (2009). *High-speed society: Social acceleration, power and modernity*. Philadelphia: Penn State University Press.

Schutte, J. (1997). *Virtual teaching in higher* education: *The new intellectual. superhighway or just another traffic jam?* Retrieved from: https://pdfs.semanticscholar.org/6ad5/30196f652b9b480ad38d50eacd8b4cdbb7b3.pdf

Slaugther, S., & Leslie, L. (1999). *Academic capitalism: Politics, policies, and the entrepreneurial university*. Baltimore, MD: John Hopkins University Press.

Smith, S. (2015). Multiple temporalities of knowing in academic research. *Social Sciences Information. Information Sur les Sciences Sociales*, *54*(2), 2149–2176. doi:10.1177/0539018414566421

Spurling, N. (2015). Differential experiences of time in academic work: How qualities of time are made in practice. *Time & Society*, *24*(3), 1–23. doi:10.1177/0961463X15575842

Taylor, S., Kiley, M., & Humphrey, R. (2017). *A handbook for doctoral supervisors*. New York: Routledge. doi:10.4324/9781315559650

Vostal, F. (2015). Academic life in the fast lane: The experience of time and speed in British academia. *Time & Society*, *24*(1), 71–95. doi:10.1177/0961463X13517537

Walker, M., & Thomson, P. (Eds.). (2010). *The Routledge doctoral supervisor's companion: supporting effective research in education and the social sciences*. Routledge. doi:10.4324/9780203851760

Wellington, J. (2005). *Succeeding with your doctorate*. London: Sage. doi:10.4135/9781849209977

Wellington, J. (2010). *Making supervision work for you: a student's guide*. London: Sage.

Wisker, G. (2012). *The good supervisor: supervising postgraduate and undergraduate research for doctoral theses and dissertations*. London: Macmillan International Higher Education. doi:10.1007/978-1-137-02423-7

Yarwood-Ross, L., & Haigh, C. (2014). As others see us: What PhD students say about supervisors. *Nurse Researcher*, *22*(1), 38–43. doi:10.7748/nr.22.1.38.e1274 PMID:25251819

Ylijoki, O. (2010). Future orientation in eGroup Leadersodic labour: Short-term academics as a case in point. *Time & Society*, *19*(3), 365–386. doi:10.1177/0961463X10356220

Ylijoki, O. (2013). Boundary-work between work and life in the high-speed university. *Studies in Higher Education*, *38*(2), 242–255. doi:10.1080/03075079.2011.577524

Zeegers, M., & Barron, D. (2012). Pedagogical concerns in doctoral supervision: A challenge for pedagogy. *Quality Assurance in Education*, *20*(1), 20–30. doi:10.1108/09684881211198211

Zerubavel, E. (1981). *Hidden rhythms: Schedules and calendars in social life.* Chicago: Chicago University Press.

KEY TERMS AND DEFINITIONS

BR: Brazil.

Deliverables Time: Time marked by the permanent need to present deliverables.

Ever Availability: Be permanently available. Lack of spatial and temporal boundaries or boundaries that prevent contact from others.

Lost Time: Time evaluated as ineffective. Does not achieve a goal.

PT: Portugal.

Screen Time: Amount and type of time passed on a screen.

Supervision Time: Time dedicated to supervising PhD thesis.

Time Acceleration: Intensifying the demands of activities for the same time interval.

Time Continuity: Subjective experience of the passage of time. Stability.

Time to PhD: Preparation time of PhD thesis.

APPENDIX

Table 1. Synthesis of the information provided by content analysis

Interview	Uses and Type	Advantages	Disadvantages
Supervisor - 1 Portugal	Email and skype. Not so frequent.	Time compression	Time losses
Supervisor - 2 Portugal	Email. Often	Temporal disciplinary frame	Time disparity and fragmentation
Supervisor - 3 Portugal	All the technologies. Be online. Very frequent	Time compression	Time disparity and fragmentation
Supervisor - 4 Portugal	Very frequent. Meetings. Skype more usual. Very frequent	Time gaining	Time losses
Supervisor - 5 Portugal	Email.very often	None	Time non(tuning)
Supervisor – 6 Brasil	Rarely. Most of the students are at the university. Very useful, to send messages and information	Time gaining	Time losses
Supervisor – 7 Brasil	Email, skype. O facebook. Very frequent	Time gaining, communication, distance	No
Supervisor– 8 Brasil	E-mail, skype, facebook, whatsapp. Very frequent	Time gaining, easiness	Time des(syntony)
Supervisor – 9 Brasil	Email and skype. Not so frequent.	Time and space compression	Constant availability
Supervisor – 10 Brasil	Email, facebook, hangout, whatsapp, all the collaborative plataforms. Often	Speed in contacts	No
Student -1 Portugal	Skype only if needing more than one regular meetig per week	Temporal disciplinary frame	No
Student - 2 Portugal	Dropbox. Rarely using skype. Face to face is more important.	Temporal disciplinary frame	Time non(tuning)
Student - 3 Portugal	Skype, hangouts. Often when in sabatics.	Time and space compression	No
Student -4Portugal	Skype, e-mail, facebook, and collabortaive plataforms. Often.	Temporal disciplinary frame	Time non(tuning)
Student - 5 Portugal	Email. Never skype.	Time and space compression	Time non(tuning)
Student – 6 Brasil	Skype, hangout, email. Very often.	Speed in contacts	Time non(tuning)
Student – 7 Brasil	Email. Whatapps. Never skype. Often	Speed in contacts	No
Student – 8 Brasil	Email, skype. Rarely	Speed in contacts	No
Student – 9 Brasil	Email, skype. Often	Speed in contacts	Time non(tuning)
Student – 10 Brasil	All of them. Often.	Time and space compression	Constant availability

Source: Author elaboration

Chapter 10

Futurization of Thinking and Behavior:
Exploring People's Imaginaries About the Future and Futurization

Anna Sircova
Time Perspective Network, Denmark

Molly Kennedy
Bowdoin College, USA

Angela E. Scharf
University of Minnesota, USA

Pinja R. Päivinen
St. Lawrence University, USA

ABSTRACT

This chapter is looking into the emerging concept of "futurization," which is being used in the context of policy making; however, without clear definition, it creates ambiguous reactions. What does "futurization of politics," "futurization of thinking," or "futurization of behavior" actually mean? This chapter looked into the associations citizens or laypeople have with terms "future" and "futurization," and what were their expressed and unexpressed hopes, dreams, fears, and anxieties. The study, using surveys and focus-groups, revealed a rather lifeless image, future without photosynthesis, without female presence, and overall a wasteland scenario. However, when speaking about "futurization" in comparison to "future," there is much less inevitability, more personal agency, and both believe in and fear the technological advancement. The working definition of "futurization" is offered in the chapter as well as a comparative analysis of "future" vs. "futurization." The implications for sustainability policymaking and curriculum development in education are discussed.

DOI: 10.4018/978-1-5225-8163-5.ch010

INTRODUCTION

Decisions made today can have profound consequences for individuals, societies, and ecosystems in the future. Yet far too often, present feelings are so powerful that our choices end up neglecting considerations of future events. This phenomena is observed in many disciplines from Psychology to Environmental Economics and its effect on decision making has far reaching implications in all aspects of human life. Adam Smith, the celebrated Economist described the struggle between our present and future selves as a "conflict between our passions and our impartial spectator" (Smith, 2010) where our impartial spectator is a fully rational version of ourselves looking in from the outside as we make choices in the present that we would not rationally choose in the future. Through the model of inter-temporal choice economists have studied and described the tradeoffs between experiencing a benefit today and experiencing a benefit with a given delay (William Senior, 1872, Lowenstein & O'Donoghue, 2002). The theory of discounted utility is the most widely used framework for analysing intertemporal choices. This framework has been used to describe actual behaviour and it has been used to prescribe socially optimal behaviour (Newman, 1998).

It is easy to understand that an immediate benefit holds a greater appeal as it neutralises the risk and uncertainty of a future benefit, nevertheless researchers have identified that the further away in time a benefit is received the more "myopic" our perception of that benefit becomes, a behaviour identified as present bias (Smith, 2010, Jevons, 1871, Delaney & Lades, 2017).

Conflicting as it may be, present bias is only part of the problem. Psychologists have observed that present bias is often accompanied by an even more alarming phenomenon called preference reversal (Green et al, 1994). Preference reversal describes changes in individual preferences when a time delay is introduced in the decision making process. Preference reversal is observed when individuals opt for a lower payout today over a higher payout in a week from today, but a higher payout in a year and a week from today over a lower payout in a year. This effect has been observed in dozens of studies covering environmental incentive programmes, pension schemes, long term health related treatments, and nutrition improvement programs amongst many others. How then can we stop our individual interests in the present from being fulfilled at the expense of future common interests? Sociologists, Psychologists and Economists alike agree that abstaining from the present enjoyment to seek delayed enjoyment is one of the most painful exertions of human will (William Senior, 1872, Hanley & Splash 1993) yet so much of the future wellbeing of our species and our environment rests on our ability to do so.

A conscious and systemic method of envisaging the future could help address the natural bias individuals exhibit when faced with intertemporal decision making.

Aware of the problems associated with present bias, the authors of this chapter explored the attitudes, thoughts, ideas and sentiments elicited when multidisciplinary participants in live scenarios were asked to futurize.

The term 'futurization' has been used in processes associated with scenario planning and scenario analysis as a way to incorporate future thinking into present decisions. However, its use in the literature has been ambiguous and widely open for interpretation (Pulver, S. & Van Deveer, S. (2007). Currently it is noted that 'futurization' is being used in the context of policy making (Hanusch, 2017). However, without clear definition it creates ambiguous reactions (Sircova, A., 2017).

Participants in the empirical studies described in this chapter responded according to their own interpretation of the term which showed ambiguity that could be categorised according to three distinct interpretations of the future: the future as a dystopic reality, the future as an extrapolation of the present and the future as a utopic result of an orchestrated intervention in the present.

Authors of the chapter believe that the importance of being able to think about the future in light of the past and the present is important for a number of disciplines and as such calls for a clear and more rigorous definition of the term. Therefore, the aim of this chapter is twofold:

1. To formalize the concept of 'futurization" in various academic contexts and to offer a definition that could be further enhanced by a formalistic approach to thinking about the future in light of the past and the present as a means for curbing the incidence of present bias and improving decision making.
2. To discuss the possible use of futurization and its prospect of being developed as a tool for behavioral design and social impact, as von Groddek (2018) observes that "the distrust in classical ideas of planning that enhances the interest in tools and instruments that allows organization to cope with an open and unclear future" (p.26).

BACKGROUND

Looking into the available definitions of the term 'futurization' did not provide much information. According to Wiktionary, 'futurization' is defined as process of futurizing (Wiktionary, 2017). The process of 'futurizing' can be defined as: "to bring into the future or make state of the art; modernize" (Wiktionary, 2018). In economics, one may find the following definition: "Futurization refers to the process of standardizing the terms of settlement and delivery of a contract" (Kurbanov, 2013). Without proper definition it is used in the context of policy making (Hanusch, 2017). Futurization was used as an educational strategy - emphasizing attention on the future;

including analyses of the important sci-fi novels in the school program; introducing school subjects that are dealing with mega-trends, especially those introducing the newest technologies and ideas of transhumanism to the humanities students (Dydrov, 2017). The term, in its current form is ambiguous, and is being used to describe activities that contemplate a future component, rather than a discrete process of incorporating the future into current decision making process. Therefore, the first author of this chapter proposed a working definition of 'futurization': "Futurization as incorporation of the future orientation or consideration of future into the process of thinking and in the acts of behaviour in the present. 'As if' perspective - having future in the focus of attention; considering how this particular action will echo in the future globally and adjusting own behaviour locally" (Sircova, 2018).

The proposed definition needs further refining, however. Furthermore, the first author argues that currently a new chronotope (time-space) is evolving in our society and thus, different methods of dealing with the future are required to be developed. The authors use chronotope in Gumbrecht's understanding of it (Gumbrecht, 2015), with the starting point of Bakhtin (Bakhtin, 1937). Gumbrecht illustrates various chronotopes in the following way. For example, the medieval chronotope considered human life and time as an episode included in the divine eternity. Between the past and future there was no relationship, no difference, and no sense of historical difference. Role of the human factor was minimal, a human was not able to change the time. In this chronotope, the temporal horizon is moved away from the human: the future is approaching, but the human is standing still. Through committing a sin, a human could break the divine order, but God would restore it, leaving the human to submit to the divine order.

Moving forward from the Renaissance times, we can see the evolution of the historical chronotope. Time became a necessary factor of change. The change occurs and the role of the human factor is great and necessary. People move through time: leaving the past behind and using it as an experience space, creating a projection into the future - a forecast. Here future becomes the open horizon of opportunities in which people move into. People have a choice: they can choose between the possible futures. In-between the past and the future there is the present - a very short time of transition (see The Clock by Baudelaire, 1857).

In the modern times the future is not an open horizon of opportunities. People do not believe in forecasts. The future is something frightening and will definitely happen, leaving people with no possibility to run away, and involving many experienced losses. At the same time, people can not leave the past behind, we witness the invasion of pastness through architecture, museums, etc. In-between the future and the past - there is the present, which is not a moment, but an expanded present of simultaneity through technology.

The first author of the current chapter argues that the current situation can be specifically characterized by the presence of technology and we can witness a new chronotope developing. The past becomes an interactive component. Furthermore, experiencing simultaneity of expanded present through technology. The future remains frightening - as the recent public opinion polls suggest. One of the latest analyses from British research institute Ipsos MORI in 2018 shows that 60 percent of people in the participating 28 nations feel their country is on the wrong track (Skinner, 2018). Roughly half or more of European Millennials "despair about the future" according to the survey by Pew Research Center in 2014 (Stokes, 2015), they lack the sense of agency; they do not feel that they can impact the world around them or their own future. This finding is not that surprising when looking at the four major worries for global citizens (Skinner, 2018): Financial/Political corruption (34%), Unemployment (33%), Poverty/Social Inequality (33%) and Crime & Violence (31%). The looming picture of the approaching 'apocalypse' is supported by a large body of research: more frequent water stress, desertification, heat waves, flooding and the global temperature increase (Sixth Assessment Report of the Intergovernmental Panel on Climate Change [IPCC-AR6-WG2]). Moreover, the climate-related health risk will more than double by the year 2030 as estimated by the World Health Organization (WHO) (McMichael et al., 2004).

Additionally the future gets a new angle due to the wider presence of robots and artificial intelligence (AI) development. For example, Volvo is developing a fully electric car that will be a driverless pod that be a hotel room, office or portable meeting room most likely to be present on the market in 2028 (A new way to travel). Otherwise a rather dramatic project among all the various futuristic developments is Sidewalk Lab's revitalization of Quayside in Toronto funded by Google (Sidewalk Toronto). It includes the self-driving cars, embedded sensors to track energy usage and automation with underground channels for garbage and utilities. However, all those developments are also bringing the sceptic and fear alive. What are the risks of exposure to unauthorized access or malicious tampering of control algorithms behind self driving public transport? People believe that they are naturally involved in the process of futurization, however, are not consciously engaged in it, it just happens and there is no control over the 'side effects' (Sircova, 2018).

This new chronotope is further supported by the semantic shift that can be traced to the early 2000's. It is a new semantics in the decision-making process, when an organization has to prepare for the completely unexpectable future. And, von Groddeck (2018) argues that it can not be done by 'planning' or 'rational analysing', but "by 'sensing' in the present how to adapt to an unknown future" (p.38), decisions become sensual decisions instead.

In contemplating definition of 'futurization' as seen from the social science's perspective and specifically from a psychological and behavioural point of view, the authors are mostly interested in the definition that incorporates an element of present behavior modification in light of a future scenario. Additionally it will take into account the time dimension, meaning how far into the future would the process of futurization need to reach into to be considered an act of futurization and not a sequential set of logically linked activities. For example: "Am I futurizing if I take a coffee this morning to avoid being tired by mid day?"

Overall, futurization of thinking and behaviour is a novel area of research. Authors believe that the applications of it can be particularly appropriate in the areas of psychology and cyberpsychology studies, environmental and sustainability studies, organizational management, policy making and it can be an important pedagogical tool as well.

MAIN FOCUS OF THE CHAPTER

Research Structure

For the purposes discussed above, the authors adopted the method, proposed by Snijders and van der Duin (2017), that actively involves citizens in theorizing about the future. It is argued that there are limitations to experts' opinions and foresights and "involving 'ordinary people' in foresight studies will increase their quality and hence their potential use in decision-making, resulting in a better future for everybody, both experts and layman" (p.33).

This chapter presents the results of the two pilot studies, both including the surveys and focus-groups, conducted with people, residing in Copenhagen, Denmark, with various backgrounds in education and professions, ensuring interdisciplinary representation. Studies concerned the concept of 'futurization' and perception of the future, exploring the concepts, associations and imagery elicited by the term 'futurization' as well as the expressed and unexpressed hopes, dreams, fears and anxieties associated with the term, which the authors believe are essential steps in formalizing the definition of the term.

Study 1 included first a focus-group and then a follow-up survey aiming at exploring the first associations people have with the term 'futurization'. Study 2 included first a survey and then a follow-up focus-group aiming at expanding on some aspects of the first impressions with the term 'futurization', introducing a working definition of the term and separating it from the notion of 'future'.

The survey in Study 1 was aimed at initial differentiation of the terms 'future' and 'futurization' and allowed gathering some first insights into those. Survey in Study

2, on the other hand, served the purpose of testing the pool of questions developed, in order to see which ones can generate valuable information in responses and select those for the follow-up focus-group.

Focus-groups, on the other hand, allowed to look into the participants' perceptions of 'future' and 'futurization' more in detail. Additionally, participants had an opportunity to interact with one another, discussing various questions offered and come up with answers otherwise not possible without the interactive part.

Study 1

Step 1

The first focus-group was developed and carried out by Anna Sircova, Martina S. Mahnke and Aglaia Michelakis in Copenhagen, Denmark, October 2017. It included a prompting lecture by an invited expert in the field of psychology of time - Marc Wittmann, Institute for Frontier Areas in Psychology and Mental Health in Freiburg, Germany, and elements of design thinking: participants were prompt to create empathy, define, ideate, prototype and share (Sircova, 2017). Participants were adults, who signed up for the focus-group via social media announcement. They were of various educational backgrounds: economists, engineers, IT specialists, bodyworkers, photographers, writers, game developers, psychologists and psychology students, architects, musicians, business owners, municipality workers, software engineers and UX designers.

One of the main issues that arose during the focus-group was that participants made an exchange of terms. Since 'futurization' was a totally new concept for them, they have exchanged it for the concept of 'future' and discussions shifted in a different direction. This confusion highlighted the need for a working definition of 'futurization' and moreover, the need to further investigate the difference between the notions of 'future' and 'futurization' held by the public.

Themes Arising and Questions for Future Explorations

1. AI as an intelligent agent programmed with human core moral values— are they the liberator to humans or a potential enemy? Would this rob mankind of the process of anticipating the the future? This proved to be a very emotionally charged topic, which the researchers then marked for deeper future exploration.
2. The setting of the focus-group allowed participants to experience the embodied present being very emotional and future in contrast being very calculative - which indicated another question for future explorations: is future emotionless?

3. The role of culture became apparent in the notion of future - all of the participants were coming from the westernized culture of linear time, which brings certain images of the future and understanding of it. However, what about the circular time or interwoven times and other cultural conceptualizations? That question remains open.

4. It was expressed that future thinking should be domain specific. The question what are the domains where it is important to have this 'futurization' aspect wasn't addressed during this focus-group.

5. Various understandings of future and 'futurization': 'Futurization' as a process of becoming futured—what are the benefits of it, but also what are the risks associated with such a process? Vs There is no future in the sense of all the future is an image, an imagination—it is a projection of something from the past, pre-existing memories.

6. Distinction between the individualistic goal centered future was made versus that of a group of people merging their goals together and dealing constructively with the uncertainty that such increased complexity brings. Future as something built collectively, co-constructed with care and having the time and space for expressing own creativity and building together in a respectful way. Could there be more possibilities? How could the two be bridged?

7. Acting for the future as a way of dealing with shame and guilt.

8. Important issue of the elitism of 'futurization'. Do all people have equal access to making choices that protect the future? Are other groups shamed for not having that ability?

9. "Are we all going to become part of the human zoo?"

10. Collective "chaos"—Can we trust one another to respect each other's actions toward the future? Is this utopian? Is considering it utopian denying mankind an intrinsically good nature?

Step 2

As a follow-up to the focus-group results the first pilot survey was developed aiming to examine people's understanding of the difference between the concepts of 'future' and 'futurization' and gather some first impressions when introduced to a term of 'futurization' (Brovich, Päivinen, & Sircova, 2017). Ten anonymous participants were recruited online and invited to answer questions on surveymonkey platform. Questions asked are presented in Appendix 1.

Thematically, the first impressions when the concept of 'futurization' was introduced, included: planning, speculation, process of making something future-like, modeling, technological innovation, ultra-modern, large-scale automation, robotization, present becoming an ideal future, making something fit into the future, flying cars, and an institution.

The colors associated with the term were mostly clustered around colorless or cold palette: white, shiny, illuminated, chrome, grey, steel grey and shining silver, with small additions of blue and deep blue, green and steel red. However, no presence of warm colors such as yellow, orange or red were observed with the exception of steel red. These findings raise questions about the connection or perhaps current disconnection many have with the natural world around. Considering the colors for example, the photosynthesis is not possible and therefore, life is not possible.

When asked to name a character, people named superheroes, robots or public figures connected to technology, such as Steve Jobs and Mark Zuckerberg, all predominantly male. There was only one female character out of ten proposed and it was a robot. That made the first author wonder - is that how the overpopulation would resolve itself in the future?

The feelings people have attached to this term are a mix of both positive and negative: curiosity (70%), optimism and uneasiness (60%), hope (50%), empowerment and strangeness (40%), disconnectedness and fear (30%).

Study 2

Step 1

The preparatory stage included creating the pool of prompting questions tapping into the various sides of 'futurization' concept and ways to distinguish it from the concept of 'future'. The survey then were gathered anonymously online which answered a number of questions pertaining to 'futurization' (Scharf, A. et al., 2018). The sample consisted of 35 participants, predominantly female (23 female, 8 male, 4 participants preferred not to indicate their gender) and was relatively young (M = 22.97, SD = 8.73) (4 participants preferred not to indicate their age). A total of 20 questions were asked (see Appendix 2). Questions that generated responses that furthered the understanding of 'futurization' were included into the focus-group discussions on Step 2.

Similarly to the results from Study 1, the colors associated with the term were mostly clustered around colorless or cold palette: silver, chrome, steel blue, blue, neon blue, with small additions of light green, green, red and brown. Additionally, respondents mentioned ethereal colors such as magic, multicolored, and vivid.

When asked to name 'futurization' as an animal, respondents named mainly creatures which are adaptable or have been around for a long time, such as: shrimp, lizard, chameleon, chimera or griffin (mythological creature). There was mention of a human and a robot, as well as a theme of animals that can survive further on or strong enough to overcome whatever future might bring; or they are genetically modified to be able to survive.

The adjectives that came to mind when thinking of 'futurization' were classified based on what type of descriptor they represent; appearance, personality, feelings, size, timing, color, and other. Of these classifications, the most adjectives are appearances (10 adjectives) including 'futuristic', 'tech-y', and 'industrial'; personality (19 adjectives) including 'innovative', 'thoughtful', and 'creative'; feelings (11 adjectives) including 'scary', 'exciting', and 'troublesome', and other (14 adjectives) including 'non-definitive', 'open-ended', and 'unknown'. The four most prevalent adjectives from the comprehensive responses are 'new', 'positive', 'unknown', and 'exciting'.

Emotions that were associated with 'futurization' were both positive and negative, passive and active: anticipation, anxiety, motivated, forward-thinking, love, cold, boredom, calmness.

When asked to name humanistic traits of 'futurization', respondents name six main characteristics: creative, intelligent, motivated, cold, ambitious, and smart.

When asked if 'futurization' was something they engage in or other people engage in, the respondents skew towards the majority of the population, if not everyone, as being engaged. The respondents answered: Everyone (58%), Everyone but not directly (17%), Most people (8%), Unsure (8%), and No (8%).

When asked if 'futurization' is a natural process, the respondents answered: No (67%), and Yes (33%).

The main concern respondents list when asked about 'futurization' are "environment" and "resources". Respondents clarify that environmental concerns range from the damage that is currently being caused, to the quality of the planet. Respondents clarify that resource concerns range from how they are protected, to the distribution, to not overusing them. Other concerns included monetary concerns such as inflation and unequal division of wealth.

The jobs that embody 'futurization' included various engineering positions (general, software, NASA), programming and computer science, and a coordinator.

Step 2

The survey served as a testing ground for the developed pool of questions. Those that proved to generate meaningful responses were then included as a warm-up prompts during the focus-group conducted next. The focus-group was developed by Anna Sircova and Chris Crespo. It was conducted in Copenhagen, Denmark in April 2018 together with Angela Scharf and Molly Kennedy. During the focus-group participants were given a framework to work with: they were introduced to a definition of 'futurization' developed by the first author and asked specifically to answer all the other follow-up questions with this definition in mind. Definition used was: "Futurization as incorporation of the future orientation or consideration of future into the process of thinking and in the acts of behaviour in the present. 'As if' perspective - having future in the focus of attention; considering how this particular action will echo in the future globally and adjusting own behaviour locally". This was done to prevent participants to present their imagery and associations that they might have with the concept of 'future'. Questions used during the focus-group and instructions are presented in Appendix 3. Participants were adults, who signed up for the focus-group via social media announcement. They were of various educational backgrounds: performance arts, sociology, elementary school teacher, electrician, psychology, dance, photography, arctic sciences, events producer, cultural studies, UX design and software engineering.

There were many similarities between the answers from the survey and those among the focus-group participants. Here, authors are highlighting some of the results they found interesting and thought provoking (see Sircova, 2018 for the report with complete results from the survey and the focus-group).

When asked what type weather would 'futurization' be, participants still also mentioned windy, rainy and stormy, however, in contrast to the survey results, some participants associated it with clear skies and sunny weather and having control on weather impact.

Additionally to the cold color palette yellow was mentioned, however, the person clarified "most likely the future will be very warm". The rationale behind choosing the green color was "I hope that 'futurization' of things will be more human".

Emotions associated with 'futurization' were mostly negative: one domain the authors labeled as Anxiety and Inevitability (those included: lost, worried, sad, anxiety, uncertainty, fear, scared, inevitable, powerless, indifference); another domain Scepticism (sceptical, cautious optimism, reflective), third domain Energetic (thrilled, excited, mobilized) and finally, Positive (calm, hopeful, positive, enthusiasm, curiosity).

Time frame associated with the term of 'futurization' ranged between 'right now' and 'infinity'.

When discussed what makes the essence of the human intelligence compared to the artificial intelligence, participants mentioned: empathy and creativity.

The main differences in how people understand 'future' and 'futurization' are: future is something static and 'futurization' is a process, more active; future is sometimes perceived as something more concrete, while 'futurization' is something from a 'sci-fi movie', moreover, 'futurization' is mostly viewed in terms of the technological progress and advancing technology (see Table 1 for more details).

Looking across the studies interesting patterns emerge, which are highlighted in the Table 2.

Table 1. Summary of survey results exploring people's understanding of the terms 'future' and 'futurization'

Future	Futurization
future is a moment of time that has not occurred yet "Future" is more of a timekeeping construct, like a minute from now or tomorrow are the Future; a place or time or thing which will be but isn't yet. Future would be time that hasn't happened yet Future is a point in time that has yet to occur, Future is a time that has not yet happened Future is the events that have not yet occurred the future is an abstract concept of a time and place at a point in the time plane that has not happened yet. future is a time	"Futurization" may be the process of **advancement towards a future goal**. Like, creating renewable energy sources (i.e. solar power) to eventually have all power renewable. Or personal improvement, self improvement over time (ex. "Today I will greet X number of people to help with social anxiety, tomorrow I will greet X more; I will do this to overcome my anxiety in the future."). whereas futurization is when we try to **actively make it happen** Futurization is an **intentional** upgrading / **changing** of lifestyle to **move away from the past**. futurization is something **you have to work for** Futurization is **taking an active role** in determining the future
The future is the end goal	is implementing a change in the present that portrays what is anticipated to happen in the future
future is a place in time The future is a notion of time The future is a time period Future is a period of time	The future is the end goal, futurization is the **process of moving towards the future** futurization is the process of moving towards the future futurization is a **process** futurization is a process
future - personal future	Futurization is preparing for the future futurization is the **process of making** something **ready** for the future...?
Future is anything after today. Future is what will happen next. the future is just in general looking forward to something that will happen at a later date.	Future would be time that hasn't happened yet, futurization would be making things resemble the future? *I.e. making things resemble a time that hasn't happened yet?* futurization is making something future-like
Future seems more concrete future is the real future Future is what we pretty much know will happen.	Futurization seems more like the idea of sci-fi like future futurization is making something from today to be perceived as futuristic, from future futurization is making us seem more like sci-fi future. Futurization is the act of becoming more futuristic?
future is abstract	futurization can happen in the present
future is a noun future is the noun Future is a thing	futurization is a verb futurization is the verb, so the making of the future. futurization an action.
future is inevitable	I don't really know what futurization is, only a few feelings about it I'm not sure what futurization is
Future: That what is to come. The future is the idea of the times to come. Future is a time, something that's coming.	**Technological progress:** Futurization: How to get there. Futurization is the advancement of a society toward a **more scientifically and technologically advanced state**. Futurization is preparing for those times by **advancing technology**. futurization - technological advancements futurization is probably the idea of making the world better via technology Futurization is to modernize something. futurization is the **development** of technology, culture, etc futurization seems like a process to **advance technology and society**
Future seems to be a time period and **something to look forward to**	futurization is visualizing your future

Table 2. Respondents' imaginaries about the future and futurization across Study 1 and Study 2 in terms of Color, Character and Emotions

Focus-Group 1	Survey 1	Survey 2	Focus-Group 2
Color			
N/A	white, shiny, illuminated, chrome, grey, steel grey and shining silver, with small additions of blue and deep blue, green and steel red	Silver, chrome, steel blue, blue, neon blue, with small additions of light green, green, red and brown. Magic, multicolored, and vivid.	In addition to the cold color palette, yellow was mentioned, however, the person clarified "most likely the future will be very warm". The rationale behind choosing the green color was "I hope that futurization of things will be more human".
Theme: Colorless, Cold, Lifeless Palette These findings raise questions about the connection or perhaps current disconnection many of us have with the natural world around us. Considering the colors for example, the photosynthesis is not possible and therefore, life is not possible.			
Character			
AI as an intelligent agent programmed with human core moral values? Rob mankind of the process of anticipating in the future.	Superheroes, robots or public figures connected to technology, such as Steve Jobs and Mark Zuckerberg, all predominantly male. Only one female character and it was a robot.	- a crazy (cool) uncle that invents crazy things (á lá Doc Brown); - that weird (cool) aunt always trying to sell you a new idea - younger cousin / sibling / toddler / grandchild / great grandkid	N/A
Theme: female-less future and robotization as a 'solution' to the overpopulation?			
Emotions			
Present is emotional and future is very calculative. Is the future emotionless?	curiosity (70%), optimism and uneasiness (60%), hope (50%), empowerment and strangeness (40%), disconnectedness and fear (30%)	both positive and negative, passive and active: anticipation, anxiety, motivated, forward-thinking, love, cold, boredom, calmness	mostly negative: one domain the authors labeled as Anxiety and Inevitability (those included: lost, worried, sad, anxiety, uncertainty, fear, scared, inevitable, powerless, indifference); another domain Scepticism (sceptical, cautious optimism, reflective), third domain Energetic (thrilled, excited, mobilized) and finally, Positive (calm, hopeful, positive, enthusiasm, curiosity).
Theme: 'Future' might be emotionless, however, current emotions about the 'future' are of a wide spectrum, both positive and negative.			

Emerging Themes and Discussion

The discussions that took place during the focus-group can be summarized into the following themes:

Overall impression can be summarized as: "thinking about the future is scary, therefore we do not do it on a day-to-day basis." However, once the emotions were expressed and discussed with others ('I am not alone, there are other people with similar fears and thoughts') then the more positive and productive emotions take over. Future as 'scary' can be due to the fact that future for humans also entails their own death, as we are the only biological species that are conscious of our own mortality. Which, according to the Terror Management Theory (Greenberg, Solomon & Pyszczynski, 1997) creates the deep ontological horror and therefore thoughts about own mortality and death, the future, are pushed away and are scary. Further, the authors believe that developing an educational workshop based on the proposed focus-group scenario could become an important pedagogical tool. The need for reform in the educational system was discussed since the current systems 'kills the creativity' and kids have no desire for future.

'Futurization' is a process that is happening now and many are part of it, however, not consciously engaged in it, it just happens and there is no control over the 'side effects'.

Alienation: Technology as tools for simplifying and facilitating connection between people, on the contrary creates disconnectedness with the immediate environment, less person-to-person contact and human communication. The role digitalization and increase in self-services (such as internet banking, self-service at the shop counters, etc.) play in this trend. Presence of screens that are viewed as 'devices that suck out all the energy, turn people into zombies, and make them soulless'.

'Futurization' seems to be associated to some degree with technology and unpredictability more than with natural and self-experienced phenomenon. It is interesting to observe how associations unfold: 'futurization' is something not widely used therefore exchanged to 'future' in respondents' minds produces associations accordingly - future associated with developments in technology, it is something unknown, and most likely should be feared of.

Increased influence of media and technology can perhaps shift the felt ability to influence the future and the more intimate connection to people influential in our lives can shift towards more disconnectedness as social media and other forms of glorifying certain individuals or ways of living become more prominent. Research suggests that loneliness can drive problematic internet use and this can further have a diminished effect on an individual's well-being (Kim, LaRose, & Peng, 2009). Other research suggests that increase in electronic communication (compared to in-person socialization or sports) and smartphone use among adolescences in the USA decreases their well-being (Twenge, Martin, & Campbell, 2018).

An important issue of privilege for future thinking was raised: as focus on the future can only be possible when the basic needs are covered - so we are in privileged position here in Denmark.

There is a split in people's perception on 'futurization'. Some believe it is about sustainability and inclusion, creating such policies and frameworks to ensure we can operate in a more equal framework. On the other hand other participants perceive 'futurization' as a grim and hopeless process of automation, dehumanisation and disintermediation. While 'futurization' is strongly associated with technology and technological advance, some participants prefer to think of it as an opportunity to show societal progress and advancement in our human quality.

One of the largest issues for working to create a better future is in getting individuals to feel a sense of responsibility and relatedness to the bigger problems of the future, without it being overwhelming. Perhaps strengthening the idea of the individual capacity to constantly affect the future and how small actions can reflect larger changes through time is one way to work on this. When 'futurization' is used in the political context among others perhaps it should aim to have a connotation of togetherness and connectedness to individual lives. This might replace the distance that a strong connection to technology and "robots rather than humans" ideology brings. If the term brings a sense of identity and belongingness to the natural world around us and an ability to direct chances at a personal and ultimately at a global level, it could be more effectively used as a force of positive environmental and political change for example.

SOLUTIONS AND RECOMMENDATIONS

The future, of course, "is fundamentally unpredictable" (Wack, 1985), however, there are some predetermined developments that should be taken into account in the present. For example, overall nuclear waste is estimated to be 6 to 50 billion tons (cumulative number from the nuclear energy reactors, military, technology and medical industries) (Donovan, 2017), which in most cases is placed in temporary storages in oceans, where it should remain untouched for at least the next 100,000 years (Madsen, 2010). Earth Overshoot Day marks the date when we (all of humanity) have used more from nature than our planet can renew in the entire year. In 2018, it fell on August 1, meaning that we currently use 1.7 Earths. Global population uses more ecological resources and services than nature can regenerate through overfishing, over-harvesting forests, and emitting more carbon dioxide into the atmosphere than ecosystems can absorb ("Earth Overshoot Day", 2018). Meaning that roughly by 2050 we would need to have two planets in order to maintain the current lifestyles.

The future is now - if we, the humanity, would like to make sure that we survive as species, we have to snap out of the 'living in the now', and enter a new cognitive default mode - of an expanded future. Where 'the new black' is to have in mind that there are tons of nuclear waste around us that will accompany us for a rather long time span, something that we can not cognitively comprehend (what is 100,000 years when compared to 2000 years that our civilization have existed?) and that we are overusing the planet's resources on a daily basis.

Therefore 'futurization of thinking and behaviour' is proposed as a framework in order to incorporate a particular future scenario which we can see already currently unfolding into the cognitive processes that would in return generate new behavioural patterns, increase the individual awareness and responsibility. 'Futurization', therefore, is envisioned as a cognitive and emotional process that brings more awareness, empathy and responsibility into the present daily actions of an individual in order to reach a non-disastrous future for all of the inhabitants of the planet.

There are a few avenues of how this can be realized. The authors see evidence that a futurised perspective cannot be achieved via promoting a future orientation. The future is too abstract, rather difficult to relate to and cannot be comprehended. The alternative mechanism for developing such a perspective is via focusing on minimizing immediacy concerns (Arnocky et al, 2014; Joireman et al., 2012), the abstract future should be made tangible in the now, in the present. Transposing the future concerns into the now as opposed to a message about maintaining the planet for individuals living generations from now.

Another way is to develop a more balanced time perspective. People partition time of their life into past, present and future, additionally, and each temporal frame can have a valence, it can be perceived as positive or negative. Time Perspective theory currently distinguishes between the following facets: Past Positive, Past Negative, Present Hedonistic, Present Fatalistic, Future Positive and Future Negative (Stolarski, Fieulaine, & van Beek, 2015; Kostić & Chadee, 2017). Furthermore, there is evidence (Wiberg et al., 2017; Wittmann & Sircova, 2018) that people with a Balanced Time Perspective profile tend to project themselves into the future and have a longer future horizon: they have a feeling of how life will be in the nearest five or six years; sometimes also have some long-term plans for the next 20-30 years. They are accepting their own mortality, and extend their future in care for the environment, so that the planet is still livable after they are gone. On another hand, those people are autonomous, self-determining and independent, they have a feeling of continued development and are open to new experiences. They have goals in life and a sense of direction and hold beliefs that give their life a purpose. They have a positive attitude toward the self; acknowledge and accept multiple aspects of the self, including good and bad qualities; and feel positive about their past life. So people, who live in harmony with themselves, are also living in harmony with the surrounding world and take care of it (Wiberg et al., 2017; Wittmann & Sircova, 2018). It's interesting how it is linked - if we are well, the world around us is also well. Therefore it would be helpful in the long run if more people would develop such a temporal perspective, which is both beneficial for individual physical health and psychological well-being, but also for the societal functioning on a larger scale.

Moreover, the experiences of conducting the focus-groups on the topic of 'futurization' have clearly indicated that creating safe space for expressing the emotions, imaginaries, hopes, and most importantly, fears associated with the future and 'futurization', allows for more productive ideas and solutions to emerge among the participants. Thinking about the future can be scary and induce fear and anxiety (Solomon, Greenberg, & Pyszczynski, 2015, Gubmrecht, 2015, Carelli, Wiberg & Åström, 2015; Zaleski, 2006), therefore we do not do it on a day-to-day basis, but once the emotions were expressed and discussed with others ('I'm not alone, there are other people with similar fears and thoughts') then more positive and productive approach and mood emerges. The authors propose that such focus groups could be further developed and included as part of school and college curriculum. Such workshops can raise awareness, foster the balanced view on the past, present and future and help participants to develop the new cognitive abilities of 'futurization'.

FUTURE RESEARCH DIRECTIONS

Putting 'futurization' of thinking and behavior in a larger context, we can observe the following trends. Taken, for example, the recent developments in the workplaces. The technological progress so far was mostly taking place in the area of mechanisation of manual tasks, requiring physical labour. Therefore, technological progress and automation processes are applied to a wide range of cognitive tasks, which, until now, have largely remained a human domain.

Most likely the computer capital will substitute most of the workers in transportation and logistics occupations, and office and administrative support workers. Industrial robots are becoming more advanced, they exhibit enhanced senses and dexterity, and soon enough they will be able to perform a wider scope of non-routine manual tasks. The market for personal and household service robots is already growing by about 20 percent annually. Thus, the technocratic future that is feared by many, has already arrived.

The effects of technology on the human development has not been extensively studied. Just to mention a few examples of the human behavior change due to the everyday presence of technology and screens. When researchers were observing passengers in public transport just a decade ago (Lyons et al., 2007; Ohmori & Harata, 2008; Russell, 2011), the variety of observed behaviour was stunning: reading newspapers, books, talking to other passengers, sleeping, listening to music / radio, window gazing, looking ahead, talking on the phone, text messaging, personal care, work computer, game (various, not on computer), romancing, eating / drinking, smoking, singing songs, thinking, using PC / video game, care of children, knitting, needlework, writing, handling wallet, etc. The vast majority of currently observed behavior in passengers and in people, who are waiting in the public spaces (hospitals, airports, bus / train stops) is being on their smartphone (Nicol, 2018). People rarely interact with strangers, conversations are observed only between people who travel together. One device has substituted all the other activities among the passengers.

Another example comes from the field of speech development. Recently it has been observed (S. Sundstedt, personal communication, November 22, 2018) that in Finland children from the Swedish speaking minority and with mild autistic disorders (such as Asperger's' syndrome) with both parents speaking Swedish as their mother tongue, do not use Swedish and instead substitute it with English. This is happening due to children's interaction with tablets and watching youtube videos in English. Particular videos attract their attention due to their simplicity, constant movement, repetition and colorfulness.

Therefore, the authors believe that 'futurization' of thinking and behaviour is becoming a burning issue to address. How interactive technologies are shaping our behaviour now and how rapidly the landscape of observed behaviour is changing. Overall, it raises the question of how to incorporate the available technologies into the daily lives without losing the essence of what makes us humans. This topic also raises the ethical questions of technology uses. The data that is being collected and how it is used, but also in general, how technological advances are at least a decade ahead of the regulative laws. And issue of the software developers and user experience designers producing various new technologies without studying how those new technologies will impact the human behavior in the greater context and historical perspective.

CONCLUSION

What images of the future people have and how those affect the daily life and behaviours? Is there a way to design such policies in sustainable development that will not be based on the reward or punishment (fear) paradigm, but rather helping overcome our amotivation? Those questions were the guidelines for the current research.

The analysis of the future imaginaries conducted in this study revealed a rather life-less image, future without photosynthesis, without female presence, and overall a waste-land scenario. And the rightful follow-up questions then arises: why would we want to bring such future to life? However, when speaking about 'futurization' in comparison to 'future', there is much less inevitability, more personal agency and both believe in and fear of the technological advancement. People believe that almost everyone is engaged in the process of 'futurization', however, at the same time people don't consider it to be a natural process. Emotions attached to the term are very mixed, however, with a slight tilt towards negative ones that invoke anxiety and inevitability. 'Futurization' is perceived as being about technological and societal advancement, sustainability and inclusion on one hand, and as a grim and hopeless process of automation, rise of AI, dehumanisation and alienation of the other hand.

In sum, the aim of the study was to show the range of emotional responses and imaginaries laypeople have regarding the terms 'future' and 'futurization'. The focus point was to show how varied the meanings are that people attach to those terms, which in turn may provide an insight into how such semantics can influence the public opinion on various policy making processes on one hand, and on the other hand how those can influence various organizational practices (organizations of various levels, from private companies to governmental structures) connected to the planning, strategies development and future foresight. The results obtained can serve as a general psychological and sociological reflection of the current semantics connected to the terms 'future' and 'futurization', they have their limitations and call for further in-depth follow-up research. However, the aim of the chapter was to show the prospects of such approach and provide the reader with the working definition of the concept of 'futurization'. "Futurization as incorporation of the future orientation or consideration of future into the process of thinking and in the acts of behaviour in the present. 'As if' perspective - having future in the focus of attention; considering how this particular action will echo in the future globally and adjusting own behaviour locally" (Sircova, 2018). Additionally, the authors argue that 'futurization' can be further developed into a tool that can help both people and organizations effectively deal with the currently developing new chronotope, when future is open, unclear, fearful and totally unknown.

ACKNOWLEDGMENT

This research was inspired by the Anna Sircova's visit to the Institute for Advanced Sustainability Studies (IASS), Potsdam, Germany in June 2017. Some questions arose after mini-symposium at IASS on "Thinking the present and the future

– psychological insights on the role of subjective time" on 22.6.2017. that was hosted by the Futurisation of Politics research group. Not finding a definition of the 'futurisation' or 'futurization' served the starting point for the current study.

The authors thank Chris Crespo, behavior economist and chief digital strategist at Nordea Bank, Copenhagen, Denmark for enriching discussions and developing ideas presented in the current chapter.

This research received no specific grant from any funding agency in the public, commercial, or not-for-profit sectors. Time Perspective Network - Denmark supported the research by providing facilities, various items required for conducting the focus-groups and snacks for the participants.

REFERENCES

Arnocky, S., Milfont, T. L., & Nicol, J. R. (2014). Time perspective and sustainable behavior: Evidence for the distinction between consideration of immediate and future consequences. *Environment and Behavior*, *46*(5), 556–582. doi:10.1177/0013916512474987

Bakhtin, M. M. (1937). Forms of Time and of the Chronotope in the Novel: Notes toward a Historical Poetics. *Narrative dynamics: Essays on time, plot, closure, and frames*, 15-24.

Baudelaire, C. (1857). L'Horloge. *Fleurs du mal*.

Brovich, J., Päivinen, P., Sircova, A. (2017, December 5). *Futurization*. doi:10.13140/ RG.2.2.22754.63683

Carelli, M. G., Wiberg, B., & Åström, E. (2015). Broadening the TP profile: Future negative time perspective. In *Time perspective theory; review, research and application* (pp. 87–97). Cham: Springer. doi:10.1007/978-3-319-07368-2_5

Day, E. O. (2018). *Global Footprint Network*. Retrieved from https://www. overshootday.org/

Donovan, B. (2017, January 6). Answer to "What is the total mass and volume of all the stored nuclear waste in the world?" *Quora*. Retrieved from: https://www. quora.com/What-is-the-total-mass-and-volume-of-all-the-stored-nuclear-waste-in-the-world/answer/Brian-Donovan-13

Dydrov, A. A. (2017). Synergy of humanitarization and futurization as a condition for the functioning of the interpretational machine. *Socium and Power*, *2*(64), 96–100. doi:10.22394/1996-0522-2017-2-96-100

Green, L., Fristoe, N., & Myerson, J. (1994). Temporal discounting and preference reversals in choice between delayed outcomes. *Psychonomic Bulletin & Review*, *1*(3), 383–389. doi:10.3758/BF03213979 PMID:24203522

Greenberg, J., Solomon, S., & Pyszczynski, T. (1997). Terror management theory of self-esteem and cultural worldviews: Empirical assessments and conceptual refinements. Academic Press. doi:10.1016/S0065-2601(08)60016-7

Gumbrecht, H.U. (2015, December 4). *Our "Broad Present" as a "Universe of Contingency": A Cultural and Epistemological Diagnostic*. Lecture during Challenging the Human Sciences Conference, Copenhagen Business School, Denmark.

Hanley, N., & Splash, C. (1993). Discounting and the Environment. In N. Hanley & C. Splash (Eds.), *Cost Benefit Analysis and the Environment*. Northampton, MA: Edward Elgar.

Hanusch, F. (2017). *Democracy and Climate Change*. Routledge. doi:10.4324/9781315228983

Jevons, W. S. (1871). *The Theory of Political Economy*. McMaster University Archive for the History of Economic Thought.

Joireman, J., Shaffer, M. J., Balliet, D., & Strathman, A. (2012). Promotion orientation explains why future-oriented people exercise and eat healthy: Evidence from the two-factor consideration of future consequences-14 scale. *Personality and Social Psychology Bulletin*, *38*(10), 1272–1287. doi:10.1177/0146167212449362 PMID:22833533

Kim, J., LaRose, R., & Peng, W. (2009). Loneliness as the cause and the effect of problematic Internet use: The relationship between Internet use and psychological well-being. *Cyberpsychology & Behavior*, *12*(4), 451–455. doi:10.1089/cpb.2008.0327 PMID:19514821

Kollmuss, A., & Agyeman, J. (2002). Mind the Gap: Why do people act environmentally and what are the barriers to pro-environmental behavior? *Environmental Education Research*, *8*(3), 239–260. doi:10.1080/13504620220145401

Kostić, A., & Chadee, D. (Eds.). (2017). *Time Perspective. Theory and Practice*. London: Palgrave Macmillan. doi:10.1057/978-1-137-60191-9

Kurbanov, R. (2013, February 13). *Swap Futurization – The emergence of a new business model or avoiding regulation and retaining the status quo?* Retrieved from https://derivsource.com/2013/02/13/swap-futurization-the-emergence-of-a-new-business-model-or-avoiding-regulation-and-retaining-the-status-quo/

Lyons, G., Jain, J., & Holley, D. (2007). The use of travel time by rail passengers in Great Britain. *Transportation Research Part A, Policy and Practice, 41*(1), 107–120. doi:10.1016/j.tra.2006.05.012

Madsen, M. (2010). *Into Eternity: A Film for the Future.* Denmark, Finland, Sweden.

Newman, P. (1998). *The new Palgrave dictionary of economics and the law.* London: Macmillan. Retrieved from https://www.volvocars.com/intl/cars/concepts/360c

Nicol, B. (2018). *Field Observation: Waiting Time in Public Spaces.* Report for Psychology of Time course, DIS: Study Abroad in Scandinavia.

Ohmori, N., & Harata, N. (2008). How different are activities while commuting by train? A case in Tokyo. *Tijdschrift voor Economische en Sociale Geografie, 99*(5), 547–561. doi:10.1111/j.1467-9663.2008.00491.x

Pulver, S., & Van Deveer, S. (2007, May). *Futurology and futurizing: a research agenda on the practice and politics of global environmental scenarios.* In *Amsterdam Conference on the Human Dimensions of Global Environmental Change Earth Systems Governance: Theories and Strategies for Sustainability*, Amsterdam, The Netherlands.

Russell, M. (2011). *Watching passengers: Using structured observation methods on public transport.* Academic Press.

ScharfA.KennedyM.EsbrookE.PäivinenP.SircovaA. (2018, May 7). *Futurization: Survey Results.* doi:10.13140/RG.2.2.28361.60000

Senior, N. W. (1938). An Outline of the Science of Political Economy (6th ed.). London: George Allen & Unwin.

Sidewalk Toronto. (n.d.). Retrieved from https://sidewalktoronto.ca/

Sircova, A. (2017, October 19). Futurization of thinking and behavior as a fine balancing act-review. *Time Perspective Network.* Retrieved from https://medium.com/time-perspective-network/futurization-of-thinking-and-behavior-as-a-fine-balancing-act-be2f44a93d62

Sircova, A. (2018, May). *Futurization-summary of results, SP18.* doi:10.13140/RG.2.2.16617.54880

Sircova, A., Karimi, F., Osin, E. N., Lee, S., Holme, P., & Strömbom, D. (2015). Simulating Irrational Human Behavior to Prevent Resource Depletion. *PLoS One*, *10*(3), e0117612. doi:10.1371/journal.pone.0117612 PMID:25760635

Sixth Assessment Report of the Intergovernmental Panel on Climate Change. (n.d.). Retrieved from https://www.ipcc.ch/reports/

Skinner, G. (2018, October 11). *What worries the world?* Ipsos MORI. Retrieved from https://www.ipsos.com/ipsos-mori/en-uk/what-worries-world-september-2018-0

Smith, A. (2010). *The theory of moral sentiments*. Penguin. doi:10.1002/9781118011690.ch10

Snijders, D., & van der Duin, P. (2017). The Future Is Ours. How Dutch People Think about Technology and the Future. *Journal of Futures Studies*, *21*(4), 19–35.

Solomon, S., Greenberg, J., & Pyszczynski, T. A. (2015). *The worm at the core: On the role of death in life*. Random House Incorporated.

Stokes, B. (2015, February 10). *U.S. and European Millennials differ on their views of fate, future*. Pew Research Center. Retrieved from http://www.pewresearch.org/fact-tank/2015/02/10/u-s-and-european-millennials-differ-on-their-views-of-fate-future/

Stolarski, M., Fieulaine, N., & van Beek, W. (Eds.). (2015). *Time perspective theory; Review, research, and application*. Springer International. doi:10.1007/978-3-319-07368-2

Twenge, J. M., Martin, G. N., & Campbell, W. K. (2018). Decreases in psychological well-being among American adolescents after 2012 and links to screen time during the rise of smartphone technology. *Emotion (Washington, D.C.)*, *18*(6), 765–780. doi:10.1037/emo0000403 PMID:29355336

von Groddeck, V. (2018). From Defuturization to Futurization and Back Again? A System-Theoretical Perspective to Analyse Decision-Making. In *How Organizations Manage the Future* (pp. 25–43). Cham: Palgrave Macmillan. doi:10.1007/978-3-319-74506-0_2

Wack, P. (1985, November). The Gentle Art of Re-Perceiving – Scenarios (part 2): Uncharted Waters Ahead. *Harvard Business Review*, 2–14.

Wiberg, B., Sircova, A., Carelli, G. M., & Wiberg, M. (2017). Developing empirical profile of the balanced time perspective (BTP) and exploring its stability over time. In A. Kostic & D. Chadee (Eds.), *Time Perspective Theory* (pp. 63–95). Palgrave. doi:10.1057/978-1-137-60191-9_4

Wiktionary, The Free Dictionary. (2017a). *Futurization*. Retrieved from https://en.wiktionary.org/wiki/futurization

Wiktionary, The Free Dictionary. (2017b). *Futurize*. Retrieved from https://en.wiktionary.org/wiki/futurize

Wittmann, M., & Sircova, A. (2018). Dispositional orientation to the present and future and its role in pro-environmental behavior and sustainability. *Heliyon (London)*, *4*(10), e00882. doi:10.1016/j.heliyon.2018.e00882 PMID:30386830

Zaleski, Z. (2006). Future orientation and anxiety. In *Understanding behavior in the context of time* (pp. 135–151). Psychology Press.

KEY TERMS AND DEFINITIONS

Delayed Gratification: The resistance to temptation of an immediate reward in preference for a later reward.

Instant Gratification: The temptation, and resulting tendency, to forego a future benefit in order to obtain a less rewarding but more immediate benefit.

Intertemporal Choice: Decisions with consequences in multiple time periods.

Preference Reversal: Observation that there are systematic changes in people's preference order between options.

APPENDIX 1

Questions Used in Study 1: Survey Questions

1. Futurization is a term that has not yet been defined. What are some first impressions that come to your mind when you hear the word?
2. If futurization was a color, which one would it be?
3. If futurization was a character in a movie, what would it be like?
4. Can you think of a specific character you already know for futurization?
5. What do you think is the difference between thinking about the future vs. thinking about futurization?
6. When you think of the term futurization, what type of emotions do you feel? (Check all that apply):
    a. Happiness
    b. Anger
    c. Sadness
    d. Curiosity
    e. Joy
    f. Fear
    g. Uneasiness
    h. Stress
    i. Empowerment
    j. Relatedness
    k. Belonging
    l. Hope
    m. Hopelessness
    n. Disconnectedness
    o. Strangeness
    p. Trust
    q. Optimism

APPENDIX 2

Questions Used in Study 2: Survey Questions

1. What is the difference between "Future" and "Futurization"?
2. If Futurization was a book or movie, what would it be?
3. How many people would it include? (Ex. The whole population? People in power?)
4. If Futurization was a food, what would it be?
5. What color would it be?
6. What does Futurization sound like?
7. Do you think it's something you engage in or other people engage in?
8. If futurization were a shape, what shape would it be?
9. If futurization was a family member, how would it be related to you?
10. If you were an expert in futurization what would be your main concern?
11. If futurization was a type of weather what would it be?
12. If your were grading futurization, what grade would you give it?
13. Is futurization a natural process? Why or why not?
14. What are the first 10 adjectives that come to mind when you think of futurization?
15. If futurization was an animal, what would it be? Why?
16. If futurization were a job what job would it be, and would you want it?
17. If futurization was an emotion, what would it be?
18. How much education would futurization have?
19. If futurization was a person, name five of their traits?
20. If futurization was in a room, where would it be standing?

APPENDIX 3

Questions Used in Study 2: Focus Group Questions

Part 1: First Impressions

Instruction:

Be fast and frivolous with your answers, don't think too much, really just give your first impressions. Please write your answer(s) one per post-it note and put it on the wall:

1.   If futurization was a type of weather what would it be?
2.   When you think of the term futurization, what type of emotions do you feel?
3.   If futurization was an animal, what animal would it be?
4.   If you are thinking of futurization what type of time frame are you imagining?
5.   If futurization was something within your professional field, what color would it be? (Pick a color and pin to the wall)
6.   Take a few minutes to reflect - list first 10 adjectives that come to mind when thinking of Futurization (write them on post-its; make clouds)
7.   If futurization was a person, name five of their traits?
8.   If futurization were an object, what would it be?

Part 2: Group Work

Instruction:

Please reflect on the following questions and write a few words / sentences. Take 5 minutes to reflect on own, make notes and afterwards discuss in small groups.

1.   Do you think it's something you engage in or other people engage in?
2.   What would I be doing if I am to futurize something?
3.   Is futurization a natural process? Why or why not?
4.   If you were an expert in futurization what would be your main concern?
5.   If futurization was a profession, which type of job would it be? - Would you want to be in that position?
6.   Based on your gut feeling, how would you define futurization? And then what de-futurization would mean?

Chapter 11
If It Ticks Like a Clock, It Should Be Time Perspective:
Shortcomings in the Study of Subjective Time

Victor E. C. Ortuño

iD https://orcid.org/0000-0002-9523-0874
Universidad de la República, Uruguay

ABSTRACT

In recent years, the concept of time perspective has acquired a prominent position within the psychology of time. After Zimbardo and Boyd´s seminal work, thousands of papers have cited its work and within the last decade; several books and papers of other authors have been dedicated to exploring and expanding its theory. Even when considering other relevant authors about this topic, such as Nuttin and Lens, among many others, Zimbardo´s theory has become a synonym of time perspective research. This chapter represents an effort to identify some of the existent shortcomings in subjective time research and more specifically in time perspective topics. This chapter intends to encourage a mostly needed discussion about what the actual state of the research being developed is and what precautions should be taken into consideration in future researches.

DOI: 10.4018/978-1-5225-8163-5.ch011

INTRODUCTION

It´s long recognized the interest of human beings about time and its impact in individual´s actions. Psychology doesn´t escape this trend, focusing in varied aspects of the individual experience of time, from its biological basis to societal behaviours structured by collective notions about time. Within Psychology of Time, exists an aggregate of topics, mostly referred as Subjective Time, which in Lloyd and Arstila´s words represent *"...the experience of temporality itself"* (2014, p. 657).

Within Subjective Time topics, Time Perspective (TP) has acquired a prominent position. After Zimbardo and Boyd´s seminal work (1999) thousands of papers have cited its work and within the last decade, several books of other authors have been dedicated to exploring and expanding its theory (Kostić & Chadee, 2017; Paixão, da Silva, Ortuño, & Cordeiro, 2013; Stolarski, Fieulaine, & van Beek, 2015). Even when considering other relevant authors about this topic, such as Nuttin and Lens (1985), among many others, Zimbardo´s theory has become a synonymous of Time Perspective research.

Previously, Paixão (1996) stated that in the domain of the study of human temporality, a multiplication of the theoretical, methodological and practical perspectives has occurred; this panorama raises difficulties to a possible effort of developing a coherent discourse about which is the better paradigm, and currently these problems are far from being solved.

This work represents an effort to identify some of the existent shortcomings in Subjective Time research and more specifically in Time Perspective topics, mostly due its theoretical dominance at this moment. The goal of this work is not to diminish or blindly criticize any author or concept, but to encourage a discussion about what the actual state of the research that´s being developed nowadays and what precautions should be taken in future researches.

HOW MANY TIME PERSPECTIVES EXIST?

A key barrier to the development of research and knowledge in Subjective Time and more specifically in Time Perspective topics is the vast aggregate of definitions and operationalisations that this concept has presented throughout the years. As Wallace (1956) points out, several temporal concepts such as time sense, time orientation, time perspective and time perception are frequently used without a proper conceptual and operational characterization. Therefore, it has been complex to reach a consensus among researchers about how many temporal dimensions exist

(Gupta et al., 2012) and which ones really matter in the study of human behaviour. Even the term "perspective" possesses various non-technical meanings, which have contributed to the existing conceptual confusion (Nuttin & Lens, 1985). Gjesme (1983, p. 445), when analysing the Future Time Orientation literature concludes that it is possible to support almost "*any conclusion you prefer to draw*", due in part to the inconsistency in the chosen methods, experimental designs and terminology.

One of the most influential authors concerning the psychology of time, Fraisse (1957) argues that, given the extensive variety of temporal concepts, it is exceptionally difficult if not impossible to unify all the "temporal phenomena" into a coherent and integrative model of human subjective temporality. Kastenbaum (1961) further complemented this idea, arguing that "there is much that could be accomplished in this direction by exploring the interrelationships between future time perspective and certain other temporal variables" (p. 215). In most cases, the research being conducted is focusing in isolated positions about subjective time, without considering how different theories can complement each other.

It is usual as well as recommendable that in any field of science, several paradigms co-exist, yet numerous problems still do persist: I) in several cases, it is not really a new paradigm or concept that is being introduced, but a simple rebranding of old and well-known concepts. II) The contrary is also true, frequently different concepts are being presented as Time Perspective, causing a totally mistaken perception about the concept amongst readers and researchers. For example, Arnocky, Milfont and Nicol (2013) considered the concept of Consideration of Future Consequences (CFC) as Time Perspective.

It is of vital importance to trace the differences among the several temporal concepts, in order to avoid misconceptions. Regarding the aforementioned case, it must be considered that the concept of Consideration of Future Consequences is a cognitive–motivational construct and has been successfully used as an individual-differences metric in the same way that Time Perspective has. Still, CFC consists of an evaluative dimension of the future, since "it enables an individual to perceive what his or her future field might require or demand behaviorally, in order to reach desired outcomes" (Petrocelli, 2003, p. 406) and is mainly related to behavioural consequences, whilst Time Perspective is a more dynamic and multifaceted process due its influence in the encoding, storing and recalling of experienced events (Zimbardo & Boyd, 1999) and motivational objects (Nuttin & Lens, 1985). This difference in the complexity and reach of those concepts, makes TP more difficult to assess than CFC, which in counterpart could make CFC assessment more precise and more adequate for situations where psychologist have to take decisions about their clients.

THE FUTURE MATTERS, PAST AND PRESENT WHO KNOWS...

Zimbardo, Keough and Boyd (1997) state that "most current research on time perspective is narrowly directed on only the future dimension by relating it to achievement motivation and anticipated action consequences" (p. 1020). Taber (2013) also stress that Vocational Psychology has focused primarily on the relation of Future Time Perspective (FTP) with career variables, neglecting the influence of the past and present time perspectives.

Obviously, it is an overstatement to affirm that this panorama constitutes a shortcoming in the study of temporal research, yet it is a limited approach if the researchers' objective is to comprehend the full impact of temporality on individuals' cognitions and behaviours. Future Time Perspective and other dimensions of subjective future are crucial in the study of concepts like motivation and learning (Andriessen, Phalet, & Lens, 2006), career planning (Janeiro, 2010; Paixão, 1996, 2004), career decision making (Walker, 2012), academic achievement (De Volder & Lens, 1982), school investment (Peetsma, 2000) and coping (Holman & Silver, 2005) among many others. In fact, Future Time Perspective is deeply rooted in well-known cognitive-motivational concepts and theories, namely expectancy-valence theories, self-determination theory and achievement goal theory (Lens, Paixão, Herrera, & Grobler, 2012). Still, as mentioned by Ortuño et al. (2013) different psychological and behavioural constructs present a different and unique relation with each one of the subjective temporal dimensions. In other words, the subjective future dimensions are not able to explain all the motivated behaviour; due to their nature, some behaviours are better explained by the other dimensions of the temporal horizon – the past and the present.

Until now we have discussed how Future Time Perspective affects or is related to a wide array of cognitions and behaviours, yet several studies enlighten about the value that Past and Present Time Perspectives have in a totally different array of cognitions and behaviours and in which Future Time Perspective has no effect. Those two temporal frames present important predictive capabilities in concepts such as:

- **Self-Esteem:** Highly and negatively associated with Past Negative and lacking a strong association with Future (Anagnostopoulos & Griva, 2012; Ortuño & Vásquez, 2013; Zimbardo & Boyd, 1999).
- **Satisfaction with Life:** From a regression analysis with seven temporal dimensions, only Past Negative was an important predictor, presenting a strong association together with a residual contribution of Future Negative and both were negatively associated with Satisfaction with Life (Ortuño et al., 2013).

- **Avoidant Procrastination:** Whose main predictor and showing a negative effect on it, is Present Fatalist (Ferrari & Diaz-Morales, 2007).
- **Risky Driving:** A dangerous activity which according to Zimbardo et al. (1997) is better predicted by Present Time Perspective (showing a positive effect on it) than Future Time Perspective.

Considering these results as well other reported in the specialized literature, we must underline that dimensions related to the past and the present temporal frames shown a crucial role in the study of cognitive and behavioural dimensions. The reported evidence demonstrates the conceptual independence of Zimbardo and Boyd´s (1999) five temporal dimensions, while it also seems to be shedding some light on the cross-sectional influence of all Time Perspectives across the different domains of the individuals' life. As such, regarding the study of subjective temporality, we recommend researchers to employ measurement techniques that allow a multi-temporal assessment, related not only to the future frame but also with the past and present frames.

MY TIME PERSPECTIVE IS BIGGER THAN YOURS!

As previously mentioned, during the development of the research on Time Perspective, various theoretical paradigms and assessment instruments have been created. According to McGrath and Kelly (1986), there exist 211 different approaches to the concept of Time Perspective. Especially if we consider other temporality-related concepts such as Consideration of Future Consequences (Strathman, Gleicher, Boninger, & Edwards, 1994), Future Anxiety (Zalesky, 1996), Sensation Seeking (Arnett, 1994; Zuckerman, 1990) and also, more current concepts like Temporal Focus (Shipp et al., 2009) which sometimes are confused with Time Perspective itself, certainly the number of TP definitions would be much higher nowadays.

However, this development has not always been accompanied by an effort by the authors to clarify either the uniqueness or the advantages of each new concept in comparison with the existing ones. Nuttin and Lens (1985) noted that the growing body of Time Perspective research in the decade of the 50s brought a *"great terminological confusion"* (p. 15). Controversially, this tendency has continued in the following years with an ever-growing number of temporal concepts or Time Perspective concepts. Almost every new concept is presented as the definitive approach to subjective temporality.

Equally important is the elaboration of comparative studies between paradigms, promoting synergies which allow us to reach a better understanding of Time Perspective as a key concept in human dynamics. It is easily possible to find research about new concepts and their statistical validity, yet authors and researchers haven't exerted the necessary caution to determine how these methods can complement the findings of previous and already validated methods.

In other words, we recommend the development of comparative studies, discussing for example why the new methods that are being presented are more adequate than the previous ones, and why it is relevant to acknowledge in which way they are complementary to already validated research techniques. An effort developed in this direction was presented by Ortuño and Janeiro's (2009) study, when analysing the assessment differences and complementarities between the Zimbardo Time Perspective Inventory (ZTPI) and the Time Perspective Scales (TPS, Janeiro, 2010).

WHAT ABOUT TOMORROW, WILL I STILL FEEL THIS YOUNG?

Most studies about subjective temporality are developed using a cross-sectional approach – comprehensible due to methodological, economic and temporal restraints. Yet, this brings consequently the existence of very few longitudinal studies being published. Hamilton, Kives, Micevski, and Grace (2003) refer to this fact as an actual limitation in temporal research, because of the restricted current understanding about aging and Time Perspective. Also, it is important to consider the statistical limitations of the cross-sectional approach, which is observational by nature. This fact raises difficulties in extracting causal inferences regarding other psychological or behavioural phenomena. For example, in a cross-sectional study developed by Ortuño, Paixão and Janeiro (2011) seven Time Perspectives amongst college students attending different years were compared to analyse differences in TP along the academic course. Although useful in an exploratory manner, using this methodology the authors are unable to truly establish a valid causal relation between TP and development in academic training.

In the longitudinal scope we would like to mention a couple of interesting studies. First, Holman and Silver (2005), studying future-oriented thinking and adjustment after a terrorist attack, observed on one hand a moderate and negative association between Future Orientation and psychological distress, and on the other hand, fear of future terrorism was moderately and positively associated with the same cognitive pattern. The same authors collecting data three years after the incident reported that subjects who engaged in active coping after the terrorist attacks, showed higher Future Orientation than those who were involved in planning or religious coping. Second and last, Peetsma, Schuitema and van der Veen (2012) when exploring the development of FTP amongst secondary school students, reported that students' long and short-term FTP regarding school and professional career decreased over a two-year evaluation, while both long and short-term leisure time FTP increased in the same period.

In a similar vein, Hamilton et al. (2003) also mention as a constraint in current temporal literature the fact that many of the research studies carried out in the Time Perspective domain use samples which are mostly formed by young adults or adolescents, the main consequence being the small amount of knowledge about age-group differences and how Time Perspective evolves across the individual's life span.

WE'RE MORE THAN OUR TEMPORAL PREFERENCES

In temporal research it is common to focus mainly on Temporal Orientation variables. Still, human behaviour is not guided only by this variable; is not enough to consider only the individual's temporal preferences to successfully predict behaviour. Other equally important temporal dimensions exist in this endeavour, such as: Temporal Extension, Temporal Density, Degree of Structuration, Level of Realism and Temporal/Time Attitude (Nuttin & Lens, 1985). Thoms and Blasko (1999) suggest that an important ability that allows individuals to successfully plan for the future is to be able to perceive the future optimistically, in other words, the affective sign associated with the Future.

There is no doubt about the impact of Future Time Perspective on motivational processes (Lens & Tsuzuki, 2007; Peetsma, 2000), but instead of studying only the individuals' tendency to think about a determined temporal frame, this knowledge could be complemented with information about how far into the future this thinking goes or how coherent this thinking is.

This shortcoming is deeply related to the measurement instruments that we use in research. Some well-known instruments such as the Zimbardo Time Perspective Inventory (ZTPI, Zimbardo & Boyd, 1999) are composed by several temporal dimensions like Present Fatalist, which measures not only temporal orientation, but also temporal affectivity (as do the remaining ZTPI dimensions, except Future Time Perspective). Yet, in a study exploring social networks, Holman and Zimbardo (2009) confirm conceptual difficulties regarding Present Fatalist, due its overlapping with negative affectivity. In the case of the Future dimension, it is frequently referred to by other authors as measuring not only temporal orientation but also time management (Webster, 2011) and planning (Worrell & Mello, 2007).

We are not advocating for one-dimension instruments; we believe that temporal instruments can and must measure different dimensions, but it is extremely important to be able to differentiate between each one of them. Each sub-scale should evaluate only one temporal dimension or be totally capable of providing differentiated scores for each dimension. This will allow research on temporal topics to move forward into a new paradigm of higher conceptual validity and consistency avoiding those overlapping conceptual issues.

HOW TIME PERSPECTIVE CAME TO BE

The evidence about what variables or conditions affect Time Perspective is scarce. Nurmi (1991) presents an interesting theoretical analysis of which variables affect the development of future temporal orientation in adolescents, and Zimbardo and Boyd (1999) also briefly mention some of the stimuli that shape individuals' temporal profile. Yet, there is a lack of comprehensive and empirically validated theoretical models that explain i) the developmental process of Time Perspective, its several dimensions and properties and ii) why individuals overemphasize a specific time zone and how this bias is maintained throughout the individual's life course.

Actually, most research has focused on exploring what variables are predicted by Time Perspective. An effort to explore possible predictor variables of TP was proposed by Dunkel and Weber (2010), using three levels of personality, life history, life history strategies, Big Five personality traits and identity; they were able to explain between 20 and 55 per cent of variance in TP, depending on which of the temporal frames were considered. The authors highlight the importance of this study arguing that individual differences on Time Perspective have been explored as important predictors of a diverse set of psychological variables, yet there is little understanding about the source of these same individual differences in Time Perspective.

The development of explanatory models of Time Perspective would aid researchers not only in knowing how Time Perspective develops and what variables participate in that process, but it would also increase our understanding of the already established relations of Time Perspective with other psychological and behavioural phenomena. As such we consider this as a crucial line of research which researchers should invest in.

ONE STUDY TO RULE THEM ALL

The use of meta-analysis has been a common practice to summarize results from numerous studies, still in Psychology of Time and more specifically Time Perspective topics, there is an important lack of studies employing this technique. Bearing in mind the increasing amount of research being produced in recent years about Time Perspective, there is an urgent need to: 1) synthesize the results of several related papers; 2) use a macro approach, allowing a broader view about the effects and associations of TP to other psychological and behavioural phenomena; and 3) facilitate the understanding of the current state-of-the-art on Time Perspective research, in order to encourage new researchers into TP-related topics.

Despite the importance and usefulness of meta-analysis as a research method, few studies have used this technique within TP topics. Some of the few carried out in recent years are presented by: Milfont, Wilson and Diniz (2012), concerning TP and environmental engagement in 19 samples from seven countries (Australia, Brazil, Germany, Mexico, New Zealand, Norway and the United States) forming a composite sample of 6301 participants. The authors found important evidence that supports the key role that Future Time Perspective plays in attitudes and behaviours towards the environment. Also, Kooij, Kanfer, Betts & Rudolph (2018) presented a meta-analysis focusing specifically on Future Time Perspective, its theory, recent advancements and some of the different techniques used to measure it. These authors presented empirical evidence about the incremental role of FTP when studying constructs like life satisfaction, depression, risk behaviour among others. The predictive power of the Big Five model of personality was increased with the inclusion of FTP ($\Delta R^2\%$ = 5.88, $\Delta R^2\%$ = 4.47, $\Delta R^2\%$ = 3.54, respectively).

Another type of analysis that could help us better understand research trends is bibliometric analysis. This quantitative method is used to analyse scientific and technological literature (De Bellis, 2009), allowing readers to explore the impact of a determined field, paper or author. Thereby, this method could assist researchers in a more complete and meaningful analysis of the scientific impact of specific Time Perspective topics. But it can also facilitate the evaluation of projects or researchers by funding agencies. As stated by Mugnaini, Jannuzzi, and Quoniam (2004), bibliometric data serves to point out the fruition of the R&D efforts, which can be measured by two means: product-barometers (or barometers of efficacy), which are related to more immediate results (such as the number of publications or quantity of patents in a determined period) and impact barometers, which are related to more long-lasting results (like impact factors and scientific developments, among others).

THE BALANCED TIME PERSPECTIVE IDEAL

The interrelations between the different temporal frames (namely past, present and future) has been mentioned by several authors related with subjective time topics. For example, Ringle and Savickas (1983) presents the notion of Balanced Time Perspective within a specific context when analysing the effects that leadership´s temporal functioning has on organizations. These authors state that leaders should promote an environment in which the tasks of remembering (past), experiencing (present) and anticipating (future) peacefully coexist; this should allow the development of an ideal organizational climate.

As previously mentioned, Time Perspective is a cognitive process composed by several temporal frames, which interrelate between themselves. Most researches usually consider how each one of these temporal frames are related and how they influence several aspects of individual´s life. One of the conceptions introduced by Zimbardo and Boyd (1999) refers to *"an idealized mental framework that allows individuals to flexibly switch temporal frames among past, future, and present depending on situational demands, resource assessment, or personal and social appraisals"* (p. 1272). According to the authors this cognitive ability is referred to as Balanced Time Perspective (BTP), which is central to an optimum psychological functioning and it is opposed to a dispositional bias towards any particular temporal frame (Boniwell & Zimbardo, 2004; Drake, Duncan, Sutherland, Abernethy, & Henry, 2008; Zimbardo & Boyd, 1999). BTP's influence is even broader, since it also contributes to physical health and societal functioning (Sircova, Wiberg, Wiberg, & Carelli, 2010, July). Among the factors that influence the development of a BTP, Stolarski, Bitner and Zimbardo (2011) point out coping strategy, emotional control and emotional application.

Since no TP is adaptive across all possible situations that individuals can find in their life, the authors highlight the added value of this broad process which consists of a combination of several Time Perspectives when analysing the relation of TP with other psychological concepts. In this case, the interpretation of individual scores is no longer fragmentary across the temporal frames; instead, it is necessary to analyse all the individual's temporal frames as a whole. The junction of all these temporal frames would result in an individualized and unique Temporal Profile, which in our view is composed not only by the temporal orientation, but also by other temporal variables such as: Temporal Extension, Temporal Orientation, Density, Emotional Valence, Continuity and Balance, as proposed by Kazakina (1999; 2013). Yet, we must stress the importance of Boniwell, Osin, Linley and Ivanchenko (2010) and Kazakina (1999) studies, who argue that there is a lack of measurement tools which consider Time Perspective in all its complexity.

At the behavioural level, individuals oriented by this metacognitive scheme should enforce a compromise between the knowledge of their own past experiences, their present desires and needs and their future expectations and consequences (Zimbardo & Boyd, 1999). To Boniwell and Zimbardo (2004), the two main mechanisms of a BTP are the flexibility and the ability to change the focus on a determined TP to another more adaptive one, considering the contextual present situation. As such, BTP depends broadly on the present situation, and Epel, Bandura and Zimbardo (1999) refer that "The optimal time perspective depends upon the demands of the situation" (p. 590).

Chronologically, the Balanced Time Perspective concept is addressed once again by Boniwell and Zimbardo in 2004. Here they complement the previous explanations defending that to achieve a Balanced Time Perspective, all the individual's temporal frames should coexist or hold simultaneously without losing the ability to activate a determined temporal frame, taking into account its adaptive value in a given present situation. Complementarily, Boyd and Zimbardo (2005) proposed that a BTP would be characterized by five theoretical TP profiles: hedonistic (high in Present Hedonist and low in Future), fatalistic (high in Present Fatalist, low in Present Hedonist and in low Future), risk-taking (high in Present Hedonist and high in Present Fatalist), future-oriented (low in Present Hedonist and high in Future) and lastly, balanced (high in Present Hedonist and high in Future). Whilst this theorization seems logical and coherent, we still agree with Boniwell et al. (2010), who state that this work's empirical validity is still missing. Nevertheless, these same authors tried to find the psychological foundations of these five profiles, and partially encountered evidence supporting the TP profile structure proposed by Boyd and Zimbardo (2005), and which were hedonistic, future, balanced, negative and risk taking.

Statistically, the Balanced Time Perspective is characterized by moderate values in Present Hedonist Time Perspective, moderate to high values in Past Positive and Future Time Perspectives, whilst presenting low values in Past Negative and Present Fatalist Time Perspectives (Kairys & Liniauskaite, 2010, July). Still this characterization of BTB is not absolute in terms of cultural and temporal contexts, since each culture values different aspects of behaviour, just as it does with the several temporal frames. For example, Boniwell and Zimbardo (2004) denote differences in the cultural notion of BTB amongst populations of the United States of America and South Africa. Sircova et al. (2010, July) proposed a way to calculate BTP introducing the idea of Level of Balance; this level is the result of the number of "adequate or adaptive" results in the five Time Perspectives, and as such an individual can score between zero and five regarding their Level of Balance.

Still further, Boniwell et al. (2010) and Zhang, Howell and Stolarski (2013) are acknowledged as the first authors that attempted to empirically operationalize the BTP concept following a proposal by Drake et al. (2008), in which they use cut-off criteria; individuals who score below the 33rd percentile in the Past Negative and Present Hedonist Time Perspectives and above this same percentile in the Past Positive, Present Hedonist and Future Time Perspectives would be considered as having a Balanced Time Perspective. Boniwell et al. (2010) criticized this approach because they consider it to be too dependent on the statistical characteristics of the collected sample, instead of having a basis of psychological differences; therefore, they proposed another method to calculate the participants' Balanced Time Perspective, which consists of a cluster analysis, the number of clusters being predefined following the theoretical considerations of Boyd and Zimbardo (2005).

A completely different approach about Balanced Time Perspective is presented by Webster (2011), who proposes a totally new and independent instrument to measure BTP, the Balanced Time Perspective Scale – BTPS, a 28-item inventory organized in two dimensions: past and future. Via this inventory it is possible to categorize participants according to their use of subjective time, such as time expansive, futurists, reminisces and time restrictive. The author found a coherent network of correlations between other subjective temporality related variables, as well as some individual difference metrics. Still, it has been pointed out that one of BTPS's major shortcomings is the lack of a dimension related to the subjective present (Stahl, 2012; Webster, 2011).

The latest addition concerning the existing methods to evaluate BTP is presented by Stolarski et al. (2011) and further validated by Zhang et al. (2013). This method, named Deviation from a Balanced Time Perspective – DBTP, consists, as the name suggests, of the calculation of a coefficient of "fit between individuals' time perceptions and the optimal time perspective profile" (Stolarski et al., 2011, p. 354) considering Zimbardo and Boyd's (2008) theorization about an adequate temporal profile or Balanced Time Perspective. The authors state that a DBTP value close to zero indicates a well-balanced time perspective, whilst a large positive value would indicate a serious deviation from the Balanced Time Perspective ideal. Through a series of comparative regression analyses, Zhang et al. (2013) defend that among the three most well-known methods of calculating BTP: Drake et al. (2008) cut-off method, Boniwell et al. (2010) hierarchical cluster analysis and Stolarski et al. (2011) Deviation of Balanced Time Perspective coefficient, the last is the most adequate. Still, as mentioned by McKay et al. (2018) the DBTP approach weights the magnitude of the differences between empirical and theoretical optimal values of each TP dimension. Which in consequence diminish its capability as an individual-difference metric since different TP profiles can exhibit similar DBTP scores. A more complete presentation about the different methods for assessing BTP and the advantages and disadvantages of each one is presented by Kairys, Liniauskaitė, Bagdonas, and Pakalniškienė (2017).

The evidence shown in previous studies suggests that if the Balanced Time Perspective is related to an optimal functioning, most of the population hasn't achieved this ideal. In a sample of 260 participants, Drake et al. (2008) reported that only 13 participants achieved BTP (most of the female gender).

Yet, even if most population doesn't achieve the BTP ideal, most studies do not effectively measure BTP; to the best of our knowledge BTP studies present a cross-sectional approach, were BTP is measured only once. Therefore, there's no possibility of assessing the temporal dimensions in different settings, which unable to assess how the individual temporal profile changes in different situations, a condition that is directly related with the BTP definition itself. In order to properly study BTP, research should follow a multi-situational approach, where individuals´ are engaged in different tasks and situations, each one with different individual requirements.

Another fundamental aspect of BTP study, refers to the characteristics of the individual temporal profile. As mentioned before, for most authors BTP consist in low levels in past negative, present fatalist, moderate levels in present hedonist and moderate to high levels in past positive and future. This conceptualization represents a unique recipe about an adaptive temporal profile, without considering cultural and situational differences. Future researches shouldn´t assume that individuals from different cultures must present the same "western and industrialized" temporal profile. Also, it ignores critical situations such as homeless, war, terminal diseases, among many other situations where the ideal temporal recipe couldn´t be the most adequate. This represent an important bias in the way time perspective research is being planned and conducted.

FINAL THOUGHTS

As previously mentioned, the main goal with this work is to mention some regular issues in the research being developed in Subjective Time and more specifically, Time Perspective topics. By doing this, it is intended to generate a debate among academics about the implications and expected results of the research that´s being (re)produced nowadays.

So far, there is no paradigm that can capture all the complexity of Time Perspective and related constructs. Future studies should focus in creating bridges between different theories and complementing its results with different instruments. The debate is still open, and consensus is far from being reached about important issues: i) Which dimensions (or temporal frames) compose Time Perspective?; ii) Temporal extension, density, as many other concepts, should be considered as independent constructs or as composite properties of Time Perspective?; iii) Time Perspective should be considered as a trait or a process?; iv) What is the stability of these constructs, not only from a temporal point of view but from a situational perspective? In TP´s definition, Zimbardo and Boyd (1999) defend that is *"a relatively stable individual-differences process"* (p. 1272). So far, no real effort has been made to define how stable is this relatively stable process; and v) Balanced Time Perspective refers to the individual ability to flexibly switch between temporal frames, something that´s being ignored in most of the research being conducted. The body of research is being focused mostly in the assessment of how distant is the individual temporal profile from an optimal temporal profile. An optimal profile that theoretically suits everyone, at all ages, cultures and situations.

More research and theoretical developments are needed in order to cover these and other questions that still exist. Due its impact and relevance at different levels, researchers certainly are going to continue working within this field of knowledge, but we should be aware that is not because something ticks like a clock, that make it Time Perspective.

REFERENCES

Anagnostopoulos, F., & Griva, F. (2012). Exploring Time Perspective in greek young adults: Validation of the Zimbardo Time Perspective Inventory and relationships with mental health indicators. *Social Indicators Research*, *106*(1), 41–59. doi:10.100711205-011-9792-y

Andriessen, I., Phalet, K., & Lens, W. (2006). Future goal setting, task motivation and learning of minority and non-minority students in Dutch schools. *The British Journal of Educational Psychology*, *76*(4), 827–850. doi:10.1348/000709906X148150 PMID:17094888

Arnett, J. (1994). Sensation Seeking: A new conceptualization and a new scale. *Personality and Individual Differences*, *16*(2), 289–296. doi:10.1016/0191-8869(94)90165-1

Arnocky, S., Milfont, T. L., & Nicol, J. L. (2013). Time Perspective and Sustainable Behavior: Evidence for the Distinction Between Consideration of Immediate and Future Consequences. *Environment and Behavior*. doi:10.1177/0013916512474987

Boniwell, I., Osin, E., Linley, P. A., & Ivanchenko, G. V. (2010). A question of balance: Time perspective and well-being in British and Russian samples. *The Journal of Positive Psychology*, *5*(1), 24–40. doi:10.1080/17439760903271181

Boniwell, I., & Zimbardo, P. G. (2004). Balancing One's Time Perspective in Pursuit of Optimal Functioning. In P. A. Linley & S. Joseph (Eds.), Positive Psychology in Practice (pp. 165-178). Hoboken, NJ: Wiley.

Boyd, J. N., & Zimbardo, P. G. (2005). Time perspective, health, and risk taking. In A. Strathman & J. Joireman (Eds.), Understanding behavior in the context of time: Theory, research, and applications (pp. 85-107). Mahwah, NJ: Erlbaum.

De Bellis, N. (2009). *Bibliometrics and Citation Analysis: From the Science Citation Index to Cybermetrics*. Plymouth: Scarecrow Press.

De Volder, M. L., & Lens, W. (1982). Academic Achievement and Future Time Perspective as a Cognitive-Motivational Concept. *Journal of Personality and Social Psychology, 42*(3), 566–571. doi:10.1037/0022-3514.42.3.566

Drake, L., Duncan, E., Sutherland, F., Abernethy, C., & Henry, C. (2008). Time perspective and correlates of wellbeing. *Time & Society, 17*(1), 47–61. doi:10.1177/0961463X07086304

Dunkel, C. S., & Weber, J. (2010). Using Three Levels of Personality to Predict Time Perspective. *Current Psychology (New Brunswick, N.J.), 29*(2), 95–103. doi:10.100712144-010-9074-x

Epel, E., Bandura, A., & Zimbardo, P. G. (1999). Escaping homelessness: The influences of self-efficacy and time perspective on coping with homelessness. *Journal of Applied Social Psychology, 29*(3), 575–596. doi:10.1111/j.1559-1816.1999. tb01402.x

Ferrari, J. R., & Díaz-Morales, J. F. (2007). Procrastination: Different time orientations reflect different motives. *Journal of Research in Personality, 41*(3), 707–714. doi:10.1016/j.jrp.2006.06.006

Fraisse, P. (1957). *Psychologie du temps* [Psychology of Time]. Paris: Presses Universitaires de France.

Gjesme, T. (1983). On the Concept of Future Time Orientation: Considerations of Some Functions´ and Measurements´ Implications. *International Journal of Psychology, 18*(1-4), 443–461. doi:10.1080/00207598308247493

Hamilton, J. M., Kives, K. D., Micevski, V., & Grace, S. L. (2003). Time Perspective and Health-Promoting Behavior in a Cardiac Rehabilitation Population. *Behavioral Medicine (Washington, D.C.), 28*(4), 132–139. doi:10.1080/08964280309596051 PMID:14663920

Holman, E. A., & Silver, R. C. (2005). Future-Oriented Thinking and Adjustment in a Nationwide Longitudinal Study Following the September 11th Terrorist Attacks. *Motivation and Emotion, 29*(4), 389–410. doi:10.100711031-006-9018-9

Holman, E. A., & Zimbardo, P. G. (2009). The Social Language of Time: The Time Perspective-Social Network Connection. *Basic and Applied Social Psychology, 31*(2), 136–147. doi:10.1080/01973530902880415

Janeiro, I. N. (2010). Motivational dynamics in the development of career attitudes among adolescents. *Journal of Vocational Behavior, 76*(2), 170–177. doi:10.1016/j. jvb.2009.12.003

Kairys, A., & Liniauskaite, A. (2010, July). The search of balanced time perspective. In A. Sircova & A. Kairys (Eds.), *Time Perspective: Methodological Issues and Relation with Different Domains of Psychological Functioning. Symposium conducted at 15th European Conference on Personality*. Brno: Czech Republic.

Kairys, A., Liniauskaitė, A., Bagdonas, A., & Pakalniškienė, V. (2017). Balanced Time Perspective: Many Questions and Some Answers. In A. Kostić & D. Chadee (Eds.), Time Perspective: Theory and Practice (pp. 97-115). London: Palgrave Macmillan.

Kastenbaum, R. (1961). The Dimensions of Future Time Perspective, an Experimental Analysis. *The Journal of General Psychology, 65*(2), 203–218. doi:10.1080/00221 309.1961.9920473 PMID:14454195

Kazakina, E. (1999). *Time perspective of older adults: Relationships to attachment style, psychological well-being and psychological distress* (Unpublished doctoral dissertation). Columbia University.

Kazakina, E. (2013). Time Perspective of Older Adults: Research and Clinical Practice. In M. P. Paixão, J. T. da Silva, V. Ortuño & P. Cordeiro (Eds.), International Studies on Time Perspective (pp. 71-86). Coimbra: University of Coimbra Press. doi:10.13140/RG.2.1.1602.0008

Kooij, D. T., Kanfer, R., Betts, M., & Rudolph, C. W. (2018). Future time perspective: A systematic review and meta-analysis. *The Journal of Applied Psychology, 103*(8), 867–893. doi:10.1037/apl0000306 PMID:29683685

Kostić, A., & Chadee, D. (Eds.). (2017). *Time Perspective: Theory and Practice*. London: Palgrave Macmillan. doi:10.1057/978-1-137-60191-9

Lens, W., Paixão, M. P., Herrera, D., & Grobler, A. (2012). Future time perspective as a motivational variable: Content and extension of future goals affect the quantity and quality of motivation. *The Japanese Psychological Research, 54*(3), 321–333. doi:10.1111/j.1468-5884.2012.00520.x

Lens, W., & Tsuzuki, M. (2007). The Role of Motivation and Future Time Perspective in Educational and Career Development. *Psychologica, 46*, 29–42.

Lloyd, D., & Arstila, V. (2014). The Disunity of Time. In V. Arstila & D. Lloyd (Eds.), Subjective time: The philosophy, psychology, and neuroscience of temporality (pp. 657-663). Cambridge, MA: MIT Press.

McGrath, J., & Kelly, J. (1986). *Time and human interaction: Towards a social psychology of time*. New York: Guildford Press.

McKay, M. T., Worrell, F. C., Zivkovic, U., Temple, E., Mello, Z. R., Musil, B., ... Perry, J. L. (2018). A balanced time perspective: Is it an exercise in empiricism, and does it relate meaningfully to health and well-being outcomes? *International Journal of Psychology*. doi:10.1002/ijop.12530 PMID:30206944

Milfont, T. L., Wilson, J., & Diniz, P. (2012). Time Perspective and enviromental engagement: A meta-analysis. *International Journal of Psychology*, *47*(5), 325–334. doi:10.1080/00207594.2011.647029 PMID:22452746

Mugnaini, R., Jannuzzi, P., & Quoniam, L. (2004). Indicadores bibliométricos da produção científica brasileira: Uma análise a partir da base Pascal [Bibliometric Indicators of Brasilian Scientific Production: An Analysis Through Pascal Basis]. *Ciência da Informação*, *33*(2), 123–131. doi:10.1590/S0100-19652004000200013

Nurmi, J. E. (1991). How do adolescents see their future? A review of the development of future orientation and planning. *Developmental Review*, *11*(1), 1–59. doi:10.1016/0273-2297(91)90002-6

Nuttin, J., & Lens, W. (1985). *Future Time Perspective and Motivation: theory and research method*. Leuven University Press.

Ortuño, V., Gomes, C., Vásquez, A., Belo, P., Imaginário, S., Paixão, M. P., & Janeiro, I. (2013). Satisfaction with life and college social integration: A Time Perspective multiple regression model. In M. P. Paixão, J. T. da Silva, V. Ortuño & P. Cordeiro (Eds.), International Studies on Time Perspective (pp. 101-106). Coimbra: University of Coimbra Press. doi:10.14195/978-989-26-0775-7_10

Ortuño, V., & Vasquez, A. (2013). Time Perspective and Self-Esteem: Negative Temporality Affects the Way We Judge Ourselves. *Annales Universitatis Paedagogicae Cracoviensis. Studia Psychologica*, *6*, 109–125.

Ortuño, V. E., & Janeiro, I. N. (2009). Estudo Comparativo de duas medidas de Perspectiva Temporal: IPT & ZTPI em foco [Comparative Study of two Measures of Time Perspective: IPT & ZTPI in Focus]. *Proceedings of X Congresso Internacional Galego-Português de Psicopedagogia*. Braga: Universidade do Minho.

Ortuño, V. E., Paixão, M. P., & Janeiro, I. (2011). Tempo e Universidade: A Evolução da Perspectiva Temporal ao Longo do Percurso Universitário [Time and University: Time Perspective's Evolution Along the University Course]. In Carreira, Criatividade e Empreendedorismo (pp. 217-225). Braga: APDC Edições.

Paixão, M. P. (1996). *Organização da Vivência do Futuro e Comportamento de Planificação. Compreensão dos Processos Motivacionais e Cognitivos na Elaboração e Avaliação de Projectos Pessoais* [The Organization of the Subjective Future and Planning Behavior. Comprehension of the Motivational and Cognitive Processes Involved in the Elaboration and Evaluation of Personal Projects] (Unpublished Doctoral Dissertation). University of Coimbra, Portugal.

Paixão, M. P. (2004). A dimensão temporal do futuro na elaboração de objectivos pessoais e organização de projectos vocacionais [The Future Temporal Dimension in the Formulation and Organization of Vocational Projects]. *Psychologica, extra-série,* 273-286.

Paixão, M. P., da Silva, J. T., Ortuño, V., & Cordeiro, P. (Eds.). (2013). *International Studies on Time Perspective.* Coimbra: University of Coimbra Press; doi:10.14195/978-989-26-0775-7

Peetsma, T. T. (2000). Future Time Perspective as a Predictor of School Investment. *Scandinavian Journal of Educational Research, 44*(2), 177–192. doi:10.1080/713696667

Peetsma, T. T., Schuitema, J., & van der Veen, I. (2012). A longitudinal study on time perspectives: Relations with academic delay of gratification and learning environment. *The Japanese Psychological Research, 54*(3), 241–252. doi:10.1111/j.1468-5884.2012.00526.x

Petrocelli, J. V. (2003). Factor Validation of the Consideration of Future Consequences Scale: Evidence for a Short Version. *The Journal of Social Psychology, 143*(4), 405–413. doi:10.1080/00224540309598453 PMID:12934832

Ringle, P. M., & Savickas, M. L. (1983). Administrative leadership: Planning and time perspective. *The Journal of Higher Education, 54*(6), 649–661. doi:10.2307/1981935

Shipp, A. J., Edwards, J. E., & Lambert, L. S. (2009). Conceptualization and measurement of temporal focus: The subjective experience of the past, present, and future. *Organizational Behavior and Human Decision Processes, 110*(1), 1–22. doi:10.1016/j.obhdp.2009.05.001

Sircova, A., Wiberg, B., Wiberg, M., & Carelli, M. G. (2010, July). Balanced Time Perspective: A Study on Operationalization of the Construct in Sweden. In A. Sircova & A. Kairys (Eds.), *Time Perspective: Methodological Issues and Relation with Different Domains of Psychological Functioning. Symposium conducted at 15th European Conference on Personality.* Brno: Czech Republic.

Stahl, M. (2012). *An exploratory study on the relation between time perspective, positive mental health and psychological distress across the adult lifespan* (Unpublished Master Dissertation). University of Twente, The Netherlands.

Stolarski, M., Bitner, J., & Zimbardo, P. G. (2011). Time perspective, emotional intelligence and discounting of delayed awards. *Time & Society*, *20*(3), 346–363. doi:10.1177/0961463X11414296

Stolarski, M., Fieulaine, N., & van Beek, W. (Eds.). (2015). *Time perspective theory; Review, research, and application*. Cham: Springer International. doi:10.1007/978-3-319-07368-2

Strathman, A., Gleicher, F., Boninger, D. S., & Edwards, C. S. (1994). The consideration of future consequences: Weighing immediate and distant outcomes of behavior. *Journal of Personality and Social Psychology*, *66*(4), 742–752. doi:10.1037/0022-3514.66.4.742

Taber, B. J. (2013). Time Perspective and Career Decision-Making Difficulties in Adults. *Journal of Career Assessment*, *21*(2), 200–209. doi:10.1177/1069072712466722

Thoms, P., & Blasko, D. (2004). Future Time Perspective As A Temporal Anchor: Applications To Organizations. *Journal of Business & Economics Research*, *2*(11), 27–40.

Walker, T. L., & Tracey, T. J. G. (2012). The role of future time perspective in career decision-making. *Journal of Vocational Behavior*, *81*(2), 150–158. doi:10.1016/j.jvb.2012.06.002

Webster, J. D. (2011). A new measure of time perspective: Initial psychometric findings for the Balanced Time Perspective Scale (BTPS). *Canadian Journal of Behavioural Science/Revue canadienne des sciences du comportement*, *43*(2), 111-118.

Worrell, F. C., & Mello, Z. R. (2007). The reliability and validity of Zimbardo time perspective inventory scores in academically talented adolescents. *Educational and Psychological Measurement*, *67*(3), 487–504. doi:10.1177/0013164406296985

Zaleski, Z. (1996). Future Anxiety: Concept, Measurement, And Preliminary Research. *Personality and Individual Differences*, *21*(2), 165–174. doi:10.1016/0191-8869(96)00070-0

Zhang, J. W., Howell, R. T., & Stolarski, M. (2013). Comparing Three Methods to Measure a Balanced Time Perspective: The Relationship Between a Balanced Time Perspective and Subjective Well-Being. *Journal of Happiness Studies*, *14*(1), 169–184. doi:10.100710902-012-9322-x

Zimbardo, P. G., & Boyd, J. N. (1999). Putting time in perspective: A valid, reliable individual differences metric. *Journal of Personality and Social Psychology, 77*(6), 1271–1288. doi:10.1037/0022-3514.77.6.1271

Zimbardo, P. G., & Boyd, J. N. (2008). *The Time Paradox: Using the New Psychology of Time to Your Advantage*. London: Rider.

Zimbardo, P. G., Keough, K. A., & Boyd, J. N. (1997). Present time perspective as a predictor of risky driving. *Personality and Individual Differences, 23*(6), 1007–1023. doi:10.1016/S0191-8869(97)00113-X

Zuckerman, M. (1990). The psychophysiology of sensation seeking. *Journal of Personality, 58*(1), 313–345. doi:10.1111/j.1467-6494.1990.tb00918.x PMID:2198341

KEY TERMS AND DEFINITIONS

Balanced Time Perspective: Individuals´ ability to modify the focus of its temporal profile, depending on situational demands.

Consideration of the Future Consequences: A personality trait within the subjective time field. It is related with the assessment and consideration of the immediate and future results of present-moment behaviors.

Psychology of Time: A general field of study within psychology. It is devoted to the study of all time-related phenomena with influence in human cognition and behavior.

Subjective Time: A specific field of study within psychology of time. It is dedicated to the study of conscious cognitive processes directly related with time, such as time perspective or time orientation.

Temporal Extension: A concept within subjective time. Refers to the psychological distance between a motivational object and the present moment.

Temporal Orientation: A concept related with subjective time. Refers to the individuals´ tendency of focusing on a particular temporal frame.

Time Perspective: A concept within subjective time field. Refers to the process of organizing and retrieving all information using a set of temporal frames which compose individuals´ temporal profile.

Chapter 12
World of Warcraft:
Screen Time and Identity Building

Diego Lourenço Sá Pinto
Universidade do Estado da Bahia, Brazil

Cláudio Xavier
Universidade do Estado da Bahia, Brazil

ABSTRACT

World of Warcraft (WoW), a game of the genre MMORPG (massive multiplayer online role playing game), has proven to be a valuable field of study for researchers interested in understanding the functioning of online communities and social relationships in those communities. This chapter seeks, through literature review and interviews conducted within the game itself, from player/researcher immersion, to discuss the relationships of a group of players in a new context of relationship and (in)formation, considering the significant screen time, communication processes, identifications, and identity building.

INTRODUCTION

In the possibility of experiencing realities empirically inaccessible to the body, we understand that the digital universe moves one of humanity's greateast longings: exceed its own limits. Become something or someone whose "nature" does not exert an impediment on any wills of the being. To be something or someone with the unlimited and unrestricted presence in time and space.

DOI: 10.4018/978-1-5225-8163-5.ch012

We observe an individual who starts to build, supported by Information and Communication Technologies – ICT, their own space-time to involve in experiences whose variables are under their control, with the processes of interactivity and choice in their hands. In this way, when they find themselves in the same virtual space in which they have decided to be, individuals converge interests, exchange information and experiences. Finally, they institute a virtual community where they participate in the production of knowledge and meaning (culture), through processes of immersion that reveal an incessant (re)construction of self.

Virtualization, empowering the creative matrix of the indivual (Lévy, 2003), opens paths to diverse spaces of socialization and collaboration, as in the case of games, platforms where it is allowed to create scenarios for fun and social interaction. That is, where there is an exchange of knowledge and recognitions, where references and identifications are constructed (Hall, 2004). Thus, attention to communicational processes and (in)formation[1] in this context is important, so that they are studied as a hermeneutic (an interpretative mediation) that can update the look on the new daily experiences, of mediations and interactions in these immersive environments (Mattos; Junior; Jacks, 2012), namely the impacts and transformations in these relations - processes of identifications and learning. This, considering the fact that the permanence of individuals in these places has increased in duration and quality, since the virtual environments, especially those sustained on platforms, in the case of games, are configured as incubators for the emergence of individuals whose online identity categorically influences their "I".

This work seeks to contribute to the visibility of a new relationship context that exists among World of Warcraft users, through mediation and interaction in a multiuser environment of players – characters, characteristics and the context itself – from where emerge (self)representation, (in)formation and authorship. In the relationships built in theses environments, information about imagery and realities is merged, as experiences lived in the online, offline and hybrid realities, predominantly lived on screen. These experiences contribute to the emergence of "selves" and "others", as identifications and collective construction of knowledge.

BACKGROUND

In the universe of games, individuals emerge that touched this border of being something beyond their "nature", seeking this critical and "no return" point of being more of oneself, like art itself that extrapolates the human condition in search of being a hero or even being a god (Maldonado, 1991). It is therefore, in this society, based on the digital technologies of information and communication, that one can perceive the presence of individuals capable of taking steps towards the construction of their identities, or identifications, in an incessant process that has the technological contribution of this potential. Contribution of technologies that allows the immersion of imaginaries in imaginaries less and less filled with realities, or realities increasingly filled or enhanced by imaginary ones (Lévy, 1993). Without being a parallel universe, but a supposed supremacy of the imaginary, this is also the universe of creativity and innovation through a new industry.

The creative industry emerges as a result of the imbrication between technology/art/culture, a conceptualization that involves the production of innovation through the creativity and the apparatus of the ICT, namely, Cyberculture. In this means of production, characteristic of contemporary society, it is possible to observe the appearance of phenomena and initiatives that centers on inventiveness and innovation, and that seekss to answer questions as they arise, as in the case of startups, incubators, as well as some aspects of research and development (R&D) that seek to understand and at the same time meet the sociocultural demands of this movement (Bolaño, 2015).

We, the authors, perceive the presence of games as a vast range of possibilities and views related to the creativity and innovation in the most diverse social sectors. A new context of relationship favorable to the processes of (self)presentation, (in) formation and authorship. Through the renewal of technique, one notices the incessant search for the breaking of the physical limits or even of the imagination. Glasses of virtual reality or enlarged reality; the evolution of artificial intelligence; cameras that capture movement, clothes that allow, in the physical body, the reproduction of sensations experienced within the games, and physically collaborative games, represent infinite possibilities for the becoming of individual and collective identities, as well as (in)formative processes to be explored (possible humanities?).

World of Warcraft, known as WoW, is a game in the market for a little more than a decade, being a reference in the games universe and nerd culture, with a player base and ex-players that exceeds 100 million spread over 244 countries and territories. WoW is a game of the genre MMORPG – Massive Multiplayer Online Role Playing Game, that is, of social character, in which multiple players can build their identities from their characters, contexts and subjective characteristics, and can live, in the representative figure of their avatars, characteristics that in their actual reality would not be possible to them, such as the physical characteristics, as well as other possible characteristics of identity, and performance through the (self)representation and the relationships/bounds that build through networking and immersion in online environment. With this it is possible to reflect on the importance that a network has in the social construction of the individual, because:

A network of people interested in the same themes is not only more efficient than any search engine, but above all, more efficient than traditional cultural intermediations, which always filters too much, without knowing in detail the situations and needs of each one. (Lévy, 2002, p.101, own translation).

This contributes to a collective thinking, represented by another logic – of network interactions, of exchanges provided by communications and immersions in online environments, such as multiplayer environments.

We understand that this logic of multiple connections and immersive encounters in these environments provides a level of interaction and exchange – of information and knowledge – unpredictable, according to Johnson (2010), in the light of symbolic interactionism,

[...] portrays the social world as generated by social interactions, interactions that in itself produces, and is modeled, by the interpretation of the participants of the world. This process of interactions is formative and creative, not composed of automatic responses to stimuli. The social order, therefore, is unstable and contingent, perpetually rebuilt by the actors. It is the temporally institutionalized product of undetermined interactions. (Johnson, 2010, pp.95-96).

Because of these characteristics, there are individual players who believe that their permanence in the virtual world can establish relationships as real or fulfilling as the relationships they establish in their life in the real world (Watkins, 2009). To the same extent, just as there are individuals who shed much of their time on online social networking screens, some players believe that screen time in a WoW environment enables relationships to be as fulfilling as offline relationships (Watkins 2009). This also explains why the on-screen time of players, especially WoW players, is so expressive given the amount of opportunities to interact with other people, since no other information system was created to support 10 million users at the same time (Bainbridge, 2010).

The sense of belonging generated by WoW makes its players feel as or more comfortable in the online reality of this environment than in their offline reality because, in addition to the simulation, virtual environments, more specifically WoW environments, provide individual conditions for representation. That is, for the (self) representation of "I's" idealized by them and by others.

The permanence of individuals in WoW seems to be a result of the experiences of relationships that can be had within the environment, and that surpass the leisure provided by the game *(per se)*, approaching much more of experiences oriented to the social interactions, something around new sociabilities (cybersociality). A social construction from efforts that are structured somewhere in the cyberspace, where real time breaks the logic of space, *deterritorializing* it, reconfiguring it or reterritorializing it (Lemos, 2013) from the collective imaginary (networks) in which individuals construct senses (culture) based on their longings, passions, goals and intersubjectivities. When added, they result in another form of Being, derived from the convergence of these individuals and their imaginary ones, through processes of identification and of the knowledge that they construct collectively.

A World of Warcraft player may, for example, not identify the "be WoW player" feature as an integral part of his offline identity. However, being a WoW player express a much more immersive connotation regarding the game, since individuals who consider themselves that way, believe that World of Warcraft is part of who they are, as if the WoW player were an identity trait that separated them from those who are not. This condition of belonging, characteristic of tribes, illustrates the sense of community that exists in the game, meaning that: WoW players are not only users of the game, but are configured as part of a universe that understands and incorporates them, since it was created in their own way, by those same players.

As O'Connor paints out, as a result of her research, this sense of community was reported as one of the best things in the game, offering a sense of belonging that may be missing in their offline lives (O'Connor, Longman, White, Obst, 2015). Still according to the authors, "These participants felt that there was something unique about being a WoW player and indicated a sense of separation between their friends who were gamers and those who were not" (O'Connor et al, 2015, p.09).

METHODOLOGY

As a qualitative methodological approach, we consider the main point of the research the immersive experience in WoW by one of the researchers. It is divided into two moments: 1) literature review in a specialized database, SCOPUS/SCIMAGO; 2) empirical research in which the multiplayer environment is used as a context for the interaction of a group of eight players through a socio-demographic questionnaire and interview, and answer the following objective: in view of the online, offline and hybrid realities in WoW player relationships, how important are these relationships in building identities and identifications for these players? This research objective is closely related to questions of social use of time, namely, screen time in contemporary social relations, and how these social relations present themselves as a new context of relationship and production of knowledge and culture – production of meaning among several networks of social relations that are woven in these realities instituted through these multiplayer environments.

1. On the review of literature in specialized database – consisted of the construction of a query that includes the expressions "World of Warcraft", "identity", "gamer", "social" and in this sense, we search for scientific articles dealing with this thematic. It is important to point out that WoW appeared in 2004. What made us think that any scientific production on the theme will have been published after this period. The literature review occurred during the months of January to April 2018, and 11 (eleven) articles were identified as search results. From the reading of their abstracts, and considering the direct relation with the subject in question, the articles entitled "The Warcraft Civilization: Social Science in a Virtual World" by Bainbridge (2010) and "The young and the Digital: What migration to social-networking Sites, games, and anytime, anywhere media means for our future" by Watkins (2009). The work of these authors has also led to new references such as Shen and Williams's "Unpacking Time Online: Connecting Internet and Massively Multiplayer Online Game Use with Psychological Well-being", by Shen and Williams (2010), and "Sense of Community, Social Identity and Social Support Among Players of Massive Multiplayer Online Games (MMOGs): A Qualitative Analysis", by O'Connor (et al, 2015). It is worth mentioning that the articles identified above share many of the references that makeup the theoretical basis of this work (Lévy, 2003; Mattos, Junior e Jacks, 2012; Watkins, 2009; Hall, 1992; Pearce, 2009; Kozinets, 2015; Fong, Mar, 2015; Nardi, 2010; Rheingold, 1997; Turkle, 2011).

The work entitled "The Warcraft Civilization: Social Science in a Virtual World" by the author William Bainbridge (Bainbridge, 2010), says "World of Warcraft is so complex, so culturally rich and so expansive, that will become a permanent part of our civilization" (Bainbridge, 2010, p.206). To accomplish its work, the author created several avatars on several servers, which are responsible for holding the WoW environment and the players. These servers, thematically called Kingdoms – since Warcraft is a fantasy game with medieval features – are categorized into four types: PVP (Player versus Player), where the player's focus is on playing against other players; PVE (Player versus Environment), in which their focus is on the player's collaborative effort to achieve goals; RP (Roleplay), in which players have to "live" in the game, remaining in the character they created and chose to represent them; and RP-PVP (Roleplay Player versus Player), which combines the characteristics of the kingdoms referred to above.

In these kingdoms, Bainbridge (2010) produced a work with several fronts related to the possibilities presented by World of Warcraft. He compared, in the game, some aspects that reflected western culture and how these aspects could influence real life, such as heritage, religion, learning, cooperation and identity, coming to see WoW as a possible form of "real" immortality. He says:

I would consider a continued existence for my main WoW character, behaving as I would behave if I still lived, as a realistic form of immortality... Ultimately, virtual world may evolve into the first real after life, not merely critiquing religion but replacing it. (Bainbridge, 2010, p. 62),

This shows the positioning of a researcher-player who, in addition to recognizing the World of Warcraft environment as a phenomenon capable of influencing society, wishes to be part of this environment, eternalizing it in his avatar.

Bainbrigde (2010), when he talks about identity, works on the subject as a social "self". For him, the social "self" is "the set of ideas individuals have about themselves, which are derived from communication with other people" (Bainbridge, 2010, p.174). For him, in an environment where the player can modify his appearance, gender and race, what prevails as "self" is the social "self". He also compares the WoW character's interpretation to real life characteristics, saying that people not only play characters in the game, but also play real life roles. And while people can interpret their characters in the game, there would be a gap between the player and the character, since in the WoW, the player can take actions that he himself would consider abhorrent in the real life, such as excessive violence. However, the author does not discuss much about it in his work.

In the article "Sense of Community, Social Identity and Social support Among Players of Massive Multiplayer Online Games (MMOGs): A Qualitative Analysis", Erin L. O'Connor, Huon Longman, Katherine White and Patricia Obst tried to examine, through a qualitative approach, the social relations on a MMOG (Massive Multiplayer Online Game). For that, they used World of Warcraft as central object of a study and interviewed 22 Australians, 15 men and 7 women, aging between 18 and 21, who have played WoW for about 3 to 85 hours every week, in a period of 6 months to 6,5 years.

The authors used three theoretical lines, from social psychology, to identify social experiences among WoW players. Psychological Feeling of Community, or the "sense of being part of group of people with whom they have something in common" (Sarason, 1977, as cited in, O'connor, 2015, p.02), Social Identity, or "how a person feels about their membership of a social group" (Tajfel, 1978 as cited in, O'connor, 2015, pp.02-03) and Social Support, "tangible and intangible resources available to someone through their relationships with others" (Cohen; Hoberman, 1973, as cited in O'connor, 2015, p.03). The literature, as painted out by the authors, also suggests that the consideration of the Psychological Feeling of Community in social relations in MMOGs environments can favor conditions of comparison between social relations inside and outside the game and how they can be formatted especially in the context of MMOGs.

The interviews were made by one of the authors of the article, either in person or by phone, at the participant's convenience. The interviews were semi-structured and consisted of open questions designed to examine the experiences of participants in the WoW. The questions derived from "Do you feel there is something that connects WoW players?" and "Would you say that being a WoW player is a part of who you are?" The interviews lasted and average of 50 minutes and were all audio recorded (O'connor et al, 2015, p.06).

The results showed the presence of the Psychological Feeling of Community among the players of the WoW as well as confirmed previous quantitative studies that player's avatars are closer to the player's ideal self than he is himself. The most important results for this work are those that showed that all participants reported a sense of belonging related to the game. A sense that connects players from WoW to each other. That sense of community has been reported as one of the best things in the game, offering a sense of belonging that may be missing in their offline lives (O'connor et al, 2015, p.08).

In addition, many participants identified themselves as WoW players and reported that the game was an important part of who they were. "These participants felt that there was something unique about being a WoW player and indicated a sense of separation between their friends who were gamers and those who were not". (O'connor et al, 2015, p.09).

Participants also reported that being part of an important guild[2], famous for great achievements within the game, was a sign of great pride and a seal of honor (O'Connor et al, 2015, p.10).

As well as giving advice on how to deal with offline issues, participants reported giving and receiving emotional support on offline issues, such as "friend's shoulders". (O'connor et al, 2015, p.11).

The conclusion of this study confirmed the quantitative researches that suggested the existence of Community Psychological Sentiment among the players and identified the existence of diverse social identities among the participants. The study also concluded that one of the key aspects of the WoW experience was the breakdown of social and geographical barriers, which allowed for greater diversity of relationships (O'Connor et al, 2015, p.13). The weaknesses, relevant to this work, indicated by the authors, point to the fact that the research was done only with Australians, since WoW is a global phenomenon and also indicated the fact that they interviewed only members of guilds, failing to analyze how individuals who do not belong to these groups behave.

From the article "The Lonely Gamer Revisited" (Schiano, Nardi, Debeauvais, Ducheneaut, Yee, 2013), which sought to visualize the stereotype of the "solitary player" or player with deficient social ties in his offline life, it is possible to conclude that the World of Warcraft can improve the social relations of an individual in his offline life, being for this individual an important influence.

The article is the result of a survey of 2865 WoW players, from various regions (Europe, United States and Hong Kong) and of a quantitative nature, drawn up in English and translated into Chinese using traditional characters, published on game sites and on social networks and with the purpose of knowing the characteristics of players such as gender, age and hours played per week and their degree of sociability, which refers to the numbers of players who play alone, with friends, co-workers, spouses and family members of offline life, and if they make friends in the WoW.

An important finding for this research is the fact that the average of 56% of the WoW players build friendship within the game. It is also suggested, from these results, that WoW can not only sustain, but may even promote social ties that link life offline to life online (Schiano, et al 2013, p.05). The article also discusses the social role of World of Warcraft, since

Typical patterns of WoW play appear to supplement, and perhaps even enhance real-life relationships, not simply subvert or destroy them. The finding that substantial percentages of players across all regions are making new RL[3] friends in the virtual world also suggests that World of Warcraft is a successful social platform with players reaching out to people they meet ingame, and incorporating them into their RL social lives. Contra Putam and the moral panic, multiplayer games may be better viewed as platforms for RL (as well as online) social interactions; whether drawing on existing RL relationships or enabling new ones, the effect is to bring people together (Schiano, et al 2013, p.05).

In this way, WoW is understood as an environment capable of mediating experiences and relationships, being configured as a social platform of relevance in the (online and offline) life of the player and behaving in a similar way around the world, in view of the proximity of the results found in the researches done in this work and the research developed in Australia. However, the article suggests that the patterns found in the relationships may be related to the way the game was developed, since the environment is substantially the same in all regions.

These works contribute to the realization that the World of Warcraft, under the watchful eye of the social bounds, is relevant to the academic community, especially in the fields of Communication and Education, because it is a mediation environment, which leads the subject to establish relationships within and experience the impacts of their online experiences in offline environments.

2.   Regarding the empirical research in the multiplayer environment itself – it is important to point out that this is a qualitative approach in which the field description is related to everyday production – culture, meaning – where one searches for evidence of flow spaces (multiplayer environments), the dynamic expression that constitutes these spaces of (self)representation, (in)formation and authorship, trying to describe them in what is challenged in this work – the relations, the construction of knowledge and identifications – taking into account the screentime in WoW and the interfaces to the online, offline and hybrid realities (Ludke & André, 2003; Cliers, 2003).

In this sense, we use the same multiplayer environment – WoW – using its characteristics as context of relationship and possibilities of (in)formation and communication, to apply a socio-demographic questionnaire and conduct interviews. Both online, through the empirical presence of the researcher/player, in the role of player-researcher, that analyzes and participates in the research process. Thus, a participatory observation posture was adopted, since it is impossible to study the virtual world without actually being there (Pearce, 2009).

From the player-researcher status, we performed the challenges presented by the game, and we raised the data for an analysis based on reflections about immersion as screen time and the relevance of interpersonal relationships within the game, the relationship between the individual and the characteristics of their character mingle.

The research has netnographic inspiration since netnography proves useful to reveal interaction styles, personal narratives, online rules, practices and rituals, discursive styles, innovative forms of collaboration and organization (Kozinets, 2015). The interviews and questionnaires were answered by 08 (eight) players, mediated by the player-researcher avatar who listened to and experienced, from the coexistence with these and other players within the game itself, about the relationships and ties made by them, understanding that the impressions passed by an avatar have social consequences (Fong, Mar, 2015).

The questionnaires were presented to the players within the game itself, in one of the central settings, the capital of the Horde, Orgrimmar, so that respondents could take on the role of player and respond to research in an immersive way. The communication for respondent players to volunteer for the survey was made through the game's general chat, in which players can have contact with a large number of other users through a single space for socialization. The volunteer players were attentive, also interested in the subject of the research. However, initial engagement proved to be problematic given the absence of volunteers, which was overcome only because of the time spent in the environment in search of participants.

The results fond in both the literature review and the questionnaire and interviews conducted in the WoW environment are presented below and analyzed in light of what constitutes our conceptual theoretical foundation on the approach presented here.

As for the socio-demographic questionnaire – was applied to the group of 08 (eight) players, made in the WoW environment, we have the following results:

The age of the players who answered it varies between 19 and 30 years. They are subjects with ongoing training in higher education, being built in a nucleus of young adults and adults, although the game is intended for an audience from 12 years of age. The male gender predominates – 1 woman and 7 men, of Brazilian nationality.

Regarding the time of the game in the World of Warcraft, the group of respondents has between 7 months and 8 years using the game as a preferred platform for multiusers games, with game times predominating over 5 years – the equivalent of 62,5%. The group of respondents also states that plays for periods between two and nine hour a day. This long screen time demonstrates, in the field of interpersonal relationships, that WoW users believe that relationships built in the environment can be as fulfilling as those that occur in the offline realities, since:

Unlike the majority of young people who spend the bulk of their time online on social sites like Facebook, synthetic-world users are much more likely to believe that online relationships can be just as fulfilling as off-line relationships. (Watkins, 2009, p.124).

This sense of belonging both corroborates the expressiveness of the World of Warcraft player's screen time and highlights the impact on their life, the social relationships built in the game.

It was also observed the predominance of players who belong to guilds – 75% of the respondents. These spaces, besides promoting the interaction between players, amplify the sense of belonging since they are places in which the players wishes to be a part of, according to the result presented by O'Connor (2015), showing reports affirming that to be part of an important guild, famous for great achievements inside the game, is a sign of great pride and seal of honor (O'Connor et al, 2015, p.10).

As for the interviews were concerned – Were conducted online, through the researcher player's empirical presence, in the role of player-researcher, from individual encounters, lasting approximately one and a half hours, in April 2018. For this, we used the game's own platform, through the general chat, which acts as a space where players can interact with other players in a massive way, or through private chat, derived from the greater chat. We used the general chat to reach a large number of players and, reaching out to interested players, we sit out to conduct interviews in a private way through the resources of the chat itself, thus seeking to answer the following objective: Taking into account the online, offline and hybrid realities in relationships among WoW players, what is the importance of these relationships in building identities and identifications of these players?

The questions that guided the interviews had as their starting point the reflections on immersion as screen time and the relevance of the interpersonal relationships within the game; the relationships between the individual and the characteristics of their avatar; and, as far as the player and the characteristics of their character mingle.

The questions and answers obtained will be presented, emphasizing the responses to immersion in the context of relationships as a representation for the social use of time – screen time – and the construction of identities or identifications.

When asking if there is a difference between the relationships built inside the WoW and those that arise in the life outside the game, we obtained the following answers:

- "Yes, but the difference is tenuous".
- "I believe that the only difference is the distance itself, to meet people from other cities, states and countries… As for the bounds of friendships it's the same thing".

These comments say there is no difference between the relationships built in offline reality and those built in World of Warcraft. For most respondents, the relationships built on the World of Warcraft do not differ significantly or differ, in a "tenuous" way, from real life, as it was perceived, which contributes to having "good friends" and friendships "for years". We believe that this view of social ties is a result of the imbrication/hybridization of realities, since respondent players seem to perceive no boundaries between them.

When we asked if the characteristics of the character contribute in some way, in the relations inside and outside the game, we obtained the following answers:

- "In the game you always want to make a character similar to you in real life".
- "I think we end up going from our personality to the characters we create, in race, class, appearance and even faction".
- "Yes, yes, of course. After all, it's an RPG. We live a little life in here. The trolls[4] show a lot of my personality, let's say "physical". Also a good guy [quiet] full of slang [laughter].
- "[...]I, for example, that I have preference for healer[5], specializations, is because I intend to go to college in a health area".

We find here answers that refer to the identifications between the respondent player and their character. We also notice comments about the longing for offline reality that were reflected in choices within the game. These answers reveal the naturalness in comparing the offline and online realities. It was also observed that there is agreement between what was identified in the O'Connor survey (2015), regarding emotional support and the building of bonds within the game.

These responses demonstrated not only the possibility of building ties that are as important as the ties established in the offline reality, but the importance that these ties have for the individual, given that, in comparative terms, they present themselves to the same extent in which social ties considered strong, that is: ties in which, as painted out by Granovetter (1973), there is a greater proximity between the pairs.

When we asked how to define a relationship built within the World of Warcraft, we obtained the following answers:

- "[...]A traditional friendship".
- "[...]I'd say that I have them as my college friends".
- "A friendship like any other, which can have different levels of intimacy depending on the friendships".
- "We build strong bonds within the game. Within the game we see people's nature. Some of them "screwed up" and others saved from "various perrengues [a difficult situation]". There are people you hate and there are people who "beat bad" [generate sadness in the player] when they stop playing".

We identified categorical responses and positions that discuss the belonging and authenticity of living/playing present in the community through pleasurable sensations generated by playing in groups or with affective partners.

We also identified the possibility of splitting the relationships, such importance that they have. From the speech of one of the respondents, we observe about the results achieved in the game, and which represent a high load of importance for some players.

All of these characteristics reiterate the importance of World of Warcraft as a space for social bonding, as well as a place where digital communication evolves to the point where the distinction between online and offline reality is tempered and even re-signified – deterritorialized and re-territorialized – as stated by Rheingold: "[…] For many people, this new medium is a way of breaking with the virtual world in which they already live" (Rheingold, 1997, pp.209-210), symbolizing that in addition to being real, relationships established and cultivated in the network, especially in the World of Warcraft, may have, as one of the characteristics, the breaking of virtual experiences experienced in offline reality.

When we asked what are the characteristics of these relationships built inside the World of Warcraft, we obtained the following answers:

- "Harmonious, reciprocal, just and honest".
- "Fellowship prevails".
- "The majority of the public is very respectful".
- "Rivalry of some friendship for others. As my girlfriend also plays there is a nice mood. When we raid[6] together several emotions, it's actually like in real life [laughter]".
- "People usually take the game to personal or put game above relationships. I have seen a lot of even long time friendships to go away because of loot[7] raid item and things like that".
- "I guess relationships have the power to develop faster than usual (you know people who love doing the same things you do - and they usually do them every day). On the other hand, relationships might end quickly if they are not cared for (at a higher level than others). For example, when we make friends in college. It is not something that happens overnight, it takes longer and when it happens, a stronger bond is created. Not that the bonds created in the wow are weaker, but it is necessary to cultivate them so that they become something else. I have friends that we have just finished playing for the day, and after that we never meet again. I have long lasting friends that although we have stopped playing that day, we still keep in touch. Thus, it depends on how friendship is built ... It takes hard work to maintain, you know?"

We find answers that reveal the perceptible influence that the relationships established within the World of Warcraft have generated in players who responded-contemporary society and culture, through their socio-technical apparatus, promote and enhance social relations, for better or worse. The composition of a social circle coming from the game demonstrates the functionality of the technological apparatuses as a viabilizer of the relations, which are sewn from an anticipated logic during the development of the game, as pointed out by Watkins (2009):

Many MMORPGs are designed to be social, insofar as they encourage interaction between players, often in the form of collaboration and teamwork. Users of MMORPGs are drawn to the platforms precisely because they afford the opportunity to engage other users in real time. (Watkins, 2009, p.107).

When we asked about the importance of the relationships built in World of Warcraft, we obtained the following answers:

- "These are people I'm going to take for a lifetime".

- "They reminded us that friends do not have to be around, and even from a distance they can make us die of laughter for the things that happen in the game".
- "They are very important friends. Some people I have already met on IRL[8], relationships that I hope to preserve as much as possible".
- "Some become as important as the ones built out of the WoW".

Moreover on this convergence of interests among users of the game, we observe answers that reiterate the difficulty in distinguishing between the relationships in the online and offline realities. In this universe, according to the players, it is possible to notice that, although their relationships were linked to the game or the geek world, the environment also allowed a real-life interaction would be less likely, as one of the respondents makes clear.

From these positions, we recall what Sherry Turkle (2011) tells us about digital identity because:

In online worlds and massively multiplayer online role-playing games, you have the virtuosity and fantasy – and something more: your performances put you at the center of a new community with virtual best friends and a sense of belonging. It is not unusual for people to feel more comfortable in an unreal place than a real one because they feel that in simulation they show their better and perhaps truer self. (Turkle, 2011, p. 212).

The digital identity, then, would portray a "self" whose ability to relate, in theory, would appear as more efficient and more satisfactory, in view of the personal interest of each one in showing their best. At the same time, we question whether this identity is actually a selection of characteristics that satisfy the "I" but which could not be considered true, in view of the clipping of the interesting part, over the rejected whole. We bring to Goffmann's (2002) discussion of the Self as an individual who believes in the role they represent. According to the author,

When an individual PERFORMS A ROLE, IMPLICITLY asks their observers to take seriously the sustained impression before them. It asks them to believe that the character they see at the moment has the attributes that appears to possess, that the role it represents will have the consequences implicitly intended by it and that, in general, things are what they appear to be. (Goffmann, 2002, p.25, own translation).

When we asked what are the main features that differentiate friends from World of Warcraft from offline friends of life, we got the following answers:

- "The focus of interest. Usually, conversations are more related to the game or geek world as a whole, while college / school friendships are things we live in these places or pop culture. Besides, I see no difference".
- "A big difference is that my Wow friends belong to very different tribes from my own. And we joined because of the wow. Who knows if we met in a bar in real life we would not become close friends? In fact, I'm sure of that".

Based on the "focus of interest" that is presented in the first response, we were able to intertwine what Lévy (1996) postulated about cyberspace, since, according to him:

In cyberspace, in return, each one is potentially emitter and receiver in a qualitatively differentiated, non-fixed, willing, participable, space. Here, it is not primarily by its name, its geographic or social position that people meet, but according to centers of interest, in a common landscape of sense or knowledge. (Lévy, 1996, p. 113, own translation).

In addition to this convergence of interests among the users of the game, we observed answers that reiterated the difficulty in distinguishing between offline and online reality relations. In this universe, according to the players, it is possible to note that although their relationships were linked to the game or the geek world, the environment also allowed an interaction that in real life would be less likely, as one of the respondents makes clear.

This final position, in the second answer, "... I am sure of that," evokes the following questions: Would it not be possible to build ties with friends in the real environment, reflecting a prejudice related to their identities? Does the virtual environment allow us to build ties from characteristics that individuals decide to present, to the detriment of other features that, in reality, offline, could not, or would be more difficult?

From these questions, we bring the thinking of Sherry Turkle (2011) regarding digital identity, when she says:

In the online world, the performances themselves place you at the center of a new community, with the best virtual friends and a sense of belonging. It is not uncommon for people to feel more comfortable in an unreal place than in the real one, because they feel that in the simulation they reveal their best and perhaps truer self. (Turkle, 2011, p. 212, own translation).

Turkle's (2011) thinking emphasizes the performativity experienced in virtual environments, in view of the incessant reconstruction of themselves through avatars and personas that emerge in the relationships and contexts of multiplayer environments, and that occurs through (self) representation - directly or indirectly, choices are made as to how to be present in these environments.

When we asked to what extent the relationships built in World of Warcraft influence offline life, we got the following answers:

- "I would say quite a lot, one of my best friends I met here helps me on a lot of subjects outside the game, like advice and help in difficult times myself, I think they make all the difference."
- ""The fact that I met all these different people, from all regions of Brazil and other countries (when I started playing a Brazilian server didn't exist yet). It took me out of some of the way I am inserted in society and I came to see other ways of thinking, other cultures ... Everything. And that was a great learning experience for me, especially considering that I started playing at age 12".
- "They influence me by showing me ideas that I often do not see in the real world".
- In a good way. My mom calls the pals for lunch here on Sunday and the atmosphere is so family like that they call my mother as their moms. I call Igor's grandmother as my grandmother. In the time of the Pandaria each one brought their laptop and we played together in the room. The coexistence within the game affected in a pleasant way even our own families".

We see in these responses an expressive influence on the lives of most respondents. This influence occurs in the relationships that the player has built with other players, in addition to recognizing a cultural, cosmopolitan value present in the environment and in their relationships. These answers reflect the importance of World of Warcraft as a social game. WoW, in addition to a socializing space, can become a bond strengthener.

This condition in which the game affects the relations of the offline reality of a player was presented by Schiano (2013), because in his viewpoint:

Typical patterns of WoW play appear to supplement, and perhaps even enhance, real-life relationships, not simply subvert or destroy them. The finding that substantial percentages of players across all regions are making new RL[9] friends in the virtual world also suggests that World of Warcraft is a successful social platform with players reaching out to people they meet ingame, and incorporating them into their RL social lives. Contra Putam and the moral panic, multiplayer games may be better viewed as platforms for RL (as well as online) social interactions; whether drawing on existing RL relationships or enabling new ones, the effect is to bring people together (Schiano, et al 2013, p.05).

Therefore, we observe the potential social aggregator that World of Warcraft has, which hybridizes referential relations from its own context, considering this context as typically characteristic for relationships in cyberculture.

As we ask how far the relationships built in offline reality influence the life of a player in World of Warcraft, we obtained the following answers:

- "The factor of helping those who need it. Real-life friends always help each other and in wow is no different".
- "My character is myself, just like everyone else. Be it in the way of talking or acting with people in here. I am what I am in my real life. I do not see a reason to be different kkk [laughter]".
- "I think I'm a little more" easygoing and quiet "because of the things I have been through in relationships outside the game. One of the reasons I happen to be casual and so on".

We observed that personality traits and personal experiences, coming from real life, can have repercussions on the life of a player, such as being supportive of other players or being a calmer player, without the duty to play with the responsibility of schedules, therefore being a casual player. Somehow, it goes back to the previous analysis in which we talked about the hybridization in this game of influences. We are not concerned, at this moment, if a reality referential, for example the online reality, influences offline reality more or vice-versa.

Our following question was if there is more time dedicated to the social relationship in WoW or reality offline, we obtained the following answers:

- "For me, I think in reality online, but without many specific reasons ... It is difficult to answer because I honestly do not know how much a relationship is in " wow "or out of the game. I think when you make real friends within the game, they end up transcending the wow environment. For example, there are days that I send message on WhatsApp with "wow stuff" all day long about issues from outside the game, hence they cease to be just wow relationships. They are as real as the others. "
- "The real relationship demands, as much time as attention, but it would not be strange to find people with relationships in the wow that overcome the relationships in reality, in the time and importance matter. It would be perfectly fitting".

We observed in laconic responses that although offline reality relationships are more relevant to respondent players, they are not easily dissociated from relationships in WoW. We also note that players understand that social relations in WoW can overcome in time and importance relationships in reality offline.

In this way, we perceive that, for the respondent players, although offline reality is supposed to have a greater influence on their lives, online reality does not pose as impossibility to their relationships. On the contrary, they are so intense and demanding, extrapolating the interface of the game, in other interfaces, and enhancing online relationships.

CONCLUSION

In contemporary times, more specifically, in the diverse environments of construction with the ITC (the so-called virtual environments, of online reality), we perceive that the subjects have become more and more present. A good part of the hours spent in social activities are in environments such as social media and multiplayer games. These environments have instituted new realities and behaviors - knowledge and production of culture (meaning). And this, unequivocally, has impacted the way we relate and learn. Each online reality environment has required one or more forms of representation through (self) representation. These forms are always resources for the relations between "I's" and "others", in a sort of game between actors (social) in a search for a better representation of themselves (Goffman, 1975). The (self) representation is, more than ever, a contemporary resource, facing the challenges of being with the other, and can be understood as a mark - record of a constructive process of a body / subject. In the specific case of multiplayer environments, a body responsible for a project that did not work: immortality (Le Breton, 2003).

World of Warcraft players develop a particular culture from a place programmed to be a place. This, understood as functionalization of the world, through which we perceive it empirically (Santos, 1996). However, what characterizes their culture is not the presence of these players in this place only, but how they are presented - whether they present themselves or (self) represent. For Bourdieu (1965), (self) representation can be understood as an action against time.

In this research in which we deal with World of Warcraft, we consider it to be a legitimate environment for the construction of identities and identifications, since the (self) representation amongst players, through their avatars, constitutes a resource not only to understand a dynamic relationship between the players and the game itself, but also to launch amongst the multiple realities as forms of Being - online, offline, hybrid.

These features make World of Warcraft an environment for the emergence of friendships and companionships, transforming the virtual space into a place where players can meet with each other without barriers and in real time. It is important to point out that the absence of a first contact in a real space does not prevent the establishment of relations of weak ties, responsible for encouraging the sharing of emotions and knowledge. It is also interesting to stand out the possibility of strengthening strong ties, because when played between members of the same family, the game provided an improvement in the quality of relationships, as well as an intensification of affective bonds (Shen, Williams, 2011).

We observed a scenario where ICTs and cyber culture shortened the distances between online and offline realities, through environments with their own characteristics and contexts, which support the construction of identities and identifications. In these environments, especially in WoW, we also noticed the birth of a new subject from their experiences of being in an imaginary world where the selves overcome the limitations of the offline world and reach the condition of being more of themselves, more possible than ideal.

We also observed the representation of self, carried out on an avatar taking features that would not be possible in an offline reality - like physical traits - projecting in the context of the game a "self" as (self) representation and mark of identifications before the relations / bonds built in WoW.

Those "selves", overlapped in offline, online and hybrid realities, through the processes of mediation and interaction, correspond to the complexity of the existence of more than one "I", due to the relativization of cultural identity, a reflection of space-time compression, the transience of the present day and the diversity of spaces and discourses (Hall, 1992), which clearly takes place within the World of Warcraft. A subject who interacts with the content that surrounds them, participating in the creation of messages that approach the single, individual, from routes elaborated by themselves, being therefore active, in a state of readiness and that connects between us and nexus, in a multilinear, multi-sequential and labyrinthine script that they themselves helped to construct by interacting with the nodes between words, images, documentation, music, video and relationships (Santaella, 2004). It configures itself as an individual who constructs and lives their construction as part of it, interacting and modifying the world in which was inserted, because instead of being a distant observer, this new subject is now implicated in the virtual world where they are immersed; their presence is active there, in the sense of triggering events and being subjected to the forces that operate in that universe.

In World of Warcraft, we analyze how players build their social relationships from their characters / avatars and their characteristics / personas and how these characteristics impact on the everyday relationships of online / offline realities of these players. In this analysis, individuals narrow the distances between online and offline worlds regarding their interpersonal relationships, since there were no significant considerations that segregated characteristics of these worlds.

We believe that the game, as a space of mediation, socialization and interaction, fosters the hybridization of realities and the identity of the individual, who is represented in World of Warcraft and filled by the relationships that comes as a result in that space.

The avatar, as an instrument of personification of the user in the context of WoW, manages to serve as representative of the individual to the extent of generating identification, despite the technical limitations, since each avatar has a certain number of selectable physical characteristics and personality. The player, therefore, assumes the characteristics of the character as their own, understanding that they corroborate their present "selves" only in an offline reality, but allows the process of building their persona online. We believe that the "mask" concept proposed by Goffman (1975) could possibly be matched to the avatar in this context, since, like masks, the avatar becomes a second nature and part of the individual personality of the individual player.

As we look into writings of correlated authors to the object of this paper, we realize the strong presence of the traces of identity and social relations established among WoW players. This made them notice the veracity of these connections and the genuine repercussion of these, to the hybrid and social life of the players. For Bainbridge (2010), "World of Warcraft is so complex, so culturally rich and so expansive that will become a permanent part of our civilization" (Bainbridge, 2010, p.) The author's perspective reinforces the findings we found through interviews, since we observe that the game has the bases to overlap realities and, in this way, to solidify its space in an increasingly digital and immersive daily life.

In order to observe the experiences of individuals in a collective way, we chose to form a focal group, however, we did not succeed in achieving it. During the time that we were occupied in carrying out this method, the environment behaved in an adverse way to the formation of the group: either because of lack of commitment of the players with the dates and schedules; or even with the difficulty of finding interest in contributing to the research. However, by changing the approach, leaving aside the collective nature of the investigation and changing to individually interviews, we were able to obtain qualitatively relevant answers to the objective of the study.

We identified in the bibliography review that a qualitative research with a significant number of participants congregating in a space of flow and action constitutes a great challenge (Santaella, 2004). In addition to this challenge in collecting data from a large number of players, we also find it difficult for players to feel comfortable responding to questionnaires and interviews dealing with age and gender, among others. We understood that in the WoW multiplayer environment, when it comes to talking about themselves through questionnaires and interviews, players are faced with fear of presenting themselves.

This work does not intend to put an end to issues related to immersion in World of Warcraft - relationships, bonds, identities and/or identifications. We aim to contribute towards the visualization of a new context of connection mediated by the interface of a multiuser environment of players - characters, characteristics and the context itself - in which (self) representation fuses information from imaginaries and realities as a lively experience, predominantly lively on screen in the sense of contributing to the emergence and / or construction of identities and identifications.

We believe that this brief analysis of the social relations built in World of Warcraft can contribute to the fields of Communication and Education. A game that is the fruit of an interconnected society and that has its ideals and values being transformed and transposed into the imaginary and intelligence in the form of data, constituent elements of this contemporary technological agency.

ACKNOWLEDGMENT

This research was supported by Bahia State University-UNEB.

REFERENCES

Bainbridge, W. S. (2010). *The Warcraft Civilization: social science in a virtual world*. Cambridge, MA: The MIT Press.

Bolaño, C. R. S. (Ed.). (2015). Cultura e desenvolvimento: reflexões à luz de Furtado. Salvador, Brasil: EDUFBA.

Bourdieu, P. (1965). *Photography, A Middle-brown Art*. Cambridge, MA: Polity Press.

Cilliers, P. (2003). Porque não podemos conhecer as coisas complexas completamente. In *Método, métodos, contramétodo* (R. L. Garcia, Trans.). São Paulo, Brazil: Cortez.

Goffman, E. (1975). *A representação do Eu na Vida Cotidiana*. Rio de Janeiro, Brazil: Ed. Vozes.

Granovetter, M. (1973). The Strength of Weak Ties. United States. *American Journal of Sociology*, 78(6), 1360–1380. doi:10.1086/225469

Hall, S. (2004). *A identidade cultural na pós-modernidade*. Rio de Janeiro, Brazil: DP&A.

Johnson, T. (2010). *Nos bastidores da Wikipédia Lusófona: Percalços e conquistas de um projeto de escrita coletiva on-line*. Rio de Janeiro, Brazil: E-papers.

Kozinets, R. (2015). *Netnography:Redefined*. Sage.

Le Breton, D. (2003). *Adeus ao corpo: Antropologia e sociedade* (M. Appenzeller, Trans.). São Paulo, Brazil: Papirus.

Lemos, A. (2013). *A comunicação das coisas: teoria ator-rede e cibercultura*. São Paulo, Brazil: Annablume.

Lévy, P. (2002). *Ciberdemocracia. Col. Epistemologia e sociedade*. Lisboa: Inst. Piaget.

Lévy, P. (2003). *O que é virtual*. São Paulo, Brazil: Editora 34.

Ludke, M., & André, E. D. A. (2003). *A pesquisa em educação: Abordagens qualitativas*. São Paulo, Brazil: EPU.

Maldonado, T. (1999). *Desenho Industrial*. Trad. José Francisco Espadeiro Martins. Lisboa: Edições 70.

O'connor, E. (2015). *Sense of Community, Social Identity and Social Support Among Players of Massively Multiplayer Online Games (MMOGs): A qualitative analysis. Journal of Community & Applied Social Psychology*. Queensland, Australia: Wiley.

Santaella, L. (2004). *Navegar no ciberespaço: o perfil cognitivo do leitor imersivo*. Brazil: Paulus.

Santos, M. (1996). *A natureza do espaço*. São Paulo, Brazil: Hucitec.

Schiano, D=. (2013). *The "lonely gamer" revisited*. Elsevier.

Shen, C., & Williams, D. (2010). Unpacking time online: Connecting internet and massively multiplayer online game use with psychological well-being. *Communication Research, 38*(1), 123–149. doi:10.1177/0093650210377196

Turkle, S. (2011). *Alone Together: Why we expect more from technology and less from each other*. Basic Books.

Watkins, S. (2009). *The Young & The Digital: What the Migration to Social-Network Sites, Games, and Anytime, Anywhere Media Means for Our Future*. Boston: Beacon Press.

ADDITIONAL READING

Bainbridge, W. S. (2010). *The Warcraft Civilization: social science in a virtual world*. Cambridge, United States: The MIT Press.

O'connor, E., Longman, H., White, K. M., & Obst, P. L. (2015). Sense of Community, Social Identity and Social Support Among Players of Massively Multiplayer Online Games (MMOGs): A qualitative analysis. *Journal of Community & Applied Social Psychology*, *25*(6), 459–473. doi:10.1002/casp.2224

Steinkuehler, C., & Williams, D. (2006). Where Everybody Knows Your (Screen) Name: Online Games as "Third Places". Oxford, United States. *Journal of Computer-Mediated Communication*, *11*(4), 885–909. doi:10.1111/j.1083-6101.2006.00300.x

KEY TERMS AND DEFINITIONS

(In)formation: Formative dimension of the information.

Healer: This is a specialization within the game which has the function of healing the injuries of other players or of oneself.

Loot: Loot, inside the game, is the same as a reward, left by a defeated enemy monster.

Raid: Raid is a game mode where several players play in a coordinated way to achieve a result that cannot be achieved individually, such as beating a very strong enemy. Raid items usually have higher quality than items purchased by other means. For Brazilian players of *World of Warcraft*, raiding means the action of playing in a raid group.

RL or IRL: These terms mean real life or in real life.

Trolls: Trolls are a playable race presented in the game.

ENDNOTES

[1] This is a study carried out between the fields of knowledge of communication and education. It concerns the contemporary forms of communication, and also the processes of (in)formation – formative dimension of the information.

[2] Guild is the space where social interaction happens widely. They are places where people with common interests join in and need to interact with each other to carry out activities in a synergistic way, obeying a leader and fulfilling, each one, their role (Rodrigues & Mustaro, 2010).

3   "RL" means Real Life.

4   Trolls are a playable race presented in the game.

5   This specialization within the game is a role which has the function of healing the injuries of other players or of oneself.

6   Raid is a game mode where several players play in a coordinated way to achieve a result that cannot be achieved individually, such as beating a very strong enemy. Raid items usually have higher quality than items purchased by other means. For the Brazilian player of World of Warcraft, raiding means the action of playing in a raid group.

7   Loot, inside the game, is the same as a reward, left by a dead enemy monster.

8   IRL means IN REAL LIFE.

9   "RL" means Real Life.

Chapter 13
Measuring the Relationship Between Time Perspective and Well-Being

Ercan Kocayörük
Çanakkale Onsekiz Mart University,
Turkey

Bekir Çelik
Çanakkale Onsekiz Mart University,
Turkey

Ömer Faruk Şimşek
İstanbul Arel University, Turkey

Pelin Buruk
Istanbul Arel University, Turkey

Emin Altintas
Université de Lille, France

ABSTRACT

The aim of this chapter is to examine the relations between time perspective and well-being considering two groups with different cultural backgrounds between Turkish and French. Instruments tapping into positive and negative affect, ontological well-being, flourishing, and five types of time perspective were administered to 615 late adolescents ages between 18 and 24 (Mean of age= 20.95, SD= 3.28). In this study, a recently created subjective well-being construct, known as ontological well-being (OWB), was utilized for measuring eudaimonic happiness based on time perspective in a cross-cultural study. Cluster analysis showed that Turkish people had higher levels of positive affect, negative affect, and psychological flourishing compared to French people, but the levels of regret and nothingness were similar in both groups. Differences between clusters in terms of negative affect were mainly driven by differences in ontological well-being (OWB).

DOI: 10.4018/978-1-5225-8163-5.ch013

INTRODUCTION

Two of the most important contributions made positive psychology define the concept of the good life and formulating what leads to an enduring level of happiness. In describing the good life, Seligman (2002) distinguishes between the hedonic approach and the eudaimonic approach, stating that a pleasant life, which perseveres positive emotions about the present, past and future, is the simplest form of a good life characterized by the hedonic approach. For enduring happiness, however, Seligman (2002) emphasizes the eudaimonic approach that focuses on the development and realization of one's signature strengths. Studies on well-being produced many constructs to measure hedonic or eudaimonic happiness. A recently created subjective well-being construct, known as ontological well-being (OWB), is utilized for measuring eudaimonic happiness in a cross-cultural study (Şimşek, 2009; Şimşek & Kocayörük, 2013). In this study, it examined the OWB and time perspective of Turkish and French cultures, while identifying its association with other widely used constructs of well-being such as flourishing, positive affect and negative affect. Moreover, the relationship between OWB and psychological time perspective and well-being are investigated in this study.

WHAT IS ONTOLOGICAL WELL-BEING?

Subjective well-being (SWB) was defined by Diener (1984; 2000) as a unity of cognitive and affective evaluations of life. Life satisfaction constituted the cognitive dimension while positive affect and the lack of negative affect represented the affective dimension, later referred to as emotional well-being. Diener et al. (1999) described subjective well-being in a broad category of constructs that includes people's emotional responses, domain satisfactions, and global judgments of life satisfaction. Each of the specific phenomenon need to be specified in their own right, considering components often related substantially, suggesting the need for the higher order factor. Accordingly, subjective well-being might be comprehended as a general area of scientific field rather than a single specific phenomenon. Main divisions could be pleasant affect (e.g. joy, affection, happiness), unpleasant affect (e.g. sadness, stress, depression), life satisfaction (e.g. desire to change life, satisfaction with past, significant others' views of one's life), and domain satisfactions (e.g. work, family, leisure health).

Many researchers have been studied the associations between subjective wellbeing and various variables. Diener (1999) highlighted that there are social and psychological indicators of subjective well-being as well as people's different reactions to the similar contexts, and they assess condition based on their personal expectations, values, and earlier experiences. For instance, Kuzu, Berk, and Aydin (2017) examined whether four factors (body image, pain, function and mental health) predicted subjective well-being variables (Positive Affect, Negative Affect, Life Satisfaction) or not. Findings of the study emphasized that body image significantly predict Positive Affect, Negative Affect, Life Satisfaction as consistent with the literature. Researchers claimed that body image is related with psychosocial concerns therefore body image is a crucial variable which is associated with subjective well-being.

Subjective well-being was criticized for not having a theoretical base on which life satisfaction and emotional well-being were integrated. In addition, the emotional well-being that incorporated the affective evaluations lacked a specific object, which caused the problem of intentionality. In other words, the positive and negative affect scales measured the frequency of feelings; however, the feelings did not have a reference to one's own life. This also caused another problem cited in the literature as conceptual overlap with personality measures (Schmutte & Ryff, 1997). Moreover, combining general life satisfaction judgments with affect measures was considered to reflect a pleasure and pain framework, which is mainly related to hedonic inclinations, but lacks eudaimonic elements such as self-actualization, growth or purpose in life.

The construct of OWB was developed by Şimşek (2009) with the aim of overcoming the shortcomings of SWB. In line with Diener's (1984) definition of SWB, OWB is also defined as a collection of affective and cognitive evaluations of one's life, but herein life is defined as "a personal project with past, present, and future parts". In order to measure OWB, the Ontological Well-Being Scale (OWBS) was developed by Şimşek and Kocayörük (2013). The OWBS requires one to rate the intensity of emotions related to his/her life considering it like a project with the completed (past), the ongoing (present) and the prospective (future) parts. The reason why the OWBS contains only affective reactions to life projects is to surpass any specific attributes about these projects that could hinder subjective evaluations. Yet, the OWBS's special feature of intentionality provides it with a cognitive dimension as well.

Intentionality implies that all mental states, including emotions, are directed towards or about something (Şimşek, 2009). The emphasis of "life as a project" in the OWBS enables one to connect affective evaluations with a cognitive stance. For example, when one is required to evaluate the affective adjectives such as regretful, proud, guilty, and disappointed related to one's past, which is the completed part of one's life project, one needs to consider the fulfillment of his or her personal project. Similarly, the OWBS asks one to evaluate affective adjectives such as hopeful, strong, confident, and ambitious when looking at the future of one's life project. It is clear that such an evaluation of a project requires a cognitive stance. As a result, the OWBS accomplishes to unite cognitive and affective evaluations of life with regard to personal goals and projects (Şimşek & Kocayörük, 2013) and still abide with subjectivity, which is a prerequisite for any definition of SWB (Diener, 1984).

One other distinguishing feature of OWB is the whole-time perspective, which gives OWB the quality of a narrative construct. Since the OWBS requires individuals to evaluate the affective adjectives about the completed, ongoing and future parts of one's life project, this evaluation facilitates the individuals to construe their own life as a story or a project, organizing all forms of critical personal goals and actions. This process is in line with what McAdams (2001) described as the life story model of identity or autobiographical memory. The personal narratives or life stories enable one to evaluate their lives from a temporal perspective, which consists of the past, present and future components (Şimşek & Kocayörük, 2013). This unification of one's life as a personal project enables one to create meaning and purpose out of this whole story. The eudaimonic dimension of OWB is generated from this process and how much meaning and purpose a person finds in life is expected to be assessed by OWB. Accordingly, the factor structure of the OWBS reveals four factors, namely regret related to past, activation, and nothingness related to present and, finally, hope related to future.

ONTOLOGICAL WELL-BEING AND TIME PERSPECTIVE

OWB can be distinguished from other SWB measures mainly because OWB considers time perspective as a whole while other SWB measures evaluate well-being in the present time (Şimşek, 2009). According to Nuttin (1985), the cognitive level of behavioral functioning is under the impact of past and future events to the extent that in a way both exist in the present time. Similarly, Bandura (1997) emphasized the importance of temporal influence on self-efficacy, stating that it has its roots in past experiences as well as current appraisals and future options. Moreover, Lens (2004) claimed that enhanced motivation, deep conceptual learning, better performance, and more intensive persistence are related with having a deep future time perspective increasing the instrumentality of one's present behavior. Psychological time was studied by Zimbardo and his colleagues (Boniwell & Zimbardo, 2004; Stolarski et al., 2014; Zimbardo & Boyd, 1999) who demonstrated that it is associated with well-being. The factor structure of psychological time revealed that time could be perceived in five categories and the dominance of any of the five categories affect the well-being of individuals. The five factors of time perspective are past-negative, past-positive, present-hedonistic, present-fatalistic and future. A proper balance in TP is generally recognized as a fundamental prerequisite for psychological health, happiness, and efficiency (e.g., Stolarski et al., 2014). The OWBS questions affect the past, present and future times, but the factor structure of the OWBS has four factors that are expected to correlate with the time perspective proposed by Zimbardo and his colleagues. The past is assessed by negative and positive adjectives such as disappointed, regretful, upset, guilty, incompetent, proud and satisfied. Therefore, we expect that people who have high levels of regret should correlate with past-negative, while people who have low levels of regret should have higher levels of past-positive dimension. The affective adjectives for the present time in the OWBS diverge into two factors: "nothingness" and "activation". These two factors are expected to correlate with the present-fatalistic and present-hedonistic dimensions of time perspective respectively. Finally, the affects evaluated for the future time in the OWBS all reveal one factor namely, hope, which is expected to be in line with the only factor defined as "future" in the time perspective of Zimbardo and his colleagues. In the present study, we searched for these expected correlations between the four factors of OWB and the five factors of time perspective.

ONTOLOGICAL WELL-BEING AND WELL-BEING (FLOURISHING)

The idea of evaluating one's life as a project in time perspective is based on existential approaches to psychology. According to Şimşek (2009), the main theme in Heidegger's *Being and Time* is the individual's existence in the world as a project. Furthermore, the basic dimension of this project is the tension between the past and the future at every single moment of now, making life a story or narration. Consequently, the evaluation of this whole life project in its temporality would require affective and cognitive appraisal of one's life with regard to the fulfillment of his/her purpose in life and the achievement of one's goals. When a person looks back at his/her past life to decide how proud, regretful, guilty or satisfied he/she feels, these decisions show how content the person is with the past. Similarly, reflecting on the present in terms of being aimless or lost or enthusiastic or motivated, all demonstrate whether or not the individual is processing according to the aims of the life project. Accordingly, feeling hopeful, confident, strong or ambitious means that the person is predicting a positive future. This conceptualization of well-being contains the elements of growth, direction and self-actualization that are the major criteria of the eudaimonic approach to happiness. Therefore, in this study we expect the OWBS to correlate with the flourishing scale (Diener et al., 2010) since it also assesses aspects of psychological well-being that go beyond positive emotions and life satisfaction. It measures the key aspects of a good life including strong social relationships, self-respect, competence, engaging in work and spirituality, all of which indicate whether one's life has a purpose and meaning. Previous research on the OWBS (Şimşek & Kocayörük, 2013) showed that all factors of the OWBS correlated with the beliefs of participants on attaining intrinsic aspirations regarding personal growth and meaningful relationships. Moreover, the OWBS explained additional variance in purpose in life and personal growth in comparison with other SWB measures including the Satisfaction with Life Scale and PANAS.

The aim of this research is to investigate whether these qualifications of the OWBS could be traced in a cross-cultural setting. First of all, the whole-time perspective of the OWBS was compared to time perspective by Zimbardo and Boyd (1999). Then, the eudaimonic features of the OWBS were investigated by seeking its associations with Flourishing Scale (Diener et al., 2010). Due to the OWBS utilizing the measurement of affect like PANAS, their relationship was also reviewed and positive correlations were expected.

METHOD

Participants

The study consisted of 615 undergraduate students, all of whom were studying in a department of either humanities or psychological counseling in France or Turkey. The participants were aged between 18 and 24 years ($\bar{x} = 20.95$, SD = 3.28). The Turkish sample was composed of 307 undergraduate students, 208 female and 99 male ($\bar{x} = 20.96$, SD = 3.15). The French sample was composed of 245 undergraduate students, 198 female and 63 male ($\bar{x} = 20.88$, SD = 3.05). Each participant was invited to complete a scales set including perceived parenting behaviors, affect, and well-being.

Instruments

- **The Positive and Negative Affect Scale (PANAS):** This scale was originally developed by Watson, Clark, and Tellegen (1988) and has been adapted to both French (Lapierre, Bouffard & Bastin, 1997) and Turkish (Gençöz, 2000). The PANAS is a 20-item self-report scale that measures the positive and negative affect, with 10 items evaluating negative affect and 10 items evaluating positive affect. Respondents indicated their score on a 5-point Likert scale ranging from 1 ("Very Slightly or Not at All") to 5 ("Extremely"). In the current study, the internal consistency of the scale was satisfactory (Turkish sample: alpha = .87; French sample: alpha = .84).
- **The Psychological Flourishing Scale (PFS):** This scale was originally developed by Diener, Wirtz, Tov, Kim-Prieto, Choi, Oishi, et al. (2010) and has been adapted to both French (Villieux, Sovey, Jung, & Guilbert, 2016)

and Turkish (Akın & Fidan, 2012). The scale is used to evaluate psychological flourishing that is described as the present subjective well-being state and includes eight items associated with one question ("Below are 8 statements with which you may agree or disagree."). Respondents indicated their scores on a 7-point Likert scale ranging from 1 ("Strong Disagreement") to 7 ("Strong Agreement") for all eight items. All of the scores of the eight items were combined into an overall psychological flourishing score. The higher the overall score is the higher the psychological flourishing. In the current study, the internal consistency of the scale was satisfactory (Turkish sample: alpha = .85; French sample: alpha = .83).

- **Short Version of the Zimbardo Time Perspective Inventory (ZTPI-short: Košťál, Klicperová-Baker, Lukavská, and Lukavský, 2016):** The ZTPI is the first comprehensive and theory-based operationalization of time perspective (TP). The ZTPI, which was developed as an individual-differences metric, assesses the fundamental dimensions of the human condition related to time (Zimbardo & Boyd, 1999). The scale is composed of 56 items after the exploratory and confirmatory factor analyses of the following five distinct time perspective factors emerged: Past-Negative (PN), Past-Positive (PP), Present-Fatalistic (PF), Present Hedonistic (PH) and Future (F). The analyses showed acceptable validity and internal, and test-retest reliability. In the current study the short version of the ZTPI has been utilized as a short-form by Košťál, Klicperová-Baker, Lukavská, and Lukavský (2016) tested both in its five-scale and six-scale forms (with and without the Future-Negative scale). The authors suggested that the five-scale ZTPI–short form with 15 items had a slightly better model fit than the six-scale version, because the Future-Negative scale correlated strongly with the Past-Negative scale. Thus within this study, 15 items in the five-scale short form by Košťál, Klicperová-Baker, Lukavská, and Lukavský (2016) (without the Future-Negative scale) was translated into Turkish culture. The authors reported that the internal consistency of the scales measured by Cronbach's alpha varied from 0.65 to 0.78.

- **The Ontological Well-Being Scale (OWBS; Şimşek & Kocayörük, 2013):** This scale was developed to measure happiness and consisted of 24 items scored on a 5-point Likert-type scale. The OWBS is comprised of four subscales: regret, activation, nothingness, and hope. The Regret subscale (7 items) assesses participants' feelings regarding the completed part of their life projects (the past). The Nothingness (6 items) and Activation (5 items) subscales measure feelings related to ongoing life projects (the present). Lastly, the Hope subscale (6 items) taps into the individual's feelings towards future life projects (the future). The original scale had good internal consistencies ranging from .78 to .90, and the test-retest reliability of the OWBS, which was conducted over a 2-week interval, showed sufficient consistency of the scores over time (ranging from .72 to .92). In this current study, Cronbach's alpha values of the OWBS varied from .61 to .73.

Statistical Analyses

Statistical analyses were realized using SPSS and Latent GOLD software. First, all the variables of the study were compared between the Turkish group and the French group with Student's t-test. Thereafter, the number of valid profiles was identified using latent profile analysis (LPA) on the Turkish and French group (Lanza et al. 2007). This procedure allowed us to detect the valid number of OWB profiles. Based on the four dimensions of the OWBS (Regret – Nothingness – Activation – Hope), an LPA was realized to determine the number of OWB profiles in both the Turkish and the French samples with the best fit and their composition. Two to six profile solutions were tested (Vermunt & Magidson, 2002). In accordance with the recommendations of Lanza et al. (2007) The Akaike Information Criterion (AIC, Akaike, 1987), Bayesian Information Criterion (BIC, Schwarz, 1978), and Entropy values were used to test the models and determine the best model fit. The lower values of AIC and BIC associated with a higher value of Entropy indicate the best model fit.

A One-way MANOVA was conducted with all of the OWB profile groups as the independent variable and the four dimensions of the OWBS as the dependent variables for confirmed that the number of profile obtained by LPA is satisfactory. In addition, ANOVA tests and New Man Keuls post hoc test were used to compare the Turkish and French profiles on each dependent variable: PANAS, Flourishing, Self-Construct and all subscales of ZTPI.

RESULTS

Preliminary Analyses

The means and standard deviations for all variables used in the study are presented in Table 1. As shown in the group comparison in Table 1, the Turkish sample (n= 307) and the French sample (n= 308) presented significant differences. The Turkish group reported higher levels of activation, past positive, past negative, present hedonic, future, PANAS negative, self-construct, and age than the French group. However, the French group reported higher levels of hope, and present fatalistic. No difference was found for regret, nothingness, Psychological flourishing and

PANAS positive between the two groups (Table 1). The differences between the Turkish group and the French group are not systematic. The results are inconsistent because the French group presented significantly higher level of hope ($\bar{x} = 3.40$) in OWB than the Turkish group ($\bar{x} = 2.91$). While the Turkish group presented significantly higher level of future ($\bar{x} = 3.78$) in ZTPI than the French group ($\bar{x} = 3.13$).

These findings are a further argument to conduct exploration into each group (Turkish and French) in light to OWB profiles. More specifically, the Turkish and French groups could both be non-homogeneous groups comprising of small homogeneous groups. Latent Profile Analyses will allow finding these small homogeneous groups in OWB.

Primary Analyses

Latent profile analysis (LPA) was performed for each group to identify the number of optimal OWB profiles (Lanza et al., 2007). These procedures enabled us to detect the valid number OWB profiles on all the subscales of the OWBS and identify the

Table 1. Comparison between the Turkish and French groups made with Student's t-test

	Mean TR	SD	Mean FR	SD	t Value	p
Age	22,88	4,68	20,80	3,16	6,47	.001
OWB						
Regret	2,46	0,82	2,40	0,87	0,80	.423
Nothingness	2,15	0,89	2,11	0,82	0,57	.566
Activation	3,48	1,04	3,24	0,82	3,24	.001
Hope	2,91	0,91	3,40	0,97	-6,41	.000
ZTPI						
Past positive	3,82	0,74	3,36	0,72	7,85	.001
Past negative	3,53	0,83	2,61	0,51	16,44	.001
Present fatalistic	2,06	0,76	2,19	0,80	-2,13	.033
Present hedonic	3,42	0,81	3,11	0,97	4,26	.001
Future	3,78	0,73	3,13	0,75	10,79	.001
Dependent Variables						
Flourishing	5,16	1,10	5,16	1,06	0,01	.995
PANAS +	3,05	0,85	3,10	0,78	-0,85	.395
PANAS -	2,09	0,76	1,92	0,74	2,87	.004

Note: TR: Turkish (n= 307), FR: French (n= 308)

groups of participants that differ on OWB. The statistical results and the extant literature tend to support that the most suitable solution for the Turkish group is a three-profile solution. The entropy, BIC and AIC suggested a well-fitted two-profile solution for OWB of the Turkish group and well-fitted three-profile solution for the French group (Table 2). For each group, the means of the OWBS subscales for each profile are reported in Table 3 and presented in Figure 1.

For the Turkish group, *Profile 1 TR* corresponded to 49.51% of the Turkish sample (n = 152, "Moderate OWB") and was characterized by moderate levels of Regret, Nothingness, Activation, and Hope. *Profile 2 TR* corresponded to 32.90% of the Turkish sample (n = 101, "High OWB") and was characterized by low levels of Regret and Nothingness and high levels of Activation and Hope. *Profile 3 TR* corresponded to 17.59% of the Turkish sample (n = 54, "Low OWB") and was characterized by high levels of Regret and Nothingness and low levels of Activation and Hope.

For the French group, *Profile 1 FR* corresponded to 34.09% of the French sample (n = 105, "Moderate OWB") and was characterized by high levels of Regret and Nothingness and moderate levels of Activation and Hope. *Profile 2 FR* corresponded to 65.91% of the sample (n = 203, "High OWB") and was characterized by high levels of Activation and Hope.

Table 2. Latent profiles analyses model fit indexes for the 2. 3. 4. 5 and 6 clusters solutions in Turkish and French sample

	LL	BIC (LL)	AIC (LL)	AIC3 (LL)	Entropy	L^2	df	p Value
French Sample								
2-cluster	-3465,85	7481,78	7123,69	7219,69	0,80	3413,04	212	.001
3-cluster	-3436,86	7452,46	7075,72	7176,72	0,71	3355,07	207	.001
4-cluster	-3417,02	7441,44	7046,05	7152,05	0,72	3315,40	202	.001
5-cluster	-3405,74	7447,53	7033,49	7144,49	0,75	3292,84	197	.001
6-cluster	-3398,22	7461,14	7028,45	7144,45	0,71	3277,80	192	.001
Turkish Sample								
2-cluster	-3566,90	7775,22	7357,81	7469,81	0,77	3625,84	195	.001
3-cluster	-3510,81	7691,67	7255,63	7372,63	0,79	3513,66	190	.001
4-cluster	-3500,40	7699,48	7244,81	7366,81	0,79	3492,84	185	.001
5-cluster	-3496,66	7720,64	7247,33	7374,33	0,75	3485,36	180	.001
6-cluster	-3484,48	7724,90	7232,96	7364,96	0,77	3460,99	175	.001

The highest levels of Regret, Nothingness and Activation were reported in the Turkish sample, with Regret and Nothingness in *Profile 3 TR* and Activation in *Profile 2 TR*. *Profile 2 TR* and *Profile 2 FR* reported the highest levels of Hope, no significant difference was found between the two profiles. Among the five OWB profiles, we found the lowest levels of OWB were found in Profile *3 TR* of the Turkish sample and the highest levels of OWB in *Profile 2 TR* of the Turkish sample.

In accordance with the profile check, a One-way MANOVA was conducted with the five OWB profile groups as the independent variable and the four dimensions of the OWBS as the dependent variables. MANOVA results showed significant differences between the five groups on the OWBS dimensions ($F_{(14, 56)} = 36.09$, $p < .001$). This latter result confirmed that the number of profiles was valid in the sample (see Figure 1).

Figure 1. OWB profiles in the French group (2 profiles) and the Turkish group (3 profiles)

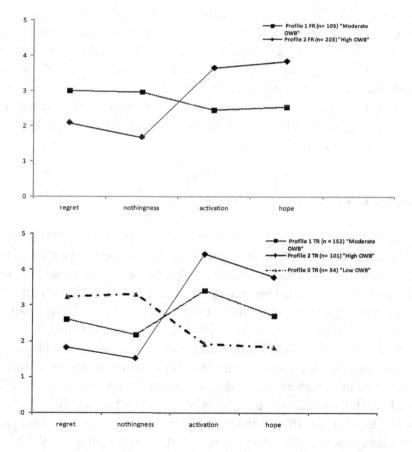

Finally, the relationships between OWB profiles and the study variables (ZTPI's dimensions, PANAS, Psychological Flourishing, Self-construct, and) were tested using an ANOVA and New Man Keuls post hoc test. The results showed a significant association between the OWB profiles and the variables of the study (Table 3). First, the High OWB profiles ("Profile 2 TR" and "Profile 2 FR") were associated with the highest level of past positive, present hedonic, future, positive affect, psychological flourishing and self-construct. These profiles were also associated with the lowest level of past negative, present fatalist, and negative affect. The Turkish sample with high OWB profile presented significantly higher levels of past positive, past negative, present hedonic and future than the French sample with high OWB profile. In this same profile, the French sample was more fatalistic than the Turkish sample. Secondly, significant differences were found between the Moderate OWB profiles ("Profile 1 TR" and "Profile 1 FR"). The Turkish sample with moderate profile presented significantly higher levels of past positive, past negative, future, psychological flourishing, and positive affect. In this same profile, the French was more fatalistic than the Turkish and presented highest negative affect. Thirdly, the Low OWB ("Profile 3 TR") was found only in the Turkish sample. This profile presented the lowest levels of positive past, present hedonic, psychological flourishing and positive affect in the Turkish sample. The same profile also presented the highest level of negative past, present fatalistic and negative affect in the Turkish sample. However, the level of future in the ZTPI scale of the Low OWB profile ("Profile 3 TR") was better than the Moderate OWB profile ("Profile 1 FR") in the French group and no significant differences were found when compared to the High OWB profile ("Profile 2 FR") in French group.

DISCUSSION

The present study investigated in what way the qualifications of OWB could be traced in a cross-cultural setting. Along with the comparison of five ZTPs to whole time perspective of OWB and the eudemonic features of OWB were investigated by seeking its connections to the psychological flourishing. As proposed in the study, results of the analyses showed significant associations between OWB profiles and the variables: TP dimensions, PANAS and psychological flourishing.

High scores on PP, PH, and F factors and low scores on the PN and PF. subscales create optimally balanced time perspective (BTP) scores which mean that past, present and future factors blend and flexibly engage (Boniwell & Zimbardo, 2004; Zimbardo, 2002). According to the evaluation of the ZTPI scores; the French group showed higher scores on PP, PH and F and lower scores on PN and PF which means that they have expected BTP scores. However, the Turkish group met the expected

Table 3. Means and standard deviations for the study variables as a function of profiles

Clusters	Profile 1 TR (n=152) "Moderate OWB" 49.51(%)		Profile 2 TR (n=101) "High OWB" (32.90%)		Profile 3 TR (n=54) "Low OWB" (17.59%)		Profile 1 FR (n=105) "Moderate OWB" (34.09%)		Profile 2 FR (n=203) "High OWB" (65.91%)		F	p	η^2
	Mean	SD	Mean	SD	Mean	SD	Mean	SD	Mean	SD			
Age	$22,93_a$	4,96	$23,39_a$	5,10	$21,80_c$	2,33	$20,34_c$	1,76	$21,03_c$	3,66	13,04	.001	0,079
OWB													
Regret	$2,60_a$	0,66	$1,82_b$	0,53	$3,23_c$	0,83	$3,00_d$	0,85	$2,09_e$	0,70	66,42	.001	0,305
Nothing	$2,17_a$	0,66	$1,52_b$	0,43	$3,30_c$	0,90	$2,96_d$	0,72	$1,67_b$	0,44	154,06	.001	0,505
Activation	$3,41_a$	0,64	$4,43_b$	0,45	$1,92_c$	0,63	$2,45_d$	0,59	$3,65_e$	0,60	238,48	.001	0,612
Hope	$2,71_a$	0,60	$3,79_b$	0,57	$1,84_c$	0,60	$2,54_a$	0,83	$3,84_b$	0,71	163,79	.001	0,520
ZTPI													
Past positive	$3,75_a$	0,69	$4,13_b$	0,59	$3,42_c$	0,89	$3,18_d$	0,80	$3,45_c$	0,65	27,64	.001	0,155
Past negative	$3,66_a$	0,69	$3,10_b$	0,90	$3,96_c$	0,74	$2,67_d$	0,60	$2,58_d$	0,45	94,13	.001	0,384
Present fatalistic	$2,15_a$	0,70	$1,79_b$	0,71	$2,30_a$	0,86	$2,47_a$	0,86	$2,05_a$	0,72	12,94	.001	0,079
Present hedonism	$3,38_a$	0,76	$3,66_b$	0,78	$3,06_c$	0,86	$2,90_c$	0,99	$3,22_a$	0,95	10,51	.001	0,065
Future	$3,72_a$	0,68	$4,17_b$	0,57	$3,23_c$	0,73	$2,96_d$	0,80	$3,22_c$	0,72	52,11	.001	0,257
Dependent Variables													
Flourishing	$5,11_a$	0,92	$5,87_b$	0,79	$4,01_c$	1,02	$4,29_d$	0,94	$5,61_e$	0,81	80,40	.001	0,347
PANAS +	$2,95_a$	0,66	$3,68_b$	0,68	$2,13_c$	0,61	$2,71_d$	0,69	$3,31_e$	0,74	57,46	.001	0,276
PANAS -	$2,16_a$	0,74	$1,76_b$	0,57	$2,50_c$	0,85	$2,36_c$	0,84	$1,69_b$	0,57	29,28	.001	0,162

Note. Turkish sample n= 307 ; French sample n= 308

For each dependent variable. means with different subscripts indicate a significant difference at $p < .05$ using New Man Keuls' post hoc test high scores on PP, PH, and F but they did not meet the lower scores on the PN factor, therefor meeting the expectations of the BTP condition is doubtful.

Latent profile analysis and extant literature yielded three OWB profiles for the Turkish group and two OWB profiles for the French group. Among the five OWB profiles, the lowest profile of OWB was found in the Turkish sample (*Profile 3 TR*), and the highest levels of OWB was also found in the Turkish sample (*Profile 2 TR*) which makes the scores of the Turkish group more diverse compared to the French group. The diversity can also be observed from the variation of the OWB scores.

As expected, participants who were in high OWB profiles scored highest on PP, PH, F, positive affect, psychological flourishing, and lowest on PN, and PF. The Turkish profile with high OWB scores presented significantly higher levels of PP, PN, PH and F than the French profile with high OWB scores. Having high scores on PN for the Turkish profile with high OWB could be questioned. People from collectivist cultures may keep negative past events on the surface and may use these events as motivation for their current and future lives. Both moderate and high Turkish OWB profiles received significantly higher flourishing scores than the corresponding French groups. The PP, F, and Hope scores varied parallel to their flourishing scores, so receiving past as positive and future as well as having hope can be related to the individual's flourishing.

The PN scores of both the moderate OWB and the high OWB Turkish profiles were significantly higher than the French profiles, however their regret scores were the opposite which means that the Turkish profiles received significantly lower scores for regret than the French profiles. The negative perception toward the past includes unpleasant emotions and regret might be one of those emotions. According to Stolarski et al. (2014) recalling an unpleasant event from the past might make present life events look better and increase people's positive perception toward their present life. The Turkish group might be focusing more on their past memories compared to the French group and this may give them more opportunity to compare their current life events; therefore, this also might explain the reason for the low regret scores of Turkish profiles. The current findings are consistent with earlier research shows that life events affect well-being, and this association is moderated by age and personality (Headey & Wearing, 1989). It is highly plausible that life events are also important in the evaluation of life projects. Future research should also focus on this association, testing the moderator effects of personality and age. Moreover, it is possible to argue, for example, that the effect of life events on well-being is mediated by the evaluation of life projects, and this mediation may be moderated by age. Since life narratives become more coherent and more based on intrinsic goals with age (Bauer & McAdams, 2004), the evaluation of life projects will become a more important mediator variable in determining the effects of life events on well-being as the aging. In other words, with increasing age, life events are more likely to be acknowledged as consistent with the evaluation of life project, and thus, in turn be more likely to contribute to well-being.

It may seem inconsistent that the Turkish participants received higher scores on both past negative and past positive and higher results on the future. However, Zimbardo argues that individuals develop a fatalistic attitude at the beginning of their life because of the difficult conditions during the childhood; yet, as the level of education rises, they begin to act towards the future (Zimbardo & Boyd, 1999). In this study, which was conducted with university students, participants' perception of the future time perspective average scores were higher than the other time perspective average scores which suggest that "education" may be related to "future time perspective". Given this finding, it is meaningful for Holman and Zimbardo (2009) to define time perspectives as "semi-flexible structures". In other words, it seems that this finding supports the fact that the time perspectives may be related to both the innate personal characteristics of the individual and the later gained experiences such as education.

In conclusion, the construct of OWB acknowledges mental health in a time perspective and considers life as a project originating in the past and extending into the future. The construct, in this respect, reflects an existential point of view and assesses mental health from a narrative/ existential perspective. Specifically, "Nothingness", as an original, existential factor emerging in this research, has been found to be strongly correlated with NA and N factors of personality, as well as other clinical variables such as depression and anxiety. These findings suggest that it could be useful in clinical settings, and therefore future research should thoroughly evaluate its relationship to such variables as depression, anxiety, and suicidal inclinations.

As one's psychological point of view, the structure and process of the culture may play an important role on one's tendency toward specific time perspective. Researchers show that individuals, who are raised in Western cultures, lean towards present and future time perspectives (Zimbardo & Boyd, 1999). A study conducted in Taiwan has shown that individuals who grow up in traditional societies can now tend to use the fatalistic time perspective, since they believe that the events in their lives have developed outside their control (Gao, 2011). According to the conclusions of the intercultural time perspective studies conducted by Sircova et al. (2015) Turkish culture differs slightly from individual and collectivistic societies, as fatalism is quite low and future time perspectives are quite high in the present. The results of this study are similar to Sircova and his colleagues' study results. It may be possible to explain the separation of Turkish culture from both individual and collectivistic cultures by the concept of related-self.

Western cultures such as France put more value on individualism and as opposed to Eastern cultures that place more value on relatedness, Turkey is a country between the East and West and its position was discussed by Kağıtçıbaşı (2005) and explained by the term "autonomous-related self", which means to be both autonomous and attached to someone. In general, people in Turkey seek autonomy but at the same time keep their connections with close people such as parents or other family members (maintain their connections with their close relations, such as parents or other family members). Individuals receive support from their related ones. Moreover, many research clarified the impact of supportive parenting for adolescents' subjective wellbeing and autonomous-self-development. In fact, the parenting climate in Turkish culture that allows supporting the adolescents' behaviors regulated on the basis of autonomous-self or self-determined represents the optimal climate for adolescent development (Kocayörük, Altıntaş & İçbay, 2014). According to Kağıtçıbaşı (2005), the Turkish family structure has changed day by day since 1970's, and the value attributed to the child has also changed. The child's value has been examined longitudinally over a 40-year data set. While families in the 1970s expected their children to be obedient and respectful to family members, families in the 2000s expect their children to be autonomous individuals and pursue their goals as well as maintain their relationship with the family. Kağıtçıbaşı evaluated this change in terms of the independent-self and dependent-self model and described it as a related-interdependent self model. In the related-interdependent self model, as described above, time perspectives may also vary according to individual and collectivist cultures. However, in order to reach such a judgment in the course of cultures, many more studies are needed.

It would be useful to repeat this research with people of different nationalities and age groups, where the relationship between university students' time perspectives, well-being, and cultural identities were examined. Kairys (2010) compared young and old individuals in terms of their time perspectives and observed that old individuals leaned towards using future perspectives more than young individuals, and they were more likely to use fatalistic and PN time perspectives. In this study, the mean scores of "future time perspective" and "past positive time perspective" of university students were higher than other time perspective average scores; "Fatalistic time perspective" mean scores were lower than the other time perspective mean scores. Cross-cultural comparisons of the differences between age groups may yield detailed information.

In conclusion, the construct of OWB acknowledges mental health in a time perspective and considers life as a project originating in the past and extending into the future. The construct, in this respect, reflects an existential point of view and assesses mental health from a narrative/ existential perspective. Specifically, "Nothingness", as an original, existential factor emerging in this research, has been found to be strongly correlated with NA and N factors of personality, as well as other l variables such as flourishing and well-being. These findings suggest that it could be useful in clinical settings, and therefore future research should thoroughly evaluate its relationship to such variables as depression, anxiety, and suicidal inclinations or happiness and well-being.

ACKNOWLEDGMENT

This research was supported by TUBITAK (The Scientific and Technological Research Council of Turkey) [Grant Number: 115K417]

REFERENCES

Akaike, H. (1987). Factor analysis and AIC. *Psychometrika, 52*(3), 317–332. doi:10.1007/BF02294359

Akın, A., & Fidan, M. (2012). The validity and reliability of the Turkish version of the Flourishing Scale. In *3rd International Conference on New Trends in Education and their Implications (ICONTE-2012)* (pp. 26-28). Academic Press.

Bandura, A. (1997). *Self-efficacy: The exercise of control*. New York: Freeman.

Bauer, J. J., & McAdams, D. P. (2004). Personal growth in adults' stories of life transitions. *Journal of Personality, 72*(3), 573–602. doi:10.1111/j.0022-3506.2004.00273.x PMID:15102039

Boniwell, I., & Zimbardo, P. G. (2004). Balancing One's Time Perspective in Pursuit of Optimal Functioning. In P. A. Linley & S. Joseph (Eds.), *Positive Psychology in Practice* (pp. 165–178). Hoboken, NJ: Wiley.

Diener, E. (1984). Subjective well-being. *Psychological Bulletin, 95*(3), 542–575. doi:10.1037/0033-2909.95.3.542 PMID:6399758

Diener, E., & Lucas, R. E. (2000). Subjective emotional well-being. In M. Lewis & J. M. Haviland (Eds.), *Handbook of emotions* (2nd ed.; pp. 325–337). New York: Guilford.

Diener, E., Suh, E. M., Lucas, R. E., & Smith, H. L. (1999). Subjective well-being: Three decades of progress. *Psychological Bulletin, 125*(2), 276–302. doi:10.1037/0033-2909.125.2.276

Diener, E., Wirtz, D., Tov, W., Kim-Prieto, C., Choi, D., Oishi, S., & Biswas-Diener, R. (2010). New measures of well-being: Flourishing and positive and negative feelings. *Social Indicators Research, 39*, 247–266.

Frijda, N. (2005). Emotion experience. *Journal of Cognition and Emotion, 19*(4), 473–497. doi:10.1080/02699930441000346

Gao, Y. (2011). Time perspective and life satisfaction among young adults in Taiwan. *Social Behavior and Personality: An International Journal, 39*(6), 729-736. doi: .2011.39.6.729 doi:10.2224bp

Gençöz, T. (2000). Pozitif ve negatif duygu ölçeği: Geçerlik ve güvenirlik çalışması [The positive and negative affect scale: validity and reliability study]. *Türk Psikoloji Dergisi, 15*(46), 19–26.

Headey, B., & Wearing, A. (1989). Personality, life events, and subjective well-being: Toward a dynamic equilibrium model. *Journal of Personality and Social Psychology, 57*(4), 731–739. doi:10.1037/0022-3514.57.4.731

Holman, E. A., & Zimbardo, P. G. (2009). The social language of time: The time perspective–social network connection. *Basic and Applied Social Psychology, 31*(2), 136–147. doi:10.1080/01973530902880415

Kağıtçıbaşı, C. (2005). Autonomy and relatedness in cultural context implications for self and family. *Journal of Cross-Cultural Psychology, 36*(4), 403–422. doi:10.1177/0022022105275959

Kairys, A. (2010). *Time perspective: Its link to personality traits, age, and gender* (Doctoral dissertation). Vilnius University.

Kocayörük, E., Altıntas, E., & İçbay, M. A. (2015). The perceived parental support, autonomous-self and well-being of adolescents: A cluster-analysis approach. *Journal of Child and Family Studies, 24*(6), 1819–1828. doi:10.100710826-014-9985-5

Košťál, J., Klicperová-Baker, M., Lukavská, K., & Lukavský, J. (2016). Short version of the Zimbardo Time Perspective Inventory (ZTPI–short) with and without the Future-Negative scale, verified on nationally representative samples. *Time & Society, 25*(2), 169–192. doi:10.1177/0961463X15577254

Kuzu, D., Berk, Ö. S., & Aydın, F. Y. (2017). Subjective well-being in idiopathic scoliosis patients. *The International Journal of Human and Behavioral Science, 3*(2), 1–6.

Lanza, S. T., Collins, L. M., Lemmon, D. R., & Schafer, J. L. (2007). PROC LCA: A SAS procedure for latent class analysis. *Structural Equation Modeling, 14*(4), 671–694. doi:10.1080/10705510701575602 PMID:19953201

Lapierre, S., Bouffard, L., & Bastin, E. (1997). Personal goals and subjective well-being in later life. *International Journal of Aging & Human Development, 45*(4), 287–303. doi:10.2190/HU3J-QDHE-LT1J-WUBN PMID:9477344

McAdams, D. P. (2001). The psychology of life stories. *Review of General Psychology, 5*, 100-122. doi: 10,1037//1089-2860.5.2.100

Nuttin, J. R. (1985). The future time perspective in human motivation and learning. *Acta Psychologica, 23*, 60–83. doi:10.1016/0001-6918(64)90075-7

Schmutte, P. S., & Ryff, C. D. (1997). Personality and well-being: Reexamining methods and meanings. *Journal of Personality and Social Psychology, 73*(3), 549–559. doi:10.1037/0022-3514.73.3.549 PMID:9294901

Seligman, M. E. P. (2002). *Authentic happiness: Using the new positive psychology to realize your potential for lasing fulfillment.* New York: Free Press.

Simons, J., Vansteenkiste, M., Lens, W., & Lacante, M. (2004). Placing motivation and future time perspective theory in a temporal perspective. *Educational Psychology Review, 16*(2), 121-139. doi: 1040-726X/04/0600-0121/0

Şimşek, Ö. F. (2009). Happiness revisited: Ontological well-being as a theory-based construct of subjective well-being. *Journal of Happiness Studies, 10*(5), 505–522. doi:10.100710902-008-9105-6

Şimşek, Ö. F., & Kocayörük, E. (2013). Affective reactions to one's whole life: Preliminary development and validation of the ontological well-being scale. *Journal of Happiness Studies, 14*(1), 309–343. doi:10.100710902-012-9333-7

Sircova, A., van de Vijver, F. J. R., Osin, E., Milfont, T. L., Fieulaine, N., Kislali, A., & Boyd, J. N. (2015). Time perspective profiles of cultures. In M. Stolarski, N. Fieulaine, & W. van Beek (Eds.), *Time perspective theory: Review, research and application* (pp. 169–188). Springer.

Stolarski, M., Matthews, G., Postek, S., Zimbardo, P. G., & Bitner, J. (2014). How we feel is a matter of time: Relationships between time perspectives and mood. *Journal of Happiness Studies, 15*(4), 809–827. doi:10.100710902-013-9450-y

Vermunt, J. K., & Magidson, J. (2002). Latent class cluster analysis. *Applied Latent Class Analysis, 11*, 89–106. doi:10.1017/CBO9780511499531.004

Villieux, A., Sovet, L., Jung, S. C., & Guilbert, L. (2016). Psychological flourishing: Validation of the French version of the Flourishing Scale and exploration of its relationships with personality traits. *Personality and Individual Differences*, *88*, 1–5. doi:10.1016/j.paid.2015.08.027

Watson, D., Clark, L. A., & Tellegen, A. (1988). Development and validation of brief measures of positive and negative affect: The PANAS scales. *Journal of Personality and Social Psychology*, *54*(6), 1063–1070. doi:10.1037/0022-3514.54.6.1063 PMID:3397865

Zimbardo, P. G., & Boyd, J. N. (1999). Putting time in perspective: A valid, reliable individual-differences metric. *Journal of Personality and Social Psychology*, *77*(6), 1271–1288. doi:10.1037/0022-3514.77.6.1271

KEY TERMS AND DEFINITIONS

Flourishing: Eudaimonic visions of well-being regarding feelings and human flourishing in relevant areas such as purpose in life, relationships, self-esteem, feelings of competence, and optimism.

Negative Affect: Unpleasant feelings such as sad, depressed and anger.

Ontological Well-Being: A collection of affective and cognitive evaluations of one's life and considered personal project with past, present, and future parts.

Positive Affect: Pleasant feelings such as strong, alert, and active.

Self-Construal: It is individuals understanding of who they are in relation to the broad set of cultural influences.

Subjective Well-Being: Cognitive and emotional evaluation of general happiness of one's personal life.

Time Perspective: An unconscious processes of assigning personal and social experiences into past, present and future events in order to give meaning and coherence to those events.

Chapter 14
The Destructuring of Time in Psychosis

Richard J. Rodriguez
Universidad de la República, Uruguay

Victor E.C. Ortuño
Universidad de la República, Uruguay

ABSTRACT

This chapter intends to interact and integrate different perspectives that address temporality as a dimension that shapes the human being's life. On the other hand, temporality as a variable or universal dimension structures both the normal and abnormal life of people, having approached the subject from the perspective of psychiatrists of the Franco-German tradition to explain and phenomenologically understand the experience of time in psychosis. At present, understanding and interdisciplinary work should be taken into account and integrated for their application in the psychosocial rehabilitation of people with this pathology, recognizing also that the subject has not obtained concrete or satisfactory answers even today.

INTRODUCTION

Many around the world have believed in the idea of an absolute time in which the event labels would be calibrated with measurements of exact and equal time intervals for all people. The Theory of Relativity posed that the location of physical events both in their space and in their time depends on the state of movement of the observers. Thus the length of an object as the instant in which an event happens will be relative and will differ with respect to the movement of those who observe

DOI: 10.4018/978-1-5225-8163-5.ch014

it. According to this idea, each observer will have their own measure of time, and the clocks of different observers will not necessarily coincide (Hawking, 1988).

It can be said that there is no single standard of time, but that each person has its own time, and that measuring it between several people allows for a certain margin of error. The theory of relativity supports the idea that there is no single way to measure the time in which all the observers of a certain event are in agreement, but that each one has its own personal valuation and measurement.

A TRANSDISCIPLINARY VARIABLE

Time may be and is approached from a philosophical, biological, physiological, psychological, neuroscientific, astronomical point of view, etc. (Dubois, 1954, Correa, 2006). Vásquez (2011) organizes different theoretical levels of the study of time, letting realize that other disciplines have focused on particular aspects of this object of study, and he achieves an integration emphasized in a "bio-cultural conception of the human psyche" (Vásquez, 2011, p. 216). This four-level model proposed by Vásquez will be used here, as a framework and a delimitation that will allow to reach the destination of the theme of this chapter.

The level of time I, or cosmological time, is the calendric time, measurable by natural and seasonal cycles. The second level or time II, covers perceptual, operational and utilitarian time. It is the essential internal estimate to operate in space and feel the passage of time. Level III of time is the subjective and historizable, it is where we build a narrative of our life, a construction of our self, of what we are, of our identity projected as reality, what we believe of us as a certainty, explicit and conscious as well as not conscious. Also included are: the internal awareness of time, the perspective of it and the subjective perception of the past and the future. The cultural time or time of societies is the time located in the fourth level time IV, and it could be seen as the different ethnographic ways of living (Vásquez, 2011).

PHYLOGENETIC AND TIME

The concept of time should be united to the idea of change, and those could be perceived by individuals while they possess the basic mechanisms to register those changes. (Correa, 2006. p.163).[1]

There is a lot of research that associates neural bases with neurophysiology of the perception of time, which allows us to affirm today that human beings, like other species, have a complex mechanism that provides us with the ability to record, predict and synchronize changes, adapting to the world surrounding with great advantages (Golombek, 2002, Correa, 2006, Gutiérrez-García, 2017). Bridging the gap between natural cycles and rhythmicity and physiological synchronization allows us to think of the survival made possible by the coordination, sequencing, timing and anticipation of mental representations and complex motor patterns (Correa, 2006). The models of perception of time are classified into: a chronobiological model based on the environment and a cognitive model based on the information stored in the memory. Likewise, three related cognitive processes are identified in temporal abilities: the *timing* of intervals where a duration must be measured; the *storage* where the interval is memorized for later, and the *decision making* that can be given from the comparison of durations between intervals. There is also a model called "spectral" in which it is proposed that the temporal codes are transferred to spatial codes; intervals of different duration that are represented in different circuits located in different areas of the brain. Currently, the existence of a versatile system is handled, that involves and reconciles structures related to automatic millisecond timing (cerebellum), work memory processes (prefrontal areas involved in the perception of seconds and minutes intervals), and attentional processes (parietal areas) (Correa, 2006).

THE PERCEPCTION OF TIME IN THE FIRST PERSON: THE SUJETIVE EXPERIENCE

The temporal interpretation of an event is affected by complex variables such as attention and mood (Gutiérrez-García, 2017). This cognitive tool allows the organization as well as mental and motor planning of action sequences based on the subjective duration of time, a quality understood and defined by the "number of temporary units accumulated over a period of time" (Gutiérrez-García, 2017, p. 86).

The contractions and temporary dilatations are given by several factors. Some of them are: the "novelty" of the stimulus and the affectivity associated with it. These are involved in most of our cognitive processes (Gutiérrez-García, 2017). This overestimation and underestimation to which we refer, are directly related to negative and positive stimuli and experiences. We go through a slowdown or temporary dilation when we face experiences of fatigue, wait times and boredom, danger, pain, illness, states of anxiety and anguish, or when the event demands a great attentional involvement. Otherwise, the experience of contraction and acceleration of intervals between events on a spatial plane, is given by joyful, motivated, shared, novel experiences and when we do not focus our attention on the event. Although the ability to estimate and predict intervals between events is an evolutionary tool with a fairly stable structure, there is a certain degree of variability among people with certain psychiatric disorders (Gutiérrez-García, 2017).

PSYCHOSIS AND TIME

Schizophrenia is a complex psychiatric disorder with multifactorial pathogenesis whose main symptoms are hallucinations associated with disorganized thoughts (Gutiérrez-García, 2017). The cognitive difficulties suffered by people with this pathology include alterations in the process of attention, memory, executive functions, perception and capture of reality, which are directly or indirectly related to various aspects of temporality.

In terms of temporality, these people lack the ability to segment their duration and imagine the passage of time. Deficiencies in the activation of the caudate nucleus and putamen produce a slowing down and overestimation of subjective time, while the loss of communication between cortico-striatal circuits makes the encoding and explicit representation of temporal information difficult. The perception of subjective time in relation to the target time in people with this pathology is still controversial (Gutierrez-García, 2017).

Certain definitions of this pathology found in manuals respond to theoretical frameworks that do not deepen the analysis or take into account the complexity that the variable subjective temporality offers.

The classifications and definitions made by neuroscience and the biological psychiatry of psychosis have a strong foundation, but it leads us to lose detail and leave out the meaning and the subjective experience of the time of those who are going through a pathology of this type. These are, as Jaspers explained, natural limits of disciplines that take the human being as an object of study:

Its limits consist in the imposibility of the dissolution of individuals in pasychological concepts. (Jaspers, 1966. p. 16).[2]

We therefore believe, in agreement with the thought of psychiatrists of German-French tradition, that philosophical contributions for the study of the subjective experience of time avoids a detention and a reductionism of knowledge. Thus, the analysis of human suffering should facilitate the encounter between various disciplines (philosophy, psychiatry, cognitive sciences, psychology, neurosciences, anthropology, etc.), to enrich and ensure more complexity in the clinical practice (Almada, 2008, Garrabé, 2017).

Importance must be given to the apprehension of the particular typical events; the phenomenology. The research on the subjective experience of time and psychopathology should capture the phenomena described by the person who lives them. In psychoses, one should make an abstraction of phenomena, of their theoretical notion, to focus on experience, the description of experiences and their states, the self-description of temporal events. Using a phenomenology of the subjective experience of time as a basis would bring individual qualities and states, not only on the subjectively experienced phenomena, but also the psychic seen directly in the expression, the facts, their manifestations and their acts (Jaspers, 1966).

Our chief help in all this comes from the patients' own self-descriptions, which can be evoked and tested out in the course of personal conversation. From this we get out best-defined and clearest data. Written descriptions by the patient may have a richer content but in this form we can do nothing else but accept them. An experience is best described by the person who has undergone it. Detached psychiatric observation with its own formulation of what the patient is suffering is not any substitute for this. (Jaspers, 1963. p. 55)

Henri Ey believes that psychosis must include in its most global definition, all mental illnesses (Ey, 1996). The states, access or acute crisis are characterized by a natural tendency to remission and by a greater or lesser destructuring of consciousness. In this category, mania and melancholy are the examples that go through this reduction and destructuring of the field of consciousness with a manifestation of the temporary ethical alteration. In its forms of delirious bouffées, acute hallucinatory psychosis and oniroid states, the person goes through a destructuring of consciousness in the form of hypnosis or fascination with the imaginary; during confusional psychosis (in its confused oniric forms, Korsakoff's syndrome and acute delirium) one suffers a clouding of consciousness that can go from blunting to stupor, with disorientation of the space-time consciousness and a psychic experience with oniroid characteristics (Ey, 1996).

The group of schizophrenias encompasses most cases of mental alienation characterized by a process of mental disintegration, intrapsychic discordance or autistic dissociation of personality. Kraepelin made reference to the non-applicability, Eugen Bleuler to the alteration of the associations, Berze made reference to the hypotony of the conscience, Eugène Minkowski to the loss of the vital contact; Kurt and Carl Schneider focused on the importance of the mental automatism syndrome or primary delirium of Clerembault and Henri Ey prioritizes the deformation and regression of the personality with alterations of the states of consciousness (Ey, 1996). Eugène Minkowski and Ludwig Biswanger studied the pathology of consciousness in the different types of psychosis, and the "way of being in the world", which is related to the subjective experience of time and its destructuring.

TIME IN THE PSYCHIATRY OF THE XX CENTURY AND IN THE PSYCHOLOGY OF TODAY

Psychitric epistemology underwent a significant transformation during the twentieth century from the positivist apogee inherited in the name of Emil Kraepelin, with its descriptive method of typical pictures and evolutions, to non-absolute semiological syndromes, where the concept of mental illness became more flexible, dynamic, complex and personal. Karl Jaspers considers, from a phenomenological and existential psychiatry, that time and space are omnipresent in the sensory perception, encompass all the objective realm, are universal. He poses that the realization and experience of existence in our inner world is achieved through space and time. The experience of existence occurs in a temporal spatial framework from which it can be separated (Jaspers, 1966).

Space and time will be organizers of normal and abnormal psychic life. They will be manifested according to a particular mode of experience, and the perception of duration and its extension can vary, materializing under basic characteristics of a quantitative experience nature. Jaspers enumerated these characteristics of time: dimension, homogeneity, continuity and unlimitedness (Jaspers, 1966). Space is the level inhabited by forms, while time is the occurrence of an event without space. The capacity of separation of these two variables is known in the daily example of moving away from oneself, contemplating oneself, imagining oneself, thinking about the abstract and successive, etc. When we abandon ourselves from our spatial experience, to live an experience without object, that experience will always be organized in a temporal axis.

Jaspers wondered about the possibility of temporary gaps during our experience. An example that he managed is the time gap experienced as a suspension in sleepwalking, where past and future become present. He made the point, in reference to the universality of time and space, that if each person has its own value and unit of measurement in space and time in a comprehensive present, its significance will be important for the behavior of each man (Jaspers, 1966).

According to Jaspers, the basic schemes' common ground for the setting of time in a general shared level are: the time lived, the objective schedule, the chronological and historical time and the time as a history of human existence. But he categorized, at the individual level, three levels of understanding of time: "Knowing about time", referred to the objective time, the appreciation of periods of time, and in its pathological case the delusional false apprehension of the essence of time. The second category was named "Time experience", referring to the *subjective experience of time* as a total awareness of it. And the third category built by Jaspers is "The deal with time": the daily and future treatment with the basic situation of temporality; to be able to wait, to postpone, to procrastinate, to decide that it has subsequent effects on the biographical consciousness of the past and its vital history (Jaspers, 1966).

Despite his constructs and ideas, Jaspers recognizes that:

We cannot explain the experience of time nor can we derive it from anything else; we can only describe it. We cannot avoid asking what are the causes of abnormal experience of time but so far demonstrable answers do not exist. (Jaspers, 1963; p. 83).

In his General Psychopathology, Jaspers uses contributions from other authors such as Bergson and Minkowski, and works on the idea of direction in a time line, experiencing a future where there is consciousness of the present and its course as an experience of continuity.

With the theory of evolutionism, Bergson sees the world through a reality of nature in a constant and dynamic development within a time frame; so he takes the concept of *becoming* as time ascribed to the progression of life. He elaborated the idea of becoming as a time creator based on three categories: the *objective time* of physics; the *subjective time* ascribed to human consciousness and existence; and the *ontological time* that treats the being as a whole (Almada, 2008). Subjective time was the work of both Bergson and Minkowski, the crossing of disciplinary boundaries being very important for the ideas of Minkowski's inspiring French philosopher (such as consciousness, freedom and interiority) to be integrated into the pillars of a psychopathology that would later prioritize existentialism and phenomenology as a method and technique.

Bergson brought to psychopathology the concept of "pure duration of time", posed as an irreversible psychological time, the personal duration from which it is not possible to return to previous situations. If you wanted to take up past events, even if you could return to such situations, you would realize that it is no longer the same as at that time (Almada, 2008).

Bergson used physics to explain that our past's weight of gravitation is condensed at this precise moment, as previous life that houses the self as a product of past experience. Pure time, as a mental process, has differentiable characteristics: quality, interiority, duration, becoming and intensity; features that will merge and penetrate every succession of psychological events that will shape the self (Almada, 2008).

Bergson can be seen as a precursor when he considers as a propitious moment for the analysis of the meaning of the pure time duration, the dream: an alteration of the communication between the self and the external world; moment where the quantitative duration ceases to be perceived to give rise to the qualitative sensation of condensation of time. He will say that the measurement of time is possible when projected onto space and by externalizing it is spatialized and degenerated;

instead, in the dream state, as a pure duration of time, all the previous states to the present merge. Time as a flow is the pillar of the perceived reality and despite the impossibility to define it because of its lack of materiality, it becomes valid as a duration of the change of the inner mental life of the psyche through consciousness (Almada, 2008).

Minkowski, based on a Husserlian phenomenological methodology, determined that temporal phenomena represent structures that determine not only the contents manifested by people but also the structures that determine human temporality (Almada, 2008). Time will be the synthesis of dynamism and stability manifested through structural phenomena. "The lived time" will be contained through memories, containers of past, desire and hope oriented towards the future (Almada, 2008). Minkowski argued phenomenologically that in the irrational character of becoming, the perception of the succession of thoughts, feelings or volitions is not enough to describe the pure perception of time. The development and creation are opposed to wear, old age and death, so it is never possible to separate the constant time of the observer, or to objectify completely (Almada, 2008). Minkowski remarked that as becoming is occurring one does not stop identifying with it.

The past has already passed, and so it doesn't exist; the future it doesn't exist yet; the present is located between two nothings; but the present, is now a point without extension, while the present is there, is not anymore; for which is contradictory and constitutes another nothing. And so, for time, reality represent a nothing between two nothings. (Almada, 2008; p. 46).[3]

He opposed a rational and spatial character of time, against another irrational and intuitive time manifested through the *intercalary phenomena* of spacetime. Those count in their structure with a rational order, but are not consciously rationalized by people, as they are perceived by consciousness as succession, continuity, similarity, stability and consistency (Almada, 2008). He will say that the duration and its flow can not be decomposed, proposing the *principle of deployment* as a connection between duration and succession, continuity and reiteration, arising the relationship between flow and continuity.

The present for Minkowski, will be different from the now: the now suffocates, while the present encompasses it within itself, it has more extension and is more homogeneous; the present manifests itself as a temporary structure that offers security, comfort and tranquility to men, pacifies them to be able to live in the present. Through the memory of the past, you can live in the now, but always thanks to a present that houses and structures it (Almada, 2008).

The author generated contributions to existentialism: the idea of direction in personal evolution and projecting oneself thanks to the vital impetus of finding a meaning to the chaos of the world. Impetus that would lead people to a meaning, to the future. The vital impetus will be creating and perceiving a perspective of a future, and through this events interconnect that enhance a sense of fullness of being that goes beyond the simple creation of a story (Almada, 2008). From this point of view, they will never finish the tasks in their life, there will always be a momentum of progress; and when the need emerges and the feeling of anguish will be due to the impasses of the progression in our objectives, the affirmation of life itself is being expressed in those same impasses (Almada, 2008).

Deshaies (1961) states that the succession of phenomena establishes a structural order in the human world, where the lifeline is temporary. He speaks about the lived duration but from the experience of the subject, of its intimate time, feeling of becoming, the intuition that we have of the homogeneous duration of the self, which when externalized is divided into moments or successive states of consciousness (Deshaies, 1961).

Pierre Janet referred to time as the regulating feeling of action, as a duration. Memory was a behavior destined to the narrative, where, if consistent and provided with a chronological order, the past is constituted. On the contrary, if it is inconsistent, a fable is produced that projects the future. The proper functioning of this allows to adapt to changes (Deshaies, 1961).

Paul Fraisse studied from an experimental psychological perspective, the perception of time, he criticized the Bergsonian perspective arguing that Bergson ignored the behavior and biological adaptations he put on three levels: 1) The conditioning to time, as synchronization of the organism to the changes of the environment through conditioned reflexes; 2) The perception of time as successive stimuli; 3) The direction of time given by the representation of the changes that organized a reconstitutive memorization of the past and an anticipation of the future. The interesting thing is that despite the criticisms, he agreed on the intuitive nature of the appreciation of duration and the existence of a psychological present, such as the organization synthesized in actualization (Deshaies, 1961).

Kurt Lewin postulated that the perception of time is one of the fundamental elements of cognition, which gives meaning to lived experiences, allows self-regulation of present behavior and anticipate the future (1942). The analysis made by the human being of the subjective temporal dimension of past and future has a key importance in the explanation of human thought and behavior, because it is always active in the present moment; and he proposed the concept of Temporary Perspective, as the way of seeing the future and the psychological past at a given moment. Under this concept came the representations of past and future materialized in representations of people concerning their fears, desires, hopes and behaviors (Lewin, 1942). A balanced temporal orientation, would allow to consider the different time frames according to the situational demands, achieving an adaptive temporal competence

(Zaleski, 1994). The alteration in the equilibrium of the Temporal Perspective can be given as a preference bias for any of the possible temporal orientations: past, present and future, thus altering the realization and homogeneity of the self.

Lewin's Perspective of Temporary Perspective was one of the last aggregates within a great plurality of twentieth century concepts (Ortuño, 2014), determining the development of a psychological time research line. To the basic concept of Temporary Perspective was added the idea of tendentially non-conscious process that gives order coherence and meaning to the experiences, forming a stable feature of the personality modifiable by external social influences (Zimbardo, 1999).

Nuttin and Lens (1985) contributed ideas to the concept of Temporal Perspective as that of the cognitive-spatial model. Cognitive to be conformed by objects or motivational events that exist in a level of behavioral, and spatial because the same objects and motivational events are located in a temporal continuum. People perceive these motivational events located in the past, present or future, even if in fact, they are thought in a present moment (Ortuño, 2014). They also tried to operationalize attributes of the Temporal Perspective: Extension, density, degree of structuring and level of realism.

According to these authors, the *temporal extension* is one of the properties that makes up the Temporary Perspective. It is the perceived psychological distance between the present moment and a certain motivational object located in the past or the future. *Density* is considered as the number of motivational objects that an individual possesses in certain time frames, it refers to the number of events, the "weight" that these generate in a person's behaviors and the moment when they occurred. The *degree of structuring* defines the existence or not of unions between several objects that occupy different time frames. The *level of realism* is the last property proposed by Nuttin & Lens (1985); it defines that the more realistic the motivational object in a given time frame, the more intense the effect on the behavior, ie the degree of realism is defined by the achievable, realistic or viable objectives (Ortuño, 2014).

Zimbardo and Boyd (1999) proposed to consider temporal perspective as an evolutionary tool manifested as an unconscious process that in the flow of personal and social experiences, are assigned to a temporary category to make order, coherence and meaning. The theoretical approach of Zimbardo and Boyd (1999) postulates that the temporal perspective contributes in the process of recovering memories of past events or motivational objects located in the past, present and future. The same time frame that serves these memory processes also serves as an affective cognitive filter that helps in determining which memories should be recovered. The information of memories, events and motivational objects that must be encoded, stored and recovered, are affected by the configuration of the individual temporary profile (Ortuño, 2014).

These theories also tried to understand the pathological or maladaptive configurations of temporal perspective since it is understood as a non-static process where individuals, consciously or not, select a particular time frame. They can develop certain fixation, under or overuse of a particular time frame, which may be influenced by family, education, society, religion and culture (Ortuño, 2014). The flexibility between several time frames to function on the basis of a type of temporary approach, should be able to adapt to the needs of the moment, understood under the concept of Temporary Balanced Perspective.

On the grounds that it can not dissolve completely the individual man into psychological concepts because of the unknowable part of him which is never reached, it happens that in the attempt to quantify and rationalize the internal time of the human being (the pure duration of Bergson) the latter is deformed in that manipulation, losing the essence of the experience. In different studies, an optimal balance of the individual time perspective has not been found. One study undertaken by Drake et al. (2008) with 260 participants, reported only 13 with ideal balance of their temporal perspective. Other studies have reported the same disparity -Kairys & Liniauskaite, 2010- (mentioned in Ortuño, 2014).

The reports following a Balanced Temporary Perspective are positively associated with mindfulness, low alcohol consumption, less consumption of cigarettes, better health evaluation, better evaluation of academic achievements, life satisfaction, psychological well-being, better performance in executive functions, low values of depression and psychopathologies, social functioning, coping strategies and emotional control (Ortuño, 2014, Boniwell & Zimbardo, 2004, Sircova, Wiberg, Wiberg & Carelli, 2010, Stolarski, Bitner & Zimbardo, 2011). Despite the lack of consensus and the need to design and improve measurement tools, all recognize a clear relevance of time in human behavior and thinking.

DISORGANIZATION OF CONSCIOUSNESS AND TEMPORALITY

Henri Ey after an exhaustive review, deduces and postulates the particularity and kinship of many acute crises, which "imposes" bringing them together in the same series of mental disorders by constructing the concept of destructuring consciousness as that involved in many of these pathological processes of personality, an implicit and common feature in all of them (Ey, 2008).

He found three major types of acute psychosis: *manic depression*; the *delirious and hallucinatory*; and the *confused oneiric*. These are levels of the same block manifested during a dissolution movement in which the shallowest or best structured level, because it involves the ethical-temporal variable, has a relation with this chapter (Ey, 2008).

We will refer in this level of weak consciousness, to the experience of time and its variability during the destructuring of consciousness. We speak about the *ethical-temporal destructuring*, typically represented in the psychopathology within *mania* and *melancholy* (and which today we could find in the Diagnostic and Statistical Manual of Mental Disorders in the category "Schizophrenia and other psychotic disorders", such as Schizoaffective Disorder of a bipolar or depressive type). Both Ey and Minkowski or Binswanger were the ones who knew how to phenomenologically describe these ways of existence. This "less deep" level of the destructuring of consciousness is traditionally associated with mood disorders, thymus disorders, affective psychoses attributed to emotions, manifestations of expansiveness or depression that a person can experience when organizing his or her lived present.

The mania is characterized by its volatility, flight of ideas, absence of conflicts. The impossibility of detention and psychic synthesis of the present forms the negative part of such a pathology. The person lives in the world as liberated from the measure of the present and released from the demands that put order to it. "...como si se burlase del tiempo... en un impulso irresistible...". The maniac is driven by an awareness that constitutes a "movement of propulsion", the ecstasy manifested in euphoric, angry, violent or mischievous form with no end or restraints, advancing and going through the forms of the present "leaping", suppressing the rules or parameters of behaviors that respond and adapt to the present (Ey, 2008, pp. 746). This disorder only alters the direction of the current of consciousness, its temporal-ethical orientation (Ey, 2008). The spontaneity of the maniac consciousness movement does not obey the demands of the present, nor does it "temporize" or adapt; only the inertia of desire drives it, leading the person farther, exceeding the limits under the sole rule of following their conveniences and their needs, escaping to the present (Ey 2008).

On the opposite, melancholy was also understood based on its negative structure. It includes inhibition, detachment, disorder of synthesis of consciousness, the absence of solution and "retrogradation", according to Ey, regarding the demands of the present (Ey, 2008, p. 746). The management that melancholy causes of the present is a blockade, an impossibility to continue and go beyond the present, opting instead to suffer tied to the fatality of the past to undermine any possibility of existence of an identity (Ey, 2008) . The positive structure of melancholy implies a vertical fall towards the nothingness imposed by consciousness. Primary anguish of existence, tragedy or metaphysical anguish, are some characteristic ways of presenting this. Temporary destructuring and its direction have been reversed with respect to mania. The "disorder of timing that alters the very meaning of existence" (Ey, 2008, pp. 747), an unstable imbalance of the present, which does not achieve an order in the construction of the gestalt of the now, the current situation, the summary and the synthesis of the past and the future that is projected.

The fact that the consciousness would be more or less balanced is then the result of the subtraction in the present, of the perspective and the projection of future, as the disposition of a time that does not exist yet, loaded with the productions of the imagination and encompassed by expansive forces, subtracting the weight of the past, all that is no longer but returns as a pattern of memory recovery, contained by depressive forces (Ey, 2008).

TIME AND CLINICAL MANIFESTATIONS: A PHENOMENOLOGICAL APPROACH

The destructuring of consciousness can be perceived clinically in different degrees and oscillations, schizophrenia being its chronic form. The person who leads his life from this "being in the world" presents a transformation in his personality that becomes visible in different ways (Ey, 1996).

Jaspers analyzed different pathological pictures, many of them located at the margin of schizophrenic psychoses. A category called *Consciousness of the momentary passage of time*, stated that the normal experience of the passage of time, which oscillates in an understandable and expected manner, does not always occur in a normal way.

Mental patients do nothing for years on end without suffering from boredom. Exhausted and tired people can have the feeling of vacuity without boredom. These are all understandable variations, but there is an abnormal experience of the time-lapse found in seizures, psychoses and poisoning. (Jaspers, 1963; p. 83)

Precipitated Time was a sub-category of *Consciousness of the momentary passage of time*, where patients describe time as if people were moving faster and the near future was precipitated:

At first you have the peculiar feeling that you have lost control over time, as if it were slipping through your fingers; as if you were no longer capable of holding on to the present in order to live it out; you try on cling on to it but it escapes you and streams away... (Jaspers, 1963; pp. 83-84).

Another subcategory was the *Loss of time consciousness*. As the synthesis of consciousness was reduced to a minimum, patients said they no longer felt time goes by, the consciousness of time disappeared to them. Under the effects of psychedelics such as mescaline, they felt a decrease in the intervals during moments of time.

The *Loss of reality in the experience of time* was a sub-category to explain that the consciousness of time involves the feeling of the present, of the presence and absence and of reality. When the temporal variable is lost, reality disappears with it as well as the current life lived (Jaspers, 1966). Jaspers relates that some depressive patients described this loss of reality as a freezing of time at one same moment, as if there were a void without time.

A depressed patient feels as if time did not want to go on. This experience has not got the elementary character of the previous cases but there is something of an elementary character in this particular feeling, which symbolizes self and time locked together... The hands of the clock move blanky, the clock ticks emptily... they are the lost hours of the years when I could not work´ ... Time goes backwards. The patient sees that the hands move forward but, for her, actual time is not going on with them but is standing still. The world is all of a piece and cannot go forward or backward; this is my great anxiety. I have lost time, the hands of the clock are so light... ´On looking back, on recovery, the patient said: ´It seems to me that January and February passed just like a blank, all of a piece, at a standstill; I couldn´t believe time really went on. As I kept working and nothing came of it, I had the feeling that everything was going backwards and I would never be done. (Jaspers, 1963; p. 84)

Another category that integrated the category of *Consciousness of the momentary passage of time* is the *Experience of detention of time*, the sense of detention:

I was suddenly caught up in a peculiar state; my arms and legs seemed to swell. A frightful pain shot through my head and time stood still. At the same time it was forced on me in an almost superhuman way how vitally important this moment was. Then time resumed its previous course, but the time which stood still stayed there like a gate. (Jaspers, 1963; p. 84)

Another sub-category in the *Consciousness of the momentary passage of time*, is the *Consciousness of the extension of time* of the recent past. The way of remembering the passage of time is not comprehensible in the pathology. Time manifests itself with a subjective, extended overestimation, where what was already experienced was perceived as distant. He also put the case where an abundance of events happens within seconds as in the dream.

Jaspers analyzed patient reports where he put on the table the contradiction of the stories in spite of a shared experience of time, and in the case of schizophrenia, it was related that brief situations were lived as with an eternal duration, entering then in this category of *Consciousness of extension of time of the recent past.*

Another category of pathological time is the *Consciousness of the present in relation to the past and the future*. Jaspers classified certain experiences and sub categories in the déjà vu and jamais vu, which are the moments related in the patients in which they feel that they see everything, that they have experienced the moment once and in the same way. Objects, people, positions and behaviors in déjà vu; and in the jamais vu everything seems to be seen for the first time. The perceived seems unknown, new and incomprehensible.

Another subcategory of the consciousness of the present in relation to the past and the future corresponds to the *discontinuity*. In schizophrenia, this sub category would be understood as the moments lived where time seems empty, without continuity; two different moments are experienced as continuous, without duration between the passage from one to another (Jaspers, 1966, pp. 108). The *shrinkage of the past*, another subcategory, includes the experience in which "a past of 29 years as of a length of at most 4 years", where other intervals also seem to shrink into extremely condensed proportions.

The next category of experience of time is the *Consciousness of the future*. The pathology may make it disappear. Jaspers describes stories of a person with depression who claimed to suffer from a terrible void:

I cannot see the future, just as if there were none. I think everything is going to stop now and tomorrow there will be nothing at all'. Patients know there is another day tomorrow but this awareness has changed from what it was like before. Even the next five minutes do not lie ahead as they used to do. Such patients have no decisions, no worries, no hopes for the future. They have also lost the feeling for past stretches of time. 'I know the exact number of years, but I have no real appreciation of how long it was. (Jaspers, 1983; p. 86)

Jaspers explains this category as a change of disposition in perception and internalization. A person is paralyzed by the conscience of already succeeded contents that he knows but does not not feel, thus submerging the future: the concept of time exists, is known but not lived.

Another category was *The schizophrenic experience of the suspension of time.* The person with schizophrenia lived very noticeably the sensory time-being with anticipations of catastrophic images in an assemblage of time.

Yesterday I looked at the clock... I felt as if! was put back, as if something past was coming to me ... I felt as if at I 1.30 a.m. it was II.0 a.m. again but not only the time went back but what had happened to me during it. Suddenly it was not just I 1.0 o'clock but a time long past was there too... midway in time I came towards myself out of the past. It was terrible. I thought perhaps the clock was put back; the attendants had played a stupid trick . . . then I had a feeling of frightful expectation that I could be drawn into the past... the play with time was so uncanny... an alien time seemed to dawn. (Jaspers, 1963; p. 86)

'There is no more present, only a backward ref- erence to the past; the future goes on shrinking-the past is so intrusive, it envelops me, it pulls me hack...I am living much faster than before...time chases me and ravenously eats itself away and I am in the middle of it all. (Jaspers, 1963; p. 86)

Minkowski formulated a temporality irreversibly lived forward due to the *vital impulse*. The *meaning of the personal work*'s plot is integrated within the area of the general sense, connecting life through *vital contact with reality*. The past for the author is the experience of memory removed from life and already related to knowledge, while the future is the direct and dynamic experience of an immediate event. He understands the future as the decay of the present in a past that gives rise to the possibilities of the future, with possibilities within an empty and stable margin that contains *personal production* and the *vital impetus* that results in a *sense*. In this way Minkowski introduces the concepts of *empty and stable margin*, and *spatialized horizon* content of experiences (Almada, 2008).

He categorized time into three levels: *activity, duration and waiting*. The *activity* is understood as the manifestation and action of the living being; the *duration* as active and oriented towards the future, lived towards the future. The duration determines the personal vital impulse and makes it aware of itself, it serves to affirm the self in space, and generates a feeling of expansion. In the activity, two dimensions are distinguished: *expansion and development;* and *maintenance of stability*.

In *waiting*, time is lived in the opposite direction; the future is directed towards us, we wait for it to become present. This waiting is the most basic elemental structure of the being, it suspends him from the activity and he remains fixed, self-anguished. The completely unknown and unexpected is left in suspension, which relates this state to death (Almada, 2008). For Minkowski, unmotivated anguish has a deeper reason of being than anxiety motivated by rational causes.

The two oppositions of the immediate levels (activity and waiting) materialize in the following way: activity through duration and waiting through instantaneity. The activity leads to an expansion of the being, and expects a contraction. The contraction that occurs as a result of waiting, reduces the being that exposes himself as little as possible to the environment; the degree of expansion and contraction determines the general attitude of the subject in the world (Almada, 2008).

Moving to the level of *mediate future*, a manifestation of it is *hope*. While waiting has a negative connotation in the Minkowskian proposal, hope is, on the contrary, positive and generates a future. On the other hand, both *desire* and hope have a clear positive character. Desire in this case is broader, it includes and contains the activity. Desire will then penetrate into the interiority, representing the activity in an intimate space that will internalize an "active self", which will form an internal and proper whole and enable to project even more in the future.

The difference between desire and hope is that the first contains the structured activity from the first immediate level. Hope has the function of freeing the being from anxious waiting by dilating the instantaneity; it expands the narrowness of the expectation from the immediate level, allowing one to look freely in the lived space, protecting from what can reveal to be painful beyond contact with the environment (Almada, 2008).

The third level is of future, that englobes the *prayer* and the *ethical act*. The prayer for Minkowski does not refer to religious faith, but is directed towards an infinite horizon beyond time and space; it contains temporality. The prayer for Minkowski may be a statement aimed at the future that surpasses hope, and bring it together with desire to a maximum point. The ethical act is the exceptional experience of freedom that surpasses the rational act of social action. The sense of the ethical act with respect to the ideal makes live the whole openness of temporality. That ideal is the future, and therefore the ethical act completes and gives meaning to the time lived (Almada, 2008). Minkowski's past derives from the future, is secondary to it and is in itself a negative temporality.

Remorse is presented as opposed to the experience of freedom lived in the impetus towards the future; it crystallizes and renews the past; it is the purest and most negative dimension of the past; it cuts out a fact and concentrates in all its negativity. For Minkowski, it will leave traces in the personal existence, positioning the remorse at the point of greater individualization, as a feeling of the most difficult to eradicate. Regret is the level that follows remorse and is applicable to less serious events that occur regardless of the direct action of being. The *futile memory*, the third and last category within the past, will be a reminiscence or production of a past fact that lacks deep content (Almada, 2008).

Minkowski considered temporality as the underlying phenomenon in psychiatric disturbances. The dynamism of temporal phenomena is distorted during a mental illness; the destructuring of personality will have its origin in the loss of the notion of lived time, in opposition against too much spatialization, altering the affects and the perceptions in a pathological level (Almada, 2008).

The cause of psychic alternation and morbid rationalism will often be this alteration in temporality, which is too spatialized by people, manifesting for example, in an acute melancholic psychosis through the search for compassion of the depressed state that puts the person in tune and vital contact with reality; while the strangeness of delusions will show a schizoid that will separate the person from his vital contact with reality. In these temporary alterations, the lived time does not appear with continuity, the facts of the past no longer suggest a projection to the future and the different events will be articulated disconnected among themselves. This alteration of temporality transpires in a general attitude towards life with respect to the future; it leads to the fact that time lived disintegrates into isolated events, losing the notion of progression.

Time is fragmented and interests are projected in space making any vision or projection towards the future impossible due to the rigidity of the experience and of the meanings of the objects and events, thus losing all possibility of improvisation. The reality is fractioned with the person losing itself in insignificant details that appear to have some richness and a latent message that does not exist.

This excessive spatialization, this altered spatial dimension will be, according to Minkowski, what impoverishes the vital impetus to the point where the surrounding world is perceived as altered. The ideo affective contents so analyzed and interpreted by psychoanalysis lose importance in this proposal, while the formal aspects of the pathological organization become relevant, as well as the destructuring of the temporal dynamism and its spatial organization that produce in the end the loss of vital contact with reality, manifested in delirious symptoms. The apparent richness of the diseased mind arises from the background of a multiplication of arbitrary elements, organized in a production of the disintegrated ego (Almada, 2008).

Minkowski described a behavior in manic activity of a disaggregated and absorbing activity, with an instantaneous contact with the world but without penetration. And given its lived duration, it lacks the deployment of its activities in time. This author, to describe the temporal movements of mania and melancholy, used the term *sliding*. The maniac slides through the land of the present, replacing it with the vertiginous desire to expand.

Deshaies (1961) takes as a basis some Bergsonian concepts of time, such as Lived Time or psychological duration (inner time); the spatialized or social time (external time). The duration of time in the pathological process is disorganized until it disappears, and within the processes of duration, the deregulation of synchronization and rhythm become characteristic in these states.

Desynchronization is presented as categorical or intersubjective. In the categorical, demential or confusional states in their socialized and spatial organization are those that manifest themselves in a pathological way. There is no possibility of orientation of behavior in relation to the history already made in the past or in relation to the possibilities offered by the future. The intersubjective desynchronization expresses the difference between what the sick person lives and what those around him live. One begins to notice in mental pathologies an *asynchronism* between on the one side the *youthful time*, living a duration oriented to the future, full of impulses, desires and hopes, what Deshaies calls the attitude of conquerors; on the opposite side, the *senile time*, in which a duration oriented towards the past imposes itself, full of memories and sorrows; all signs that declare the vital double and the progressive narrowing of the horizon and activity. It is the time of the dispossessed who were once possessors (Deshaies, 1961). The mental illness creates obstacles in the feelings of duration, thus generating an incomplete link with the real action.

The painful tone arises and the prolongation of the action. The experience of the morbid duration has its own rhythm. Delirious activity will generate accelerations, delays or suspensions of duration there, which will result in a disturbance of expression and communication.

Deshaies analyzed the *chronotimia*, the affective effect of the temporary disturbance. States such as tedium, sadness and melancholic depression generate a lengthening of durations. As to the enjoyment, hypomania, full delusions and expansiveness, they will shorten the duration of time. You can get to see in pathologies such as schizophrenia, the absence of feeling of aging due to a lack of historical regression for not integrating the morbid experiences.

They do not age subjectively because they do not live historically. In a melancholic psychosis and morbid anxiety, there is a denial of the future, a feeling of intense aging due to an excess of historical anticipation. Asthenia, abandonment, disinterest, depreciation, punishment, apathy and anhedonia can be related and phenomenologically understood as the way of being in the world that excessively anticipates the future while being lost in those thoughts (Deshaies, 1961).

The loss of rhythm, or dysrhythmia, manifests itself as fragmentation or immediacy of the duration of mobility; the rejection of the past and the dictatorship of the instant are some of the forms found in the susceptibility of the maniac. This pathological figure of acute psychosis (mania), will manifest itself in the form of non-duration, of the experience of the fast, multiple and incomplete act, without any capacity of relationship with the previous act and with no perspective of future.

The acceleration of duration can be found in the phases of euphoric excitement, in the onirism and in the fecund moments of delirium, during which hectic events are experienced in a hasty and disorderly manner. The rapid durations are perceived excessive. In toxic psychoses, both an acceleration of duration and a delay can occur. On the other hand, the delay of duration as a semiological entity, in hypochondria, depression and anguish, arises as a manifestation of difficulty and rarity of action, as well as a painful, empty and indissoluble form of adherence to the present.

Deshaies also mentioned Eugène Minkowski in his work, who, when undertaking the analysis of detention in schizophrenia, stated as statism and spatialization, in melancholy as crystallization and in melancholic delirium for its temporal order (Deshaies, 1961). In delirium, Minkowski (quoted by Deshaies) analyzes and phenomenologically identifies in that structure of temporal consciousness the absolute slavery to the past, the immobilization, the feeling of guilt, of self-accusation, the denial of the present time, the ideas of ruin of unworthiness, barriers to the future, punishment, imminent catastrophe, lack of desires and lack of hope (Deshaies, 1961, p. 132).

Deshaies also refers to the temporality of the suicidal behavior, lived as a halt in the becoming, with the abolition of desires and hopes, the annihilation of the future, the withdrawal from the past that is feeled as oppressive, unbearable and vain (Deshaies, 1961, p. 133). In suicide, the author identifies a denial of being and a suppression of duration in nothing; sometimes an impulse is experienced to a beyond time, from a past lived with great tension.

The deep disorganizations of reality such as dementia, stupor, catatonic states, deep autism, epileptic accesses, etc., contain an abolition of the duration of time. In other behavioral states such as sleep or coma, the duration is eliminated: nothing is recorded because there is nothing to realize the registration *with*, due to anesthesia and the altered state of destructuring of consciousness. Just as death, eternity, according to these states of detainment of psychic activity, is absence of duration (Deshaies, 1961).

Another appreciation of Deshaies, refers to the mention made of Henri Ey where many future advances are predicted, leading us towards nowaday's knowledge in the area of memory. The morbid duration as a characteristic of the pathological temporality posed by Deshaies in his treatise, refers to the way of life of the pathological personality; phenomenologically speaking, we speak of "how the past weight is lightened or increases according to the orientation of the future; and how the future unfolds or retreats under the pressure of the past "(Deshaies, 1961, p. 133). The morbid duration includes then the disturbances of memory, since the mnemonic activity usurps the organization of the lived duration (See Figure 1.).

ORGANIZATIONAL CHARTS WITH AUTHORS FROM A PSYCHIATRY OF THE FRANCO-GERMAN TRADITION WHO MADE REFERENCE TO TEMPORALITY: CONCEPTUAL GENERALITIES AND SUBCATEGORIES

See Figures 2-5.

THERAPEUTIC POSSIBILITIES

As we could observe, there are several currents and theoretical lines that directly or indirectly address the issue of the subjective experience of time. Psychoanalysis, referring to past events in order to rethink the present; the behavioral cognitive line, using planning and the establishment of strategies that organize certain objectives,

Figure 1. Authors of the twentieth century who have theorized from different disciplines about temporality

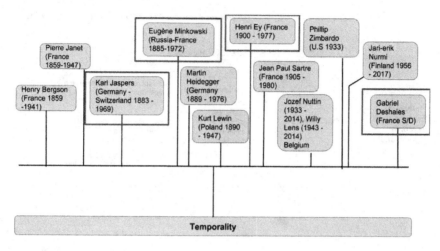

Figure 2.

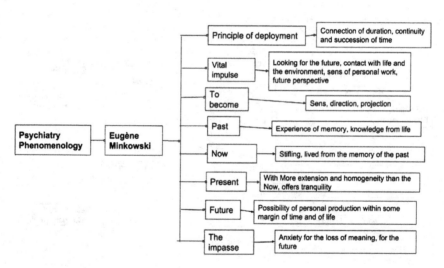

takes place on a temporary and structural basis that is more clearly counted during a number of pre-established sessions; the logotherapy or the existential analysis from the present, pretends to find a possible and optimistic sense in the future, etc. Clearly it will not be possible to refer to all the theoretical lines of psychotherapy, but it is necessary to discuss and problematize the importance and place that may be occupying in clinical work the subjective experience of time, understood as *becoming* for more philosophical orientations of the human being, or as a *Temporary Perspective* for more cognitive behavioral perspectives.

Figure 3.

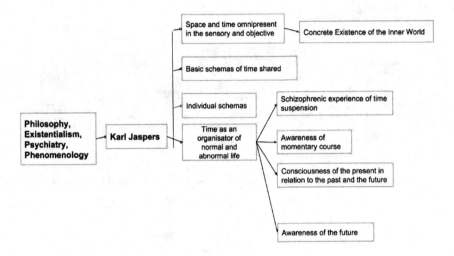

Figure 4.

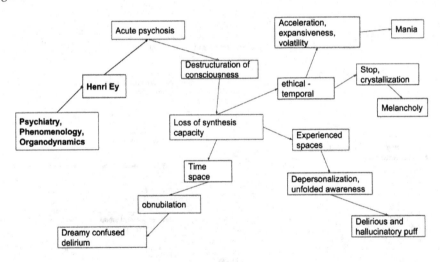

Theoretical currents such as logotherapy or existential analysis put an explicit and constant emphasis on time, which is becoming an important part of the treatments. The past according to the Viktor Frankl school for example, is eternal, indelible and not transitory. That is where are recorded our choices of meaning already fulfilled, which are taken optimistically by the strength they offer to the identity. The fact of *having been* in the past, is a safe *way of being*, that does not take away meaning from life due to the difficulties of the current existence. The evocation of moments full of meaning already lived in the past provides security and serenity (Almada,

Figure 5.

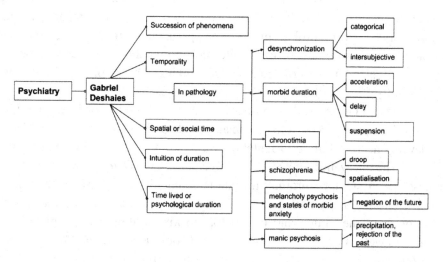

2008). Frankl, unlike psychoanalysis, will transform the past's negative and traumatic valence of the Freudian current, to think it as a possibility of meaning. Minkowski for his part marked the optimism of the future as a possibility and as an activity of fulfillment, also ensuring in the future the positivity of the meaning of life, and the establishment of a certain distance from the horizon will give possibility to the feeling of hope.

The current research and theoretical proposals refering to the Temporary Perspective based on the definition given by Zimbardo and Boyd (1999) include the temporal characteristic of the human being as a relatively stable dimension, but which can be affected and modified by external influences of a social, political, religious, economic and psychological nature. From this perspective, proposals for psychotherapeutic intervention can be clustered into two categories: that defined by objectives (based on extending and deepening a Temporary Perspective of the individual Future); or that intended to fully develop a balance of the entire individual time profile (Ortuño, 2014). Lens & Tsuzuki (2007), argued that the Future Time Perspective should be developed so that the patient can formulate his own objectives over a more extended period of time and elaborate more mid-end facilitating structures (Ortuño, 2014). Thoms & Blasko argued that the Future Time Perspective can be manipulated through training, even if it could consider that this temporal dimension is relatively stable due to the culture, the personality and the stage of individual development.

An important influence has also been observed on the adaptability of the professional career, on its development and importance within the Perspective of Future Time. Ferrari, Nota and Soresi (2012) designed an investigation based on an intervention of 10 sessions in which it was meant to increase in adolescents the ability to project in the future. The results of this pilot confirmed differences in future thinking between the control group and the experimental group. This intervention was based on didactic sessions that allowed participants to understand several deep psychological theories rooted in future thinking (Theory of decision conflict, interests, self-efficacy, objectives, decision strategies and others).

According to Ortuño (2014), previous attempts to modify or intervene in the Individual Temporary Perspective were also made by Marko and Savickas (1998). The development of Future Orientation was proposed as the main intervention objective. The intervention consisted of three phases: the *Orientation* phase, which was based on an attempt to promote the Future Orientation and the sense of optimism towards the future; *Differentiation*, in which an attempt was made to create a sense of reality about the future, and to develop positive attitudes in the planning of activities as well as in the definition of projects or objectives; and the third phase called *Integration*, where the objective was to cognitively connect the participants with a present behavior heading to future results, putting into practice the newly acquired planning tools and developing greater awareness of their projects. The results yielded data that indicated that the experimental group presented significant increases in the Orientation to the Future and optimism towards it. Although most of the research was conducted in educational contexts, the development of a Futur Orientation has been transferred to clinical situations to work with patients who do not have such guidance.

On the other hand, Hall and Fong (2003) developed a process of three short 30 minutes sessions in which the participants were instructed on the long-term implications of their habitual behaviors. In this investigation there was an intervention group, another group of "no treatment" and another intervention but controlled, intervening from the standardized cognitive behavioral orientation without components reported in a long-term Temporary Perspective.

When comparing these three groups in relation to the number of hours that the participants devoted to intense physical activity, they found that those who had received the Temporary Perspective intervention reported a greater number of hours of physical activity during the 10 weeks following the intervention (Ortuño, 2014). This study and others have shown that an intervention focused on improving the Temporary Perspective in the long term provided significant results and improvements (Ortuño, 2014).

Van Beek, Kerkhof and Beekman (2009), as mentioned in Ortuño (2014) created a group approach of 10 sessions applied to the psychopathological clinical context with the aim of reducing suicidal thinking through the development of a more realistic future thinking. It was based on psychoeducation and sought to influence individual dysfunctional cognitive aspects such as: dichotomous thinking and the modification of the locus of control. According to the authors, the development of the Future Temporal Perspective can help to modify cognitive patterns of dysfunctional behaviors (Ortuño, 2014). Kazakina presented a network of Temporal Perspectives over various dimensions, based on the concept of a Balanced Temporary Perspective. He considers it important to frame clinical objectives in psychotherapy. Although he does not mention an empirical analysis of the efficacy of this proposal in a context of psychotherapy based on temporality, his work is considered of important value in the theoretical and interventions context (Ortuño, 2014).

FINAL COMMENTS

In this chapter a kind of interdisciplinary dialogue was carried out referring to the subjective experience of time in psychosis, both current and classic, from a psychological, neuroscientific and psychopathological point of view. The temporal variable still generates intrigue, its comprehension is not complete and that is the reason why an approach from different disciplines is totally valid. Many professionals from different fields and sometimes some clinicians do not take much into account the Temporary Perspective and the personal experience of it that a patient suffering from some form of psychosis can have. Throughout experiences in classic authors with vast experience and analytical skills, as well as in the current clinic of psychotherapy and rehabilitation of people with Schizophrenia, we see that the "dysfunctional use" or the pathological structuring of time are still as valid as in the classic psychopathological descriptions. These are in line with the categories and concepts made by Lewin, Zaleski and Zimbardo among others (Ortuño, 2014, Vasquez, 2011).

The subjective experience of time in psychopathology thereby recovers new relevance. The current clinic and the daily coexistence with populations with this pathology only confirm these experiences of a subjective nature, although perhaps manifested with less acuity thanks to the current treatments. The vividly updated memory of events that took place decades ago, morbid anxiety or anxiety in the future, the prevailing and preponderated perception of a life prior to pathology, the planning of unrealistic, unattainable plans or objectives in short, structured periods of time along a limited and dysfunctional temporal extension, are some examples.

The neural complexity involved in the biological processes of perception, sequencing and temporal planning are determining factors in a large part of our daily performance. However, in psychotherapeutic work, the technical data provided by basic research lines related to neural functioning are not tools directly applicable to the patient. This requires an opening, an interdisciplinary integration and acceptance, and the basic research undertaken at the moment is not enough. It is too difficult (at least to this day) to generate a psychoactive drug capable of solving symptoms and psychotic syndromes of great complexity such as morbid rationalism, schizoid and withdrawal of vital contact with reality, autism and experience subjective of maladaptive time. However, neither is it acceptable to realize a clinical encounter about rehabilitation from a position that ignores current theoretical contributions of neuroscience and basic research (Pomi, Valle-Lisboa, Mizraji, Cabana, 2010), as well as critically accepted and well-founded contributions of disciplines or sister theoretical lines. As Florit Robles says, "not anything goes" (Florit-Robles, 2006).

Enzo Tagliazucchi says that we are the only species with the capacity to think metacognitively with an identity, a conscience and some characteristics that make us think that we are unique beings (Tagliazucchi, 2018). A species in which, in the pathology, the morbid conscience appears in the clinical through speech, misused metaphors, descriptions, lax associations and affections that must be professionally received, worked with adequate tools for analysis and work in rehabilitation. The anchoring of the state of consciousness will be given to us by means of the temporal space axis, and therefore, the temporality and its perception will be relevant information for the clinician. Some studies will contribute in the future new data and information about the destructuring and the subjective experience of time in psychosis (Rodriguez, Ortuño, & Pezzani, 2018).

Based on studies of this type and with the use of clinical tools and theoretical currents based on evidence, with sustenance and theoretical argument, it will be possible to validate and recognize human suffering from a personal and personal description of these pathological experiences. It is still necessary to rethink and adjust the effectiveness of Mental Health policies and programs, carry out research, design interventions and not discard the phenomena experienced by the patients themselves, recognize them in their existence and recognize their suffering in order to advance a little more in the understanding of pathologies and structures that are articulated and installed, modifying all the temporary events of people. To reestablish a temporary balance, a modification in the affective valencies awarded by a person with a pathological picture such as psychosis or schizophrenia, and enable a temporary optimism, an active attitude, hopeful and meaningful towards the future; a more homogeneous and adaptive identity, that makes a synthesis of the autobiography of the most balanced person. Enable a better quality of life and a better self-perception.

This work was wrote as a unifier within a book related with screen time in a online society. In our days it´s possible to foresee the acceleration and speed in people´ lives. Nowadays, the temporal dynamism and variability is no longer questioned. Live elapse in several spaces at the same time. It´s possible to communicate with people from different places at the same moment. Suddenly, every activity generates discomfort if it is not perfomed at new generations speeds. The anxiety and rush are dominant forces instead of the goals, objectives or the contents.

Within this premise, what is the place and validity that psychological therapy settings still have? How a therapist can understand and generate empathy with people with any kind of severe psychological disorder? The actual society imposes us a rithym and a cadence. It defines us and restring our empty spaces for waiting, making us less and less patients, less tolerants and definitely less empathetic with other ways of experiencing time. These are questions for clinical professionals, who receive people with different kind of difficulties, which can be related with a disfunctional experience of time. Time and the way we experience it is not the same for everyone, but that is not an issue per se. The real question lies in about what the place that the actual society and mental health professionals left to people who present different time experiences.

REFERENCES

Almada, R. (2008). *Fenomenología y Psicopatología del tiempo vivido en Eugène Minkowski*. Retrieved from www.robertoalmada.com/blog/wp-content/.../01/minkowski.pdf

American Psychiatric Association. (2002). *Diagnostic and statistical manual of mental disorders: DSM-IV-TR*. Washington, DC: Author.

Castro, S. (2018). *Estudio de las oscilaciones gamma del EEG durante la vigilia, el sueño y en un modelo farmacológico de psicosis (Tesis de Doctorado)*. Montevideo: Universidad de la República.

Correa, A., Lupiáñez, J., & Tudela, P. (2006). La percepción del tiempo: Una revisión desde la Neurociencia Cognitiva. *Cognitiva*, *18*(2), 145–168. doi:10.1174/021435506778148667

de la Iglesia, H. O., Meyer, J., Carpino, A., & Schwartz, W. J. (2000). Antiphase oscillation of the left and right suprachiasmatic nuclei. *Science*, *290*(5492), 799–801.

Deshaies, G. (1961). *Psicopatología General*. Buenos Aires: Kapelusz.

Ey, H. (1996). *Tratado de Psiquiatría*. Barcelona: Masson.

Ey, H. (2008). *Estudios Psiquiátricos. In Estructura de las Psicosis agudas y desestructuración de la conciencia. Volumen I y II*. Buenos Aires: Polemos.

Ferrari, L., Nota, L., & Soresi, S. (2012). Evaluation of an Intervention to Foster Time Perspective and Career Decidesdness in a Group of Italian Adolescents. *The Career Development Quarterly, 60*(1), 82–96. doi:10.1002/j.2161-0045.2012.00007.x

Florit-Robles, A. (2006). La rehabilitación psicosocial de pacientes con esquizofrenia crónica. *Apuntes de Psicología, 24*(1-3), 223–244.

Garrabé, J. (2017). La phénoménologie de langue allemande et la psychiatrie française. *L'Évolution Psychiatrique, 82*(1), 17–37. doi:10.1016/j.evopsy.2016.05.003

Golombek, D. A., & Yannielli, P. C. (2006). Organización del sistema circadiano en vertebrados. In J. A. Madrid & M. A. Rol de Lama (Eds.), *Cronobiología Básica y Clínica* (pp. 191–222). Madrid: Editeca Red.

Gutierrez-García, A., Reyes-Platas, D., & Picazo, O. (2017). Percepción del tiempo en la neuropsicopatología: Una revisión sistemática. *Psiquiatría Biológica, 24*(3), 85–96. doi:10.1016/j.psiq.2017.10.002

Hawking, S. (1988). *A Brief History of Time: From the big bang to black holes.* New York: Bantam Books.

Jaspers, K. (1963). *General Psychopathology.* Chicago, IL: University of Chicago Press.

Jaspers, K. (1996). *Psicopatología General.* Buenos Aires: Beta.

Lewin, K. (1943). Defining the fiels at a given time. *Psychological Review, 50*(3), 292–310. doi:10.1037/h0062738

Minkowski, E. (1966). *Traité de Psychopathologie.* Paris: Presses Universitaires de France.

Minkowski, E. (2002). *Écrits Cliniques.* Érès: Saint – Agne.

Ortuño, V. E. (2014). *Time Perspective Stability: Studies with a multidimensional model in the University Context* (Doctoral dissertation). University of Coimbra, Coimbra, Portugal. Retrieved from https://estudogeral.sib.uc.pt/handle/10316/24324

Rodríguez, R., Ortuño, V. E., & Pezzani, G. (2018). *Desestructuración de la vivencia del tiempo en la psicosis y Rehabilitación Psicosocial.* Work presented at Primer Congreso Internacional de Psicología, Universidad de la República. Montevideo, Uruguay. Retrieved from https://www.researchgate.net/publication/328736314_Desestructuracion_del_Tiempo_en_l a_Psicosis_y_Rehabilitacion_Psicosocial_Presentacion_oral_dada_en_el_Primer_Congres o_Internacional_de_Psicologia_en_la_Universidad_de_la_Republica

Suddendorf, T. & Corballis, M. (2009). *Mental time travel and the evolution of the human mind*. University of Auckland.

Tagliazuchi, E. (2017). *Psicodélicos. En El Gato y La Caja: Un libro sobre drogas.* Retrieved from https://elgatoylacaja.com.ar/sobredrogas/

Vásquez, A. (2011). Experiencia subjetiva del tiempo y su influencia en el comportamiento: Revisión y modelos. *Psicologia: Teoria e Pesquisa, 27*(2), 2015–2223.

Zimbardo, P., & Boyd, J. (1999). *The Time Paradox: the new psychology of time that will change your life*. New York: Free Press.

KEY TERMS AND DEFINITIONS

Existentialism: Philosophical current that emerges as a rupture to positivist and mechanistic dogmas. This current analyzes and studies the very existence of the human being thrown into the world. Within this current, temporality is a category of great importance.

Franco-Germanic Psychiatry: Denomination assigned to a line within the psychiatry of more philosophical and humanistic perspective. It takes contributions from existentialism and phenomenology.

Phenomenology: Philosophical current that is dedicated to the analysis and study of the lived phenomena, the experiences, and the contents of the conscience.

Psychology of Time: A general field of study within psychology. It is devoted to the study of all time-related phenomena with influence in human cognition and behaviour.

Psychosis: Serious mental disorder that affects more than 21 million people worldwide. It can cause serious deterioration and loss of autonomy and one of the aspects that shows disruptions is the perspective and the temporary experience.

Psychosocial Rehabilitation: Rehabilitation intervention model designed and applied to serious disorders such as schizophrenia or piscosis. In the same work on the project of life of the person and their reintegration into society.

Time Perspective: A concept within subjective time field. Refers to the process of organizing and retrieving all information using a set of temporal frames which compose individuals´ temporal profile.

ENDNOTES

[1] "El concepto de tiempo debe ir unido indefectiblemente a la idea de cambio, y estos podrán ser percibidos por un individuo en tanto este posea los mecanismos básicos que posibiliten un registro de tales cambios" (Correa, 2006. p. 163).

[2] "Sus límites consisten en que no puede disolver nunca enteramente al hombre individual en conceptos psicológicos" (Jaspers, 1966. p. 16).

[3] "El pasado ha pasado, por lo tanto ya no existe; el futuro no existe todavía; el presente por ello se encuentra entre dos nadas; pero el presente, el ahora es un punto sin extensión; en cuanto el presente está ahí ya no es; por tanto el ahora es contradictorio y constituye por ello otra nada. Y así, para el tiempo, la realidad se reduce a una nada situada entre dos nadas" (Almada, 2008; p. 46).

Compilation of References

Abbott, C. (2003). *ICT: Changing education*. New York: Routledge.

Abreu, J., Nogueira, J., Becker, V., & Cardoso, B. (2017). Survey of Catch-up TV and other time-shift services: A comprehensive analysis and taxonomy of linear and nonlinear television. *Telecommunication Systems, 64*(1), 57–74. doi:10.100711235-016-0157-3

Adam, B. (1990). *Time and Social Theory*. Philadelphia: Temple University Press.

Adams, H. (2005). A Law of Acceleration. In The Education of Henry Adams (pp. 473–482). San Diego, CA: Icon.

Adams, F., & Aizawa, K. (2008). *The Bounds of Cognition*. London: Blackwell.

Adams, J., & Nettle, D. (2009). Time perspective, personality and smoking, body mass, and physical activity: An empirical study. *British Journal of Health Psychology, 14*(1), 83–105. doi:10.1348/135910708X299664 PMID:18435866

Agarwal, R., & Karahanna, E. (2000). Time Flies When You're Having Fun: Cognitive Absorption and Beliefs about Information Technology Usage. *Management Information Systems Quarterly, 24*(4), 665–694. doi:10.2307/3250951

Agger, B. (2011). iTime: Labor and life in a smartphone era. *Time & Society, 20*(1), 119–136. doi:10.1177/0961463X10380730

Aghaee, N. (2013). Finding potential problems in the thesis process in higher education: Analysis of e-mails to develop a support system. *Education and Information Technologies, 20*(1), 1–16.

Aghaee, N., Hansson, H., Tedre, M., & Drougge, U. (2014). Learners' perceptions on the structure and usefulness of e-resources for the thesis courses. *European Journal of Open, Distance and E-Learning, 17*(1), 154–171. Retrieved from: https://www.degruyter.com/downloadpdf/j/eurodl.2014.17.issue-1/eurodl-2014-0011/eurodl-2014-0011.pdf

Aghaee, N., Karunaratne, T., Smedberg, A., & Jobe, W. (2015). Communication and collaboration gaps among phd students and ict as a way forward: results from a study in sweden. In *Proceedings of E-Learn: World Conference on E-Learning in Corporate, Government, Healthcare, and Higher Education 2015* (pp. 237-244). Association for the Advancement of Computing in Education (AACE). Retrieved from: https://www.learntechlib.org/primary/p/152016/

Aghaee, N., Jobe, W. B., Karunaratne, T., Smedberg, A., Hansson, H., & Tedre, M. (2016). Interaction gaps in PhD education and ICT as a way forward: Results from a study in Sweden. *International Review of Research in Open and Distributed Learning, 17*(3), 360–383. doi:10.19173/irrodl.v17i3.2220

Ahrens, M. B., & Sahani, M. (2011). Observers exploit stochastic models of sensory change to help judge the passage of time. *Current Biology, 21*(3), 200–206. doi:10.1016/j.cub.2010.12.043 PMID:21256018

Akaike, H. (1987). Factor analysis and AIC. *Psychometrika, 52*(3), 317–332. doi:10.1007/BF02294359

Akın, A., & Fidan, M. (2012). The validity and reliability of the Turkish version of the Flourishing Scale. In *3rd International Conference on New Trends in Education and their Implications (ICONTE-2012)* (pp. 26-28). Academic Press.

Albion, P., & Erwee, R. (2011). Preparing for doctoral supervision at a distance: Lessons from experience. In Proceedings of Society for information technology & teacher education international conference 2011 (pp. 82-89). Academic Press.

Alhadeff-Jones, M. (2017). *Time and the Rhythms of Emancipatory Education - Rethinking the temporal complexity of self and society.* Routledge.

Almada, R. (2008). *Fenomenología y Psicopatología del tiempo vivido en Eugène Minkowski.* Retrieved from www.robertoalmada.com/blog/wp-content/.../01/minkowski.pdf

Almeida, P., Abreu, J., Silva, T., Varsori, E., Oliveira, E., Velhinho, A., … Oliveira, D. (2018). Iterative User Experience Evaluation of a User Interface for the Unification of TV Contents. In *Applications and Usability of Interactive Television* (pp. 44–57). Aveiro: Springer. Retrieved from https://www.springer.com/us/book/9783319901695

Almeida, P., Abreu, J., Silva, T., Guedes, R., Oliveira, D., Cardoso, B., & Dias, H. (2018). UltraTV: an iTV content unification prototype. In *Proceedings of the ACM International Conference on Interactive Experiences for TV and Online Video - TVX '18*. Seoul: ACM. 10.1145/3210825.3213558

Alstyne, M. V., & Brynjolfsson, E. (1997). *Electronic Communities: Global village or cyberbalkans?* Retrieved May 12, 2017, from https://www.mediensprache.net/archiv/pubs/2809.pdf

American Psychiatric Association. (2002). *Diagnostic and statistical manual of mental disorders: DSM-IV-TR.* Washington, DC: Author.

American Psychological Association (APA). (2006). *Multitasking: Switching costs.* APA.

ANACOM. (2017). *Serviço de Distribuição de Sinais de Televisão por subscrição – 3º trimestre 2017.* Retrieved from https://www.anacom.pt/streaming/TVS3T2017public11dez2017.pdf?contentId=1423909&field=ATTACHED_FILE

Anagnostopoulos, F., & Griva, F. (2012). Exploring Time Perspective in greek young adults: Validation of the Zimbardo Time Perspective Inventory and relationships with mental health indicators. *Social Indicators Research*, *106*(1), 41–59. doi:10.100711205-011-9792-y

Anderson, B. (1989). *Nação e Consciência Nacional*. São Paulo, SP: Ática.

Anderson-Fye, E. P. (2012). Anthropological Perspectives on Physical Appearance and Body Image. In *Encyclopedia of Body Image and Human Appearance* (Vol. 1, pp. 15–22). San Diego, CA: Academic Press. doi:10.1016/B978-0-12-384925-0.00003-1

Andrew, M. (2012). Supervising doctorates at a distance: Three trans-Tasman stories. *Quality Assurance in Education*, *20*(1), 42–53. doi:10.1108/09684881211198239

Andriessen, I., Phalet, K., & Lens, W. (2006). Future goal setting, task motivation and learning of minority and non-minority students in Dutch schools. *The British Journal of Educational Psychology*, *76*(4), 827–850. doi:10.1348/000709906X148150 PMID:17094888

Appadurai, A. (1996). *Modernity at large: cultural dimensions of globalization*. University of Minnesota Press.

Araújo, E., Oliveira, A., & Bianchetti, L. (2014). *Formação do investigador: reflexões em torno da escrita/pesquisa/ autoria e orientação*. Braga: CECS - Centro de Estudos de Comunicação e Sociedade Universidade do Minho / Braga. Portugal e CED - Centro de Ciências da Educação Universidade Federal de Santa Catarina / Florianópolis-SC, Brasil. Retrieved from: https://docs.wixstatic.com/ugd/18e49d_ddbc2b1dbe624a359281ea921dec573e.pdf

Araújo, E. (2007). O desaparecimento do tempo nas sociedades modernas. In *Quando o tempo desaparece: Tempo e simultaneidade*. Porto: Edições Ecopy.

Araújo, E., & Bento, S. (2007). *Como fazer um doutoramento? Práticas institucionais e gestão do tempo*. Porto: Ecopy.

Arnett, J. (1994). Sensation Seeking: A new conceptualization and a new scale. *Personality and Individual Differences*, *16*(2), 289–296. doi:10.1016/0191-8869(94)90165-1

Arnocky, S., Milfont, T. L., & Nicol, J. R. (2014). Time perspective and sustainable behavior: Evidence for the distinction between consideration of immediate and future consequences. *Environment and Behavior*, *46*(5), 556–582. doi:10.1177/0013916512474987

Ashkanasy, N. M., Gupta, V., Mayfield, M. S., & Trevor-Roberts, E. (2004). Future orientation. In R. J. House, P. J. Hanges, M. Javidan, P. W. Dorfman, & V. Gupta (Eds.), Culture, Leadership, and Organizations: The GLOBE study of 62 societies (pp. 282-342). Thousand Oaks, CA: Sage Publications.

Autoridade Nacional das Comunicações (ANACOM). (2015). *Evolução da penetração dos serviços de comunicações eletrónicas*. ANACOM.

Aylmer, B. (2013). *Continuity and Change in Time Perspective: A Longitudinal Field Study of Youth Workers* (Doctoral dissertation). Dublin City University, Business School.

343

Babic, M. J., Morgan, P. J., Plotnikoff, R. C., Lonsdale, C., Eather, N., Skinner, G., ... Lubans, D. R. (2015). Rationale and study protocol for "Switch-off 4 Healthy Minds" (S4HM): A cluster randomized controlled trial to reduce recreational screen time in adolescents. *Contemporary Clinical Trials, 40,* 150–158. doi:10.1016/j.cct.2014.12.001 PMID:25500220

Babic, M. J., Smith, J. J., Morgan, P. J., Eather, N., Plotnikoff, R. C., & Lubans, D. R. (2017). Longitudinal associations between changes in screen-time and mental health outcomes in adolescents. *Mental Health and Physical Activity, 12,* 124–131. doi:10.1016/j.mhpa.2017.04.001

Babic, M. J., Smith, J. J., Morgan, P. J., Lonsdale, C., Plotnikoff, R. C., Eather, N., ... Lubans, D. R. (2016). Intervention to reduce recreational screen-time in adolescents: Outcomes and mediators from the 'Switch-Off 4 Healthy Minds' (S4HM) cluster randomized controlled trial. *Preventive Medicine, 91,* 50–57. doi:10.1016/j.ypmed.2016.07.014 PMID:27471018

Badura, P., Madarasova Geckova, A., Sigmundova, D., Sigmund, E., van Dijk, J. P., & Reijneveld, S. A. (2017). Do family environment factors play a role in adolescents' involvement in organized activities? *Journal of Adolescence, 59,* 59–66. doi:10.1016/j.adolescence.2017.05.017 PMID:28582651

Bainbridge, W. S. (2010). *The Warcraft Civilization: social science in a virtual world.* Cambridge, MA: The MIT Press.

Baker, F., & Mackinlay, E. (2006). Sing, soothe and sleep: A lullaby education programme for first-time mothers. *British Journal of Music Education, 23*(2), 147–160. doi:10.1017/S0265051706006899

Bakhtin, M. M. (1937). Forms of Time and of the Chronotope in the Novel: Notes toward a Historical Poetics. *Narrative dynamics: Essays on time, plot, closure, and frames,* 15-24.

Baldi, V. (2011a). Oltre il presentismo. *Critica Sociologica, 45*(178), 75–80.

Baldi, V. (2011b). Su tiempo! Más allá de la ubiquidad del presente. *Interartive. A Platform for Contemporaney Art and Thought, Abril/Maio*(31–32).

Bandura, A. (1997). *Self-efficacy: The exercise of control.* New York: Freeman.

Bapat, R., van Geel, M., & Vedder, P. (2017). Socio-Economic Status, Time Spending, and Sleep Duration in Indian Children and Adolescents. *Journal of Child and Family Studies, 26*(1), 80–87. doi:10.100710826-016-0557-8 PMID:28111517

Barber, L., & Santuzzi, A. (2016). Telepressure and College Student Employment: The Costs of Staying Connected Across Social Contexts. *Stress and Health.* Retrieved from http://onlinelibrary.wiley.com/doi/10.1002/smi.2668/pdf

Baudelaire, C. (1857). L'Horloge. *Fleurs du mal.*

Bauer, J. J., & McAdams, D. P. (2004). Personal growth in adults' stories of life transitions. *Journal of Personality, 72*(3), 573–602. doi:10.1111/j.0022-3506.2004.00273.x PMID:15102039

Baumgartner, S., Weeda, W., van der Heijden, L., & Huizinga, M. (2014). The Relationship Between Media Multitasking and Executive Function in Early Adolescents. *The Journal of Early Adolescence, 34*(8), 1120–1144. doi:10.1177/0272431614523133

Baym, N. K. (2010). New relations, new selves. In N. K. Baym (Ed.), *Personal Connections in the Digital Age* (pp. 99–121). Cambridge, UK: Polity Press.

Becker, H. J. (2000). Who's Wired and Who's Not: Children's Access to and Use of Computer Technology. *The Future of Children, 10*(2), 44–75. doi:10.2307/1602689 PMID:11255709

Bergmann, W. (1992). The Problem of Time in Sociology. *Time & Society, 1*(1), 81–134. doi:10.1177/0961463X92001001007

Bermúdez, J. L. (2007). *Thinking without Words*: An Overview for Animal Ethics. *The Journal of Ethics, 11*(3), 319–335. doi:10.100710892-007-9013-8

Bhagwat, V. R. (2002). Cryptochromes and biological clocks. *Resonance, 7*(9), 36–48. doi:10.1007/BF02836184

Bianchetti, L., & Machado, A. (2005). *Orientação/escrita de dissertações e teses em questão: produção científica e estratégias de orientadores e Coordenadores de PPGEs. Relatório final de projeto do CNPq, Edital Universal (Processo 479166/01-3)*. Florianópolis: PPGE/UFSC.

Bianchetti, L., Turnes, L., & Cunha, R. (2016). O tempo de doutorado e o papel das TICS, questões para a pesquisa e análise. *Conjetura. Filosofia e Educação, 3*, 628–644.

Blanco, S. R., Miguel, F. J. R. S., & Arraz, F. G. (2016). Los millenials universitarios y su interacción con el social mobile. *Journal of Communication*, 97–116.

Blatchley, B., Dixon, R., Purvis, A., Slack, J., Thomas, T., Weber, N., & Wiley, C. (2007). Computer use and the perception of time. *North American Journal of Psychology, 9*(1), 131–142.

Block, R. A., & Zakay, D. (2001). Retrospective and prospective timing: Memory, attention, and consciousness. *Time and Memory: Issues in Philosophy and Psychology*, 59-76.

Bluedorn, A. (1998). An Interview with Anthropologist Edward T. Hall. *Journal of Management Inquiry, 7*(2), 109–115. doi:10.1177/105649269872003

Bluedorn, A., Kalliath, T., Strube, M., & Martin, G. (1999). Polychronicity and the Inventory of Polychronic Values (IPV). *Journal of Managerial Psychology, 14*(3/4), 205–231. doi:10.1108/02683949910263747

Bolaño, C. R. S. (Ed.). (2015). Cultura e desenvolvimento: reflexões à luz de Furtado. Salvador, Brasil: EDUFBA.

Boltanski, L., & Thévenot, L. (2006). *On justification: economies of worth*. Princeton, NJ: Princeton University Press.

Boniwell, I., & Zimbardo, P. G. (2004). Balancing One's Time Perspective in Pursuit of Optimal Functioning. In P. A. Linley & S. Joseph (Eds.), Positive Psychology in Practice (pp. 165-178). Hoboken, NJ: Wiley.

Boniwell, I., Osin, E., Linley, P. A., & Ivanchenko, G. V. (2010). A question of balance: Time perspective and well-being in British and Russian samples. *The Journal of Positive Psychology*, *5*(1), 24–40. doi:10.1080/17439760903271181

Boniwell, I., & Zimbardo, P. G. (2004). Balancing One's Time Perspective in Pursuit of Optimal Functioning. In P. A. Linley & S. Joseph (Eds.), *Positive Psychology in Practice* (pp. 165–178). Hoboken, NJ: Wiley.

Borghi, A. M., Scorolli, C., Calisiore, D., Baldassarre, G., & Tummolini, L. (2013). The embodied mind extended: Using words as social tools. *Frontiers in Psychology*, *4*, 214. doi:10.3389/fpsyg.2013.00214 PMID:23641224

Borsen, T., Antia, A. N., & Glessmer, M. S. (2013). A case study of teaching social responsibility to doctoral students in the climate sciences. *Science and Engineering Ethics*, *19*(4), 1491–1504. doi:10.100711948-013-9485-9 PMID:24272332

Boschma, R., Marrocu, E., & Paci, R. (2015). Symmetric and asymmetric effects of proximities. The case of M&A deals in Italy. *Journal of Economic Geography*, *16*(2), 505–535. doi:10.1093/jeg/lbv005

Boud, D., & Lee, A. (Eds.). (2008). *Changing practices of doctoral education*. London: Routledge.

Bourdieu, P. (1965). *Photography, A Middle-brown Art*. Cambridge, MA: Polity Press.

Boyce, M. (2001). *Zoroastrians: Their Religious Beliefs and Practices*. New York, NY: Routledge.

Boyd, J. N., & Zimbardo, P. G. (2005). Time perspective, health, and risk taking. In A. Strathman & J. Joireman (Eds.), Understanding behavior in the context of time: Theory, research, and applications (pp. 85-107). Mahwah, NJ: Erlbaum.

Boyd, D. (2014). *It's Complicated: The Social Lives of Networked Teens*. New Haven, CT: Yale University Press. doi:10.100710615-014-0512-3

Brislin, R. W., & Kim, E. S. (2003). Cultural diversity in people's understanding and uses of time. *Applied Psychology*, *52*(3), 363–382. doi:10.1111/1464-0597.00140

Brodersen, N. H., Steptoe, A., Williamson, S., & Wardle, J. (2005). Sociodemographic, developmental, environmental and psychological correlates of physical activity and sedentary behavior at age 11 to 12. *Annals of Behavioral Medicine*, *29*(1), 2–11. doi:10.120715324796abm2901_2 PMID:15677295

BrovichJ.PäivinenP.SircovaA. (2017, December 5). *Futurization*. Doi:10.13140/RG.2.2.22754.63683

Brown, S. W. (1995). Time, change, and motion: The effects of stimulus movement on temporal perception. *Perception & Psychophysics*, *57*(1), 105–116. doi:10.3758/BF03211853 PMID:7885802

Buckingham, D. (2008). *Youth, identity and digital media*. Cambridge, MA: MIT Press.

Busch, V., Loyen, A., Lodder, M., Schrijvers, A. J. P., van Yperen, T. A., & de Leeuw, J. R. J. (2014). The Effects of Adolescent Health-Related Behavior on Academic Performance: A Systematic Review of the Longitudinal Evidence. *Review of Educational Research*, *84*. doi:10.3102/0034654313518441

Cameron, J. D., Maras, D., Sigal, R. J., Kenny, G. P., Borghese, M. M., Chaput, J. P., ... Goldfield, G. S. (2016). The mediating role of energy intake on the relationship between screen time behaviour and body mass index in adolescents with obesity: The HEARTY study. *Appetite*, *107*, 437–444. doi:10.1016/j.appet.2016.08.101 PMID:27545672

Campbell, A. J., Cumming, C. R., & Hughes, I. (2006). Internet use by the socially fearful: Addiction or therapy? *Cyberpsychology & Behavior*, *9*(1), 69–81. doi:10.1089/cpb.2006.9.69 PMID:16497120

Campos, S. (2016). *StudentSurfer: Afinal o que fazem os estudantes universitários com a Internet?* Universidade de Aveiro.

Candiotto, L. (2016). Extended affectivity as cognition of primary intersubjectivity. *Phenomenology and Mind*, *11*, 232–241. doi:10.13128/Phe_Mi-20122

Cao, H., Qian, Q., Weng, T., Yuan, C., Sun, Y., Wang, H., & Tao, F. (2011). Screen time, physical activity and mental health among urban adolescents in China. *Preventive Medicine*, *53*(4-5), 316–320. doi:10.1016/j.ypmed.2011.09.002 PMID:21933680

Capdeferro, N., Romero, M., & Barberà, E. (2014). Polychronicity: Review of the literature and a new configuration for the study of this hidden dimension of online learning. *Distance Education*, *35*(3), 294–310. doi:10.1080/01587919.2015.955249

Cardoso, G. (Ed.). (2013). *A Sociedade dos Ecrãs*. Lisboa: Tinta da China Edições.

Carelli, M. G., Forman, H., & Mäntylä, T. (2008). Sense of time and executive functioning in children and adults. *Child Neuropsychology*, *14*(4), 372–386. doi:10.1080/09297040701441411 PMID:17852120

Carelli, M. G., Wiberg, B., & Åström, E. (2015). Broadening the TP profile: Future negative time perspective. In *Time perspective theory; review, research and application* (pp. 87–97). Cham: Springer. doi:10.1007/978-3-319-07368-2_5

Carelli, M. G., Wiberg, B., & Wiberg, M. (2011). Development and Construct Validation of the Swedish Zimbardo Time Perspective Inventory (S-ZTPI). *European Journal of Psychological Assessment*, *27*(4), 220–227. doi:10.1027/1015-5759/a000076

Carlson, S. A., Fulton, J. E., Lee, S. M., Foley, J. T., Heitzler, C., & Huhman, M. (2010). Influence of limit-setting and participation in physical activity on youth screen time. *Pediatrics*, *126*(1), e89–e96. doi:10.1542/peds.2009-3374 PMID:20547642

Carpenter, J. (2012). Researchers of tomorrow: The research behaviour of generation y doctoral students. *Information Services & Use*, *32*(1), 3–17. doi:10.3233/ISU-2012-0637

Carr, N. (2012). *Os Superficiais - O que é que a Internet está a fazer aos nossos cérebros?* Lisboa: Gradiva Publicações.

Carroll-Scott, A., Gilstad-Hayden, K., Rosenthal, L., Peters, S. M., McCaslin, C., Joyce, R., & Ickovics, J. R. (2013). Disentangling neighborhood contextual associations with child body mass index, diet, and physical activity: The role of built, socioeconomic, and social environments. *Social Science & Medicine*, *95*, 106–114. doi:10.1016/j.socscimed.2013.04.003 PMID:23642646

Carson, V., & Kuzik, N. (2017). Demographic correlates of screen time and objectively measured sedentary time and physical activity among toddlers: A cross-sectional study. *BMC Public Health*, *17*(1), 1–11. doi:10.118612889-017-4125-y PMID:28193271

Castells, M. (2000). *A sociedade em rede - volume I* (8ª). Paz e Terra.

Castells, M. (2003). A sociedade em rede. In D. Moraes (Ed.), *Por uma outra Comunicação. Mídia, mundialização cultural e poder* (pp. 255–287). Rio de Janeiro, RJ: Record.

Castells, M. (2009a). *The Rise of the Network Society: The Information Age - Economy, Society, and Culture: 1 (Information Age Series)*. Oxford, UK: Wiley-Blackwell.

Castells, M. (2009b). *The Power of Identity: The Information Age - Economy, Society, and Culture: 2 (Information Age Series)*. Oxford, UK: Wiley-Blackwell.

Castells, M. (2010). Globalisation, networking, urbanisation: Reflections on the spatial dynamics of the information age. *Urban Studies (Edinburgh, Scotland)*, *47*(13), 2737–2745. doi:10.1177/0042098010377365

Castells, M. (2010). *The Rise of the Network Society*. Blackwell Publishing. doi:10.2307/1252090

Castoriadis, C. (1991). Time and creation. *Chronotypes: The Construction of Time*, 38–64.

Castro, S. (2018). *Estudio de las oscilaciones gamma del EEG durante la vigilia, el sueño y en un modelo farmacológico de psicosis (Tesis de Doctorado)*. Montevideo: Universidad de la República.

Cevasco, A. M. (2008). The effects of mother's singing on full-term and preterm infants and maternal emotional responses. *Journal of Music Therapy*, *45*(3), 273–306. doi:10.1093/jmt/45.3.273 PMID:18959452

Chabot, P. (2013). *The Philosophy of Simondon Between Technology and Individuation*. London: Bloomsbury.

Chang, F.-C., Chiu, C.-H., Chen, P.-H., Miao, N.-F., Chiang, J.-T., & Chuang, H.-Y. (2018). Computer/Mobile Device Screen Time of Children and Their Eye Care Behavior: The Roles of Risk Perception and Parenting. *Cyberpsychology, Behavior, and Social Networking*. doi:10.1089/cyber.2017.0324

Cheung, C. H. M., Bedford, R., Saez De Urabain, I. R., Karmiloff-Smith, A., & Smith, T. J. (2017). Daily touchscreen use in infants and toddlers is associated with reduced sleep and delayed sleep onset. *Scientific Reports*, 7(May). doi:10.1038rep46104 PMID:28406474

Chittaro, L., & Vianello, A. (2013). Time perspective as a predictor of problematic Internet use: A study of Facebook users. *Personality and Individual Differences*, 55(8), 989–993. doi:10.1016/j.paid.2013.08.007

Chorianopoulos, K. (2008). User interface design principles for interactive television applications. *International Journal of Human-Computer Interaction*, 24(6), 556–573. doi:10.1080/10447310802205750

Chowhan, J., & Stewart, J. M. (2007). Television and the behaviour of adolescents: Does socio-economic status moderate the link? *Social Science & Medicine*, 65(7), 1324–1336. doi:10.1016/j.socscimed.2007.05.019 PMID:17587476

Christakis, D. A. (2009). The effects of infant media usage: What do we know and what should we learn? *Acta Paediatrica (Oslo, Norway)*, 98(1), 8–16. doi:10.1111/j.1651-2227.2008.01027.x PMID:18793294

Chung, L.-Y., & Lim, S. S. (2005). From Monochronic to Mobilechronic – Temporality in the Era of Mobile Communication. In K. Nyiri (Ed.), *A Sense of Place: The Global and the Local in Mobile Communication* (pp. 267–282). Vienna: Passagen Verlag.

Cilliers, P. (2003). Porque não podemos conhecer as coisas complexas completamente. In *Método, métodos, contramétodo* (R. L. Garcia, Trans.). São Paulo, Brazil: Cortez.

Clark, A. (1997). *Being There. Putting Brain, Body and World together again*. Cambridge, MA: MIT Press.

Clark, A. (2003). *Natural-Born Cyborgs. Minds, Technologies, and the Future of Human Intelligence*. Oxford, UK: Oxford University Press.

Clark, A., & Chalmers, D. (1998). The extended mind. *Analysis*, 58(1), 7–19. doi:10.1093/analys/58.1.7

Clowes, R. W. (2013). The Cognitive Integration of E-Memory. *Review of Philosophy and Psychology*, 4(1), 107–133. doi:10.100713164-013-0130-y

Cohen, A. K. (2018). An instrumental variables approach to assess the effect of class size reduction on student screen time. *Social Science and Medicine*, 201, 63–70. doi:10.1016/j.socscimed.2018.02.005

Collaboration, C. (2001). *Guidelines for preparation of review protocols*. Retrieved from https://scholar.google.com/scholar?hl=en&btnG=Search&q=intitle:Guidelines+for+Preparation+of+Review+Protocols#8

Comscore. (2016). *Cross-Platform Future in Focus 2016*. Retrieved from https://www.comscore.com/Insights/Presentations-and-Whitepapers/2016/2016-US-Cross-Platform-Future-in-Focus

Correa, A., Lupiáñez, J., & Tudela, P. (2006). La percepción del tiempo: Una revisión desde la Neurociencia Cognitiva. *Cognitiva*, *18*(2), 145–168. doi:10.1174/021435506778148667

Couclelis, H. (2004). Pizza over the Internet – E-commerce, the fragmentation of activity and the tyranny of the region. *Entrepreneurship and Regional Development*, *16*(1), 41–54. doi:10.1080/0898562042000205027

Csikszentmihaiyi, M. (1990). *Flow: The Psychology of Optimal Experience*. New York, NY: Harper and Row.

Csordas, T. J. (1999). Embodiment and Cultural Phenomenology. In G. Wiess & H. F. Haber (Eds.), *Perspectives on Embodiment: The Intersections of Nature and Culture* (pp. 143–164). New York, NY: Routledge.

CTUR. (n.d.). *Centre for Time Use Research*. Retrieved December 5, 2018, from https://www.timeuse.org

Cummings, H. M., & Vandewater, E. A. (2007). Relation of adolescent video game play to time spent in other activities. *Archives of Pediatrics & Adolescent Medicine*, *161*(7), 684–689. doi:10.1001/archpedi.161.7.684 PMID:17606832

Day, E. O. (2018). *Global Footprint Network*. Retrieved from https://www.overshootday.org/

De Bellis, N. (2009). *Bibliometrics and Citation Analysis: From the Science Citation Index to Cybermetrics*. Plymouth: Scarecrow Press.

de la Iglesia, H. O., Meyer, J., Carpino, A., & Schwartz, W. J. (2000). Antiphase oscillation of the left and right suprachiasmatic nuclei. *Science*, *290*(5492), 799–801.

De Preester, H. (2011). Technology and the Body: The (Im)Possibilities of Re-embodiment. *Foundations of Science*, *16*(2-3), 119–137. doi:10.100710699-010-9188-5

De Volder, M. L., & Lens, W. (1982). Academic Achievement and Future Time Perspective as a Cognitive-Motivational Concept. *Journal of Personality and Social Psychology*, *42*(3), 566–571. doi:10.1037/0022-3514.42.3.566

Delamont, S., Atkinson, P., & Parry, O. (2004). *Supervising the doctorate: A guide to success*. United Kingdom: McGraw-Hill Education.

Deshaies, G. (1961). *Psicopatología General*. Buenos Aires: Kapelusz.

Dewey, J. (1925). *Experience and Nature*. Chicago: Open Court.

Diener, E. (1984). Subjective well-being. *Psychological Bulletin, 95*(3), 542–575. doi:10.1037/0033-2909.95.3.542 PMID:6399758

Diener, E., & Lucas, R. E. (2000). Subjective emotional well-being. In M. Lewis & J. M. Haviland (Eds.), *Handbook of emotions* (2nd ed.; pp. 325–337). New York: Guilford.

Diener, E., Suh, E. M., Lucas, R. E., & Smith, H. L. (1999). Subjective well-being: Three decades of progress. *Psychological Bulletin, 125*(2), 276–302. doi:10.1037/0033-2909.125.2.276

Diener, E., Wirtz, D., Tov, W., Kim-Prieto, C., Choi, D., Oishi, S., & Biswas-Diener, R. (2010). New measures of well-being: Flourishing and positive and negative feelings. *Social Indicators Research, 39*, 247–266.

Domingues-Montanari, S. (2017). Clinical and psychological effects of excessive screen time on children. *Journal of Paediatrics and Child Health, 53*(4), 333–338. doi:10.1111/jpc.13462 PMID:28168778

Donovan, B. (2017, January 6). Answer to "What is the total mass and volume of all the stored nuclear waste in the world?" *Quora*. Retrieved from: https://www.quora.com/What-is-the-total-mass-and-volume-of-all-the-stored-nuclear-waste-in-the-world/answer/Brian-Donovan-13

Drake, L., Duncan, E., Sutherland, F., Abernethy, C., & Henry, C. (2008). Time perspective and correlates of wellbeing. *Time & Society, 17*(1), 47–61. doi:10.1177/0961463X07086304

Dron, J. (2012). The pedagogical-technological divide and the elephant in the room. *International Journal on E-Learning, 11*(1), 23–38.

Duffy, J. F., Rimmer, D. W., & Czeisler, C. A. (2001). Association of intrinsic circadian period with morningness–eveningness, usual wake time, and circadian phase. *Behavioral Neuroscience, 115*(4), 895–899. doi:10.1037/0735-7044.115.4.895 PMID:11508728

Dunkel, C. S., & Weber, J. (2010). Using Three Levels of Personality to Predict Time Perspective. *Current Psychology (New Brunswick, N.J.), 29*(2), 95–103. doi:10.100712144-010-9074-x

Durand, G. (1988). *A Imaginação Simbólica*. São Paulo, SP: Cultrix.

Durkin, K., & Barber, B. (2002). Not so doomed: Computer game play and positive adolescent development. *Journal of Applied Developmental Psychology, 23*(4), 373–392. doi:10.1016/S0193-3973(02)00124-7

Dydrov, A. A. (2017). Synergy of humanitarization and futurization as a condition for the functioning of the interpretational machine. *Socium and Power, 2*(64), 96–100. doi:10.22394/1996-0522-2017-2-96-100

Egli, E. A., & Meyers, L. S. (1984). The role of video game playing in adolescent life: Is there reason to be concerned? *Bulletin of the Psychonomic Society, 22*(4), 309–312. doi:10.3758/BF03333828

Elder, C. R., Gullion, C. M., Funk, K. L., DeBar, L. L., Lindberg, N. M., & Stevens, V. J. (2012). Impact of sleep, screen time, depression and stress on weight change in the intensive weight loss phase of the LIFE study. *International Journal of Obesity*, *36*(1), 86–92. doi:10.1038/ijo.2011.60 PMID:21448129

Eliade, M. (1949). *Le Mythe de l'éternel retour*. Paris: Les Essais.

Entidade Reguladora para a Comunicação Social. (2016). *As novas dinâmicas do consumo audiovisual em Portugal 2016*. Retrieved from http://www.erc.pt/documentos/Estudos/ConsumoAVemPT/ERC2016_AsNovasDinamicasConsumoAudioVisuais_web/assets/downloads/ERC2016_AsNovasDinamicasConsumoAudioVisuais.pdf

Epel, E., Bandura, A., & Zimbardo, P. G. (1999). Escaping homelessness: The influences of self-efficacy and time perspective on coping with homelessness. *Journal of Applied Social Psychology*, *29*(3), 575–596. doi:10.1111/j.1559-1816.1999.tb01402.x

Ericsson-Consumerlab. (2016). *TV and Media 2016: The evolving role of TV and media in consumers' everyday lives*. Retrieved from https://www.ericsson.com/assets/local/networked-society/consumerlab/reports/tv-and-media-2016.pdf

Ericsson-Consumerlab. (2017). *TV and Media 2017: A consumer-driven future of media*. Retrieved from https://www.ericsson.com/assets/local/careers/media/ericsson_consumerlab_tv_media_report.pdf

Escobosa, A. (2012). Los Usos Del Tiempo En La Relación: Familia, Trabajo Y Género. *Contribuciones a Las Ciencias Sociales*. Retrieved from http://www.eumed.net/rev/cccss/18/ape.pdf

European Broadcasting Union - Media Intelligence Service (MIS). (2014). *VISION 2020 - Media Consumption Trends*. Retrieved from https://www.ebu.ch/files/live/sites/ebu/files/Publications/EBU-Vision2020-Connect_EN.pdf

Ey, H. (1996). *Tratado de Psiquiatría*. Barcelona: Masson.

Ey, H. (2008). *Estudios Psiquiátricos. In Estructura de las Psicosis agudas y desestructuración de la conciencia. Volumen I y II*. Buenos Aires: Polemos.

Farr, W., Price, S., & Jewitt, C. (2012). *An introduction to embodiment and digital technology research: Interdisciplinary themes and perspectives*. NCRM Working Paper. NCRM. Retrieved from http://eprints.ncrm.ac.uk/2257/

Felt, U. (2015). *The temporal choreographies of participation: Thinking innovation and society from a time-sensitive perspective*. Vienna: Department of Studies of Science and technology, University of Vienna. Retrieved from: https://www.researchgate.net/publication/270451756_The_temporal_choreographies_of_participation_Thinking_innovation_and_society_from_a_time-sensitive_perspective

Ferrari, J. R., & Díaz-Morales, J. F. (2007). Procrastination: Different time orientations reflect different motives. *Journal of Research in Personality, 41*(3), 707–714. doi:10.1016/j.jrp.2006.06.006

Ferrari, L., Nota, L., & Soresi, S. (2012). Evaluation of an Intervention to Foster Time Perspective and Career Decidesdness in a Group of Italian Adolescents. *The Career Development Quarterly, 60*(1), 82–96. doi:10.1002/j.2161-0045.2012.00007.x

Field, A. (2018). *Discovering Statistics Using IBM SPSS Statistics (5ᵗʰ ed.).* London: Sage Publications.

Florit-Robles, A. (2006). La rehabilitación psicosocial de pacientes con esquizofrenia crónica. *Apuntes de Psicología, 24*(1-3), 223–244.

Fortunati, L. (2005). The mobile phone: Towards new categories and social relations. *Information Communication and Society, 5*(4), 513–528. doi:10.1080/13691180208538803

Fraisse, P. (1957). *Psychologie du temps*. Paris: Presses Universitaires de France.

Fraisse, P. (1984). Perception and estimation of time. *Annual Review of Psychology, 35*(1), 1–37. doi:10.1146/annurev.ps.35.020184.000245 PMID:6367623

Francis-Smythe, J., & Robertson, I. (1999). Time-related individual differences. *Time & Society, 8*(2-3), 273–292. doi:10.1177/0961463X99008002004

Fraser, J. T. (1987). *Time - The Familiar Stranger*. University of Massachusetts Press.

Friedman, W. J., & Jenssen, S. M. J. (2010). Aging and the speed of time. *Acta Psychologica, 134*(2), 130–141. doi:10.1016/j.actpsy.2010.01.004 PMID:20163781

Frigotto, G., & Ciavatta, M. (Eds.). (2001). Teoria e educação no labirinto do capital. Petrópolis, RJ: Vozes.

Frigotto, G. (1993). *A produtividade da escola improdutiva: um (re) exame das relações entre educação e estrutura econômico-social capitalista* (4th ed.). São Paulo: Cortez.

Frigotto, G. (1996). *Educação e a crise do capitalismo real* (2nd ed.). São Paulo: Cortez.

Frijda, N. (2005). Emotion experience. *Journal of Cognition and Emotion, 19*(4), 473–497. doi:10.1080/02699930441000346

Froese, T., Gershenson, C., & Rosenblueth, D. A. (2013). *The Dynamically Extended Mind. A Minimal Modeling Case Study*. Retrieved from https://www.researchgate.net/publication/236661591_The_Dynamically_Extended_Mind_--_A_Minimal_Modeling_Case_Study

Fuchs, C. (2014). Digital prosumption labour on social media in the context of the capitalist regime of time. *Time & Society, 23*(1), 97–123. doi:10.1177/0961463X13502117

Gallagher, S. (2005). *How the Body Shapes the Mind*. Oxford, UK: University Press. doi:10.1093/0199271941.001.0001

Gallagher, S. (2017). *Enactivist Interventions. Rethinking the Mind*. Oxford, UK: Oxford University Press. doi:10.1093/oso/9780198794325.001.0001

Gallagher, S., Martínez, S. F., & Gastelum, M. (2012). Action-Space and Time: Towards an Enactive Hermeneutics. In B. B. Janz (Ed.), *Place, Space and Hermeneutics, Contributions to Hermeneutics 5* (pp. 83–96). New York, NY: Springer.

Gallagher, S., & Zahavi, D. (2008). *The Phenomenological Mind*. London: Routledge.

Gao, Y. (2011). Time perspective and life satisfaction among young adults in Taiwan. *Social Behavior and Personality: An International Journal, 39*(6), 729-736. doi: .2011.39.6.729 doi:10.2224bp

García Canclini, N. (2015). *Consumidores e Cidadãos: conflitos multiculturais da globalização* (8th ed.). Rio de Janeiro, RJ: UFRJ.

Garcia, J. M., Sirard, J. R., Deutsch, N. L., & Weltman, A. (2016). The influence of friends and psychosocial factors on physical activity and screen time behavior in adolescents: A mixed-methods analysis. *Journal of Behavioral Medicine, 39*(4), 610–623. doi:10.100710865-016-9738-6 PMID:27055818

García, T. (2010). La mercantilización de la educación. *Revista Electrónica Interuniversitaria de Formación del Profesorado, 13*(2), 16–21.

Gärdenfors, P., & Lombard, M. (2018). Causal Cognition, Force Dynamics and Early Hunting Technologies. *Frontiers in Psychology, 9*, 1–10. doi:10.3389/fpsyg.2018.00087 PMID:29483885

Garrabé, J. (2017). La phénoménologie de langue allemande et la psychiatrie française. *L'Évolution Psychiatrique, 82*(1), 17–37. doi:10.1016/j.evopsy.2016.05.003

Garton, L., Haythornthwaite, C., & Wellman, B. (1999). Studying On-line Social Networks. In S. Jones (Ed.), *Doing Internet Research: Critical issues and methods for examining the Net* (pp. 75–105). Thousand Oaks, CA: Sage Publications. doi:10.4135/9781452231471.n4

Gavazzi, G., Bisio, A., & Pozzo, T. (2013). Time perception of visual motion is tuned by the motor representation of human actions. *Scientific Reports, 3*(1), 1–8. doi:10.1038rep01168 PMID:23378903

Gençöz, T. (2000). Pozitif ve negatif duygu ölçeği: Geçerlik ve güvenirlik çalışması [The positive and negative affect scale: validity and reliability study]. *Türk Psikoloji Dergisi, 15*(46), 19–26.

Gentile, D. A., Nathanson, A. I., Rasmussen, E. E., Reimer, R. A., & Walsh, D. A. (2012). Do You See What I See? Parent and Child Reports of Parental Monitoring of Media. *Family Relations, 61*(3), 470–487. doi:10.1111/j.1741-3729.2012.00709.x

Gibson, J. J. (2015). *The Ecological Approach to Visual Perception*. New York, NY: Taylor and Francis.

Gibson, W. (2016). *Neuromancer* (5th ed.). São Paulo, SP: Aleph.

Giddens, A. (2002). *Modernidade e Identidade*. Rio de Janeiro: Jorge Zahar Editor.

Giddens, A. (1984). *The Constitution of the Society: Outiline of the Theory of Structuration. Bulletin of the British Society for the History of Science* (Vol. 1). Cambridge, UK: Polity Press; doi:10.1017/S0950563600000038

Gillmor, D. (2005). *Nós, os médias*. Lisboa: Editorial Presença.

Gjesme, T. (1983). On the Concept of Future Time Orientation: Considerations of Some Functions´ and Measurements´ Implications. *International Journal of Psychology, 18*(1-4), 443–461. doi:10.1080/00207598308247493

Goffman, E. (1975). *A representação do Eu na Vida Cotidiana*. Rio de Janeiro, Brazil: Ed. Vozes.

Golombek, D. A., & Yannielli, P. C. (2006). Organización del sistema circadiano en vertebrados. In J. A. Madrid & M. A. Rol de Lama (Eds.), *Cronobiología Básica y Clínica* (pp. 191–222). Madrid: Editeca Red.

Granovetter, M. (1973). The Strength of Weak Ties. United States. *American Journal of Sociology, 78*(6), 1360–1380. doi:10.1086/225469

Gray, P. W., & Jordan, S. R. (2012). Supervisors and academic integrity: Supervisors as exemplars and mentors. *Journal of Academic Ethics, 10*(4), 299–311. doi:10.100710805-012-9155-6

Greenberg, J., Solomon, S., & Pyszczynski, T. (1997). Terror management theory of self-esteem and cultural worldviews: Empirical assessments and conceptual refinements. Academic Press. doi:10.1016/S0065-2601(08)60016-7

Green, L., Fristoe, N., & Myerson, J. (1994). Temporal discounting and preference reversals in choice between delayed outcomes. *Psychonomic Bulletin & Review, 1*(3), 383–389. doi:10.3758/BF03213979 PMID:24203522

Greif, H. (2017). What is the extension of the extended mind? *Synthese, 194*(11), 4311–4336. doi:10.100711229-015-0799-9 PMID:29200511

Gumbrecht, H.U. (2015, December 4). *Our "Broad Present" as a "Universe of Contingency": A Cultural and Epistemological Diagnostic*. Lecture during Challenging the Human Sciences Conference, Copenhagen Business School, Denmark.

Gutierrez-García, A., Reyes-Platas, D., & Picazo, O. (2017). Percepción del tiempo en la neuropsicopatología: Una revisión sistemática. *Psiquiatría Biológica, 24*(3), 85–96. doi:10.1016/j.psiq.2017.10.002

Haesbaert, R. (2004). *O Mito da Desterritorialização*. Rio de Janeiro, RJ: Bertrand Brasil.

Haggard, P., Clark, S., & Kalogeras, J. (2002). Voluntary action and conscious awareness. *Nature Neuroscience, 5*(4), 382–385. doi:10.1038/nn827 PMID:11896397

Hall, E. (1959). *The Silent Language*. Garden City, NY: Doubleday.

Hall, E. (1983). *The Dance of Life: The Other Dimension of Time*. Anchor Press/Doubleday.

Hall, E. T. (1984). *La Danse de la Vie - Temps culturel, temps vécu*. Paris: Seuil.

Hall, E. T. (1989). *Beyond Culture*. New York: Anchor Books Edition.

Hall, E. T., & Hall, M. R. (1990). *Understanding Cultural Differences: Germans, French, and Americans*. Yarmouth, ME: Intercultural Press.

Hall, S. (2004). *A identidade cultural na pós-modernidade*. Rio de Janeiro, Brazil: DP&A.

Hall, S. (2014). *A Identidade Cultural na Pós-modernidade*. Rio de Janeiro, RJ: Lamparina.

Hamilton, J. M., Kives, K. D., Micevski, V., & Grace, S. L. (2003). Time Perspective and Health-Promoting Behavior in a Cardiac Rehabilitation Population. *Behavioral Medicine (Washington, D.C.)*, *28*(4), 132–139. doi:10.1080/08964280309596051 PMID:14663920

Han, B.-C. (2016a). *A Salvação do Belo*. Lisboa: Relógio D' Água.

Han, B.-C. (2016b). O Aroma do Tempo - Um Ensaio Filosófico sobre a Arte da Demora. Lisboa: Relógio D' Água.

Hanley, N., & Splash, C. (1993). Discounting and the Environment. In N. Hanley & C. Splash (Eds.), *Cost Benefit Analysis and the Environment*. Northampton, MA: Edward Elgar.

Hanusch, F. (2017). *Democracy and Climate Change*. Routledge. doi:10.4324/9781315228983

Hardie, E., & Tee, M. Y. (2007). Excessive Internet Use: The Role of Personality, Loneliness, and Social Support Networks in Internet Addiction. *Australian Journal of Emerging Technologies and Society*, *5*(1), 34–47.

Hartley, R. (2010). *Living on the Screen: Disembodiment to Embededness*. Retrieved from http://riahartley.com/wp-content/uploads/2013/07/Living-on-the-Screen-Disembodiment-to-Embededness.pdf

Harvey, D. (1999). Time-Space Compression and the postmodern condition. *Modernity: Critical Concepts*. doi:10.1037/0278-7393.11.1-4.629

Hassan, R. (2003). Network time and the new knowledge epoch. *Time & Society*, *12*(2/3), 225–241.

Hassan, R. (2009). *Empires of speed: Time and the acceleration of politics and society*. Leiden, Boston: Brill. doi:10.1163/ej.9789004175907.i-254

Hassan, R. (2010). Social acceleration and the network effect: A defence of social "science fiction" and network determinism. *The British Journal of Sociology*, *61*(2), 356–374. doi:10.1111/j.1468-4446.2010.01316.x PMID:20579058

Hassoun, D. (2012). Costly attentions: Governing the media multitasker. *Continuum*, *26*(4), 653–664. doi:10.1080/10304312.2012.698041

Hauer, T. (2016). Globalization and Political Economy of Speed. In M. S. Eva Kovářová, Lukáš Melecký (Ed.), *3rd International Conference on European Integration 2016* (pp. 319–325). Ostrava: VŠB - Technical University of Ostrava.

Hawking, S. (1988). *A Brief History of Time: From the big bang to black holes.* New York: Bantam Books.

Haythornthwaite, C., & Wellman, B. (2005). Introduction: Internet in the everyday life. In B. Wellman & C. Haythornthwaite (Eds.), *The Internet in Everyday Life* (pp. 3–40). Hong Kong: Blackwell.

Headey, B., & Wearing, A. (1989). Personality, life events, and subjective well-being: Toward a dynamic equilibrium model. *Journal of Personality and Social Psychology, 57*(4), 731–739. doi:10.1037/0022-3514.57.4.731

Heidegger, M. (2003). O conceito de tempo. Lisboa: Fim de Século.

Heidegger, M. (1996). *Sein und Zeit, 1927. Being and Time: A Translation of Sein und Zeit.* SUNY Press. (Original work published 1927)

Helman, C. H. (2005). Cultural aspects of time and ageing. Time is not the same in every culture and every circumstance; our views of aging also differ. *EMBO Reports, 6,* S54–S58. doi:10.1038j. embor.7400402 PMID:15995664

Henkel, L. A. (2014). Point-and-Shot Memories. The Influence of Taking Photos on Memory for a Museum Tour. *Psychological Science, 25*(2), 396–402. doi:10.1177/0956797613504438 PMID:24311477

Hergert, P. (2017). How tangible is cyberspace? *Digital Culturist.* Retrieved from https://digitalculturist.com/how-tangible-is-cyberspace-dce550c52248

Hiniker, A., Suh, H., Cao, S., & Kientz, J. A. (2016). Screen time tantrums: how families manage screen media experiences for toddlers and preschoolers. In *Proceedings of the 2016 CHI Conference on Human Factors in Computing Systems* (pp. 648-660). ACM 10.1145/2858036.2858278

Hofstede, G. (2011). Dimensionalizing Cultures: The Hofstede Model in Context. *Online Readings in Psychology and Culture, 2*(1), 8. doi:10.9707/2307-0919.1014

Hofstede, G., & Minkov, M. (2010). Long-versus short-term orientation: New perspectives. *Asia Pacific Business Review, 16*(4), 493–504. doi:10.1080/13602381003637609

Holman, E. A., & Silver, R. C. (2005). Future-Oriented Thinking and Adjustment in a Nationwide Longitudinal Study Following the September 11th Terrorist Attacks. *Motivation and Emotion, 29*(4), 389–410. doi:10.100711031-006-9018-9

Holman, E. A., & Zimbardo, P. G. (2009). The Social Language of Time: The Time Perspective-Social Network Connection. *Basic and Applied Social Psychology, 31*(2), 136–147. doi:10.1080/01973530902880415

Hutto, D., & Myin, E. (2013). *Radicalizing Enactivism: Basic Minds whitout Content.* Cambridge, MA: MIT Press.

Hyndman, B. P. (2017). Perceived social-ecological barriers of generalist pre-service teachers towards teaching physical education: Findings from the GET-PE study. *Australian Journal of Teacher Education*, *42*(7), 26–46. doi:10.14221/ajte.2017v42n7.3

Ihde, D. (2001). *Bodies in Technology*. Minneapolis, MN: University of Minnesota.

Innis, H. A. (1950). *Empire and Communications*. Toronto: Toronto University Press.

Jameson, F. (1991). *Postmodernism, or The Cultural Logic of Late Capitalism*. Durham, NC: Duke University Press. Retrieved from http://socium.ge/downloads/komunikaciisteoria/eng/Jameson.Postmodernism,orTheculturallogicoflatecapitalism(1991).pdf

Janeiro, I. N. (2010). Motivational dynamics in the development of career attitudes among adolescents. *Journal of Vocational Behavior*, *76*(2), 170–177. doi:10.1016/j.jvb.2009.12.003

Jaspers, K. (1963). *General Psychopathology*. Chicago, IL: University of Chicago Press.

Jevons, W. S. (1871). *The Theory of Political Economy*. McMaster University Archive for the History of Economic Thought.

Johnson, M. (1987). *The Body in the Mind. The Bodily basis of Meaning, Imagination, and Reason*. Chicago, IL: University of Chicago Press.

Johnson, M. (2007). *The Meaning of the Body. Aesthetics of Human Understanding*. Chicago, IL: University of Chicago Press. doi:10.7208/chicago/9780226026992.001.0001

Johnson, M. (2017). *Embodied Mind, Meaning, and Reason. How our Bodies give rise to Understanding*. Chicago, IL: University of Chicago Press. doi:10.7208/chicago/9780226500393.001.0001

Johnson, N. F., & Keane, H. (2017). Internet addiction? Temporality and life online in the networked society. *Time & Society*, *26*(3), 267–285. doi:10.1177/0961463X15577279

Johnson, T. (2010). *Nos bastidores da Wikipédia Lusófona: Percalços e conquistas de um projeto de escrita coletiva on-line*. Rio de Janeiro, Brazil: E-papers.

Joireman, J., Shaffer, M. J., Balliet, D., & Strathman, A. (2012). Promotion orientation explains why future-oriented people exercise and eat healthy: Evidence from the two-factor consideration of future consequences-14 scale. *Personality and Social Psychology Bulletin*, *38*(10), 1272–1287. doi:10.1177/0146167212449362 PMID:22833533

Kağıtçıbaşı, C. (2005). Autonomy and relatedness in cultural context implications for self and family. *Journal of Cross-Cultural Psychology*, *36*(4), 403–422. doi:10.1177/0022022105275959

Kairys, A. (2010). *Time perspective: Its link to personality traits, age, and gender* (Doctoral dissertation). Vilnius University.

Kairys, A., & Liniauskaite, A. (2010, July). The search of balanced time perspective. In A. Sircova & A. Kairys (Eds.), *Time Perspective: Methodological Issues and Relation with Different Domains of Psychological Functioning. Symposium conducted at 15th European Conference on Personality*. Brno: Czech Republic.

Kairys, A., Liniauskaitė, A., Bagdonas, A., & Pakalniškienė, V. (2017). Balanced Time Perspective: Many Questions and Some Answers. In A. Kostić & D. Chadee (Eds.), Time Perspective: Theory and Practice (pp. 97-115). London: Palgrave Macmillan.

Kastenbaum, R. (1961). The Dimensions of Future Time Perspective, an Experimental Analysis. *The Journal of General Psychology, 65*(2), 203–218. doi:10.1080/00221309.1961.9920473 PMID:14454195

Kazakina, E. (1999). *Time perspective of older adults: Relationships to attachment style, psychological well-being and psychological distress* (Unpublished doctoral dissertation). Columbia University.

Kazakina, E. (2013). Time Perspective of Older Adults: Research and Clinical Practice. In M. P. Paixão, J. T. da Silva, V. Ortuño & P. Cordeiro (Eds.), International Studies on Time Perspective (pp. 71-86). Coimbra: University of Coimbra Press. doi:10.13140/RG.2.1.1602.0008

Keightley, E. (2013). From immediacy to intermediacy: The mediation of lived time. *Time & Society, 22*(1), 55–75. doi:10.1177/0961463X11402045

Khan, K. S., Kunz, R., Kleijnen, J., & Antes, G. (2003). Five steps to conducting a systematic review. *JRSM, 96*(3), 118–121. doi:10.1177/014107680309600304 PMID:12612111

Kim, J., LaRose, R., & Peng, W. (2009). Loneliness as the cause and the effect of problematic Internet use: The relationship between Internet use and psychological well-being. *Cyberpsychology & Behavior, 12*(4), 451–455. doi:10.1089/cpb.2008.0327 PMID:19514821

Kocayörük, E., Altıntas, E., & İçbay, M. A. (2015). The perceived parental support, autonomous-self and well-being of adolescents: A cluster-analysis approach. *Journal of Child and Family Studies, 24*(6), 1819–1828. doi:10.100710826-014-9985-5

Kollmuss, A., & Agyeman, J. (2002). Mind the Gap: Why do people act environmentally and what are the barriers to pro-environmental behavior? *Environmental Education Research, 8*(3), 239–260. doi:10.1080/13504620220145401

König, C., & Waller, M. (2010). Time for Reflection: A Critical Examination of Polychronicity. *Human Performance, 23*(2), 173–190. doi:10.1080/08959281003621703

Kononova, A., & Chiang, Y. (2015). Why do we multitask with media? Predictors of media multitasking among Internet users in the United States and Taiwan. *Computers in Human Behavior, 50*, 31–41. doi:10.1016/j.chb.2015.03.052

Kononova, A., Zasorina, T., Diveeva, N., Kokoeva, A., & Chelokyan, A. (2014). Multitasking goes global: Multitasking with traditional and new electronic media and attention to media messages among college students in Kuwait, Russia, and the USA. *The International Communication Gazette*, *76*(8), 617–640. doi:10.1177/1748048514548533

Kooij, D. T., Kanfer, R., Betts, M., & Rudolph, C. W. (2018). Future time perspective: A systematic review and meta-analysis. *The Journal of Applied Psychology*, *103*(8), 867–893. doi:10.1037/apl0000306 PMID:29683685

Košťál, J., Klicperová-Baker, M., Lukavská, K., & Lukavský, J. (2016). Short version of the Zimbardo Time Perspective Inventory (ZTPI–short) with and without the Future-Negative scale, verified on nationally representative samples. *Time & Society*, *25*(2), 169–192. doi:10.1177/0961463X15577254

Kostić, A., & Chadee, D. (Eds.). (2017). *Time Perspective. Theory and Practice*. London: Palgrave Macmillan. doi:10.1057/978-1-137-60191-9

Kozinets, R. (2015). *Netnography:Redefined*. Sage.

Kranjec, A., & McDonough, L. (2011). The implicit and explicit embodiment of time. *Journal of Pragmatics*, *43*(3), 735–748. doi:10.1016/j.pragma.2010.07.004

Kubiszewski, V., Fontaine, R., Rusch, E., & Hazouard, E. (2014). Association between electronic media use and sleep habits: An eight-day follow-up study. *International Journal of Adolescence and Youth*, *19*(3), 395–407. doi:10.1080/02673843.2012.751039

Kurbanov, R. (2013, February 13). *Swap Futurization – The emergence of a new business model or avoiding regulation and retaining the status quo?* Retrieved from https://derivsource.com/2013/02/13/swap-futurization-the-emergence-of-a-new-business-model-or-avoiding-regulation-and-retaining-the-status-quo/

Kurek, A., Jose, P. E., & Stuart, J. (2017). Discovering unique profiles of adolescent information and communication technology (ICT) use: Are ICT use preferences associated with identity and behaviour development? *Cyberpsychology (Brno)*, *11*(4). doi:10.5817/CP2017-4-3

Kuzu, D., Berk, Ö. S., & Aydın, F. Y. (2017). Subjective well-being in idiopathic scoliosis patients. *The International Journal of Human and Behavioral Science*, *3*(2), 1–6.

Lakoff, G., & Johnson, M. (1999). *Philosophy in the Flesh. The Embodied Mind and its Challenge to Western Thought*. New York, NY: Basic Books.

Lanningham-Foster, L., Jensen, T. B., Foster, R. C., Redmond, A. B., Walker, B. A., Heinz, D., & Levine, J. A. (2006). Energy expenditure of sedentary screen time compared with active screen time for children. *The Journal of Pediatrics*, *118*(6), e1831–e1835. doi:10.1542/peds.2006-1087 PMID:17142504

Lanza, S. T., Collins, L. M., Lemmon, D. R., & Schafer, J. L. (2007). PROC LCA: A SAS procedure for latent class analysis. *Structural Equation Modeling*, *14*(4), 671–694. doi:10.1080/10705510701575602 PMID:19953201

Lapierre, S., Bouffard, L., & Bastin, E. (1997). Personal goals and subjective well-being in later life. *International Journal of Aging & Human Development, 45*(4), 287–303. doi:10.2190/HU3J-QDHE-LT1J-WUBN PMID:9477344

Laroche, J., Berardi, A. M., & Brangier, E. (2014). Embodiment of intersubjective time: Relational dynamics as attractors in the temporal coordination of interpersonal behaviors and experiences. *Frontiers in Psychology, 5*, 1180. doi:10.3389/fpsyg.2014.01180 PMID:25400598

Lastowka, F. G., & Hunter, D. (2003). *The Laws of the Virtual Worlds*. Public Law and Legal Theory, Research Paper Series, Pennsylvania, PA. Retrieved May 12, 2017, from http://papers.ssrn.com/abstract=402860

Lauer, R. (1981). *Temporal man: the meaning and uses of social time*. New York: Praeger.

Lauer, R. H. (1980). *Temporal Man: The Meaning and Uses of Social Time*. New York: Praeger.

Laurson, K. R., Eisenmann, J. C., Welk, G. J., Wickel, E. E., Gentile, D. A., & Walsh, D. A. (2008). Combined influence of physical activity and screen time recommendations on childhood overweight. *The Journal of Pediatrics, 153*(2), 209–214. doi:10.1016/j.jpeds.2008.02.042 PMID:18534231

Le Breton, D. (2003). *Adeus ao corpo: Antropologia e sociedade* (M. Appenzeller, Trans.). São Paulo, Brazil: Papirus.

Leatherdale, S. T., & Ahmed, R. (2011). Screen-based sedentary behaviours among a nationally representative sample of youth : Are Canadian kids couch potatoes? Screen-based sedentary behaviours among a nationally repre- sentative sample of youth : are Canadian kids couch potatoes? *Chronic Diseases and Injuries in Canada, 31*(September), 141–147. PMID:21978636

Leatherdale, S. T., & Harvey, A. (2015). Examining communication- and media-based recreational sedentary behaviors among Canadian youth: Results from the COMPASS study. *Preventive Medicine, 74*, 74–80. doi:10.1016/j.ypmed.2015.02.005 PMID:25732538

Leatherdale, S. T., & Papadakis, S. (2011). A Multi-Level Examination of the Association Between Older Social Models in the School Environment and Overweight and Obesity Among Younger Students. *Journal of Youth and Adolescence, 40*(3), 361–372. doi:10.100710964-009-9491-z PMID:20013351

Leite, U., Tamayo, Á., & Günther, H. (2003b). Organização do uso do tempo e valores de universitários. *Avaliação Psicológica*. Retrieved from http://pepsic.bvsalud.org/scielo.php?script=sci_arttext&pid=S1677-04712003000100007

Leite, U., Tamayo, Á., & Günther, H. (2003a). Organização do uso do tempo e valores de universitários. *Avaliação Psicológica, 1*, 57–66. Retrieved from http://pepsic.bvsalud.org/scielo.php?pid=S1677-04712003000100007&script=sci_arttext&tlng=en

LeMay, S., Costantino, T., & O'Connor, S., & ContePitcher, E. (2014, June). Screen time for children. In *Proceedings of the 2014 Conference on Interaction Design and Children* (pp. 217-220). ACM.

Lemos, A. (2003). Cibercultura. Alguns pontos para compreender a nossa época. In A. Lemos, & P. Cunha, P. (Ed.), Olhares sobre a Cibercultura (pp. 11-23). Porto Alegre, RS: Sulina.

Lemos, A. (2006). Ciberespaço e Tecnologias Móveis: processos de territorialização e desterritorialização na cibercultura. In *Anais do Encontro Anual da Associação Nacional dos Programas de Pós-Graduação em Comunicação* (vol. 15., pp. 1-17). Bauru, SP: UNESP. Retrieved May 12, 2017, from http://www.facom.ufba.br/ciberpesquisa/andrelemos/territorio.pdf

Lemos, A. (2009). Cultura da mobilidade. *Mídia. Cultura e Tecnologia, 16*(40), 28–35.

Lemos, A. (2013). *A comunicação das coisas: teoria ator-rede e cibercultura*. São Paulo, Brazil: Annablume.

Lemos, A. (2016). *Cibercultura, Tecnologia e Vida Social na Cultura Contemporânea* (8th ed.). Porto Alegre, RS: Sulina.

Lens, W., Paixão, M. P., Herrera, D., & Grobler, A. (2012). Future time perspective as a motivational variable: Content and extension of future goals affect the quantity and quality of motivation. *The Japanese Psychological Research, 54*(3), 321–333. doi:10.1111/j.1468-5884.2012.00520.x

Lens, W., & Tsuzuki, M. (2007). The Role of Motivation and Future Time Perspective in Educational and Career Development. *Psychologica, 46*, 29–42.

Levine, R. (1997). *A geography of time: The temporal misadventures of a social psychologist, or how every culture keeps time just a little bit differently*. New York: Basic Books.

Levine, R. (2015). Keeping Time. In M. Stolarski & N. Fieulaine (Eds.), *Time Perspective Theory; Review, Research, and Application* (pp. 189–196). Cham: Springer International.

Lévy, P. (2000). *Cibercultura*. Lisboa: Instituto Piaget. Retrieved from http://www.google.com/books?hl=pt-PT&lr=&id=7L29Np0d2YcC&oi=fnd&pg=PA11&dq=cibercultura&ots=ghVxxEUwbm&sig=-39WptJB1He-abTbu0DdGCkBGOQ

Lévy, P. (2003). *O que é virtual*. São Paulo, Brazil: Editora 34.

Lévy, P. (1996). *O que é o Virtual?* São Paulo, SP: Editora 34.

Lévy, P. (2002). *Ciberdemocracia. Col. Epistemologia e sociedade*. Lisboa: Inst.Piaget.

Lévy, P. (2004). O Ciberespaço como um Passo Metaevolutivo. In F. M. Martins & J. M. Silva (Eds.), *A Genealogia do Virtual: comunicação, cultura e tecnologias do imaginário* (pp. 157–170). Porto Alegre, RS: Sulina.

Lewin, K. (1943). Defining the fiels at a given time. *Psychological Review, 50*(3), 292–310. doi:10.1037/h0062738

Lewis, R. D. (1996). *When cultures collide: Managing successfully across cultures*. London: N. Brealey Pub.

Lima, L. (2010). Investigação e investigadores em educação – Anotações críticas. *Sísifo: Revista de Ciências da Educação, 12,* 63–72.

Lin, L., Cranton, P., & Lee, J. (n.d.). Research Methodologies for Multitasking Studies. *Handbook of Research on Scholarly Publishing and Research Methods,* 329-348. doi:10.4018/978-1-4666-7409-7.ch017

Lindquist, J., & Kaufman-Scarborough, C. (2007). The Polychronic—Monochronic Tendency Model. *Time & Society, 16*(2-3), 253–285. doi:10.1177/0961463X07080270

Lipovetsky, G. (2016). *Da Leveza - para uma civilização do ligeiro.* Lisboa: Edições 70.

Lipovetsky, G. (2016). *Da leveza: Para uma civilização do ligeiro.* Lisboa: Edições 70.

Lipovetsky, G., & Serroy, J. (2010). *O ecrã global.* Lisboa: Edições 70.

Lissak, G. (2018). Adverse physiological and psychological effects of screen time on children and adolescents: Literature review and case study. *Environmental Research, 164,* 149–157. doi:10.1016/j.envres.2018.01.015 PMID:29499467

Livingstone, S. (2002). *Young people and new media: childhood and the changing media environment.* London: SAGE Publications Ltd.

Livingstone, S. (2009). Children and the Internet. *Polity.*

Livingstone, S., & Helsper, E. J. (2008). Parental mediation of children's internet use. *Journal of Broadcasting & Electronic Media, 52*(4), 581–599. doi:10.1080/08838150802437396

Lloyd, D., & Arstila, V. (2014). The Disunity of Time. In V. Arstila & D. Lloyd (Eds.), Subjective time: The philosophy, psychology, and neuroscience of temporality (pp. 657-663). Cambridge, MA: MIT Press.

Loizou, A. (2000). *Time, embodiment and the self.* Aldershot, UK: Ashgate.

Ludke, M., & André, E. D. A. (2003). *A pesquisa em educação: Abordagens qualitativas.* São Paulo, Brazil: EPU.

Lyons, G., Jain, J., & Holley, D. (2007). The use of travel time by rail passengers in Great Britain. *Transportation Research Part A, Policy and Practice, 41*(1), 107–120. doi:10.1016/j.tra.2006.05.012

Lyotard, J.-F. (1998). *A Condição Pós-moderna.* Rio de Janeiro, RJ: José Olympio.

Lypovetsky, G. (2007). *A Felicidade Paradoxal - ensaio sobre a sociedade do hiperconsumo.* Lisboa: Edições 70.

Madsen, M. (2010). *Into Eternity: A Film for the Future.* Denmark, Finland, Sweden.

Madzia, R. (2013). Chicago Pragmatism and the Extended Mind Theory. Mead and Dewey on the Nature of Cognition. *European Journal of Pragmatism and American Philosophy, 5*(1), 279–297.

Maffesoli, M. (1996). *No Fundo das Aparências.* Petrópolis, RJ: Vozes.

Maffesoli, M. (1998). *O Tempo das Tribos: o declínio do individualismo nas sociedades de massa*. Rio de Janeiro, RJ: Forense Universitária.

Maffesoli, M. (2004). A Comunicação sem fim (teoria pós-moderna da comunicação). In F. M. Martins & J. M. Silva (Eds.), *A Genealogia do Virtual: comunicação, cultura e tecnologias do imaginário* (pp. 20–32). Porto Alegre, RS: Sulina.

Maffesoli, M. (2016). From society to tribal communities. *The Sociological Review, 64*(4), 739–747. doi:10.1111/1467-954X.12434

Magalhães, R. L., dos Santos, N. S., da Costa, R. F., Bones, V., & Martins Kruel, L. F. (2017). Effects of two types of low impact physical training on screen time among overweight adolescents. *Journal of Human Growth and Development, 27*(3), 294–299. doi:10.7322/jhgd.118505

Malafouris, L. (2013). *How Things Shape the Mind. A Theory of Material Engagement*. Cambridge, MA: MIT Press.

Maldonado, T. (1999). *Desenho Industrial*. Trad. José Francisco Espadeiro Martins. Lisboa: Edições 70.

Maloney, A. E., Bethea, T. C., Kelsey, K. S., Marks, J. T., Paez, S., Rosenberg, A. M., & Sikich, L. (2008). A pilot of a video game (DDR) to promote physical activity and decrease sedentary screen time. *Obesity (Silver Spring, Md.), 16*(9), 2074–2080. doi:10.1038/oby.2008.295 PMID:19186332

Manathunga, C. (2007). Supervision as mentoring: The role of power and boundary crossing. *Studies in Continuing Education, 29*(2), 207–221. doi:10.1080/01580370701424650

Manovich, L. (2002). Generation Flash. *Black Box White Cube, 2007*(2/10), 1–18. doi:10.1007/3-7643-7677-5_6

Maor, D., Ensor, J., & Fraser, B. (2015). *Doctoral supervision in virtual spaces: a review pf wev-basedtools to develop collaborative supervision*. Retrived from: https://espace.curtin.edu.au/bitstream/handle/20.500.11937/41864/236299.pdf?sequence=2

Mark, A. E., & Janssen, I. (2008). Relationship between screen time and metabolic syndrome in adolescents. *Journal of Public Health, 30*(2), 153–160. doi:10.1093/pubmed/fdn022 PMID:18375469

Marktest. (2018). *3 em 4 utilizadores de telemóvel usa smartphone*. Retrieved from https://www.marktest.com/wap/a/n/id~2350.aspx

Massey, D. (1991). A Global Sense of Place. *Marxism Today, 35*(June), 315–323. doi:10.1016/j.pecs.2007.10.001

Matin, N., Kelishadi, R., Heshmat, R., Motamed-Gorji, N., Djalalinia, S., Motlagh, M. E., ... Qorbani, M. (2017). Joint association of screen time and physical activity on self-rated health and life satisfaction in children and adolescents: The CASPIAN-IV study. *International Health, 9*(1), 58–68. doi:10.1093/inthealth/ihw044 PMID:27836949

Mavoa, J., Gibbs, M., & Carter, M. (2017). Constructing the young child media user in Australia: A discourse analysis of Facebook comments. *Journal of Children and Media, 11*(3), 330–346. doi:10.1080/17482798.2017.1308400

McAdams, D. P. (2001). The psychology of life stories. *Review of General Psychology, 5*, 100-122. doi: 10,1037//1089-2860.5.2.100

McCallin, A., & Nayar, S. (2012). Postgraduate research supervision: A critical review of current practice. *Teaching in Higher Education, 17*(1), 63–74. doi:10.1080/13562517.2011.590979

McGrath, J. E., & Tschan, F. (2004). *Temporal matters in social psychology: Examining the role of time in the lives of groups and individuals.* American Psychological Association.

McGrath, J., & Kelly, J. (1986). *Time and human interaction: Towards a social psychology of time.* New York: Guildford Press.

McKay, M. T., Worrell, F. C., Zivkovic, U., Temple, E., Mello, Z. R., Musil, B., ... Perry, J. L. (2018). A balanced time perspective: Is it an exercise in empiricism, and does it relate meaningfully to health and well-being outcomes? *International Journal of Psychology.* doi:10.1002/ijop.12530 PMID:30206944

Mcluhan, M. (1996). Os meios de comunicação como extensões do homem. *Buscalegis, 407.* doi:10.1590/S0034-75901969000300009

Melro, A., & Oliveira, L. (2017). Screen Culture. In Encyclopedia of Information Science and Technology (4th ed.). Hershey, PA: IGI Global.

Melro, A., & Silva, L. (2013). A ecrãcultura emergente nas vivências dos jovens portugueses: poderá falar-se de uma geração de ecrãs? *Observatorio (OBS*).* Retrieved from http://obs.obercom.pt/index.php/obs/article/view/694

Menary, R. (Ed.). (2010). *The Extended Mind.* Cambridge, MA: MIT Press. doi:10.7551/mitpress/9780262014038.001.0001

Menzies, H., & Newson, J. (2007). No time to think: Academics' life in the globally wired university. *Time & Society, 16*(1), 83–98. doi:10.1177/0961463X07074103

Menzies, H., & Newson, J. (2008). Time, stress and intellectual engagement in academic work: Exploring gender difference. *Gender, Work and Organization, 15*(5), 504–522. doi:10.1111/j.1468-0432.2008.00415.x

Merleau-Ponty, M. (2012). *Phenomenology of Perception.* London: Routledge.

Meyrowitz, J. (2005). The Rise of Glocality: New Senses of Place and Identity in the Global Village. In K. Nyiri (Ed.), *A Sense of Place: The Global and the Local in Mobile Communication.* Vienna: Passagen Verlag.

Milfont, T. L., Wilson, J., & Diniz, P. (2012). Time Perspective and enviromental engagement: A meta-analysis. *International Journal of Psychology*, *47*(5), 325–334. doi:10.1080/00207594.2011.647029 PMID:22452746

Mills, S. (2016). *Gilbert Simondon: Information, Technology & Media*. London: Rowman & Littlefield International.

Minkowski, E. (2002). *Écrits Cliniques*. Érès: Saint – Agne.

Minkowski, E. (1966). *Traité de Psychopathologie*. Paris: Presses Universitaires de France.

Moffat, P. (2014). Screen time. How much is healthy for children? *Community practitioner: The journal of the Community Practitioners' & Health Visitors'. Association*, *87*(11), 16–18.

Moore, J., & Harre, N. (2007). Eating and activity: The importance of family and environment. *Health Promotion Journal of Australia*, *18*(2), 143–148. doi:10.1071/HE07143 PMID:17663650

Morden, T. (1999). Models of national culture – a management review. *Cross Cultural Management*, *6*(1), 19–44. doi:10.1108/13527609910796915

Morin, E. (2002). *O Método 4. As ideias*. Porto Alegre, RS: Sulina.

Morin, E. (2004). A Comunicação pelo meio (teoria complexa da comunicação). In F. M. Martins & J. M. Silva (Eds.), *A Genealogia do Virtual: comunicação, cultura e tecnologias do imaginário* (pp. 11–19). Porto Alegre, RS: Sulina.

Morin, E. (2005). *O Método 5. A humanidade da humanidade*. Porto Alegre, RS: Sulina.

Morita, N., Nakajima, T., Okita, K., Ishihara, T., Sagawa, M., & Yamatsu, K. (2016). Relationships among fitness, obesity, screen time and academic achievement in Japanese adolescents. *Physiology & Behavior*, *163*, 161–166. doi:10.1016/j.physbeh.2016.04.055 PMID:27150913

Mugnaini, R., Jannuzzi, P., & Quoniam, L. (2004). Indicadores bibliométricos da produção científica brasileira: Uma análise a partir da base Pascal [Bibliometric Indicators of Brasilian Scientific Production: An Analysis Through Pascal Basis]. *Ciência da Informação*, *33*(2), 123–131. doi:10.1590/S0100-19652004000200013

Muller, R. (2014). Racing for what? Anticipation and acceleration in the work and career practices of academic life science postdocs. *Qualitative Social Research*, *15*(3). Retrieved from: http://www.qualitative-research.net/index.php/fqs/article/view/2245/3726

Munaro, H. L. R., Silva, D. A. S., & Lopes, A. D. S. (2016). Prevalence of excessive screen time and associated factors in a school from a city in the northeast of Brazil. *Journal of Human Growth and Development*, *26*(3), 360–367. doi:10.7322/jhgd.122821

Munn, L. (2015). *Digital Disembodiment*. Retrieved from http://www.lukemunn.com/2015/digital-disembodiment/

Murray, C. D. (2000). Towards a phenomenology of the body in virtual reality. *Research in Philosophy and Technology*, *19*, 149–173.

Myíri, K. (2005). *A sense of place: the global and the local in mobile communication.* Vienna: Passagen Verlag.

Nassehi, A. (1994). No Time for Utopia: The Absence of Utopian Contents in Modern Concepts of Time. *Time & Society, 3*(1), 47–78. doi:10.1177/0961463X94003001003

Nather, F. C., Bueno, J. L. O., Bigand, E., & Droit-Volet, S. (2011). Time Changes with the Embodiment of another's Body Posture. *PLoS One, 6*(5), e19818. doi:10.1371/journal.pone.0019818 PMID:21637759

Negroponte, N. (1995). *A Vida Digital.* São Paulo, SP: Companhia das Letras.

Nevski, E., & Siibak, A. (2016). The role of parents and parental mediation on 0–3-year olds' digital play with smart devices: Estonian parents' attitudes and practices. *Early Years, 36*(3), 227–241. doi:10.1080/09575146.2016.1161601

Newman, P. (1998). *The new Palgrave dictionary of economics and the law.* London: Macmillan. Retrieved from https://www.volvocars.com/intl/cars/concepts/360c

Nicol, B. (2018). *Field Observation: Waiting Time in Public Spaces.* Report for Psychology of Time course, DIS: Study Abroad in Scandinavia.

Nielsen. (2018). *The Nielsen Total Audience Report.* Retrieved from: https://www.nielsen.com/us/en/insights/reports/2018/q1-2018-total-audience-report.html

Nielsen-Company. (2015). *Screen wars: The battle for eye space in a TV-everywhere world. Nielsen Insights.* Retrieved from http://www.nielsen.com/apac/en/insights/reports/2015/screen-wars-the-battle-for-eye-space-in-a-tv-everywhere-world.html%5Cnhttp://www.nielsen.com/content/dam/corporate/us/en/reports-downloads/2015-reports/nielsen-global-digital-landscape-report-march-2015

Noë, A. (2004). *Action in Perception.* Cambridge, MA: MIT Press.

Noë, A. (2012). *Varieties of Presence.* Cambridge, MA: Harvard University Press. doi:10.4159/harvard.9780674063013

Noonan, J. (2015). Thought-time, money-time and the conditions of free academic labour. *Time & Society, 24*(1), 109–128. doi:10.1177/0961463X14539579

Norman, D. A. (2008). Signifiers, not affordances. *Interactions (New York, N.Y.), 15*(6), 18–19. doi:10.1145/1409040.1409044

Norman, D. A. (2013). *The Design of Everyday Things.* New York, NY: Basic Books.

Noys, B. (2014). *Malign Velocities - Acceleration and Capitalism.* Zero Books.

Nurmi, J. E. (1991). How do adolescents see their future? A review of the development of future orientation and planning. *Developmental Review, 11*(1), 1–59. doi:10.1016/0273-2297(91)90002-6

Nuttin, J. R. (1985). The future time perspective in human motivation and learning. *Acta Psychologica, 23*, 60–83. doi:10.1016/0001-6918(64)90075-7

Nuttin, J., & Lens, W. (1985). *Future Time Perspective and Motivation: theory and research method*. Leuven University Press.

Nyberg, L., Salami, A., Andersson, M., Eriksson, J., Kalpouzos, G., Kauppi, K., ... Nilsson, L. G. (2010). Longitudinal evidence for diminished frontal cortex function in aging. *Proceedings of the National Academy of Sciences of the United States of America, 107*(52), 22682–22686. doi:10.1073/pnas.1012651108 PMID:21156826

O'connor, E. (2015). *Sense of Community, Social Identity and Social Support Among Players of Massively Multiplayer Online Games (MMOGs): A qualitative analysis. Journal of Community & Applied Social Psychology*. Queensland, Australia: Wiley.

Obercom. (2015). *Anuário da Comunicação*. Retrieved from https://www.ofcom.org.uk/__data/assets/pdf_file/0020/102755/adults-media-use-attitudes-2017.pdf

OECD. (2018). *Hours worked (indicator)*. Retrieved from https://data.oecd.org/emp/hours-worked.htm

Ofcom. (2015). *Adults' media use and attitudes Report 2015*. Retrieved from; https://www.ofcom.org.uk/__data/assets/pdf_file/0014/82112/2015_adults_media_use_and_attitudes_report.pdf

Ohmori, N., & Harata, N. (2008). How different are activities while commuting by train? A case in Tokyo. *Tijdschrift voor Economische en Sociale Geografie, 99*(5), 547–561. doi:10.1111/j.1467-9663.2008.00491.x

Okazaki, S., & Hirose, M. (2009). Effects of displacement–reinforcement between traditional media, PC internet and mobile internet. *International Journal of Advertising, 28*(1), 77–104. doi:10.2501/S026504870909043X

Okuda, J., Fujii, T., Ohtake, H., Tsukiura, T., Tanji, K., Suzuki, K., ... Yamadori, A. (2003). Thinking of the future and past: The roles of the frontal pole and the medial temporal lobes. *NeuroImage, 19*(4), 1369–1380. doi:10.1016/S1053-8119(03)00179-4 PMID:12948695

Oliveira, L. (2017). Hiperconexão: o pensamento na era da canibalização do tempo. In H. Pires, M. Curado, F. Ribeiro, & P. Andrade (Eds.), Circum-navegações em Redes Transculturais de Conhecimento, Arquivos e Pensamento (pp. 73–84). Famalição: Edições Húmus.

Oliveira, L., & Baldi, V. (Eds.). (2014). *Insustentável leveza da Web: retóricas, dissonâncias e práticas na Sociedade em Rede*. Salvador da Bahia: Edufaba.

Orlikowski, W. J., & Yates, J. (2002). It's about time: Temporal structuring in organizations. *Organization Science, 13*(6), 684–700. doi:10.1287/orsc.13.6.684.501

Ortuño, V. E. (2014). *Time Perspective Stability: Studies with a multidimensional model in the University Context* (Doctoral dissertation). University of Coimbra, Coimbra, Portugal. Retrieved from https://estudogeral.sib.uc.pt/handle/10316/24324

Ortuño, V. E., & Janeiro, I. N. (2009). Estudo Comparativo de duas medidas de Perspectiva Temporal: IPT & ZTPI em foco [Comparative Study of two Measures of Time Perspective: IPT & ZTPI in Focus]. *Proceedings of X Congresso Internacional Galego-Português de Psicopedagogia.* Braga: Universidade do Minho.

Ortuño, V. E., Paixão, M. P., & Janeiro, I. (2011). Tempo e Universidade: A Evolução da Perspectiva Temporal ao Longo do Percurso Universitário [Time and University: Time Perspective's Evolution Along the University Course]. In Carreira, Criatividade e Empreendedorismo (pp. 217-225). Braga: APDC Edições.

Ortuño, V., Gomes, C., Vásquez, A., Belo, P., Imaginário, S., Paixão, M. P., & Janeiro, I. (2013). Satisfaction with life and college social integration: A Time Perspective multiple regression model. In M. P. Paixão, J. T. da Silva, V. Ortuño & P. Cordeiro (Eds.), International Studies on Time Perspective (pp. 101-106). Coimbra: University of Coimbra Press. doi:10.14195/978-989-26-0775-7_10

Ortuño, V., & Vasquez, A. (2013). Time Perspective and Self-Esteem: Negative Temporality Affects the Way We Judge Ourselves. *Annales Universitatis Paedagogicae Cracoviensis. Studia Psychologica, 6,* 109–125.

Osiurak, F., Navarro, J., & Reynaud, E. (2018). How Our Cognition Shapes and Is Shaped by Technology: A Common Framework for Understanding Human Tool-Use Interactions in the Past, Present, and Future. *Frontiers in Psychology, 9,* 293. doi:10.3389/fpsyg.2018.00293 PMID:29563891

Owen, G. S., Freyenhagen, F., Hotopf, M., & Martin, W. (2015). Temporal inabilities and decision-making capacity in depression. *Phenomenology and the Cognitive Sciences, 14*(1), 163–182. doi:10.100711097-013-9327-x

Pais, J. M. (2007). Cotidiano e reflexividade. *Educação & Sociedade, 28*(98), 23–46. doi:10.1590/S0101-73302007000100003

Paixão, M. P. (1996). *Organização da Vivência do Futuro e Comportamento de Planificação. Compreensão dos Processos Motivacionais e Cognitivos na Elaboração e Avaliação de Projectos Pessoais* [The Organization of the Subjective Future and Planning Behavior. Comprehension of the Motivational and Cognitive Processes Involved in the Elaboration and Evaluation of Personal Projects] (Unpublished Doctoral Dissertation). University of Coimbra, Portugal.

Paixão, M. P. (2004). A dimensão temporal do futuro na elaboração de objectivos pessoais e organização de projectos vocacionais [The Future Temporal Dimension in the Formulation and Organization of Vocational Projects]. *Psychologica, extra-série,* 273-286.

Paixão, M. P., da Silva, J. T., Ortuño, V., & Cordeiro, P. (Eds.). (2013). *International Studies on Time Perspective.* Coimbra: University of Coimbra Press; doi:10.14195/978-989-26-0775-7

Parent, J., Sanders, W., & Forehand, R. (2016). Youth Screen Time and Behavioral Health Problems: The Role of Sleep Duration and Disturbances. *Journal of Developmental and Behavioral Pediatrics, 37*(4), 277–284. doi:10.1097/DBP.0000000000000272 PMID:26890562

Patel, I. (2017). *Portugal TV Update*. Retrieved from https://ovum.informa.com/resources/product-content/me0003-000831

Peelo, M. (2011). *Understanding Supervision and the PhD*. A&C Black. Retreived from: http://www.siecon.org/online/wp-content/uploads/2014/10/Boschman-Marrocu-Paci-106.pdf

Peetsma, T. T. (2000). Future Time Perspective as a Predictor of School Investment. *Scandinavian Journal of Educational Research, 44*(2), 177–192. doi:10.1080/713696667

Peetsma, T. T., Schuitema, J., & van der Veen, I. (2012). A longitudinal study on time perspectives: Relations with academic delay of gratification and learning environment. *The Japanese Psychological Research, 54*(3), 241–252. doi:10.1111/j.1468-5884.2012.00526.x

Pentzold, C. (2018). Between moments and millennia: Temporalising mediatisation. *Media Culture & Society, 40*(6), 927–937. doi:10.1177/0163443717752814

Petrocelli, J. V. (2003). Factor Validation of the Consideration of Future Consequences Scale: Evidence for a Short Version. *The Journal of Social Psychology, 143*(4), 405–413. doi:10.1080/00224540309598453 PMID:12934832

Pew Research Center. (2017). *Mobile Fact Sheet*. Retrieved from: http://www.pewinternet.org/fact-sheet/mobile/

Piaget, J. (1968). *Genetic Epistemology*. New York, NY: Columbia University Press.

Primack, B. A., Swanier, B., Georgiopoulos, A. M., Land, S. R., & Fine, M. J. (2009). Association between media use in adolescent and depression in young adulthood: A longitudinal study. *Archives of General Psychiatry, 66*(2), 181–188. doi:10.1001/archgenpsychiatry.2008.532 PMID:19188540

Przybylski, A. K., & Weinstein, N. (2017). A Large-Scale Test of the Goldilocks Hypothesis: Quantifying the Relations Between Digital-Screen Use and the Mental Well-Being of Adolescents. *Psychological Science, 28*(2), 204–215. doi:10.1177/0956797616678438 PMID:28085574

Pulver, S., & Van Deveer, S. (2007, May). *Futurology and futurizing: a research agenda on the practice and politics of global environmental scenarios*. In *Amsterdam Conference on the Human Dimensions of Global Environmental Change Earth Systems Governance: Theories and Strategies for Sustainability*, Amsterdam, The Netherlands.

Putnam, R. D. (2000). *Bowling Alone: The collapse and revival of American community*. New York, NY: Simon & Schuster.

Radich, J. (2013). Technology and interactive media as tools in early childhood programs serving children from birth through age 8. *Every Child, 19*(4), 18–19.

Reinecke, K., Nguyen, M. K., Bernstein, A., Näf, M., & Gajos, K. Z. (2013, February). Doodle around the world: Online scheduling behavior reflects cultural differences in time perception and group decision-making. In *Proceedings of the 2013 conference on Computer supported cooperative work* (pp. 45-54). ACM. 10.1145/2441776.2441784

Rheingold, H. (1993). *The virtual community: Homesteading on the electronic frontier*. Reading, MA: Addison-Wesley Publishing Co.

Richardson, I. (2005). *Mobile Technosoma: some phenomenological reflections on itinerant media devices. The Fibreculture Journal*. Sydney, Australia: TFJ Inc.

Richardson, I. (2007). Pocket Technospaces: The Bodily Incorporation of Mobile Media. *Continuum, 21*(2), 205–215. doi:10.1080/10304310701269057

Richards, R., McGee, R., Williams, S. M., Welch, D., & Hancox, R. J. (2010). Adolescent screen time and attachment to parents and peers. *Archives of Pediatrics & Adolescent Medicine, 164*(3), 258–262. doi:10.1001/archpediatrics.2009.280 PMID:20194259

Ricoeur, P. (1984). *Time and Narrative* (Vol. 1). Chicago, IL: The University of Chicago Press.

Rideout, V. (2016). Measuring time spent with media: The Common Sense census of media use by US 8- to 18-year-olds. *Journal of Children and Media, 10*(1), 138–144. doi:10.1080/17482 798.2016.1129808

Ringle, P. M., & Savickas, M. L. (1983). Administrative leadership: Planning and time perspective. *The Journal of Higher Education, 54*(6), 649–661. doi:10.2307/1981935

Rivoltella, P. C. (2010). *A sociedade Multi-ecrãs: Das recomendações educativas à nova mídia-educação*. Retrieved from http://www.maxwell.vrac.puc-rio.br/acessoConteudo. php?nrseqoco=52514

Robinson, H., & Kalafatis, S. (2017). The 'Polychronicity - Multiple Media Use' (P-MMU) scale: A multi-dimensional scale to measure polychronicity in the context of multiple media use. *Journal of Marketing Management, 33*(17-18), 1421–1442. doi:10.1080/0267257X.2017.1383297

Rodríguez, R., Ortuño, V. E., & Pezzani, G. (2018). *Desestructuración de la vivencia del tiempo en la psicosis y Rehabilitación Psicosocial*. Work presented at Primer Congreso Internacional de Psicología, Universidad de la República. Montevideo, Uruguay. Retrieved from https://www. researchgate.net/publication/328736314_Desestructuracion_del_Tiempo_en_l a_Psicosis_y_ Rehabilitacion_Psicosocial_Presentacion_oral_dada_en_el_Primer_Congres o_Internacional_ de_Psicologia_en_la_Universidad_de_la_Republica

Roenneberg, T., Allebrandt, K. V., Merrow, M., & Vetter, C. (2012). Social jetlag and obesity. *Current Biology, 22*(10), 939–943. doi:10.1016/j.cub.2012.03.038 PMID:22578422

Rooksby, J., Asadzadeh, P., Rost, M., Morrison, A., & Chalmers, M. (2016). Personal tracking of screen time on digital devices. In *Proceedings of the 2016 CHI Conference on Human Factors in Computing Systems* (pp. 284-296). ACM. 10.1145/2858036.2858055

Rosa, H. (2011). Aceleración social: consecuencias éticas y políticas de una sociedad de alta velocidad desincronizada. *Revista Persona y Sociedad, 1*(25), 9–49. Retrieved from http:// onlinelibrary.wiley.com/doi/10.1111/1467-8675.00309/abstract

Rosa, H. (2010). *Alienation and acceleration: towards a critical theory of late-modern temporality*. Malmo: NSU Press.

Rosa, H. (2013a). *Accélération - Une critique social du temps*. Paris: La Découverte. doi:10.7312/rosa14834

Rosa, H. (2013b). *Aliénation et accélération: vers une théorie critique de la modernité tardive*. Paris: La Découverte.

Rosa, H. (2015). *Social Acceleration: A New Theory of Modernity*. New York: Columbia University Press.

Rosa, H., & Scheuerman, W. E. (2009). *High-speed society: Social acceleration, power and modernity*. Philadelphia: Penn State University Press.

Rowlands, M. (2010). *The New Science of the Mind*. Cambridge, MA: MIT Press. doi:10.7551/mitpress/9780262014557.001.0001

Russell, M. (2011). *Watching passengers: Using structured observation methods on public transport*. Academic Press.

Ryle, G. (1949). *The Concept of Mind*. London: Hutchinson.

Saint-Georges, C., Chetouani, M., Cassel, R., Apicella, F., Mahdhaoui, A., Muratori, F., ... Cohen, D. (2013). Motherese in Interaction: At the Cross-Road of Emotion and Cognition? (A Systematic Review). *PLoS One, 8*(10), e78103. doi:10.1371/journal.pone.0078103 PMID:24205112

Salvucci, D., Taatgen, N., & Borst, P. (2009). Toward a unified theory of the multitasking continuum: from concurrent performance to task switching, interruption, and resumption. In *Proceedings of the SIGCHI Conference on Human Factors in Computing Systems* (CHI '09). ACM. 10.1145/1518701.1518981

Sami-Ali, M. (1974). *L'Espace imaginaire*. Paris: Gallimard.

Sanders, W., Parent, J., Forehand, R., Sullivan, A. D. W., & Jones, D. J. (2016). Parental perceptions of technology and technology-focused parenting: Associations with youth screen time. *Journal of Applied Developmental Psychology, 44*, 28–38. doi:10.1016/j.appdev.2016.02.005 PMID:27795603

Santaella, L. (2004). *Navegar no ciberespaço: o perfil cognitivo do leitor imersivo*. Brazil: Paulus.

Santos, E. (1992). *Time, Affect and Project* (Unpublished doctoral thesis). University of Coimbra.

Santos, E., Almeida, J. G., Santos, G., Frontini, R., & Ferreira, J. A. (2012). Tempos e Afectos: para um paradigma ecossistémico na construção de projectos. In E. Santos, J. A. Ferreira & Colaboradores (Eds.), Mudanças e Transições: pessoas em contextos (pp. 11-24). Viseu: Psicosoma.

Santos, M. (1996). *A natureza do espaço*. São Paulo, Brazil: Hucitec.

Scharf A. Kennedy M. Esbrook E. Päivinen P. Sircova A. (2018, May 7). *Futurization: Survey Results.* Doi:10.13140/RG.2.2.28361.60000

Schiano, D=. (2013). *The "lonely gamer" revisited.* Elsevier.

Schmid, H. (2017). The Embodiment of Time. In S. Broadhurst & S. Price (Eds.), *Digital Bodies. Palgrave Studies in Performance and Technology* (pp. 97–109). London: Palgrave Macmillan; doi:10.1057/978-1-349-95241-0_7

Schmutte, P. S., & Ryff, C. D. (1997). Personality and well-being: Reexamining methods and meanings. *Journal of Personality and Social Psychology, 73*(3), 549–559. doi:10.1037/0022-3514.73.3.549 PMID:9294901

Schreck, M., Althoff, R., Sibold, J., Giummo, C., Hudziak, J., Bartels, M., ... Rubin, D. (2016). Withdrawn behavior, leisure-time exercise behavior, and screen-time sedentary behavior in a clinical sample of youth. *Journal of Clinical Sport Psychology, 10*(3), 206–221. doi:10.1123/jcsp.2015-0031

Schutte, J. (1997). *Virtual teaching in higher* education: *The new intellectual. superhighway or just another traffic jam?* Retrieved from: https://pdfs.semanticscholar.org/6ad5/30196f652b9b480ad38d50eacd8b4cdbb7b3.pdf

Searle, J. R. (1983). *Intentionality. An Essay in the Philosophy of Mind.* Cambridge, UK: Cambridge University Press. doi:10.1017/CBO9781139173452

Selfhout, M. H. W., Branje, S. J. T., Delsing, M., ter Bogt, T. F. M., & Meeus, W. H. J. (2009). Different types of Internet use, depression, and social anxiety: The role of perceived friendship quality. *Journal of Adolescence, 32*(4), 819–833. doi:10.1016/j.adolescence.2008.10.011 PMID:19027940

Seligman, M. E. P. (2002). *Authentic happiness: Using the new positive psychology to realize your potential for lasing fulfillment.* New York: Free Press.

Selwyn, N. (2013). *Education in a Digital World: Global Perspectives on Technology and Education.* New York: Routledge. doi:10.4324/9780203108178

Senior, N. W. (1938). An Outline of the Science of Political Economy (6th ed.). London: George Allen & Unwin.

Shapiro, L. (2011). *Embodied Cognition.* London: Routledge.

Shapiro, L. (Ed.). (2014). *The Routledge Handbook of Embodied Cognition.* London: Routledge. doi:10.4324/9781315775845

Sharkins, K. A., Newton, A. B., Albaiz, N. E. A., & Ernest, J. M. (2016). Preschool Children's Exposure to Media, Technology, and Screen Time: Perspectives of Caregivers from Three Early Childcare Settings. *Early Childhood Education Journal, 44*(5), 437–444. doi:10.100710643-015-0732-3

Sharma, S. (2017). Temporality. In Keywords for media studies. New York: NY UP.

Sharma, S. (2014). In the Meantime. *Temporality and Cultural Politics, 9*, 2014–2016. doi:10.1215/9780822378334

Shen, C., & Williams, D. (2010). Unpacking time online: Connecting internet and massively multiplayer online game use with psychological well-being. *Communication Research, 38*(1), 123–149. doi:10.1177/0093650210377196

Shields, M., Gorber, S. C., & Tremblay, M. S. (2008). Estimates of obesity based on self-report versus direct measures. *Health Reports, 19*(2), 61–76. PMID:18642520

Shields, M., & Tremblay, M. S. (2008). Screen time among Canadian adults: A profile. *Health Reports, 19*(2), 31–43. PMID:18642517

Shipp, A. J., Edwards, J. E., & Lambert, L. S. (2009). Conceptualization and measurement of temporal focus: The subjective experience of the past, present, and future. *Organizational Behavior and Human Decision Processes, 110*(1), 1–22. doi:10.1016/j.obhdp.2009.05.001

Sidewalk Toronto. (n.d.). Retrieved from https://sidewalktoronto.ca/

Silva, J. M. (2012). *As Tecnologias do Imaginário* (3rd ed.). Porto Alegre, RS: Sulina.

Simmel, G. (1986). Como la sociedad es possible. In *Sociología: estudios sobre las formas de socialización* (pp. 37–56). Madrid: Alianza.

Simons, J., Vansteenkiste, M., Lens, W., & Lacante, M. (2004). Placing motivation and future time perspective theory in a temporal perspective. *Educational Psychology Review, 16*(2), 121-139. doi: 1040-726X/04/0600-0121/0

Şimşek, Ö. F. (2009). Happiness revisited: Ontological well-being as a theory-based construct of subjective well-being. *Journal of Happiness Studies, 10*(5), 505–522. doi:10.100710902-008-9105-6

Şimşek, Ö. F., & Kocayörük, E. (2013). Affective reactions to one's whole life: Preliminary development and validation of the ontological well-being scale. *Journal of Happiness Studies, 14*(1), 309–343. doi:10.100710902-012-9333-7

Sircova, A. (2017, October 19). Futurization of thinking and behavior as a fine balancing act-review. *Time Perspective Network*. Retrieved from https://medium.com/time-perspective-network/futurization-of-thinking-and-behavior-as-a-fine-balancing-act-be2f44a93d62

Sircova, A. (2018, May). *Futurization-summary of results, SP18*. Doi:10.13140/RG.2.2.16617.54880

Sircova, A., Wiberg, B., Wiberg, M., & Carelli, M. G. (2010, July). Balanced Time Perspective: A Study on Operationalization of the Construct in Sweden. In A. Sircova & A. Kairys (Eds.), *Time Perspective: Methodological Issues and Relation with Different Domains of Psychological Functioning. Symposium conducted at 15th European Conference on Personality*. Brno: Czech Republic.

Sircova, A., Karimi, F., Osin, E. N., Lee, S., Holme, P., & Strömbom, D. (2015). Simulating Irrational Human Behavior to Prevent Resource Depletion. *PLoS One*, *10*(3), e0117612. doi:10.1371/journal.pone.0117612 PMID:25760635

Sircova, A., van de Vijver, F. J. R., Osin, E., Milfont, T. L., Fieulaine, N., Kislali, A., & Boyd, J. N. (2015). Time perspective profiles of cultures. In M. Stolarski, N. Fieulaine, & W. van Beek (Eds.), *Time perspective theory: Review, research and application* (pp. 169–188). Springer.

Sircova, A., van de Vijver, F. J., Osin, E., Milfont, T. L., Fieulaine, N., Kislali-Erginbilgic, A., & Zimbardo, P. G. (2015). In M. Stolarski & N. Fieulaine (Eds.), *Time Perspective Theory; Review, Research, and Application* (pp. 169–187). Cham: Springer International.

Sixth Assessment Report of the Intergovernmental Panel on Climate Change. (n.d.). Retrieved from https://www.ipcc.ch/reports/

Skinner, G. (2018, October 11). *What worries the world?* Ipsos MORI. Retrieved from https://www.ipsos.com/ipsos-mori/en-uk/what-worries-world-september-2018-0

Slaugther, S., & Leslie, L. (1999). *Academic capitalism: Politics, policies, and the entrepreneurial university*. Baltimore, MD: John Hopkins University Press.

Smart, P. R. (2012). The Web-Extended Mind. *Metaphilosophy*, *43*(4), 446–463. doi:10.1111/j.1467-9973.2012.01756.x

Smith, A. (2010). *The theory of moral sentiments*. Penguin. doi:10.1002/9781118011690.ch10

Smith, S. (2015). Multiple temporalities of knowing in academic research. *Social Sciences Information. Information Sur les Sciences Sociales*, *54*(2), 2149–2176. doi:10.1177/0539018414566421

Snijders, D., & van der Duin, P. (2017). The Future Is Ours. How Dutch People Think about Technology and the Future. *Journal of Futures Studies*, *21*(4), 19–35.

Solomon, S., Greenberg, J., & Pyszczynski, T. A. (2015). *The worm at the core: On the role of death in life*. Random House Incorporated.

Sora, C. (2016). *Temporalidades Digitales - Análisis del Tiempo en los New Media y las Narrativas Interactivas*. Barcelona: Editorial UOC.

Sora, C., Jordà, S., & Codina, L. (2017). Chasing real-time interaction in new media: Towards a new theoretical approach and definition. *Digital Creativity*, *28*(3), 196–205. doi:10.1080/14626268.2017.1355323

Southerton, D., & Tomlinson, M. (2005). "Pressed for time" - The differential impacts of a "time squeeze.". *The Sociological Review, 53*(2), 215–239. doi:10.1111/j.1467-954X.2005.00511.x

Soylu, F., Brady, C., Holbert, N., & Wilensky, U. (2014). *The thinking hand: Embodiment of tool use, social cognition and metaphorical thinking and implications for learning design.* Paper presented at the AERA Annual Meeting (SIG: Brain, Neurosciences, and Education), Philadelphia, PA. Retrieved from https://ccl.northwestern.edu/2014/Soylu-2014-ThinkingHand.pdf

Sparrow, B., Liu, J., & Wegner, D. M. (2011). Google Effects on Memory: Cognitive Consequences of Having Information at Our fingertips. *Science, 333*(6043), 776–778. doi:10.1126cience.1207745 PMID:21764755

Spurling, N. (2015). Differential experiences of time in academic work: How qualities of time are made in practice. *Time & Society, 24*(3), 1–23. doi:10.1177/0961463X15575842

Stahl, M. (2012). *An exploratory study on the relation between time perspective, positive mental health and psychological distress across the adult lifespan* (Unpublished Master Dissertation). University of Twente, The Netherlands.

Stamatakis, E., Hamer, M., & Dunstan, D. W. (2011). Screen-based entertainment time, all-cause mortality, and cardiovascular events: Population-based study with ongoing mortality and hospital events follow-up. *Journal of the American College of Cardiology, 57*(3), 292–299. doi:10.1016/j.jacc.2010.05.065 PMID:21232666

Stamatakis, E., Hamer, M., & Lawlor, D. A. (2009). Physical activity, mortality, and cardiovascular disease: Is domestic physical activity beneficial? The Scottish Health Survey—1995, 1998, and 2003. *American Journal of Epidemiology, 169*(10), 1191–1200. doi:10.1093/aje/kwp042 PMID:19329529

Stoetzel, J. (1983). *Les Valeurs du Temps Présent: une enquête européen.* Paris: Presses Universitaires de France.

Stokes, B. (2015, February 10). *U.S. and European Millennials differ on their views of fate, future.* Pew Research Center. Retrieved from http://www.pewresearch.org/fact-tank/2015/02/10/u-s-and-european-millennials-differ-on-their-views-of-fate-future/

Stolarski, M., Bitner, J., & Zimbardo, P. G. (2011). Time perspective, emotional intelligence and discounting of delayed awards. *Time & Society, 20*(3), 346–363. doi:10.1177/0961463X11414296

Stolarski, M., Fieulaine, N., & van Beek, W. (Eds.). (2015). *Time perspective theory; Review, research, and application.* Springer International. doi:10.1007/978-3-319-07368-2

Stolarski, M., Matthews, G., Postek, S., Zimbardo, P. G., & Bitner, J. (2014). How we feel is a matter of time: Relationships between time perspectives and mood. *Journal of Happiness Studies, 15*(4), 809–827. doi:10.100710902-013-9450-y

Strasburger, V. C., Hogan, M. J., Mulligan, D. A., Ameenuddin, N., Christakis, D. A., Cross, C., ... Moreno, M. A. (2013). Children, adolescents, and the media. *Pediatrics, 132*(5), 958–961. doi:10.1542/peds.2013-2656 PMID:28448255

Strathman, A., Gleicher, F., Boninger, D. S., & Edwards, C. S. (1994). The consideration of future consequences: Weighing immediate and distant outcomes of behavior. *Journal of Personality and Social Psychology*, *66*(4), 742–752. doi:10.1037/0022-3514.66.4.742

Suchert, V., Hanewinkel, R., & Isensee, B. (2016). Screen time, weight status and the self-concept of physical attractiveness in adolescents. *Journal of Adolescence*, *48*, 11–17. doi:10.1016/j.adolescence.2016.01.005 PMID:26854729

Suchert, V., Pedersen, A., Hanewinkel, R., & Isensee, B. (2017). Relationship between attention-deficit/hyperactivity disorder and sedentary behavior in adolescence: A cross-sectional study. *ADHD Attention Deficit and Hyperactivity Disorders*, *9*(4), 213–218. doi:10.100712402-017-0229-6 PMID:28378132

Suddendorf, T. & Corballis, M. (2009). *Mental time travel and the evolution of the human mind.* University of Auckland.

Sum, S., Mathews, M. R., Hughes, I., & Campbell, A. (2008). Internet Use and Loneliness in Older Adults. *Cyberpsychology & Behavior*, *11*(2), 208–211. doi:10.1089/cpb.2007.0010 PMID:18422415

Sutton, J. (2009). Remembering. In P. Robbins & M. Aydede (Eds.), *Cambridge Handbook of Situated Cognition* (pp. 217–235). New York, NY: Cambridge University Press.

Svoboda, E., & Richards, B. (2009). Compensating for anterograde amnesia: A new training method that capitalizes on emerging smartphone technologies. *Journal of the International Neuropsychological Society*, *15*(04), 629–638. doi:10.1017/S1355617709090791 PMID:19588540

Szpunar, K. K. (2010). Evidence for an implicit influence of memory on future thinking. *Memory & Cognition*, *38*(5), 531–540. doi:10.3758/MC.38.5.531 PMID:20551334

Taber, B. J. (2013). Time Perspective and Career Decision-Making Difficulties in Adults. *Journal of Career Assessment*, *21*(2), 200–209. doi:10.1177/1069072712466722

Tagliazuchi, E. (2017). *Psicodélicos. En El Gato y La Caja: Un libro sobre drogas.* Retrieved from https://elgatoylacaja.com.ar/sobredrogas/

Taylor, S., Kiley, M., & Humphrey, R. (2017). *A handbook for doctoral supervisors.* New York: Routledge. doi:10.4324/9781315559650

Thoms, P., & Blasko, D. (2004). Future Time Perspective As A Temporal Anchor: Applications To Organizations. *Journal of Business & Economics Research*, *2*(11), 27–40.

Þórarinsdóttir, J. A. (2015). *The Impact of Screen-Use on Cognitive Function: A Pilot Study.* Retrieved from http://hdl.handle.net/1946/22566

Torres, F. (2016). A secular acceleration: Theological foundations of the sociological concept "social acceleration.". *Time & Society*, *25*(3), 429–449. doi:10.1177/0961463X15622395

Triphon, A., & Vonèche, J. (Eds.). (1996). *Piaget-Vygotsky. The Social Genesis of Thought*. New York, NY: Psychology Press.

Tsai, H.-T., & Babozzi, R. P. (2014). Contribution behavior in virtual communities: Cognitive, emotional, and social influences. *Management Information Systems Quarterly, 38*(1), 143–163. doi:10.25300/MISQ/2014/38.1.07

Tsakiris, M., Prabhu, G., & Haggard, P. (2006). Having a body versus moving your body. How agency structures body ownership. *Consciousness and Cognition, 15*(2), 423–432. doi:10.1016/j.concog.2005.09.004 PMID:16343947

Tsakiris, M., Shcütz-Bosbach, S., & Gallagher, S. (2007). On agency and body-ownership: Phenomenological and neurocognitive reflections. *Consciousness and Cognition, 19*(3), 645–660. doi:10.1016/j.concog.2007.05.012 PMID:17616469

Tsatou, P. (2009). Reconceptualising 'time' and 'space' in the Era of Electronic Media and Communications. *PLATFORM: Journal of Media and Communication, 1*, 11–52.

Tulving, E., & Szpunar, K. K. (2012). Does the future exist? In B. Levine & F. I. Craik (Eds.), *Mind and the frontal lobes: Cognition, behavior, and brain imaging* (pp. 248–263). OUP USA.

Turkle, S. (2011). *Alone Together: Why we expect more from technology and less from each other*. Basic Books.

Turkle, S. (2011). *Alone Together: why we expect more from technology and less from each other*. New York: Basic Books.

Turkle, S. (2011). *Alone Together: Why We Expect More from Technology and Less from Each Other*. New York: Basic Books.

Turkle, S. (2015). *Reclaiming Conversation - The Power of Talk in a Digital Age*. New York: Penguin Press.

Turvey, M. T. (1992). Affordances and prospective control: An outline of the ontology. *Ecological Psychology, 4*(3), 173–187. doi:10.120715326969eco0403_3

Twenge, J. M., Joiner, T. E., Rogers, M. L., & Martin, G. N. (2018). Increases in Depressive Symptoms, Suicide-Related Outcomes, and Suicide Rates Among U.S. Adolescents After 2010 and Links to Increased New Media Screen Time. *Clinical Psychological Science, 6*(1), 3–17. doi:10.1177/2167702617723376

Twenge, J. M., Martin, G. N., & Campbell, W. K. (2018). Decreases in psychological well-being among American adolescents after 2012 and links to screen time during the rise of smartphone technology. *Emotion (Washington, D.C.), 18*(6), 765–780. doi:10.1037/emo0000403 PMID:29355336

Van der Ploeg, H. P., Chey, T., Korda, R. J., Banks, E., & Bauman, A. (2012). Sitting time and all-cause mortality risk in 222 497 Australian adults. *Archives of Internal Medicine, 172*(6), 494–500. doi:10.1001/archinternmed.2011.2174 PMID:22450936

Van Everdingen, M., & Waarts, E. (2003). The effect of national culture on the adoption of innovations. *Marketing Letters, 14*(3), 217–232. doi:10.1023/A:1027452919403

Vanattenhoven, J., & Geerts, D. (2015a). Broadcast, Video-on-Demand, and Other Ways to Watch Television Content. In *Proceedings of the ACM International Conference on Interactive Experiences for TV and Online Video - TVX '15* (pp. 73–82). Brussels: ACM. 10.1145/2745197.2745208

Vanattenhoven, J., & Geerts, D. (2015b). Designing TV Recommender Interfaces for Specific Viewing Experiences. In *Proceedings of the ACM International Conference on Interactive Experiences for TV and Online Video - TVX '15* (pp. 185–190). Brussels: ACM. 10.1145/2745197.2755522

Varela, F. J., Thompson, E., & Rosch, E. (1991). *The Embodied Mind. Cognitive Science and Human Experience*. Cambridge, MA: MIT Press.

Varsori, E. (2016). *Os Dispositivos-Ecrã no Quotidiano dos Jovens Portugueses - A mediação-ecrã no uso social do tempo*. Universidade de Aveiro. Retrieved from http://hdl.handle.net/10773/17738

Varsori, E. (2016). *Os dispositivos-ecrã no quotidiano dos jovens portugueses: a mediação-ecrã no uso social do tempo*. Universidade de Aveiro. Retrieved from https://ria.ua.pt/bitstream/10773/17738/1/Dissertacao__Enrickson_Varsori.pdf

Varsori, E., & Oliveira, L. (2015). Ecrã-quotidiano: Epifania do ausente. In *Atas do IX Congresso Sopcom*. Coimbra: SOPCOM.

Varsori, E., Oliveira, L., & Melro, A. (2017). Jovens nos ecrãs : A fronteira invisível no quotidiano metodologia. In *CIBERCULTURA Circum-navegações em redes transculturais de conhecimento, arquivos e pensamento* (pp. 217–228). Braga: Edições Húmus. Retrieved from http://www.lasics.uminho.pt/ojs/index.php/cecs_ebooks/article/view/2803/2710

Vásquez, A. (2011). Experiencia subjetiva del tiempo y su influencia en el comportamiento: Revisión y modelos. *Psicologia: Teoria e Pesquisa, 27*(2), 2015–2223.

Vaz, P. (2004). Mediação e tecnologia. In F. M. Martins & J. M. Silva (Eds.), *A Genealogia do Virtual: comunicação, cultura e tecnologias do imaginário* (pp. 216–238). Porto Alegre, RS: Sulina.

Vermunt, J. K., & Magidson, J. (2002). Latent class cluster analysis. *Applied Latent Class Analysis, 11*, 89–106. doi:10.1017/CBO9780511499531.004

Verto Analytics. (2017). *Multitasking and Mobile Apps: New Ways to Measure Consumer Behavior*. Retrieved from https://www.vertoanalytics.com/chart-week-multitasking-rise/

Villieux, A., Sovet, L., Jung, S. C., & Guilbert, L. (2016). Psychological flourishing: Validation of the French version of the Flourishing Scale and exploration of its relationships with personality traits. *Personality and Individual Differences, 88*, 1–5. doi:10.1016/j.paid.2015.08.027

Virilio, P. (1989). *Esthétique de la disparition. Collection l'Espace Critique*. Retrieved from http://www.sudoc.fr/00151766X%5Cnhttp://www.worldcat.org/search?q=no%3A300078551

Virilio, P. (2000). *Cibermundo: a política do pior*. Lisboa: Editorial Teorema.

von Groddeck, V. (2018). From Defuturization to Futurization and Back Again? A System-Theoretical Perspective to Analyse Decision-Making. In *How Organizations Manage the Future* (pp. 25–43). Cham: Palgrave Macmillan. doi:10.1007/978-3-319-74506-0_2

Voorveld, H., Segijn, C., Ketelaar, P., & Smith, E. (2014). Investigating the Prevalence and Predictors of Media Multitasking across Countries. *International Journal of Communication, 8*(23).

Vostal, F. (2015). Academic life in the fast lane: The experience of time and speed in British academia. *Time & Society, 24*(1), 71–95. doi:10.1177/0961463X13517537

Vygotsky, L. S. (1978). *Mind in society: The development of higher psychological processes*. Cambridge, MA: Harvard University Press.

Wack, P. (1985, November). The Gentle Art of Re-Perceiving – Scenarios (part 2): Uncharted Waters Ahead. *Harvard Business Review*, 2–14.

Wahi, G., Parkin, P. C., Beyene, J., Uleryk, E. M., & Birken, C. S. (2011). Effectiveness of interventions aimed at reducing screen time in children: A systematic review and meta-analysis of randomized controlled trials. *Archives of Pediatrics & Adolescent Medicine, 165*(11), 979–986. doi:10.1001/archpediatrics.2011.122 PMID:21727260

Wajcman, J. (2008). Life in the fast lane? Towards a sociology of technology and time. *The British Journal of Sociology, 1*(59), 59–77. doi:10.1111/j.1468-4446.2007.00182.x PMID:18321331

Walker, M., & Thomson, P. (Eds.). (2010). *The Routledge doctoral supervisor's companion: supporting effective research in education and the social sciences*. Routledge. doi:10.4324/9780203851760

Walker, T. L., & Tracey, T. J. G. (2012). The role of future time perspective in career decision-making. *Journal of Vocational Behavior, 81*(2), 150–158. doi:10.1016/j.jvb.2012.06.002

Wasiak, J. (2009). Being-in-the-City: A Phenomenological Approach to Technological Experience. *Culture Unbound, 1*(2), 349–366. doi:10.3384/cu.2000.1525.09121349

Waterman, D., Sherman, R., & Wook Ji, S. (2013). The economics of online television: Industry development, aggregation, and "TV Everywhere." *Telecommunications Policy, 37*(9), 725–736. doi:10.1016/j.telpol.2013.07.005

Watkins, S. (2009). *The Young & The Digital: What the Migration to Social-Network Sites, Games, and Anytime, Anywhere Media Means for Our Future*. Boston: Beacon Press.

Watson, D., Clark, L. A., & Tellegen, A. (1988). Development and validation of brief measures of positive and negative affect: The PANAS scales. *Journal of Personality and Social Psychology, 54*(6), 1063–1070. doi:10.1037/0022-3514.54.6.1063 PMID:3397865

Webster, J. D. (2011). A new measure of time perspective: Initial psychometric findings for the Balanced Time Perspective Scale (BTPS). *Canadian Journal of Behavioural Science/Revue canadienne des sciences du comportement, 43*(2), 111-118.

Wellington, J. (2005). *Succeeding with your doctorate.* London: Sage. doi:10.4135/9781849209977

Wellington, J. (2010). *Making supervision work for you: a student's guide.* London: Sage.

Wheeler, M. (2005). *Reconstructing the Cognitive World: the Next Step.* Cambridge, MA: MIT Press.

Wiberg, B., Sircova, A., Carelli, G. M., & Wiberg, M. (2017). Developing empirical profile of the balanced time perspective (BTP) and exploring its stability over time. In A. Kostic & D. Chadee (Eds.), *Time Perspective Theory* (pp. 63–95). Palgrave. doi:10.1057/978-1-137-60191-9_4

Wiecha, J. L., Peterson, K. E., Ludwig, D. S., Kim, J., Sobol, A., & Gortmaker, S. L. (2006). When children eat what they watch: Impact of television viewing on dietary intake in youth. *Archives of Pediatrics & Adolescent Medicine, 160*(4), 436–442. doi:10.1001/archpedi.160.4.436 PMID:16585491

Wiktionary, The Free Dictionary. (2017a). *Futurization.* Retrieved from https://en.wiktionary.org/wiki/futurization

Wiktionary, The Free Dictionary. (2017b). *Futurize.* Retrieved from https://en.wiktionary.org/wiki/futurize

Wilbur, S. P. (2000). An Archaeology of Cyberspaces: virtuality, community, identity. In D. Bell & B. M. Kennedy (Eds.), *The Cybercultures Reader* (pp. 45–55). New York, NY: Routledge.

Wisker, G. (2012). *The good supervisor: supervising postgraduate and undergraduate research for doctoral theses and dissertations.* London: Macmillan International Higher Education. doi:10.1007/978-1-137-02423-7

Wittmann, M. (2009). The inner experience of time. *Philosophical Transactions of the Royal Society of London. Series B, Biological Sciences, 364*(1525), 1955–1967. doi:10.1098/rstb.2009.0003 PMID:19487197

Wittmann, M. (2017). *Felt Time: The Science of How We Experience Time.* The MIT Press.

Wittmann, M., Dinich, J., Merrow, M., & Roenneberg, T. (2006). Social jetlag: Misalignment of biological and social time. *Chronobiology International, 23*(1-2), 497–509. doi:10.1080/07420520500545979 PMID:16687322

Wittmann, M., & Sircova, A. (2018). Dispositional orientation to the present and future and its role in pro-environmental behavior and sustainability. *Heliyon (London), 4*(10), e00882. doi:10.1016/j.heliyon.2018.e00882 PMID:30386830

Wolton, D. (2012). *Internet, e depois? Uma teoria crítica das novas mídias* (2nd ed.). Porto Alegre, RS: Sulina.

Worrell, F. C., & Mello, Z. R. (2007). The reliability and validity of Zimbardo time perspective inventory scores in academically talented adolescents. *Educational and Psychological Measurement, 67*(3), 487–504. doi:10.1177/0013164406296985

Wu, X., Tao, S., Rutayisire, E., Chen, Y., Huang, K., & Tao, F. (2017). The relationship between screen time, nighttime sleep duration, and behavioural problems in preschool children in China. *European Child & Adolescent Psychiatry, 26*(5), 541–548. doi:10.100700787-016-0912-8 PMID:27822641

Yarwood-Ross, L., & Haigh, C. (2014). As others see us: What PhD students say about supervisors. *Nurse Researcher, 22*(1), 38–43. doi:10.7748/nr.22.1.38.e1274 PMID:25251819

Yilmaz, G., Caylan, N. D., & Karacan, C. D. (2015). An intervention to preschool children for reducing screen time: A randomized controlled trial. *Child: Care, Health and Development, 41*(3), 443–449. doi:10.1111/cch.12133 PMID:24571538

Ylijoki, O. (2010). Future orientation in eGroup Leadersodic labour: Short-term academics as a case in point. *Time & Society, 19*(3), 365–386. doi:10.1177/0961463X10356220

Ylijoki, O. (2013). Boundary-work between work and life in the high-speed university. *Studies in Higher Education, 38*(2), 242–255. doi:10.1080/03075079.2011.577524

Zaleski, Z. (1996). Future Anxiety: Concept, Measurement, And Preliminary Research. *Personality and Individual Differences, 21*(2), 165–174. doi:10.1016/0191-8869(96)00070-0

Zaleski, Z. (2006). Future orientation and anxiety. In *Understanding behavior in the context of time* (pp. 135–151). Psychology Press.

Zani, L., & Kaivanara, M. (2015). Teaching Embodiment through Technology. Teaching Tools. *Cultural Anthropology*. Retrieved from https://culanth.org/fieldsights/682-teaching-embodiment-through-technology

Zeegers, M., & Barron, D. (2012). Pedagogical concerns in doctoral supervision: A challenge for pedagogy. *Quality Assurance in Education, 20*(1), 20–30. doi:10.1108/09684881211198211

Zelazo, P. D. (2013). The Oxford Handbook of Developmental Psychology: Vol. 1. *Body and Mind*. Oxford, UK: Oxford University Press.

Zenith Media. (2018). *Mobile internet to reach 28% of media use in 2020*. Retrieved from: https://www.zenithmedia.com/mobile-internet-to-reach-28-of-media-use-in-2020/

Zerubavel, E. (1981). *Hidden rhythms: Schedules and calendars in social life*. Chicago: Chicago University Press.

Zhang, J. W., Howell, R. T., & Stolarski, M. (2013). Comparing Three Methods to Measure a Balanced Time Perspective: The Relationship Between a Balanced Time Perspective and Subjective Well-Being. *Journal of Happiness Studies, 14*(1), 169–184. doi:10.100710902-012-9322-x

Zimbardo, P., & Boyd, J. (2008). *The Time Paradox - Using the new Psychology of Time to your advantage*. London: Rider.

Zimbardo, P. G., & Boyd, J. N. (1999). Putting Time in Perspective: A Valid, Reliable Individual-Differences Metric. *Journal of Personality and Social Psychology, 77*(6), 1271–1288. doi:10.1037/0022-3514.77.6.1271

Zimbardo, P. G., & Boyd, J. N. (2008). *The Time Paradox: Using the New Psychology of Time to Your Advantage*. London: Rider.

Zimbardo, P. G., Keough, K. A., & Boyd, J. N. (1997). Present time perspective as a predictor of risky driving. *Personality and Individual Differences, 23*(6), 1007–1023. doi:10.1016/S0191-8869(97)00113-X

Zimbardo, P., & Boyd, J. (1999). *The Time Paradox: the new psychology of time that will change your life*. New York: Free Press.

Zimbardo, P., & Boyd, J. (2009). *The time paradox: The new psychology of time that can change yout life*. New York: Free Press.

Zuckerman, M. (1990). The psychophysiology of sensation seeking. *Journal of Personality, 58*(1), 313–345. doi:10.1111/j.1467-6494.1990.tb00918.x PMID:2198341

About the Contributors

Lídia Oliveira has a degree in Philosophy from the University of Coimbra (1990), a Master's degree in Educational Technology from the University of Aveiro, in partnership with the University of Valenciennes (France) and Mons (Belgium) (1995), and a PhD in Sciences and Technologies of Communication from the University of Aveiro (2002). Her research focuses on individual, collective and institutional behaviour on the internet. The areas of interest are: Social Network Analysis, Cyberculture Studies, Sociology of Communication, Science and Technologies of Communication, ICT and Education, Multimedia, Information Systems, Digital Libraries, Science Communication, Communication in the Scientific Community (theoretical and empirical studies). ORCID: http://orcid.org/0000-0002-3278-0326. | ResearchGate: https://www.researchgate.net/profile/Lidia_Oliveira5.

* * *

Emin Altintas is an Associate Professor in Psychology department at Université de Lille, France since 2010. He received a Master Degree in Cognitive and Behavioral Therapy in 2005, and Ph.D. in Psychology in 2008 from Université de Lille 3 in France. His principal current research field is well-being in a life span perspective.

Emilia Araujo holds a PhD in sociology. She is teacher at the Department of Sociology at the Institute of Social Sciences, in the University of Minho. She teaches in the field of methodologies, culture and technoscience and has been researching on sociology of time, PhD, academic careers, and gender. She was the Principal Investigator of the project "Mobiscience - trajectories of Portuguese researchers and knowledge circulation. She has many international and national publication addressing the importance of gender in science and sustainability (http://orcid.org/0000-0003-3600-3310).

Jose Azevedo received his PhD from Cardiff University and University of Minho. He is currently Professor at University of Porto and was a Fulbright scholar. He writes on issues of digital divide, science communication and media literacy. He has a large experience of coordination of research projects both at national and European level.

Ralph Ings Bannell is an Associate Professor in the Department of Education, Pontifícia Universidade Católica do Rio de Janeiro (PUC-Rio). Past Director of the Department (2014-2018). Also founder and past President of the Sociedade Brasileira de Filosofia da Educação (sofie) and past Coordinator of the Philosophy of Education Working Group of the Associação Nacional de Pesquisa e Pós-Graduação em Educação, Brazil (ANPEd). Research interests are in two broad fields: theories of cognition and learning; political theory and its implications for education.

Cláudia Barbosa has a graduate degree in Teaching of English and German, from the University of Aveiro, where she is currently working towards a PhD in Multimedia in Education. She has been involved as project manager in several FP7, H2020 and other international and national funded projects. Her current research interests lie in the use of technologies to support language teaching and learning and media multitasking.

Pelin Buruk is working as an Instructor and Researcher at Arel University. She completed her BA in Bogazici University Economics Department and Master's degree at Marmara University Organizational Behavior. Currently, she is enrolled in the doctoral program at Arel University in Clinical Psychology. She also has 16 years of experience as Human Resources Manager in various sectors.

Bekir Çelik completed his B.Sc. degree in Guidance and Psychological Counseling with honor degree in 2007, and was awarded with a scholarship by the Ministry of National Education of Turkey to pursue a graduate degree in the United States of America. He received his M.Ed. in Community Agency Counseling in 2011 and Ph.D. in Educational Psychology in 2014 from Auburn University in the United States of America. Besides publishing numerous articles in national and international journals, he conducted workshops and taught many courses in college levels. Bekir Çelik currently work as an assistant professor in the department of Educational Sciences at Çanakkale Onsekiz Mart University.

Kadydja Karla Nascimento Chagas holds a PhD in Education (Federal University of Rio Grande do Norte) She is teacher at the Federal Institute of Education, Science and Technology of Rio Grande do Norte (IFRN/BRAZIL). She is also academic coordinator of the international educational studies partnership UMinho/ IFRN. She has developed several research projects on education, mostly in the context of under graduation.

Cynthia H. W. Corrêa is an Associate Professor of Information and Communication Technologies at the School of Arts, Sciences and Humanities, University of São Paulo (USP), Brazil. The leader of the Humanitas Digitalis Research Group, linked to the National Council for Scientific and Technological Development (CNPq Brazil), and a member of the Association of Internet Researchers (AoIR). Dr. Cynthia has coordinated research projects with the support of USP and CNPq Brazil with emphasis on digital culture, online marketing, and technological innovation, involving students in undergraduate and graduate levels. Also, her research results have been published in peer-reviewed journals and books, both nationally and internationally.

Jorge Trinidad Ferraz de Abreu got his graduation and Master's degree in Electronic and Telecommunication by the University of Aveiro, Portugal. After his participation in several European projects he joined the Department of Communication and Arts and concluded his PhD in Sciences and Communication Technologies. Currently he teaches in the three levels of courses offered by its department: Undergraduate course, Master and PHD program. As a member of the research unit Digimedia (CIC.Digital), he develops his research activities in new media, cross-platform content and Interactive Television with particular interest in the development and evaluation of Social iTV applications.

Camila De Paoli Leporace is a journalist experienced in digital media and researcher in the areas of education, digital technologies and cognition. Collaborates with the E-Minds Lab at the University of Coimbra in research on new approaches to cognition and their implications for education. Currently a post-graduate student in the Education Department at the Pontifical Catholic University of Rio de Janeiro.

Pedro Alexandre dos Santos Almeida graduated in New Communication Technologies by the University of Aveiro and his PhD in the same university in Sciences and Communication Technologies. Currently, he is a lecturer in the Communication and Art Department in undergraduate, master and doctoral courses. As a member of the research unit Digimedia (CIC.Digital), he develops his research activities in new media, cross-platform and context-aware content and Interactive Television. He has special interests in multimedia communication systems and applications aiming the promotion of social practices around AV content in iTV, web or mobile. He has also been working in social media applied to education and organizational scenarios.

Molly Kennedy is an undergraduate student at Bowdoin College who is studying economics and psychology. She has also studied at DIS Copenhagen in Denmark. She has worked for a small nonprofit dedicated to the economic development of local businesses and is currently the business manager and an illustrator for her school newspaper.

Ercan Kocayörük has a PhD from the Middle East Technical University (Ankara) in Psychological Counseling and Guidance. He received M.S. degrees in Psychological Counseling and Guidance from Ankara University in 2000. He had worked as a school counselor in Ankara from 1996 to 2008. He has experience about counseling applications and practices in school over 15 years. He has been working as an Assistant Professor at the Çanakkale Onsekiz Mart University since 2008. He is a researcher in the field of relationship between parents and children and the role of parents on healthy adolescent development. His main areas of research interest are subjective well-being and its relation to narrative processes, time perspective, mental health, personal and self-construal He has presented at numerous international conferences about the effects of parents on the children and adolescent development.

Victor E. C. Ortuño received his Ph.D. in Psychology of Motivation and Personality in the Faculty of Psychology and Education Sciences, University of Coimbra (FPCE-UC). Works as Assistant Professor at the Faculty of Psychology, University of the Republic, Uruguay. He is a Researcher of the Cognitive and Behavioural Center for Research and Intervention at FPCE-UC. Member of Researchers National System (Uruguay), and the International Thematic Research Network on Time Perspective. Editor of the book International Studies on Time Perspective and organizer of the Ist International Conference on Time Perspective (ICTP2012), held in Coimbra, Portugal. His main research interests are time perspective, subjective temporality, psychometrics and motivation.

Luís Pedro holds a PhD in Didactics-Educational Technology (2005, University of Aveiro, Portugal). He currently is an Assistant Professor at the Department of Communication and Arts, University of Aveiro, Portugal. His research interests are related with social media development, integration and assessment in educational and training contexts, which have been developed in several MSc and PhD supervisions and through the coordination and participation in externally funded research projects.

Sara Pereira is an Associate Professor at the Communication Sciences Department and researcher at the Communication and Society Research Centre at the University of Minho, Portugal. Director of the Communication and Sciences Department since July 2013. Director of the Master's Degree on 'Communication, Citizenship and Education' (2010-2015).

Richard Rodriguez is a clinical psychologist and researcher psychologist specialized in psychosocial rehabilitation of people with psychosis or schizophrenia.

Eduardo Santos is Associate Professor with Aggregation, Scientific Coordinator of the Institute of Cognitive Psychology, Human and Social Development of the University of Coimbra. His current research interests center on the processes of constitution of new subjectivities, namely digital ones, in the light of new cognitive theories of the mind and with implications for the psychotherapeutic processes.

Ivone Neiva Santos is a PhD student in Digital Media at University of Porto. She received her BSc and Ma in Sociology from University of Porto where she is currently working as a researcher in projects related to science communication. She has also several years of experience in education and human resources management.

Angela Scharf is a recent graduate from the University of Minnesota - Twin Cities. Angela has a fascination with solving puzzles. To this she owes her tolerance for ambiguity, drive to understand complex systems, and passion for creative solutions and strategic thinking. Her current project is "Futurization of Thinking and Behaviour: Exploring People's Imaginaries about the Future and Futurization."

Ömer Faruk Şimşek is a professor of counseling psychology at Istanbul Arel University, department of psychology. His main areas of research interest are subjective well-being and its relation to narrative processes, language use and mental health, personal sense of uniqueness, and self-consciousness. He is also interested in using advanced statistical analyses such as multi-trait multi-method analyses and growth curve modeling.

Anna Sircova is an independent researcher, visual artist, event organizer and educator, currently based in Copenhagen, Denmark. She is passionate for cross-disciplinary approach and does research and creative projects about concept of time. She holds a PhD in Psychology and is the Chair of the Board for the Time

Perspective Network. Her research is published in various scientific articles and book chapters. She has teaching experience in cross-cultural psychology, psychology of time, and creativity development. Her artwork has been exhibited in Denmark, Sweden, Latvia, Tunisia, Croatia and France.

Enrickson Varsori is a PhD student in Communication Sciences at University of Minho. Graduated in Social Communication at State University of Londrina and Master´s degree in Multimedia Communication at University of Aveiro. The current research interests focus on issues related with social use of time and screen devices, cyberculture. Currently works as a research fellow in the project UltraTV, on DIGIMEDIA (Digital Media and Interaction).

Ana Velhinho is a communication designer, with a five-year BA in Communication Design (2005, FBAUL), a MA in Design and Visual Culture (2008, IADE) and is a PhD student in Image Theory at the Faculty of Fine Arts of the University of Lisbon, with her research project hosted by the CIC-Digital/Digimedia research unit. Currently, she is an interaction design researcher of the Ultra TV project and a member of the Social iTV group at the Department of Communication and Art of the University of Aveiro. As a designer, she develops graphic, editorial and multimedia projects focusing her research on post-internet culture and the influence of media and networking on image-driven practices and literacies.

Britt Wiberg is a Ph.D., Associate professor in psychology. She is a licensed clinical psychologist, a licensed psychotherapist and also an authorized supervisor of psychotherapy. Her clinical and research interests and expertise are in attachment, psychopathology, time-perspective and the outcome and processes in psychotherapy, where she has published many articles. She has an affiliation to the Department of Psychology, Umeå University, SE-901 87, Umeå, Sweden.

Mikael Wiberg is a full professor of informatics at Umeå University, Sweden. He has held positions as a chaired professor in HCI at Uppsala University and as research director for Umeå Institute of Design. His research interests focus on the materiality of interaction and ways of integrating architectural thinking with interaction design. His is author of "The Materiality of Interaction" MIT Press.

Index

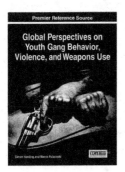

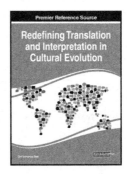

Ensure Quality Research is Introduced to the Academic Community

Become an IGI Global Reviewer for Authored Book Projects

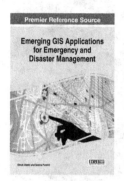

Premier Reference Source

Emerging GIS Applications for Emergency and Disaster Management

Premier Reference Source

Managerial Strategies and Green Solutions for Project Sustainability

Premier Reference Source

Comparative Approaches to Using R and Python for Statistical Data Analysis

Premier Reference Source

Solutions for High-Touch Communications in a High-Tech World

The overall success of an authored book project is dependent on quality and timely reviews.

In this competitive age of scholarly publishing, constructive and timely feedback significantly expedites the turnaround time of manuscripts from submission to acceptance, allowing the publication and discovery of forward-thinking research at a much more expeditious rate. Several IGI Global authored book projects are currently seeking highly qualified experts in the field to fill vacancies on their respective editorial review boards:

Applications may be sent to:
development@igi-global.com

Applicants must have a doctorate (or an equivalent degree) as well as publishing and reviewing experience. Reviewers are asked to write reviews in a timely, collegial, and constructive manner. All reviewers will begin their role on an ad-hoc basis for a period of one year, and upon successful completion of this term can be considered for full editorial review board status, with the potential for a subsequent promotion to Associate Editor.

If you have a colleague that may be interested in this opportunity, we encourage you to share this information with them.